Development As Social Transformation

Reflections on the Global Problematique

contributions by: Herb Addo
Samir Amin
George Aseniero
Andre Gunder
Frank
Mats Friberg
Folker Fröbel
Jürgen Heinrichs
Björn Hettne
Otto Kreye
Hiroharu Seki

Westview Press/Boulder, Colorado

in association with the United Nations University

Published in the United States of America in 1985 by
Westview Press, Inc.
5500 Central Avenue
Boulder, Colorado 80301
Frederick A. Praeger, Publisher

Copyright © 1985 by the United Nations University

Library of Congress Catalog Card Number: 84–52653

ISBN (Westview) 0-8133-0200-X (pb)

Printed in Great Britain

Contents

About the Contributors

Herb Addo, Institute of International Relations, University of the West Indies, St. Augustine, Trinidad, West Indies.

Samir Amin, United Nations Institute for Training and Research (UNITAR), Project 'Strategies for the Future of Africa', Dakar, Senegal.

George Aseniero, United Nations University, Tokyo, Japan.

Andre Gunder Frank, Institute for the Socio-Economic Studies of Developing Regions, University of Amsterdam, Netherlands.

Mats Friberg and Björn Hettne, Department of Peace and Conflict Research, University of Gothenburg, Sweden.

Folker Fröbel, Jürgen Heinrichs and *Otto Kreye*, Starnberg Institute for the Study of Global Structures, Developments and Crises, Federal Republic of Germany.

Hiroharu Seki, Institute for Asia Pacific Peace Policy, Tokyo, Japan.

Foreword

I am pleased to write the foreword to this research product of the United Nations University's Goals, Processes, and Indicators of Development Project (UNU-GPID).

This book is one of comprehensive findings of the group of researchers within the GPID which concerned itself principally with the macro aspects of the development content of the global problematique.

Even though readers will know this from the description of the authors, it is important that I point out the prominent fact that the authors come from, and have lived in, different parts of the world, from where they have gathered their perspectives on the developmental implications of the overall conception(s) of the global problematique.

While the richness of the contents of the book is amply demonstrated in the individual chapters, I would like to draw readers' attention to the integrative coherence of the work. It is noteworthy that, despite the diverse nature of the chapter topics, there is the underlying unity of purpose and shared concerns in the treatments of these topics.

As a product of the UNU-GPID, we must know that all the chapters in this book were presented and discussed at several GPID Meetings, at different stages of their construction.

However, in their final forms, the arguments and views expressed in each of the chapters owe a lot to the two GPID Meetings held in Starnberg, July-August 1982, and in Colombo, August 1982. It was at these meetings that the coherence between the individual chapters in this book were discussed and agreed upon from the integrative point of view.

This book then is one of the authentic results of the GPID, which was initiated and brought together by Johan Galtung, the Co-ordinator of the project from 1979 to 1981. As the Co-ordinator of the project during its integrative phase, 1981–1983, I am not only proud to pronounce this book as such, but at the same time also as a set of serious reflections on the developmental implications of the global problematique.

Carlos Mallmann

Introduction

The global problematique

Two common motives unite the contributors to this volume: on the one hand, a deep concern to understand the world as a unity, as an inter-related totality, and on the other, a commitment to transform it. Transformation here is understood as the unfolding, or preservation, of structures and processes which can yield and secure the bases of life for *all* the world's inhabitants under just, equitable and therefore *humane* conditions: only such a transformation merits the designation 'development'.

Underlying the separate contributions, therefore, is a collective, reflective and critical endeavour to understand the origins of, and contemporary requirements for, realizing the idea of development and the relationship between this idea and the *global problematique* What then is the global problematique?

Considered empirically, the global problematique can be specified as a complex set of interacting elements which *in toto* characterize the current state of the world. And by virtue of the fact that the world-system does not provide those who compose and populate it with the preconditions for an existence consonant with the minimum demands of *humanity*, both the elements in the global problematique and the global problematique itself as a whole are loaded with negative and even life-threatening properties.

Each of the chapters in this book deals with different aspects and outcomes of this all-embracing problematique: the nature of the current crisis in the world economy; deteriorating North-South and East-West relations; new advances in militarization under the threat of war; distinctive European political options in the face of intensifying super-power rivalry; the 'development of under-development' versus 'genuine development' in the Third World; the relations between emerging and existing social movements; evaluation of the developmental strengths of anti-systemic forces; and philosophical and historical critiques of the foundations of standard development thinking.

In exploring the systematic interrelationships between these aspects and outcomes, each seeks to demonstrate why standard or dominant development thinking and practice are not only ineffective, but actually generate further underdevelopment. In their individual ways, the authors proceed to indicate some of the conditions, alternatives, and derivative political choices open to the future, which have to be confronted if the realization of the development objective, as a final project, is ever to be achieved.

Despite evident differences in approach, the contributions are organically cohesive in the sense that they share both the assumption and conclusion that any serious reflection on development must culminate in the idea that development – as defined above – entails a global social transformation. Development is not global in scope because it is simply 'the common concern of all', or because 'it affects us all' but in the primordial sense that it is only in terms of the historical evolution and continuing dynamics of the world-system as a whole that the development-underdevelopment relation can be grasped; and that, consequently, it is only through a full confrontation with the logic and dynamics of the world-system that authentic and realistic alternative development policies and perspectives can be conceived. Finally, the problem of development is global in the sense that it refers not only to the plight of the peoples of the 'underdeveloped' countries but equally to the urgent concerns of those of the 'developed' countries as well, both in the West and in the East, as they strive to grapple with their own socio-economic and political problems.

Whatever the specific topic chosen, each discussion leads to the same general conclusion that the prospects of mitigating, much less solving, the pressing problems of humanity within the present world-system are practically nil – a situation likely to deteriorate still further as the global crisis continues to intensify and deepen. The bankruptcy of dominant development models, the deterioration of living conditions virtually everywhere, the sharpening of conflicts within and between nations, and the destruction of the natural foundations of existence should overwhelm the illusion held for so long of the possibilities of developmental transformation *within* the capitalist world-system. As these possibilities dwindle in the face of facts, the conclusion becomes increasingly inescapable: that development is conceivable only in an anti-systemic perspective; that it must be pursued *against* the constitutive logic and structural constraints of the all-encompassing capitalist world-system; and that in effect it is synonymous with social transformation understood globally. Development as defined above, can only mean the institution of different modes of production and different forms of society: hence *development as social transformation*.

The perspective of 'development as social transformation' offers a point of departure for grasping how and why capitalist development and underdevelopment coexist as intrinsic elements and as a dialectical expression of the world-system in evolution. And this, in turn, provides the key to understanding why programmes and political proposals directed towards individual factors or spheres (such as industrialization, technologization of agriculture, export-orientation) are utterly irrelevant and inappropriate to the historical nature of the causes of the present crisis of the world-system. The permanent crisis of the Third World, and the current acute global crisis, are not mere peripheral or epi-phenomena, whose threat to run out of control is some kind of unfortunate accident: they are the expression of a crisis of the system *as such*, a crisis rooted in the dynamics of the system's own development.

Such an approach offers a further, practical-political advantage for assessing those oppositional forces which the system itself calls into being. It implies that political initiatives aimed at development can only be successful, can only yield a genuine development of the type outlined above, if they are, at root, *anti-systemic*: that is, if they direct themselves at the core features of the world-system which give the global problematique its non-random character. But what are these features, and at what points can opposition to individual facets of the system flower into resistance to the system itself?

Capitalist world-system

The shaping of the globe into a single, coherent system – built on exploitation – is first and foremost the product of the pursuit of the valorization of capital. The current state of the world-system must, therefore, be seen as the product of both the exigencies of the valorization of capital *and* the degrees of resistance to it encountered or engendered in the course of the history of the modern period.

Since its inception, the capitalist system has combined the pursuit of valorization with unrestrained, or not easily restrainable, geographical expansion. It is this physical, where necessary militarily aggressive, conquest which has given capitalism its world-wide systemic character. Sheer territorial extent does not, of course, imply homogeneity or equal incidence in all parts of the globe.

The capitalist world-system is not confined to those parts of the globe which can formally be designated as the capitalist countries. Some, although not all, of the contributors see the existing socialist countries as part of the capitalist world-system to the extent either that their internal organization follows capitalist criteria of efficiency and/or they participate in the world economy on terms set by capitalist competition and the law of value. And in this sense, and to this degree, they are not only victims of those ominous military, ecological, and social developments and threats propelled by the dictates of capitalist accumulation which, in combination, make up the global problematique: they also bear their due proportion of responsibility for not hampering social transformation, in the sense employed above.

This conceptualization of the capitalist world-system – with the exception of the understanding of the socialist countries, over which the group still enjoys a healthy divergence of views – represents a fundamental position to which all the contributors, in their individual ways, are committed. This should not be construed as a caprice, an expression of scientific hubris, or political naivity. On the contrary, such an approach is suggested, if not demanded, by the object of analysis itself – the unfolding of the capitalist system. The deterioration of the conditions under which the mass of the population has to live in many areas of the world, the increase in conflicts between and within countries, the intensification of the world economic crisis, are now showing once again – if more proof were needed – that unequal and uneven development, with all the forms of immiseration and alienation which it creates, cannot be surmounted within the capitalist world-system.

This argument should in no way serve as an excuse for relapsing into fatalistic determinism, nor is it born simply out of the desire to produce a historical explanation. An appreciation of the exigencies of the capitalist world-system also embraces an awareness of the contradictions which this system repeatedly generates. And these contradictions constitute the sites at which anti-systemic forces can crystallize points of leverage, as it were, for an open future.

Analyzing aspects of the development problematique

The dominant conceptions of theories of development are themselves a fundamental part of the global problematique. For this reason, critiques of the foundations of development thinking are not only important, they are indeed necessary, if we are to move on towards alternative formulations of development as social transformation. Issue is taken with these theories in a number of chapters. However, it is the first two chapters which attempt to lay bare the methodological-ideological and the historical-ideological foundations of prevailing theories of development.

In 'Beyond Eurocentricity', Addo argues that all the dominant theories of development can be shown to be Eurocentric in nature, a persistent tendency in which the world-system is observed from standpoints within the European, that is, Western domination of this system. Global validities are then claimed for these highly specific perceptions of the world-system and its development requirements. Understandings of development are therefore cast in European lights which offer the evolution of European history and culture as models for development, which the rest of the world is then exhorted to imitate. This appropriation of the concept 'development' serves the Western aim of establishing, in perpetuity, the West's dominance in the world. Third World countries are therefore placed in an absurd position: by opening up themselves to some of the changes that these models require of them, they contribute to the perpetuation of the structures of domination in the world-system.

The author demands that history be understood in ways which allow interventions to influence how the future is to be shaped. But who will be responsible for such a social transformation? Who are the agents of change? Certainly not those forces whose aim is to change the societies of the periphery in accord with the dominant conceptions of development, since their activities merely contribute to perpetuating the given state of the world-system, and with it the status of the world-system's peripheries.

Whereas it is the peoples and groupings of the countries themselves who are responsible for effecting social transformation – as is the case everywhere in the world – Addo singles out the intellectuals, and points to their conjunctural responsibility for charting new, and possibly novel, ways towards conceiving and effecting transition from past history, through present history, to a desired future history.

In his 'Reflection on Developmentalism' Aseniero shows that underlying the apparent diversity of contending development theories is a deep and unquestioned consensus over key ideas that collectively make up what may be called the philosophy or paradigm of developmentalism. The two central tenets of developmentalism are firstly that history unfolds as progress, and secondly that this historical progression itself is manifested as development in and of nation-states. However, to designate the nation-state as the basic unit of development is to lose sight of the fact that it is the *world-system* which has been developing through the global accumulation of capital, unevenly as between its structural parts (core-periphery) and cyclically (expansion-stagnation phases), and that it is by virtue of their role in the *global capital accumulation* process that individual nation-states either 'develop' (the core) or 'underdevelop' (the periphery).

The developmentalist strategies currently being pursued by Third World countries are therefore supportive of the world-system because they are perfectly consistent with its organizational logic. They reproduce, in effect, the exploitative conditions of capital accumulation internally, while intensifying these countries' dependency within the world-economy.

The failure of developmentalist strategies to improve the living conditions of the impoverished majority of the world's population, even in cases where national growth rates are high, is cited as proof that development via deeper integration into the world-system represents an utterly false trail. It is an unbearably costly delusion. Aseniero proposes that only by abandoning the developmentalist paradigm can the route be opened up to grasping the concept of development as social transformation.

In 'Dead End' Fröbel, Heinrichs and Kreye examine the prospects of success facing the various crisis policies proposed, considered, or already implemented in the Western industrialized countries. The questions raised by the authors are the following: can these policies surmount the current economic crisis, if so, at whose expense, and whether, at the same time, these solutions facilitate first steps towards development as social transformation?

The mainly negative answers given by the authors raise fundamental and legitimate doubts as to whether economic policy, in the conventional narrow sense of the term, can ever be successful under current circumstances. The authors argue that it is well-nigh impossible for such policies to overcome the current economic crisis, and simultaneously lay the ground-work for the first long-overdue steps towards mitigating, and in the longer term solving, the pressing problems facing humanity without jettisoning the post-war model of capitalist development, and with it possibly the capitalist character of the economy and society in general.

For Fröbel, Heinrichs and Kreye this conclusion should not lead to resignation, but rather the demand for the restoration of the primacy of politics over the primacy of economics. The radical reorganization of economy and society, relations between nations, the relationship between humanity and nature, and relations between individuals which constitutes the necessary prerequisite for successfully tackling global problems in turn requires that society be liberated from the grip of capitalist economics. The first necessary and feasible steps must be judged by the extent to which they ease the way and prepare the success of subsequent steps.

'Dead End' does not imply the end of *all* politics: on the contrary, the crisis is charted as a period of great uncertainty, a period in which decisions will be taken as to who will bear the long-term costs of resolving the crisis, and in consequence decisions as to the future model of the intra- and inter-national political order. In such a period of uncertainty and perplexity, the likelihood of acts of desperation and insanity born of the world's rulers' sense of looming danger to themselves and their continuing capacity to wield decisive means of power is heightened enormously.

A time of crisis is a breeding-ground for calamity. But it also justifies and demands optimism, and a seizure of the initiative for the future course of events: a time of crisis can also therefore be a springboard for positive change.

'The Global Crisis and the Developing Countries', the second contribution by Fröbel, Heinrichs and Kreye examines the effects of the crisis of the capitalist world-system on the countries and peoples of the Third World. The deep and persistent economic, social, and political crisis provides a very clear demonstration of the fact that capitalist development, that is greater integration into the world-market, allows neither autonomous, self-reliant development nor any gradual surmounting of underdevelopment. Instead, many countries in the Third World are now hovering on the brink of economic bankruptcy.

The economic crisis has its counterpart in the political crisis both of the bourgeois-democratic state in the periphery, inasmuch as it has managed to survive, and the bourgeois-military state. Bourgeois-democratic states have not been able to fulfil the hopes and promises of an improvement in popular welfare attached to greater integration into the world-market. Bourgeois-military states are forced into closer collaboration with the imperialist powers, at the cost of the complete abandonment of state responsibility for the direction of the economy within the world-system – a role assigned to transnational corporations.

However, in many countries and regions of the Third World, the economic crisis of the capitalist world-system is not only giving renewed impetus to new alliances between and within the urban and rural proletariat; these alliances are also extending to the middle classes. And where this happens, the crisis may engender political forces strong enough to make further changes in the international power structures, and push ahead with the transformation of the developing countries' all too unequal incorporation into the international division of labour.

Frank's 'From Atlantic Alliance to Pan-European Entente' considers the viability of the political and economic arrangements and alignments of the post-war period in the wake of the current world economic crisis, and explores the possibility of the emergence of profound changes in the relations between nation-states and blocs. The author advances the thesis that the continued existence of the political and economic groupings and alliances established after the Second World War is entering a phase of heightened instability, undermining their former rationale.

Frank examines the growing confusion and dissatisfaction in the Atlantic Alliance, together with the changes in the balance of power between Europe and North America which have become particularly evident in the economic sphere. Concurrently growing economic and political conflicts are also beginning to show through inside the Soviet Union and Eastern Europe. The author examines whether an economic basis can be found for a pan-European economic and strategic political alternative, which might open up possibilities for a movement for world peace and the creation of a nuclear-free zone in Europe.

The author does not rule out the possibility of a reordering of the world political scene in which close co-operation between Eastern and Western Europe, with the abandonment of the Atlantic and other Alliances, including the growing Washington-Peking-Tokyo axis, could play significant roles.

Such a new order in East-West relations would be unlikely to liberate the South from its dependency: in fact, the stabilization of the world system which this might bring about could reinforce the Third World's subordinate status. Nevertheless, in the period of transition to such an amended world order, the South might find that it had some additional room for manoeuvre which could be exploited to obtain concessions from the competing powers.

Seki's 'Militarization and Development' deals with the question of war and peace, and their relationship to development and under-development. The author observes that, whereas the recent past was dominated by efforts to ease international tension, with the threat to survival coming from the issues of food, energy, raw materials and conservation, the breakdown of detente policies has now pushed the danger of war back into the forefront. The process of worldwide milita-rization, centred on the nuclear arms race between the great powers and the transfer of military equipment from the First and Second to the Third World, now represents the greatest threat to survival.

Seki points out that militarization, represented by the nuclear arms race at the top layer of the present world structure, and militarization in the form of arms transfers to the Third World to bolster the forces of repression, are not independent processes. They are the expression and the outcome of top level international rivalry, and characterize a politi-cal-military crisis which is likely to be exacerbated by the world eco-nomic crisis: militarization is the antithesis of development. Any theory or policy of development which rests on the perpetuation of militarization is not worthy of the name. And any theory of global disarmament and demilitarization must, perforce, constitute an alter-native theory of development, compatible with the conception of devel-opment as social transformation considered in this volume.

The elaboration of concepts of development based on demilitariza-tion requires first and foremost that scientists in universities and other research institutions create and insist on one vital precondition: the demilitarization of these institutions themselves.

Whether progressive forces in Japan can succeed in maintaining their country's post-war tradition of arms limitation, and extend this to support for peace-building forces, will play a major role in the current process of worldwide crisis and transformation: at present the question turns on whether Japan can be compelled by the hegemonic United States to build up and expand as a deputizing military presence.

The concluding two chapters by Friberg and Hettne, and Amin, debate the viability of a 'Green perspective' on development. Friberg and Hettne, arguing for such a perspective, present a critique of the evolutionist character of dominant theories and strategies of develop-ment, according to which development aims at a pre-given goal, is fixed and irreversible, progressivist, and cast within the confines of the nation-state. The authors trace the evolutionist tendencies in a number of historical and structural aspects of the modern Western world-system and relate them to their corresponding ideologies and cultural projects.

They reason that such a mechanistic and impersonal conception of development lapses into total determinism, foreclosing any role for human action and freedom. The goal of development, the authors argue, is precisely the full realization of the individual in every aspect of their being. A radical humanist approach to development requires rejection of the determinist models of evolutionist development theories, and must restore to human beings their freedom to choose the future and to act accordingly. The 'Green' approach to development thinking aims to do just this.

Development as social transformation understood from a Green perspective therefore requires withdrawal from the capitalist world-system, and the construction of a new, non-modern, non-capitalist model of development which can root itself in the progressive elements of pre-capitalist and post-materialist social orders, value systems, and experiences. The Green Movement is accordingly viewed as a world-wide movement, borne by the diverse attempts to resist enforced modernization observable throughout the world. The authors contend that its support comes from three main strands of resistance to modernization and capitalist expansion, located at different points in the centre-periphery structure of the world-system. The first are the traditionalists of various kinds in non-western structures, within the peasantry and in the 'informal' sector. The second are those marginalized individuals and groups with no stable foothold in the modern sector. And the third are the post-materialists, who are searching for new values and new forms of self-realization.

Amin's reply to the Green view begins with the observation that the aim of the Green Movement as formulated by its ideologists – liberation from the dictates of the system and human self-realization – is so fundamentally similar to the communism of Marx that it is incomprehensible why the Green position attempts to differentiate itself from Marxist socialism as much as it does from capitalism. Amin concedes that the traditional left – as we now encounter it – has either postponed these aims to the indefinite future or even denounced them as 'utopian', or – as Amin contends has happened in the Soviet Union – has distorted them. Although the Greens may have succeeded in formulating new problems, barely touched on in Marxism, this does not negate Marxism, and can in fact be seen as a possible enrichment and extension of it.

The aims of the Greens are not, therefore, new: moreover, they were also not the discovery of Marxism. Amin observes that the resistance of the oppressed and exploited has always given rise to counter-systems characterized by freedom, equality, and justice. Following the models of eighteenth century thought, Green ideology has a tendency to refer to the nature of humanity in isolation from the social forms of organization of material production. For Amin this is a barren undertaking, offering no increase in either our knowledge of the world or our capacity to change it.

What the Greens term the Utopia of the total domination of nature is attributed to European culture and the Christian religion. In contrast, religions such as Hinduism and Buddhism see humanity as an integral part of nature. For Amin such an approach is unsatisfactory since it represents a step backwards from the approach embodied in historical materialism. The weaknesses contained in the Green's theory of society then reappear as weaknesses in their strategy for changing society.

Amin does not see the existence of the Green Movement as particularly surprising at this conjuncture: it represents a response to the mistakes in the strategy of the European Left over the last few decades. Like forms of religious fundamentalism, the Green theory of transformation does not represent a solution to the current crisis. It should rather be seen as a symptom of this very crisis.

Movements and forces for system change

In periods during which capitalist development is viable, that is, when it is possible to secure an adequate level of valorization despite its inherent contradictions, the system is highly resistant to the advance of political alternatives. The current global crisis is an indicator of the rundown of a once successful model, as yet without replacement by an alternative successful model. But the very intractability and persistence of this crisis creates new space, and demands, for decisions: we are impelled to re-think escapes from our collective human predicament!

By its nature the capitalist world-system constantly generates exploitation and oppression: but at the same time it also engenders oppositional political forces and programmes. However, to effect a social transformation such forces firstly need to act in concert or alliance, and secondly need to act in a context in which the immanent logic and dynamics of the system have rendered it untenable as a model of social and economic organization.

Social movements should therefore be looked at in terms of their potential for changing the system, that is in terms of their contributions to social transformation. And movements with such a potential have emerged, and are still being generated, at the points of conflict and contradiction in the system. In addition to the traditional labour and trade union movements in the industrialized countries, whose changing composition reflects changes in the historic composition of the working class, movements of workers' opposition have arisen in the Third World, adding their strength to peasant movements and struggles. The intensified despoliation of nature has produced a mass ecological movement with growing political power. The threat of war and the accumulation of weapons of mass destruction have prompted the emergence of the peace movement. And the contradictory demands of the system as regards women's role in production and reproduction have formed the basis for a feminist movement which is challenging patriarchal power at all levels.

Long-term and large-scale systems cannot be transformed in one historic stroke. Rather, historic transitions and transformations are the product of a combination of diverse forces acting in mutually reinforcing ways.

The critical state of the capitalist world-system in the 1980s shows more clearly than in previous decades the obsolescence of traditional development policies, and of problem-solving strategies which remain bound within the parameters of the current system. The crisis reveals, with particular poignancy, the system's urgent need for transformational change; and at the same time nourishes the tantalizing hope that the world-system will, in fact, be amenable to change.

It has become accepted in our decadent system that it is normal for the world to wink at dishonesty. But with our increasing ability not only to describe but to understand the sources of our global problems is it merely dishonesty or is it a crime to wink at the persistence of dehumanization?

1

Beyond Eurocentricity: Transformation and Transformational Responsibility*

Herb Addo

A cause for reflection

A reflection on any aspect of life involves the pleasant, or unpleasant, recall of certain sets of related problems and their silent but *honest* reconsideration in the light of a meaningful puzzle. This chapter is a reflection on fundamental aspects of the interrelated set of problems which appears to explain the poverty of development thinking and the ineffectiveness of development policies. It is meant to be read as if the reader were intruding on the mental soliloquy of a disenchanted believer in the current dominant traditions of development thought and practice.

The basis of this reflection involves a critical look at the epistemological foundations of the dominant world-view from the perspective of world-system methodology.[1] It is often unappreciated that understanding the nature of these – faulty – epistemological foundations is the key to understanding both the poverty of development thinking and the ineffectiveness of development policies. If we want to know where to

Author's Note: This essay is a product of the Structural Interpretation of International Inequality Project (S3IP) located at the Institute of International Relations, University of the West Indies, St. Augustine, Trinidad. The S3IP is a sub-project within the United Nations University's Project on Goals, Processes, and Indicators of Development (UNU/GPID). This chapter is a statement emerging from attempts within the GPID Project to integrate approaches to the development problematique. Thanks to the many who made this chapter possible, especially Lily Addo and all the authors of this volume. All errors and inadequacies are my own.

look and what we have to do fashion a viable development philosophy, an examination of these foundations of current development thinking is the source to which we must first turn.

Approaching this question from the perspective of world-system methodology makes a number of issues clear. Firstly, that the global and development problematiques are more or less co-terminous. The basic unicity of the world-system, fundamental to this methodology, compels us to recognize that the development of any one part of the world implies the development/underdevelopment of other parts too. Additionally, as I understand it, the very notion of global problematique carries with it a *humanizing* meaning and relevance when we consider the implications of the interrelatedness of social problems within the development of a given macro-historical system for the human condition. In our case this macro-system is the capitalist world-system, whose historic theme is the accumulation of capital and whose historic force is the purposive exploitation of human and non-human resources in the creation of surplus-value and profit.[2]

Secondly, once we have grasped the development component in the global problematique, it becomes clear that under our current historical circumstances, and if *development* is to have any meaning at all for our times, development has to be conceived as *global social transformation*. The need to recover such a meaning for the notion of development is rooted in the deception practised by the currently dominant concept of development with its professed attainability and masquerading desirability. The pursuit of this concept intensifies the dehumanizing meaning of our given world, as it perpetuates the system itself – rather than transcending it in order to enhance the feasibility of increasing humanization.

Thirdly, it becomes clear that we need to address the crying urgency for a reconsideration of the rigidities inherent in the dominant conceptions of 'approved' development images, and how these rigidities explain the limited span of the dominant conceptions of the 'transformational responsibility'. Included here is the over-determinist interpretation of the nature of future history. What is involved here is a confrontation with the determinist-voluntarist dialectic.

All the observations sketched out should also be seen in the context of the worrisome malaise creeping into debates on development thinking, occasioned by the belief that all that can be said about development has already been said. While this may be true, the question is whether all that *needs* to be said about development has in fact been said.[3]

The meaningful puzzle posed by the global problematique is at once both comprehensive, intimidating and elusive. What is intriguing, however, is the interrelatedness of the lesser curiosities which make up the puzzle. The first difficulty we encounter when dealing with the global problematique is, consequently, the choice of the proper point of entry into the cluster of curiosities. Each lesser curiosity may serve as a convenient point of entry into the subject, but I prefer to capture the comprehensiveness of the subject from the broadest possible base. I therefore opt to approach the global problematique via a discussion of the partisan foundations of its epistemology – an appropriate starting point since our concern is to understand the common characteristics shared by the dominant interpretations of reality in order to set about the matter of the transformation of this reality.

The manner of reflection[4]

There is no single, generic term offering an uncontroversial portrayal of all the methods (sciences, disciplines and theories) which deal with the study of human beings in societies since the *meanings* and *values* placed on societies by social individuals and groups change as these societies unfold as cultures in space and time. There are at least three clearly discernible methods within the dominant interpretations of social reality: the social sciences (or liberal political economy), radical political economy, and historical materialism.

Each of these three methods brings a distinctive approach to the area and object of study. The social sciences compartmentalize the subject matter into separate parts, with only rare attempts at approaching the subject as a whole. In such rare instances the *via media* takes the form of the superficial multi-disciplinary approach. The effective divorce of the political and the economic succeeds in impoverishing both: where this is realized casual attempts are made to slap the study of the political together with that of the economic to create what is best described as liberal political economy, with little regard for the organic and intricate relationships between these two and other areas as they bear on the understanding of epochal transformations.

Although radical political economy is much more aware that its subject-matter is complex and exists as an interconnected whole, its theoretical categories nevertheless remain extremely limited. Elaborated within the specific context of the capitalist mode of production, they fail us by not providing much of a theory of epochal transformation. This method tends to be analytic and usually stops once it has reached the significance of class conflicts and relations, and intimated the strategic importance of class struggle. What it shares in common with the third method, Marx's historical materialism, is a mere product of the fact that it provided the real point of departure and object of critique for Marx. The fact that some radical political economists consider themselves marxist, because of this critical bond and their mutual demarcation from liberal political economy, owes much to the fact either that they continue to subscribe to the conception of marxism as positivist social theory, or because the term 'political economy' retains, at least in English language and culture, a certain inherited nineteenth century radical aura which is not found in other linguistic renditions, such as French or Spanish.[5]

Marx's historical materialism was propounded not simply as a critique of a misapplication of science or method, otherwise capable of producing better analytical results, but as a critique of the status of the economic in social life;[6] and it was essentially meant to inject, not merely introduce, Marx's discovery[7] that social life can *only* be understood by going beyond the purely economic and advancing towards a dialectical grasp of the laws of motion of society and their transformations, and of the forms of alienation which tend to prevail in any historically given social system.[8]

Our central concern here is not, however, to provide a rejoinder to some of the typical criticisms levelled against marxism – that it is 'economistic', 'over-deterministic' and so on. Instead we wish to engage in the proposition that, despite their differences, all three methods share certain fundamental characteristics, which by virtue of these methods' *loyal subscription to a common European (or Western) world-view* open *all* of these methods to the charge of *Eurocentricity*.

Thus, in addition to the strong criticism of marxist orthodoxy, which identifies it as *positivist*, *idealist* (and perhaps analytical), *revisionist* and *developmentalist*,[9] a further criticism can be levelled – that it is also Eurocentric. If this criticism is to be voiced, then one purpose of this chapter is to advance the thesis, in fact to make it plain, that Third World problems and perspectives[10] raise certain questions which ought not to be beyond the scope of historical materialism, and which only appear to be so because of orthodox marxism's Eurocentric rigidities. Our argument is intended as a provocative confrontation with marxist orthodoxy, the kind of critical confrontation marxism may well need if it is to move on, and live up to its claim to universal validity.

The Eurocentric world-view is not a science with epistemological innocence[11]

Our initial concern is with the basic principles underlying the relationships within and between cultures with respect to the production and the appropriation of both material and non-material human needs. These basic principles may appear simple and uncomplicated, but the modes of their study are complex and even confusing, given that the basic puzzle which informs the basic principles and their lesser curiosities is this: *why do human beings in given societies, within large-scale historical systems, produce what they produce in the way they produce it; and why do they appropriate what they produce in such a way as to fail to meet maximum humanizing conditions?*[12] This puzzle refers to the key properties of large-scale long-term historical systems in terms of the historic referrents which define the systems' historic identities.

The two parts of this initial puzzle deliberately hide more than they reveal, as the real source of concern lies in the *interlink* between the two parts. Neither in fact nor in the realm of ideas is this link a peaceful one. In both realms it is full of tensions, conflicts and struggles.

At one level, this interlink is concerned with how a given culture, at a particular time, conceives of what it is to be a human being, and how this conception deviates from the fundamental notions of value in that culture, and further how epistemology, theory and construction of knowledge, sets about understanding and eliminating this gap between a culture's ontology and its axiology. At another level the interlink appears to involve a deep and intricate organic relationship between the science and philosophy of production on the one hand, and the science and philosophy of distribution or appropriation on the other with the objective of pursuing humanity's sempiternal ontological vocation – the confronation of dehumanization by increasing humanization, with the goal of fully humanized societies.[13]

The fact that the whole area is so value-laden means that methods employed are of necessity ridden with controversy, and do not contain a single question (or statement) that can be considered *objectively* innocent, and hence uninteresting. All those entering this field and remaining in it long enough sooner or later acquire their own strong convictions as to what the initial puzzle and the interlink between its two parts *should be*. This leads to a situation where no hands in this endeavour can remain clean for too long, all protestations to the contrary notwithstanding. Seeking equity in the scientific context, therefore, becomes so difficult that, ideally, separate courts of equity must exist to cater for different scientific pleas of objective innocence.[14]

The absence of such courts raises a problem. It is that some particular courts not only claim, but also appear to have, real jurisdiction over all that goes on in the discipline. These courts claim to be authoritative and legitimate because they are *established* and that other courts are not because they are only pretenders to legitimate and authoritative jurisdiction. This is what brings about the everpresent struggles and tensions within schools of thought and between their higher courts in the discipline. As a result of this, a discourtesy persists in the establishment. It is that for works to be considered scientific and therefore scholarly, they must be deemed neutral and objective. However, the criteria for being neutral and objective are either *unspecified, misleading, or deliberately deceptive* as regards some of their universal claims. The sources of motivation, provocation, encouragement and sympathies which inform the criteria of the neutral and objective are, in most cases, either never boldly expressed or highly partisan in their foundations.

To be fair, there are different ideas of what constitute the scientific, the neutral, and the objective in the different methodological/

ideological camps within the establishment itself. But then our argument is precisely that, despite the ideological divisions, liberals, radicals
and orthodox marxists are part of the establishment by virtue of the
common claims to neutrality and objectivity which all three make.

I raise these issues at the outset not so that they can be forgotten, but
so that their further discussion will lead to a critical consideration of the
nature, the motive, and the methods of the commonality between the
different ideological camps within the establishment. Principally, I
raise these issues so that I can argue that the problem for us is not so
much that there are many contending orthodoxies, but that, because of
the history of our present large-scale historical system, these orthodoxies operate consciously or unconsciously toward the realization of a
purpose. These orthodoxies, liberal, radical, and orthodox marxist,
have a commonality in motive and methods that make them more
similar than is often recognized. I have two forwarding propositions to
make in this regard.

The first is that the claims to scientific neutrality and objectivity
come easily to the establishment; indeed they are natural to it because,
apparent ideological divisions notwithstanding, the establishment
holds fast to a deep-seated common world-view: a common theoretical
structure of what the world *is like* and *ought to be like*; and what *it is
about* and *ought to be about*. It is because of this common world-view
that most works share the common characteristics of being extremely
anti-sceptic and highly predictable. They are anti-sceptic in the sense
that they lack the honest individual indications of the deep-seated
motive behind the works; and they are predictable because the theoretical structure of the common world-view is so deeply hidden in the very
epistemological pores of the establishment that it is taken for granted in
ways which can be counted upon to inhibit new insights into the complexity of the articulation of the interlink between the two parts of the
basic puzzle.

The second proposition is that, because the common world-view
takes so much for granted, the different ideological options within it,
which are strictly no more than mere variations on the common theme
of a world-view, are uncritically promoted to the ranks of radically
opposite and contending world-views.

It is this common theme of a world-view that I call *Eurocentric*. The
term Eurocentric, as used here, is meant to express the belief that the
dominant world-view within the establishment, all ideological hues
within it considered, holds fast to the common fallacy of mistaking the
European dominance in the world-system – world-economy and
world-history – for the world-system itself.

I have long suspected that the dominant views in the establishment
share two prominent properties. One is the propensity, even perhaps a
conscious conspiratorial understanding, to illuminate the world for
Europeans and Europeanized elements in the world only; and the other
is the propensity, even the vocational predilection, to obscure the world

for Non-Europeans. This suspicion, even if it were to be proved infallibly correct, would amount to very little, as Eurocentrics, as much as any other centric, should not be denied the right to understand the world in their own fashion.

However, there is a problem. It is that, when we consider this suspicion together with the undeniable European dominance in the modern world-system, then we happen upon a very serious intellectual charge, a charge serious enough to amount to the 'indictable' offence of Eurocentrics using European dominance in the world-system wittingly or unwittingly to mislead the entire world into thinking as though all its inmates were European, Europeanized, or ought to be Europeanized.

This charge will be hard to prosecute, especially if Eurocentrics plead that, given the world for what it is, it is perfectly legitimate, indeed it is only to be expected, that Eurocentrics, or any others, will try to influence the rest of the world intellectually and otherwise in their own interests.

A successful prosecution of this charge, therefore, will have to base its arguments on the unfairness of the *methods* used by Eurocentrics to mislead the world.

One aspect of the establishment's Eurocentric method is to fashion the ideas about the world and to formulate categories, concepts, and their interrelationships into frameworks, theories etc. in such ways as to explain the world only to Europeans and Europeanized elements. The other aspect is that, while the process of obscuring the world for Non-Europeans is going on, there is to be a severe vigilance against non-Eurocentric and anti-Eurocentric views and ideas about the world.

This is done in two ways. First, any ideas outside the Eurocentric conceptions of the world are decried vehemently, whatever their sources. This is intended to strike terror into the hearts of the carriers of un-Eurocentric ideas. Second, should such ideas prove useful to European interests they should then be deliberately and consistently interpreted in such ways that they can be co-opted into the ideological options within the common Eurocentric world-view. This is meant to ensure the permanence of European dominance in the realm of ideas. The adage appears to be – let a thousand ideas contend, as long as they are all of the Eurocentric kind, useable by, or compatible with Eurocentric ambitions.[15]

All this does not make Eurocentricity and its methods necessarily guilty. It is the purpose behind the Eurocentric methods that makes it guilty, intellectually dishonest, and, therefore, unacceptable as a way of explaining the entire world-system, of which Europe is only a part, even if the dominant part, to the entire world. The purpose appears to be the maintenance of European dominance in this world and its preservation in any transformed future world. The motive component of this purpose appears to be that the European culture, through the dominance of its ideas, will continue to dominate this world and any transitional processes in the present world-system so as to ensure that the inevitable transformation of this world will still assure European dominance in any ensuing new world-order. But then, there are two sides to the story. If the motive is what makes the Eurocentric world-view guilty, dishonest, and therefore unacceptable, then I suggest that what makes it pathetic, in the humiliating sense of the word, are the meek acceptance and blind implementation of this world-view by most intellectuals in the world, especially those in the periphery of the world-system.

This to my mind is a serious indictment of both sides. But I do not think it is the kind of indictment that would or should be passed on to a higher court for an impartial and just trial by the establishment. Why? Because any representative grand jury will be heavily loaded in favour of the establishment. At best, such a jury will consist of fair representations from the liberal, radical, and orthodox marxist variants of the establishment – all of them Eurocentric.

The intention, therefore, is not to refer the Eurocentric indictment to any higher court. My concern in this regard is to address my arguments to those who, for one good reason or another, suspect the validity and seriousness of the Eurocentric charge. It is addressed to those who have good reasons to be critical of the contending orthodoxies, and especially of the Eurocentric vestiges lurking within the potentially promising basis offered by marxism. I shall discuss this charge with reference to the development problematique. But before this, let me state the nature of my world-system critique of Eurocentricity. It is an objection to the dominant interpretation of the global problematique or the 'world reality problem'. The essence of it is that *dominant conceptions of the world reality consider the Non-European parts of the world as merely underdeveloped Europe. These conceptions pretend to be explaining the world to the entire world, while in fact they explain Europe and the world to Europeans and their Europeanized trustees in other parts of the world in pursuit of the goal of perpetuating European dominance in the world-system.*

An analogy may be useful at this juncture. Let us imagine an 'epistemological coin' for our area of endeavour. If we let one face represent the methodology of the discipline, then it is perhaps appropriate to let the other face represent its theory. This can mean that the *reality* which the discipline deals with can be conceived of as the matter between the two faces of the coin, contained by its edge. From this, it can be argued that method and theory are inseparable and that they are perhaps more important than the matter they claim to explain. To push the analogy a step further, we can reason that, generally, faces of coins display their imprimatur and their money values, with little reference to the actual value of the metal composing the coin; and that because of this, perhaps, methods and theories should alert us to, if not tell us about, their sources of origin and therefore the nature of their dominance and their motives.

This should indicate how much the epistemological basis of our field of endeavour should be worth to different students of this discipline, depending, of course, upon their particular situations and persuasions. This is to say that, because of its dominant imprimatur, the real value of the dominant epistemology must, in the best of circumstances, differ for different students, again depending on their particular persuasions. Different persuasions should lead to different curiosities *vis-à-vis* the basic puzzle and the interlink between its two parts.

From this, I shall ask an important rhetorical question to prevent the reader from dismissing these arguments prematurely. This is not so much for what these arguments say in terms of finality, but more for what they illustrate, intimate and provoke. The question is: *given the European dominance in evolving the modern large-scale historical system since the late fifteenth century, is it all that woefully untenable to suggest that the epistemology and the derivative theories and methodologies in establishment political economy are Eurocentric?*

We should note that the dominant pretence of explaining the world to the world, on its own terms, is not fallacious. On its own terms, it is not necessarily unscientific or unobjective. What it is and means is that, on the world-scale *of explanation*, the dominant explanation is partisan because of the motive of its adherents. And the argument is that the dominant conception of the world reality problem, that is the global problematique, is partisan in all its different but established interpretations.

The partisan point of entry

If we can agree that there is nothing resembling an impartially interpreted social reality, then we can also agree that one partisan interpretation of reality cannot call for anything less than another partisan interpretation. The adherents of each interpretation must have their own motive and their own methodology. In fact, it is the motive which in all cases dictates the appropriateness of the methodology. In our field of endeavour, at least, methodology is no more than a way of approaching the interpretation of a reality problem. Invariably, a prescribed methodology is inherent in a theory – the structure of explanation – of a reality problem. Every partisan interpretation of a reality problem, therefore, has something crucial about it, which I shall refer to as the partisan point of entry into the understanding of that reality.

If we can agree that the dominant partisan point of entry into the world reality problem is the perpetuation of European dominance in the world-system, then we must agree that the overriding dominant methodological concern is how to approach the interpretation of the modern world-system in order to make it safe for – that is amenable or conducive to – the perpetuation of European dominance in this world-system. What, then, is my point of entry into the world reality problem?

It is one which is, first of all, unabashedly partisan, best expressed through the following complex question: why was it that the Third World was dominated, oppressed, and exploited; and having been so treated in the past, continues to be so treated, even if the modes of the treatment have changed with time? Specifically, *why do these parts of the world continue to make it possible for this treatment to persist at this late post-independence phase of world capitalism*? Clearly, the motive behind this question is to understand the world-system in such a way that we can set about the task of making it impossible for the centre to dominate and exploit the periphery in the future.

It is true that, during the past twenty-five years or so, the ever-present uneasiness which breeds the ever-present contentions in our field of endeavour has come to centre prominently on the plight of the periphery in what is now becoming increasingly seen as the *capitalist* world-system and its *capitalist* world-economy.[16]

There have been many related questions discussed in connection with the plight of the periphery in the world-system. These questions have in the main dealt with the nature of the internal conditions of the societies of the periphery, the nature of the internal conditions of the centre societies, and the extent to which the former is not like the latter. Causal relationships between the two internal conditions were not considered interesting problematics. What became known as development studies, or modernization, therefore concerned itself largely with one question, which was how the internal conditions of the societies of the periphery could be made similar to those of the centre societies. This question was considered adequate to all intents and purposes, because it was held that development or modernization had to do with how the non-European world could be Europeanized. Development studies and modernization did ask *why* some parts of the world were supposedly developed and other parts were not. This question had to be asked, and yet from the dominant perspective, the establishment had known the answer to it all along in world-history: the non-European areas and their cultures were not Europeanized enough for them to develop to look like the European areas of the world.

This was the axiom from which all deductions flowed. The scientific answer was that, to *develop*, the non-European areas must change to look like Europe by imitating Europe and European history. This way of looking at the world reality problem is long-standing in European philosophy of social change.

Robert Nisbet, for example, treats this matter very well, but only as an aspect of the western theory of development, in his *Social Change and History*.[17] What this book most reveals, in terms of transformation and transition, is that European philosophy of history is *developmentalist* and *developmental*, and that this philosophy has its material basis in the emergence of the capitalist world-system.[18]

These two terms, developmentalist (from developmentalism) and developmental (from development) differ in their philosophical roles, even though the first term incorporates the second, and they both share a common etymology.

Developmentalism refers to a philosophy of history, the philosophy informing the articulations within and between cultures as they unfold through time. The developmentalist conception of history has three crucial dimensions to it. Firstly, it holds the *progressivist* notion of history. Secondly, it rides on the *derogatory* comparison with other cultures. And thirdly, it is, by combined derivation from the other two dimensions, *expansionist*, seeking to dominate and exploit, by enculturalizing others. These three dimensions combine to mean that developmentalism is by nature dominance-prone and exploitation-oriented. These are not its defining criteria, however. Many, if not most, culturally specific social philosophies may display these tendencies. In the case of developmentalist social philosophy, its defining criteria are that it is *limitless*, not so much in fact as in its *progressivist*, *derogatory* and *expansionist* ambitions.

For a social philosophy to be developmentalist, it must display limit-less ambitions in these three dimensions in its real history. Carriers of a developmentalist philosophy of history consider their culture to be the vanguard of the progressivist movement in universal history and, there-fore, they consider their culture superior to all other cultures. This is a blinding world-view which may take similar but exaggerated forms even in its apparent opposites. This world-view compels expansion, but falsely justifies its expansionist impulses in pursuit of exploitation, no matter how thinly veiled, as civilising missions which are not in any way related to the historic theme of historic periods.

Development, as a distinct and core component within a develop-mentalist philosophy, deals with the specifics of the concrete and the actualizing aspects of this philosophy at particular times within a his-toric period. It deals essentially with what is to be done, or not to be done, within the developmentalist philosophy to assist (through updating and legitimizing) the continuity of the dominance of the dominating culture.

One thing ought to be clear. Many cultures may have harboured developmentalist ambitions, some may have even displayed develop-mentalist pretensions, and yet, as far as we know, only the Western (I prefer the term European) civilization has succeeded in actualizing and universalizing these ambitions and pretensions over the past five hun-dred years or so. Our contemporary world is nothing, if we do not conceive it as in large part formed by the relentless pursuit of the world-scale ambitions of European developmentalist philosophy, together with the effects of this pursuit. We know this pursuit will end in collapse some day – the product of the escalating contradictions which inhabit this pursuit. I suppose we can at least be grateful for this benign knowledge. But my question is, will this eventually impending collapse also be the end of Eurocentricity?

Not necessarily. There is nothing in history, or elsewhere, which indicates that the collapse of world capitalism will also mean the end of Eurocentricity. The present world-system is capable of collapsing and a new system arising in its ashes, still bearing an Eurocentric imprint. What this new imprint will look like is beside the point: it can still be Eurocentric.[19]

The immediate post-Second World War liberal wing within the establishment conceived the modern world as one of an uncompromising *duality*, rather than as a set of related *contradictions* and their implied paradoxes.[20] The world economy consisted of dual economies of developed and underdeveloped sectors, both within and between societies. But nowadays, because of certain influences,[21] even the liberal view of the world reality has tempered itself enough to adopt the argument that the two sets of economies and societies are not necessarily unrelated; nevertheless, they continue to stress that the dual nature of the two realities within the modern world reality is more important than any relationships between the separate realities within the dualistic whole. The only time when it is legitimate to breach the sacred duality of the world reality is when it comes to the diffusion of the exogenous sources of 'progressive' change from the centre into the periphery. This liberal view was severely criticized by Andre Gunder Frank in his classic essay, 'Sociology of Development and Underdevelopment of Sociology'.[22]

From the point of view of development, and with the increasing demonstration of the difficulties inherent in the liberal conception of the duality of the world reality problem, the question confronting this brand of Eurocentrics became why, despite their theories, the development-underdevelopment duality persisted in its traditional or unmodern perversity. This question centred around the lack of evidence indicating that the Third World countries were getting more complex in social structures and growing economically toward 'taking off' on their predicted self-sustained paths of development, just as the European countries had done earlier.

The pursuit of this question has been very interesting, even if as a career it has been rather inauspicious. The debates which this question engendered became something akin to battlegrounds for inner-Eurocentric ideologies. The positions taken by the different Eurocentric ideological camps are what are often presented as immaculate universal theories and explanation of the underdevelopment of the Third World, and often as the basis for the hopeful Eurocentric predictions regarding the dissolution of underdevelopment.

While in general everybody in the establishment contemplated *what* was responsible for underdevelopment in terms of endogenous Third World societies' deficiencies and prescribed exogenously diffusionist

Eurocentric solutions, the radical/marxist alliance within the establishment contemplated in particular *who* was responsible for the underdevelopment of the Third World societies. This latter question did not exclude the question of '*what* was responsible'. The alliance had known the answer all along: it was capita*lism* of the centre societies. Rather, it emphasized '*who* was responsible' and came out with the startling discovery that capita*lists* of the centre were responsible.

We should note two things very carefully at this point. The first is that neither of these views sees underdevelopment as the property of the world-system itself. It remains the property of the periphery of the world-system. That both views see underdevelopment as the property of the peripheral parts of the system, even if they locate the sources of the causes differently, is important to note. Second, both views conceive development as the progressive *imitation* of the social history of the centre by the periphery: Europeanization is synonymous with development.

And yet the radical/marxist way of putting the question seems to indicate something very crucial. It seems to indicate how far we have come towards posing the right question. We seem to be moving away from regarding underdevelopment as the property of parts of the world-system due to some sort of a natural law, the explanation for which must be sought in inanimate and superstitious realms. I say 'we seem to be moving', because it is not yet clear whether we have moved far enough away from Eurocentric mystifications of development, as understood in terms of the crude contest for primacy between 'endogenous' and 'exogenous' factors. All this is true, and yet nobody can gainsay the fact that we seem to have come a long way from viewing underdevelopment as some stage which some parts of the world, for one silly reason or the other, must go through and which will consume itself provided some simple Eurocentric precepts of imitation, planning, and revolutionary rhetorics are indulged in.

Lately, if we have come nearer to formulating the proper question with the respect to underdevelopment, we did not come this far easily. It has taken an intense struggle against conventional wisdoms to establish the baseline that underdevelopment of parts of the world, in contrast to the development of parts of it, has something to do with the actions of groups of individuals as they have interacted on the face of the earth over the last few centuries in a particular history which has benefited some groups and hurt others. This is no mean achievement, considering the initial one-sided nature of the struggle between ideas.

The developmental relations between the centre and the periphery in the flow of modern world history which had been discussed by Marx in *Capital*[23] rightly became the basis for opposing the liberal orthodoxy in the explanation of the persistence of poverty in the periphery. The persistence and the insistence of the liberal orthodoxy, we should note, only encouraged the intransigence and the rigidity of marxist orthodoxy. The problem with marxism in this regard, however, became not so much that there threatened to be as many orthodoxies as there were marxists, but that a certain reverential deference towards the alleged meaning of Marx's corpus inhibited the opening up and reconsideration of a number of crucial matters in the light of developments in the global development-underdevelopment contradiction.

Marx's method of historical materialism now runs the risk of being turned into marxology. Rather than serve as the solid and open basis it should be for a fresh wave of intellectual assault on crucial problems, it has now become nothing less than a formidable obstacle to such an assault.

The problem facing orthodox marxism at present is not that it has become fashionable for all those finding the liberal irrationalities and rationalizations of conventional wisdom repugnant to call themselves marxist. The problem is precisely that orthodox marxism continues to be guarded by a viscous legion of versatile Eurocentric adherents who appear well-versed in every scratch in the huge marxist corpus. This legion is ever-alert to the slighest dissonance between its tensile interpretations of 'what Marx meant' and the most well-intended attempts at extending, reviewing, or even merely re-reading, Marx in the light of the non-fulfilment of marxist expectations and the emergence and discovery of new *real* problems.[24]

This orthodox marxist rigidity inhibits the timely realization that, from the point of view of the periphery, many marxist categories, their derivative concepts, their endowed contents, and the interrelationship between them, need urgent up-dating if that hint of dualism in marxism, which is masked by the belief in the universal and progressive mission of Eurocentric capitalism, is to be exposed as a handicap in the proper conception of the world-system for the purpose of facilitating the understanding of its transformation.

As we move from Eurocentric consciousness to world-system consciousness, our categories and concepts must be reconsidered in the light of rendering them useable at the world-system level. For example, the bourgeois-proletarian class contradiction remains a *primary* contradiction, and yet approaching the issue from the world-system perspective,[25] it becomes clear that this primary contradiction is meaningful, as primary, only if we associate it very closely with a *major* contradiction: the centre-periphery contradiction in the world-system. In fact, the class contradiction is primary precisely because it causally incorporates or implies, without any denigration to it, the major contradiction between the centre and periphery at the world-level. This suggests that, in explaining the developed-underdeveloped contradiction, first, we must put emphasis on the historical tensions and forces which distinguish between the centre and the periphery; and second, we must explain the articulation and the persistence of these tensions and forces in terms of class interests and alliances *within* and *between* the centre and periphery with respect to the persistence (or reproduction) of the relations between centre-centre, periphery-periphery, and centre-periphery societies.

Approached in this way, we are alerted with enhanced sensitivity to the characters of internal-centre and internal-periphery class identities and interests. This heightened sensitivity is necessary if we are going to be able to appreciate the thinkable possibility, at least, of some of the orthodox marxist unthinkables at this point in world history. We may come to understand, for example, that in periphery societies the proletariat is very privileged indeed, as Frantz Fanon argued,[26] compared to the many proletarianized, unemployed, and other exploited groups, outside the industrial workers proper, who remain a minority in most cases. This indicates that to talk of 'proletariat' (in most societies) in the periphery is not quite the same thing as to talk of 'proletariat' in the centre. And from this, we may come to the question as to whether the fetish attachment to the proletariat as the revolutionary class in the periphery, to the exclusion of the other exploited majority classes may not itself be a Eurocentric factor with its roots in the nineteenth century.[27]

Further, if indeed the centre-periphery contradiction is really a historical process, the product of the capitalist world-system in evolution, and not due to any magical presence of dualism and its stubborn interference with the effectiveness of the progressive mission of capitalism, then it may be that the fluctuating, but all the same abating, class confrontation in the centre societies indicates that perhaps 'international workers' solidarity' may not have much of an objective basis on the world-scale.[28] It may well be that this much touted solidarity has always been no more than a clever Eurocentric deception.[29]

The *need* for such an objective solidarity may be there. But for it to be transformationally meaningful, should there not be, subjectively, an *immediately perceived* commonality of interests between workers of the world? Truly, is there such commonality of interests? Indeed, has there ever been, as between centre and periphery societies?

Let us reconstruct this important argument, in order to be sure we are absolutely clear. Nation-states are time-specific balances of contending social forces, the external appearances (their characterization by others) of which are the results of internal class contradictions. This means that class contradictions are primary. We can agree on this. But we can also agree that, given the peripheral capitalist nature of certain societies and the very existence of 'advanced' but 'external' class conflicts in other nation-states, we should attempt to understand the transformational relevance of class alliances in terms other than the validity of the objective primacy of class contradictions : in terms of the close link between the *major* and the *primary* contradictions as described above.

In anti-colonialist and anti-imperialist struggles, alliances are probable, in fact common, between the local elites and the masses. These alliances do not detract from the primacy of class contradiction. It remains valid all the time and moreover it determines the directions and contents of these struggles. Such alliances are, however, always perilous. If this is so, then what grounds do we have other than the objective validity of the primacy of class contradiction, to expect an abiding alliance between the proletariat of the centre and the proletariat of the periphery?

Subjectively, it must be extremely difficult for the proletariats of the centre to appreciate the *objective* need for solidarity with the proletariats of the periphery and vice versa. This is all because of the major contradiction of the centre-periphery, differing circumstances within the world-system, nationalist ideologies, and the very logic of the system itself.

For instance, as the present crisis deepens and unemployment rises in the centre, while transnational corporations continue to transfer production processes to low-wage areas in the periphery, workers in the centre should realize that it is through the logical consequence of the transnationalization of capital that they are losing their jobs to such areas, and that it is the transnationals' manipulation of wage differentials in the world economy which enables them to resist demands for higher wages from workers in the centre, indeed to punish them by depriving them of their jobs.

On this specific issue, the anti-imperialist resistance of the Third World and the fight by centre-workers against the export of jobs *should find some objective common ground*. However, the fact that the subjective differences intervene to obscure the objective validity of the common ground should lead us to be concerned with the extent of the objective realization of this valid objective basis. If the transformational validity of this crucial transitional basis is not subjectively grasped – because of ideological and other interventions – then this is simply an indicator of how far workers' action and consciousness-raising, 'international workers' solidarity' still has to go for it to start making transitional sense. In this regard, there is one question which we should not evade: if international workers' solidarity has so far only advanced this far, then are we not correct in questioning the theoretical-methodological (epistemological) basis of its imputation?

The main problem, then, is whether the societies of the periphery are to view their historic reality and its transformation in terms of their own critical interpretation of history, for which they may find marxist and other referents useful, or whether they are to blind themselves with the uncritical adoption of Eurocentric formulae. This is important to consider, if we are to move on.

Does the powerful marxist thesis of unequal development have any relevance outside national confines, then? If it does, why the orthodox reluctance to break away from the conception of the *world* as no more than a set of nations nebulously related only through European dominance, in fact and in ideas?[30] Why then, the predilection to confuse the impure notion of 'social formations' with the purity of 'modes of production' in criticizing the correct view that the world-system, whose dominance is capitalist, has an impure nature but an identity of its own, and as such must be approached on its own distinct terms?[31]

Is it not true that 'long-distance trade', in both its exotic forms as well as in the changing natures of trade and commerce themselves, has always had something to do with the continuing violent contact between European and non-European cultures?[32] Has this violent contact not remained ever since it started in the late fifteenth century to shape our modern world and has it not taken the changing forms of the plundering of valuables through formal colonizations to the present huge differentials in the integrated rewards for labour-power – wages – as between the centre and the periphery economies, 'unequal exchange'?

But most importantly, in the course of all this, have most of the peripheral states which have emerged lately not proved themselves competent accomplices in the exploitation of the peripheral societies by the centre through believing that they can repeat the 'European transitions' in European fashions by imitating European values in their frantic efforts to live up to the Eurocentric belief that modern non-European history is not much more than Europeanization processes in peripheral societies? Can we ignore this matter?

These are questions we cannot avoid asking, if the intention is to approach the reality problem from the totality of the world as a large-scale historical system and not from the Eurocentric perspective.

The oppressive hand of Eurocentricity appears to lie as heavily on the orthodox marxist mode of thought as it lies on the liberal and radical modes. In the marxist case, however, nowhere is this clearer than in the 'great transition debate' initiated by Maurice Dobb and Paul Sweezy in 1950.[33] The fact that this debate has been resurrected at different times since the original debate (Laclau-Frank, Bettelheim-Emmanuel, and Brenner-Wallerstein debates)[34] indicates that if there is any challenge in marxism today it does not lie in reading classical marxist sources in order to provide orthodox statements of what the sources mean or actually intended to say.

The challenge in marxism, then, it would appear, lies in reading classical and other marxist sources and having the courage to apply *interpretations* of and *insights* from these sources to various social problems in ways that transcend the Eurocentric orthodoxies which confine aspects of marxism and threaten to reduce its immense value as a philosophy of transformation: a mode of practical analysis of *apparently changing* realities to reveal their *constancies* and *continuities* and *apparently constant* realities to reveal their *changingness* and *variations*.

The real problem here is the need to recognize that even a highly developed critical social philosophy can very easily become under-developed in its *anti-systemic* critical functions by becoming a prisoner of its own orthodoxy in the changing circumstances of the world reality problem. Marxism was initially a critical anti-systemic philosophy. But it is rapidly slipping from its *anti-systemic* critical role to a comfortable *anti-regime* role.[35] It lacks the honest and fluid ability to update itself through internal criticism. As it is in history, in medicine, and in the sciences today, what is interesting in marxism is not where marxism is right, but in discovering where it is wrong: in discovering its Eurocentric rigidities. There is an unfortunate mystification going on and it is Eurocentric mystification within orthodox marxism.

Ashis Nandy argues that it is possible to visualize an alternative ethics of scientific interpretation which would admit no end of demystification. He says that the credo of such ethics, 'could well be summarized as "unending interpretation" . . . where the interpretation which the interpreter provides is ultimately seen as both self-interpretative and self-enriching'.[36] Nandy argues that in the case of marxism, to the extent that it 'proclaims itself a science, it too might have to give up its faith in the conscientizing vanguard and in the revolutionary consciousness that the masses are supposed to acquire as the pupils of a new priesthood. Only then could marxism, as a science, hope to be a powerful critique of everyday commonsense, standing for conventionality and conformity.'[37] Nandy argues further that marxism is bound to a particular conception of the limits of interpretation or demystification. In marxism, demystification 'stops once it reaches the level of the mode of production or class relations'.[38] The biggest worry, in my view, is the European purity with which marxism endows these and other categories.

But, can there be a clear world-view without a distinctive and supportive historiography? Can there be a dominant world-view without a characteristic dominant historiography? Of course not! To the extent that there is such a historiography and to the extent that the dominant world-view is in fact Eurocentric, the argument cannot be that conventional European history – the methodical narration and chronology of European events and other events involving Europe – is Eurocentric.

The argument is that dominant historiography – the science or the art (not excluding the possibility of magic) of the construction of historical knowledge for universal consumption – is what is Eurocentric; and that Eurocentricity is to be understood in terms of the methods employed and the motive these methods serve in the evolution of the modern world-system, with specific reference to the undisputable European dominance in the history of this system. To the extent that history is the stuff from which we derive our knowledge about our world, its workings and its transformation, then it is the common fibre through the enormous intricacy and the all-pervading complexity of establishment historiography in its efforts to explain the world to the entire world that we should, I believe, call here Eurocentric.

Scholarship in the people's history movement[39] indicates efforts at departure from the Eurocentric conception of modern history as the immaculate presentation of the poetics and heroics of *supermen* portrayed by the 'use of categories which remain wholly external to the object they purport to account for'.[40] This movement strives to bring history closer to the lives of the majority of the people who actually make it.

There are many problems in this effort, however. The biggest problem is the sweetly tempting danger to swing the pendulum from the worship of heroes in history to the worship of 'the people' in the manner of Rousseauian worship of the noble savage. Another danger is the difficulty of inserting the particulars of 'the people' into the flow of the general in the articulation of historical forces while allowing for the historical movements and moments within the prominence of a specific and precise historic boundary. This is particularly worthy of note if historiography is to concern itself with what it should focus on, namely the transformation of our contemporary capitalist large-scale historical system. To do this, dominant historiography must move from the conception and construction of history as 'struggle between virtue and vice'[41] and a story of endless justified revenges.[42] Because of its transformational focus, historiography should concern itself with the effective narrowing of the ontological-axiological gaps at all levels within the world-system, as it moves on.

People's history, broadly and properly understood, shows that the most fascinating thing in the study of history today is not in the reinstatement of where history went right, but ironically in discovering where it went wrong and still continues to go wrong.[43]

The historiography informing the world-system methodology shares much in common with the people's history movement, but it has much more of its own. This method of approaching the global problematique realizes that the dominant basis and terms of ascertaining the validity of knowledge suffers from the dead and oppressive hand of a bygone era in the European tradition and even beyond that into the very antiquity and classical origins of European civilization.[44] Wallerstein puts it aptly, even if somewhat differently, when he states that, 'we have begun to open up, for the first time since the 1850s both the epistemological and historiographical premises of social science'.[45] Specifically,

In terms of epistemology, we are seeing a serious challenge to both universalization and sectorialization and an attempt to explore the methodology of holistic research, the implementation of that *via media* that had been excluded by the nomothetic-ideographic pseudo-debate of the nineteenth century. For the first time, the imagery of the route of scientific advance is being inverted. Instead of the assumption that knowledge proceeds from the particular towards ever more abstract truths, there are some who wish to argue that it proceeds from the simple abstractions towards ever more complex interpretations of empirical, that is historical, reality. This epistemological challenge has been made before as we have already noted, but is being made systematically and solidly today. What is really new, however, is the historiographical challenge. Once our unit of analysis shifts from the society-state to that of economic worlds, the entire reification of states, of nations, of classes, of ethnic groups, even of households falls away. They cease being primordial entities, Platonic ideals, whose real nature we must somehow intuit or deduce. They become constantly evolving structures resulting from the continuing development of long-term large-scale historical systems.[46]

Put this way, the message is that we should avoid developmentalist ideals, constructs, and abstractions; and instead we should pay heed to the important matter raised by Husserl and by Frank, at different times, to the effect that theory is history:[47] the theory explaining the development of a long-term large-scale historical system cannot exist outside the system's own actual development and its own historical meaning: the world-system is its own methodology.

Once we appreciate the meaning of the above, we should begin to suspect the validity of the dominant response(s) to the partisan question raised above as to why the exploitation of the periphery persists. The common meaning of the seemingly different responses within the establishment would be that, inasmuch as such exploitation exists at all, the centre exploits the periphery because the periphery is still trying to manage the business of imitating European traditions and conditions of industrialization. The major concern of the dominant development agencies is, therefore, how to manage this business successfully. The failure of development policies based on this belief is an ample indication of the invalidity of the belief. But the demonstration of this invalidity is to be sought in the histories of the peripheral and the central formations within the common mould of the world capitalist formation. Both the centre and the periphery are, in their respective ways, nothing more, or less, than what they, as products of historical processes and representations within the global problematique, have encountered in the common mould of world-history.

If, in fact, it is true that theory is history, then what we are confronted by is the need to change our world-view of history, our historiography, just enough to realize that Eurocentric developmentalist tenets may be invalid. Why? Because the enforced or adopted imitation of Europe may be the reason why the exploitation of the periphery by the centre persists, and if we wish to tackle this exploitation component of the global problematique – to eliminate it in fact – we need a grasp of theory able to indicate the possibilities for influencing future history.

Historic absurdities of the developmentalist conception of transformation

My point of entry into the global problematique was a critical discussion of the dominant world-view, and how it nourishes a particular understanding of the question and concept of development, and the plight of the periphery in the world system. It might be argued that the broad features of developmentalist thinking are too well known to merit yet another elaboration. I would not agree, and would argue that we have attempted to do more than that. Merely pointing to the abject failure of the developmentalist strategy cannot transcend the limitations of its basic philosophy. Therefore, all that has been said has had to be said to show up some of the fundamental absurdities of the developmentalist conception of transformation.

Specifically, our intention is to show how these absurdities cohere into a historic tautology which inhibits the vital distinction being drawn between the conception of development as the imitation of the dominance of the world and the conception of development as transformation, the transcendence of the major limitations of the present world.

The developmentalist precept is that the so-called underdeveloped parts of the world should imitate European ways and history, in the belief that, once this imitation succeeds, all will be developed – looking like Europe. There will be no more gap between centre and periphery to bridge. All will be humanized at a higher level. The world will therefore be *transformed* through the *development* of its underdeveloped parts. The tactical imperative of this strategy is the vigorous Europeanization of everything in the periphery.

Any good intentions in such a strategy cannot, however, excuse its absurdities. Try as hard as we may, we cannot *avoid* asking whether this view of future history is desirable, whether European culture is so much more humanizing than all other cultures, that all cultures ought to imitate it, and whether it is not sheer Eurocentric arrogance, understandable though it may be, which encourages this view of a universal future, and in doing so manages to limit the span of choices of future alternatives. We do not argue that Europe has *no* humanizing traits: nothing could be further from the truth. The argument is rather that, notwithstanding the *equality* of all cultures and national differences by virtue of the fact that they exist, it is false to believe in the *equal desirability* of all aspects of all cultures and national differences: all cultures are equal because they exist, but, from our transformational perspective, all cultures need not be equally desirable. The ethical basis of this argument resides in the fact that no existing culture is maximally humanizing and the fact that we regard existing specific cultures and societal differences as specific expressions of the influences of a common world-view of a historic ontological-axiological deficiency.

The desirability of this image of future history aside, it is the impossibility of it as a strategy that demands serious contemplation. What was considered developmentally of 'limited' possibilities in the early 1970s had, by the end of the decade, come to be seen as plain 'impossible'.[48] Can we avoid asking the question why? We need to know what has caused the limited possibilities to dwindle to plain impossibility.[49] This is what *needs* to be explained. In my opinion, this is the question of questions, if there is such a thing in this enquiry. This reflection, then, must consider what it is about the tactic of developmentalist imitation that negates its own strategy of universal developmentalist achievement. Two relevant questions are in order:

1. Which agencies are assumed by the developmentalist philosophy to carry the transformational responsibility?
2. Why did they fail to carry this responsibility successfully?

The point is either we explain the failure, worse still the self-negation, of the developmentalist strategy by the fact that the developmentalist imitation precept is impossible to realize in itself, or that the agencies of the developmentalist transformation are incapable and/or that they were wrongly identified, or that this precept, no matter how well-intentioned, is part of a subtle historic plot calculated to perpetuate Eurocentric dominance. And which is it?

I shall argue that it is all these factors in cadence, all in support of the historical unfolding of the capitalist order, the capitalist historic theme of accumulating capital in the centre and away from the periphery: the purposive and efficient accumulation of capital to the paradoxical and irrational dehumanization of humankind. Truly, this is the essence of the developmentalist chicanery we confronted earlier in this chapter as Eurocentricity.

This chicanery is made up of many absurdities. The first one is the Eurocentric regard of the periphery parts of the world as mere objects of history. From this emerges the absurd expectation that these areas of the world can be Europeanized by development. Another absurdity is that, while enforced and adopted Europeanizing processes weaken non-European cultures and drain them of all self-confidence, these cultures are expected to be confident in their imitations of European ways and history. Yet another absurdity lies in the nature of the imitation itself. This imitation calls for the non-European cultures to be turned into something similar to the European culture; and yet precisely by doing this these cultures become less autonomous and easier to exploit. This imitation precept is absurd because it seems to say that for the Third World cultures to develop they must imitate everything European including even the underdeveloped aspects of European culture. When we put all these absurdities together, they begin to cohere into the fallacy of developmentalist tautology; and we begin to get near to answering why the precept of imitation must, necessarily, be self-negating. But perhaps the biggest absurdity is the uncritical adoption of the developmentalist philosophy by the institutions which compose Third World states, especially their intellectual components.

What is frightening, however, is the limited and Eurocentric nature of the images of development inherent in the developmentalist philosophy. We are offered a choice between capitalism, socialism, and their combinations as the developmental paths to increasing humanization. The question at this point is not that these paths are not different or that they cannot ever lead to increasing humanization; it is whether, given their common Eurocentric world-view and developmentalist philosophy, they are the only alternative paths available. They emerged from European experiences and therefore the simple question is why they should be the only alternatives for other cultures in the world whose experiences and realities differ from those of Europe within the common mould of the global problematique.

The argument is not, therefore, that other cultures cannot gain, or have not gained, in a humanizing sense from Europe: in this sense, all cultures can and must learn from one another.[50] Rather, the excessive imitation of European ways and history compound dehumanizing realities in most non-European areas, increasing global dehumanization rather than decreasing it.

The non-European parts of the world can never become Europe, because at the moment they are not underdeveloped Europe, and never were in the past. All they have encountered in world history (and are likely to encounter) has turned them into something which defies any sense of development as maximum Europeanization. The self-contained logic of our capitalist world-system defies the realization of this developmental dream. The failure here then is not the failure of development policies, but the failure of developmental philosophy. This is what we seek to make clear: that development, as it is conventionally understood, is an impossible dream – an impossibility rooted in its faulty, partisan, philosophical foundations. Understanding development as a vocation for increasing humanization entails conceiving of development as the *social transformation* of our present world.

If the right question is now, what should we do, and how should we begin, the correct starting-point must be to make use of the absurdities of developmentalism to arrive at a re-interpretation of the history which has culminated in the present dehumanized world – the global problematique: in doing this, it is impossible to avoid a head-on confrontation with the Eurocentric allocation of transformational responsibility. To go forward, we first have to go back to the drawing-board, so to speak, to capture the dehumanizing content of our reality in the light of the observation that theory is history. This is necessary if – within the new and necessary conception of development as social transformation – all the images of development which we derive from history are to be deemed valid until demonstrated to be opposed to the requirement of increasing humanization. And in this endeavour we should not shy away from the need to determine *ourselves* what *appears* to be determined historically, in order to move history along some preferred paths.

A historic representation of the conception of theory as history will show that when we talk about the global problematique, we are not talking about something remote and abstract. It will show that at any one time the humanization-dehumanization contradiction, as presented earlier in this chapter, is located in the concreteness of a historic dominance; that the developments within a particular historic formation are not necessarily the same thing as the transformational development of that given historic formation; and above all it will show that it is impossible to consider the transformation of a given system without the explicit acceptance that what is finally meant is the transcendence of the cardinal limitation of a given system, as this limitation *is* the historic theme of the system, to be understood in terms of the basic puzzle stated at the beginning of the chapter.

The essential point here is that the dominant conception of development rests on the fundamental assumption that change is both possible and compatible with the retention of the historic theme of the accumulation of capital. In fact, the ineffectiveness of current development policies rests on the fact that retaining this theme imposes a logic incompatible with real social transformation – and hence development. In the kindest terms, the fallacy of developmentalism can be seen as the desire to change everything in order that it remains the same – to the immediate benefit of Europe and the small Europeanized parts of the non-European world.

However, if one chooses to leave kindness aside and state matters as they are, what is involved is a complex situation in which, while things change and the changes are claimed to be reducing dehumanization, dehumanization not only persists but intensifies and deepens on a world-scale. Why? Very simple – because of the developmentalist precept that to develop, the so-called underdeveloped must change to look like the so-called developed; and it is in this process that the level of dehumanization increases on a world-scale.

Transformation and transformational responsibility

If we are reasonable, we will ask the honest question as to what we are to do and how we are to proceed. But if we are sensibly attuned to the complexity of what we must do, we will know that we should avoid any procedure which promises immediate answers to the many questions raised. As little as we may know and understand the problem, we know enough to appreciate that we are involved in attempts to influence the unfolding of future history along lines that we prefer because those lines promise to set in train reinforcing processes which will move history toward maximum humanized conditions. This position appears to suggest that people make their own history: but, as we all know, Marx has said they do not do so just as they please.

> They do not make it under circumstances chosen by themselves, but under circumstances directly encountered, given and transmitted from the past. The tradition of all the dead generations weighs like a nightmare on the brain of the living. And just when they seem engaged in revolutionizing themselves and things, in creating something that has never yet existed, precisely in such periods of revolutionary crisis they anxiously conjure up the spirits of the past to their service and borrow from them names, battle cries and costumes in order to present the new scene of world history in this time-honoured disguise and this borrowed language.[51]

As much as this is true, it is also true that as we make the conscious effort to understand ourselves and our world, more and more, we can manipulate those 'circumstances directly encountered, given and transmitted from the past' in order to shape the future into a preferred form, into something 'that has never yet existed'. In 'revolutionary crisis' we may 'conjure up the spirits of the past' and even borrow from the past to convince ourselves that a new scene of world history does not differ much from an old scene. All this may be true, but are we in a revolutionary crisis? Are we in the throes of transformational change? Has the *kairos* arrived – that conception of the 'right time' for social transformation which bears the paradoxical essence of being there all the time and yet not being there; and the actualization of which becomes the more real, the more it is searched for consciously?[52]

These are not idle questions. I have no doubt that when the time comes the commentary that will be history will be very critical of our present understanding of the idea of *development* as it should mean *transformation*, the transcending of the limitations within our present large-scale long-term historical system. The historical criticism will hinge on the disapproving fact that we should have known better, given all that we know about our world and all that we have available for use in the service of increasing humanization.

Setting to one side what we do have, we know both so much and yet so little to give what we know a meaning, a transformational directive: we lack ways of seeing ourselves and the totality of our reality in a philosophically coherent manner, conceived so as to present us both with our historic limitations and at the same time intimate our historic-transformational potential, our capacity for self-salvation. Our blink-eredness to both these aspects must, amongst other things, lie in our inability to work our visions derived from an honestly critical appreciation of our *epochal* circumstances into truly constructive-negative definitions. Why this is so is neither hard to see nor difficult to comprehend: it is our insensitivity to the evolving dialectics of the real meaning of history. Principally, we cannot distinguish between the *historical* and the *historic*; and within this we cannot distinguish between the dialectically *celebratory* and dialectically *condemnatory* aspects in our history in terms of their historic meanings.

And yet this is exactly what it should be, seeing that we are involved in a very puzzling enterprise known for its uncertainty and unpredictability. We are not engaged in merely interpreting future history, but in determining it along preferred lines. The main problem here is how to approach the voluntarist-determinist dialectic: how we come to understand past history and its relationship to preferred future history in ways that do not make this dialectic insurmountable.

In this endeavour we are interested in *what is it?*, *how is it?*, and *what will it be?*[53] only to prepare to tackle the questions of *what shall it be?* and *who shall it be?* We are involved in nothing less than the attempt to understand theory as history in order to capture, the best we can, the historical genetic code of the determinist meaning of the present in order to shape the future in a transformational way. This is why it is important to make the crucial methodological distinction between the interpretation of history as either a matter of *congratulatory celebration* or a *solemn invocation*.

Those who find a lot to be pleased about in past history would tend to value it as a congratulatory matter of, and cause for, *celebration*. Such people would tend to appreciate past history in terms of the past poetics and heroics which they would like to see more or less emulated at a particular time and extrapolated into a particular future. In this conception of *history as celebration*, the present as it mediates between the past and the future, is evaluated in terms of its departures from, and insufficiencies in, the glories of the past.

Those who find little to be pleased about in a particular past history tend to place more emphasis on *preferred* future history, basing this preference on the few redeeming aspects of past and present histories. This is the conception of *history as invocation*. In this latter conception of history, the present, as it mediates between the past and preferred future, is invariably found wanting in the few redeeming aspects of past history. It is for this reason that the conception of history as invocation has that slight touch of the *prophetic*, in that this conception of history tends to warn about dire future history consequences which will issue from the non-application of the few basic redeeming factors in past history, as portrayed in present history.

The methodological device of distinguishing between history as celebration and history as invocation provides us with a critical point of entry into the evaluation of the transformational utility of historical elements: whether they promote or arrest movement towards our preferred transformational objectives. It forces us to keep in mind constantly the invocative question *of what shall it be*?

It should be made very clear, however, that we do not pretend to be able to determine the future in full. We only attempt to use understandings of history to *influence* 'determined' futures along some preferred lines. This is why we should reject both *uni-linearity* of social time and the *historical instant* as the sole determining seeds of the future, even where the conception of the historical instant includes invocatory praxis.[54] There is nothing in any present which *fully* assures us of its determined future; and therefore, the flexibility which we need to influence the multiple images of the future to some degree counsels caution and encourages us to reject the rigid adoption of these two concepts. Social time and historical instants are always pregnant with multiple futures even within their historic unicity; but because the explanatory relationship between a particular future and its present is largely an *ex post facto* affair, we should not surrender our ability, no matter how limited, to influence the future: the futures which the present hold or portend should not be deemed totally immutable, inalterable, or immune to present thoughts and actions.

The multiplicity of images of development, filtered through the multiplicity of current historical instants, forces us to recognize the concept of the multiplicity of 'overlapping histories'. Our concern is precisely how to affect the individual histories and overlaps between them in order to advance the human vocation of humanizing our world. This is why, when we approach history as a matter of preferred transformed future, we are not indulging in prophecy. Prophecy may have a lot to do with invocation, but the two are not the same. Invocation, inasmuch as it has any connection with prophecy, attempts to will the future as much as it can through changing thought and action toward an end. Invocation differs from well-founded prediction, but only to the extent that one ignores or undervalues the arguments upon which the invocation is based.

Crucial to this way of thinking is the answer to the question of *who will it be*?, the agents to carry the transformational responsibility. This occurs in all images of preferred futures, ranging from God Himself and His acts through such chosen agents as monarchs, elites, workers, the unemployed, the oppressed, to even the magic of the sheer force of time. But the choice of the transformational agent always depends upon the particular understanding of the existing situation and the images of the preferred future. Viewed in their multiplicity and substitutability, transforming agents are therefore less important perhaps than what is preferred and the particular understanding of the existing situation.[55]

In reference to this matter, we must make mention of the capitalist-socialist transition as *the* transformational path. In context, criticism does not attach to the idea(1) or the image of socialism as equal to transformation. Criticism attaches to the practicalities and realities of developmentalist *transition* which are rationalized and blindly imitated as being the socialist transition itself.

There is more to this matter. The capitalist-socialist transformation path, as the dominant ideology of transformation, was conceived out of the exigencies of European experiences in the development of world capitalism; and while Amin is right to argue that socialism as a philosophy for transforming societies, in order to enhance human dignity, is not the gift of any people to any other people,[56] the dominant means to and visions of socialism have their roots very much sunk in the European tradition and its secular visions of desirable worlds and their composite societies. If the dominance of European images of development is the direct consequence of the undebatable European dominance of the world-system from its inception to date, the lack of non-European-rooted images of development is also due to this dominance, and hence in general the poverty of the multiplicity of these images, as they have been added to by what non-European parts of the world have become through their encounters in world-history.

However viewed, the argument is that it is dangerous to confront the transformation of the capitalist world-system (any large-scale historical system for that matter) as though it is the primary historic duty of its dominant part to negate the system and its dominance with it. This is why, when we come to the discussion of transformational responsibility, it is important to raise the question as to whether the images of development that are emerging and can emerge from the experiences of societies in the periphery are not to be encouraged.

I am referring to the need to reconsider the developmentalist conception of transformational responsibilities in the light of our increasing consciousness deriving from the historic interpretation of the global problematique. The progressivist view of the matter derives from the developed-underdeveloped distinction (or duality) upon which the entire developmentalist philosophy is based; and accordingly, the transformational agencies are located, in the diffusionist tradition, in the form of their equivalents in the periphery. But is it possible that these transformational agents, by virtue of what world-history has made of periphery societies, and because of that fallacy of developmentalist tautology, operate to perpetuate existing conditions?

The argument is that, although possessing a peripheral commonality within the world-system, societies of the periphery are historically distinct, and therefore transformational responsibility need not be borne by the same agencies as in the centre of world capitalism. And further, since these agencies subscribe to the developmentalist image of development, they are exposed to the charge of being merely developmental, rather than transformational in their effects.

The arguments so far must indicate that I consider these agencies as developmental. It can be argued that to the extent that peripheral states can be transformational agents, the validity of their transformational qualities is so strained (the gap between what they claim to be about and what they are actually about is so large) that they function in reality to fulfil the dominant motive of perpetuating the capitalist world-system.[57] Some peripheral states may function more so than others, but essentially they all operate in that vein.

Given the developmentalist tradition of the dominant world-view, what is required is the development of other world-views which, beginning with the question as to why the exploitation component of the global problematique persists, raise the question of what peripheral societies must do so as to contribute to the elimination of exploitation on all levels in the current system as a contribution to augmenting humanizing processes. This will entail the fashioning of new images of development hingeing four-squarely on the conscious negation of the historic theme of our current historicity – the accumulation of capital. It is these images which will show the need to reconsider the transformational responsibility, in the light of Sartre's view that, 'truth comes into being out of non-being, into the present out of the practical future'.[58]

Questioning the organic credentials of intellectuals of the periphery

It should be clear from what has been said that those who are not dissatisfied with the nature of the world will have no need to worry about the forms of future histories. The elaborate contemplation of these histories will be done only by those who have fundamental reasons to consider the continuation of world capitalism to be unacceptable and who, therefore, believe that only fundamentally critical appraisals of world-views, in terms of images of desirable worlds and societies, are what is required. Initially this task cannot be the *immediate* responsibility of all in world society. While a large measure of the responsibility may fall on the people on the whole, or groups such as states, it is the direct and immediate vocational responsibility of the intellectual components of these groups to develop new, perhaps even novel, approaches to the conception of how to mediate past history, through present history, to preferred future history. Meanwhile, it will not be out of place for us to pose the fundamental aspect of the overall problem as residing in the qualities of intellectual traditions in the periphery as well as in the centre of world capitalism.

What are the organic credentials of the intellectuals of the periphery? Are they *organic* products of the real plight of the periphery of the world system, in the sense used by Gramsci? Do they realize that, in the words of Sartre, we do not live in an era of the universal but rather in that of the 'universalizing endeavour'?[59] These questions refer to a series of other questions relating to the objective status of these intellectuals, in terms of their role in the overall socio-historical praxis of negating the system: their links to the oppressed, who, while not representing a universality, represent the immense majority;[60] their alienation as a social category, themselves victims of Eurocentric ideology; the intellectual tools available to them in the conscious and critical recasting of the development component of the global problematique; but above all, do they have the courage to at least indicate the paths towards the future both to themselves and to others? Is the main problem that they are falling into the principal trap of 'universalizing too fast'?[61]

For those who consider it their timely vocation to attempt to de-Eurocentricize social thought before it becomes impossible, before we do anything at all, I suggest that they should gather, if not take, courage in the face of the ever-present fear that we may be wrong. The source of our courage must be clear, however: in the long run we shall all be dead; and if by some miracle we are not, we shall definitely be too old for it to matter. In any case, the vocation of de-Eurocentricizing thought is more important than anybody's fear of being wrong. Eurocentrics have been wrong all along but that does not appear to have done them much harm.

The courage needed will have to come in the fresh part from the intellectuals, if it is to come at all, and principally from the intellectuals of the periphery of the world-system. I am calling, then, for a cynical, perhaps even for a reasoned nihilistic posture toward existing Eurocentric conventional wisdom. I am not necessarily calling for their total, and certainly not for their cavalier, rejection.

The call is not an idle call for mere words either. It is not a call for words to the exclusion of action. If it is anything at all, it is a call for new words, new idioms, and new tools. They don't have to be correct: they only have to exist and contest with other words, idioms, tools and *actions*. It is a call for whatever is needed to be derived from the collective experiences in the unfolding of our common history. It is a call for praxis, words that shape actions and actions that shape words for human betterment. If anything at all, it is a call for a start to confront the shaping of *our* collective experiences in exploitation and subordination into *a* distinct philosophy dedicated to the negation of exploitation in our concrete circumstances of world capitalism. As Ayi Kwei Armah puts is:

> Minds don't stay in the past . . . They can find the truths of the past, come back to the present and look forward to the future. That's not getting lost. The present is when we get lost – if we forget our past and have no visions of the future.[62]

Could the truths of the past be those of the future? This will always be a contentious question. But whatever the truths are, they must ride on a *maji*[63] created especially for their actualization. Who then are to create the *maji* upon which the truths will ride?

It is of course the responsibility of us all. But, at the same time, it is not too much to expect that intellectuals of the periphery will recognize the complex uniqueness and the very subtlety of the plight of the periphery in the capitalist world-system for what it is; and at the very least do the 'initial unveiling'[64] of the truths for us all. Whether we like it or not, our intellectuals are among the 'hearers, seers, imagers, thinkers, rememberers . . . called to communicate truths of the living'.[65] This must be so, if the present plight is not to grow into a blighted and bloody confusion from which we cannot salvage 'even a broken ring of meaning'.[66]

To reconstruct the 'broken ring of meaning', even to salvage its broken parts, we need to agree with Husserl that in our respective scientific endeavours, 'we lack the real awareness by which the cognitive subject (of the peripheral kind) can account for itself – not only in its effective actions and innovations, but also in the dimensions whose meaning is obscure and sedimented, the underlying presuppositions of its instruments, notions, propositions and theories'.[67] And if it is true, as Husserl further argues, that science and scientific method today resemble a machine which is obviously rendering useful service, and which anyone can learn to manipulate correctly, without having the least idea of its basics and necessity, then we must admit and, by doing so, agree with him that:

> The scientific method, having developed into the progressive accomplishment of a job, is a technique which can be transmitted, but which does not thereby necessarily transmit its true meaning. Thereafter theoretical work can only dominate the infinity of its themes by an infinity of methods, and an infinity of methods only by meaningless technical thought and activity. It is for this reason that theory can remain genuinely and pristinely meaningful if the man of science has developed the capacity to return to the original meaning of all his ideas and methods: to their basis in history.[68]

And finally, if what is at stake is the necessity to lay the basis of the Third World's contribution to social knowledge, then we need to bring to social scientific thought our original experiences as they inhere in our authentic world-views. Essentially, this will mean ceaselessly questioning inherited and imposed social scientific knowledge from the standpoint of the periphery. We will need to ask in all circumstances: is this meaningful to *us*? Is this *our* truth? And does this or that promise the possibility of enabling *us* and *our* groups within the world-system to become 'subjects of world-history', instead of mere objects of thought and manipulation?[69] All this is not easy to do, but then nobody said it would be; and besides if it were, it would not be written about at such length.

Notes

1 See volumes of *Review* and *Political Economy of World-System Annuals* for expositions of this methodology. For my particular interpretation of this methodology see my 'Illustrating World-System Critique of Eurocentric Conceptions: The Continuity of Imperialism Thesis', mimeo, June 1982.

2 For a fuller discussion of this see my 'Prologue: Eurocentric State of the Discipline', HSDRGPID-69/UNUP-385, 1981. The reader is referred to Aseniero, 'A Reflection on Developmentalism: From Development to Transformation' in this volume.

3 This matter is discussed in my 'Multiplicity of Images of Development in the Single Transformation of the World-System', mimeo, April-May, 1982.

4 This section owes a lot to critical comments on an earlier draft received at a UNU/GPID Meeting in Starnberg, July 1982. In particular, to the strong objection by Samir Amin to the use of the term 'political economy' as a generic term covering social science, radical political economy and historical materialism on the grounds that such a usage is not only a contradiction in terms, but also a faulty usage in the English language, not to be found in other languages. The present form of this section is the result of correspondence between George Aseniero and myself on our chapters in this volume. The subtleties of the arguments are due to Aseniero's influence.

5 See note 4 above. Such usage is kept alive in the English language by marxian groups such as the Union of Radical Political Economy.

6 At least the titles of three of his main works attest to this: *Capital: A Critique of Political Economy, Grundrisse: Foundations of the Critique of Political Economy*, and *A Contribution to the Critique of Political Economy*.

7 Embryonically presented in the *Economic and Philosophical Manuscripts of 1844*.

8 See the further development of this by Samir Amin in his *Unequal Development: An Essay on the Social Transformation of Peripheral Capitalism*, The Harvester Press, Brighton, 1976 and *Class and Nation, Historically and in the Current Crisis*, Monthly Review Press, New York, 1980.

9 See the relevant works by such critics, including Amin, Sartre, Mao Tse-Tung, and Wallerstein.

10 These views may be many, but must include Mao, Ho Chi Minh, Frantz Fanon, Kim Il-Sung, Che Guevara, Amical Cabral, etc. These views may be wrong, but must we reject them on Eurocentric methodological premises?

11 This section is a revised version of my essay cited in note 2 above, and is intended as a chapter in my forthcoming volume, *Imperialism: Who Underdevelops Whom, How and Why?*

12 We recognize that 'maximum humanizing conditions' are open to a variety of interpretations, relating to the allocation of resources, distribution of wealth, political rights, access to the means to meet basic needs, the definition of 'basic needs' and so on. We cannot address these arguments here. Suffice to say that by way of a negative definition, the conditions of life for the bulk of the population of the Third World (inadequate nourishment,

health, hygiene, security) will be located at the opposite end of the spectrum.

13 See Paolo Freire, *Pedagogy of the Oppressed*, The Seabury Press, New York, 1968; *Cultural Action for Education*, Penguin, New York, 1972.

14 The old English legal precept that those seeking equity must have clean hands does not seem to apply in political economy.

15 For a convincing discussion of this matter see Ashis Nandy, 'Science in Utopia: Equity, Plurality and Openness', paper presented at the meeting of the Alternative Visions of Desirable Societies Group of the UNU/GPID, Mexico City, April 1981, p. 16. See also his paper 'Emancipating Science', presented at a conference on Science, Technology and Development, Berlin, May 1979, and his 'The Traditions of Technology', *Alternatives*, 4:4, 1978–1979, pp. 165–180.

16 See reference in note 1 above.

17 Robert A. Nisbet, *Social Change and History*, Aspects of the Western Theory of Development, Oxford University Press, London, 1969. See also D.C. Somervell's two volume abridgement of Arnold J. Toynbee's *A Study of History*, Oxford University Press, London, 1957.

18 There are others who will attribute these orientations to the very cosmological sources of western philosophy itself. See Johan Galtung, Tore Heiestad and Eric Ruge, 'On the Decline and Fall of Empires: The Roman and Western Imperialism Compared', HSDRGPID-1/UNUP-53, 1979.

19 Some will delude themselves with a shining socialist world order rising to replace the old capitalist one. I am not impressed by such visions. They denude very little of the Eurocentric world-view. Socialism (Utopian, humanistic, or otherwise) is still Eurocentric, if I am to judge by its origins, its philosophy, and its currently operational variants. All the socialist variants I can think of still bear the Eurocentric imprint of the continuing accumulation of capital through the excessive exploitation of either human beings or nature. See the section headed 'Transformation and Transformational Responsibility' on pages 35–40 of this chapter.

20 In my manuscript, 'Dialogue as Development: A Critique of Freire's Philosophy of Education', 1981, I try to argue that European epistemology and social philosophy do not accord the proper role to the paradoxes which intimate social contradictions, ignoring the role that persisting paradoxes can play in indicating the exchange of one set of contradictions for a similar set of contradictions.

21 These influences derive mainly from the dependency school of thought. For an essay contrasting the modernization and dependency perspectives see J.S. Valenzuela and A. Valenzuela, 'Modernization and Dependency: Alternative Perspective in the Study of Latin American Underdevelopment', in Heraldo Munoz (ed.), *From Dependency to Development: Strategies to Overcome Underdevelopment and Inequality*, Westview Press, Boulder, Col., 1981, pp. 15–41. And for a comprehensive view of the history of the matter, see Robert L. Bach, 'On the Holism of a World-System Perspective', in Hopkins and Wallerstein (eds.), op. cit.

22 *Latin America: Underdevelopment or Revolution*, Monthly Review Press, 1969, pp. 21–94. All the essays in Frank's book are relevant in this regard, in particular 'Functionalism and Dialectics', pp. 95–107.

23 Karl Marx, *Capital*, Vol. I, Penguin Books, Harmondsworth, 1976, pp. 579–80.

24 See for example the massive orthodox marxist onslaught on Andre Gunder
   Frank's continuing work on world capitalism, and his response in *World
   Accumulation 1492-1789*, Macmillan, London, 1978, pp. 238–271. See
   too the following reviews of Frank: Geoffrey Hawthorn, 'Case
   Unproven', *New Society*, 48, 1979, p. 863; Cecilia Green in *Two Thirds*,
   1:3, 1978–79; Quentin Skinner, 'Taking Off', *New York Review of Books*,
   22nd March 1979, pp. 15–16; Martin Bronfenbrenner, in *Journal of Economic Literature*, 18; David Booth, mimeo of a review for *Journal of
   Development Studies*; Kit Sims Taylor, in *Science and Society*, 63:4,
   1979–1980, pp. 490–492; Ruth Pike, in *Journal of Economic History*,
   September 1979, pp. 805–806.
25 On this matter see Terence Hopkins, 'World-system Analysis: Methodological Issues' in Kaplan (ed.), *Social Change in the Capitalist World
   Economy*, where he says on p. 217 that, 'so far as constructing inter-
   pretative accounts is concerned, we have barely begun to appreciate the
   power of the 'internal'/'external' sets of contradictions – let alone sketch
   a 'logic' for them'. In particular see Wallerstein, 'World-system Analysis'
   in Kaplan (ed.), op. cit., in response to Walter L. Goldfrank 'Fascism and
   world economy' in the same volume.
26 See Wallerstein, 'Fanon and the Revolutionary Class' in his *Capitalist
   World Economy*, pp. 250–268, for a good treatment of Fanon's views and
   orthodox marxist critiques of them.
27 See Gareth Stedman Jones, 'Utopian Socialism Reconsidered' in Samuel
   (ed.) *People's History and Social Theory*, London, 1981, pp. 140–41.
28 Emmanuel, *Unequal Exchange*, Monthly Review Press, 1972, especially
   pp. 271–431, for exchanges between Emmanuel and Bettelheim.
29 Or at best just a harmless Eurocentric phrase for gurgling in the throats of
   wishful intellectuals, who believe in the duplication of Europe in the non-
   European parts of the world, a cause for alienated dissidents looking for
   causes to uphold, and a platform for self-conscious radical activists at
   social democratic annual conventions.
30 Emmanuel, op. cit. p. 263.
31 See Amin, *Unequal Development* and *Class and Nation*.
32 There have always been violent contacts between cultures. The significance of this particular contact lies in its world-wide scope and historic
   meaning.
33 For the nature of the original debate, see Rodney Hilton (ed.), *The Transition from Feudalism to Capitalism*, New Left Books, London, 1976.
34 See Ernesto Laclau, 'Feudalism and Capitalism in Latin America', *New
   Left Review*, 67, 1971; Emmanuel, *Unequal Exchange*, pp. 271–431;
   Ernesto Laclau, *Politics and Ideology in Marxist Theory*, New Left
   Books, London, 1977, pp. 15–50; Frank, *World Accumulation,
   1492-1789*, pp. 238–271; Wallerstein, *The Capitalist World-Economy*,
   pp. 138–151; R. Brenner, 'Dobb on the Transition From Feudalism to
   Capitalism', *Cambridge Journal of Economics*, 2, 1978; and Brenner,
   'The origins of capitalist development: a critique of neo-smithian
   marxism', *New Left Review*, 104, 1977, pp. 25–93. And many more.
35 Surely the time has come for us to assess the distinction we need to make
   between anti-systemic and anti-regime movements and forces. The former
   and transformationally-oriented in that they aim to turn the system into a
   genuinely *different system*, while the latter aim to change not so much the

system, but incumbent political regimes, without necessarily doing much about the nature of the system. Given our conception of the world-system as capitalist, this distinction is important to make in identifying radical carriers of genuine change.

36 Nandy, 'Science in Utopia', op. cit., pp. 33–34.

37 Ibid. pp. 34–35.

38 Ibid. p. 32.

39 See Raphael Samuel (ed.), *People's History and Socialist Theory*, Routledge, London, 1981.

40 Samuel, 'Editorial Preface' in Samuel (ed.) op. cit. p. xxxi.

41 Peter Burke, 'People's History or Total History', in Samuel (ed.) p. 8.

42 See the contribution of Mihailo Markovic in Eleonora Masini (ed.), *Vision of Desirable Societies*, Pergamon Press, Oxford, 1983.

43 See Eric Williams, *British Historians and the West Indies*, Andre Deutsch, London, 1966.

44 See reference in note 16 above.

45 Immanuel Wallerstein, 'The Development of the Concept Development', a talk delivered at Brown University, October 9th 1981, p. 13.

46 Ibid.

47 Edmund Husserl, *The Crisis of the European Sciences*, 1936; Frank, *World Accumulation, 1492–1789*, p. 13.

48 See Wallerstein, 'Dependence in an Interdependent World: the Limited Possibilities of Transformation with the Capitalist World-economy', in Heraldo Munoz (ed.), *From Dependence to Development: Strategies to Overcome Underdevelopment and Inequality*, Westview Press, Boulder Col., 1981, pp. 267–293; Samir Amin, *Unequal Development: An Essay on the Social Formation of Peripheral Capitalism*, Harvester Press, Sussex, 1976 and *Class and Nation, Historically and in the Current Crisis*, Monthly Review, New York, 1980; and Andre Gunder Frank, 'Crisis and Transformation of Dependency in the World-system', in Dale Johnson and Ronald Chilcote (eds.), *Mode of Production or Dependency? Alternative Perspectives on Peripheral Social Formations*, Sage (forthcoming). See too the contributions to this volume by Fröbel, Heinrichs and Kreye.

49 See my 'The Dwindling Nature of the Limited Transformation Possibilities: The Caribbean Case', paper delivered at CEESTEM, Mexico City, March 17th 1981.

50 See in this connection the contribution by Friberg and Hettne, and the reply by Amin in this volume.

51 Karl Marx, *The Eighteenth Brumaire of Louis Bonaparte*, Progress Publishers, Moscow 1967, p. 11

52 For a discussion of *kairos* see *Wallerstein, The Capitalist World-Economy*, pp. 269–282.

53 See Ramkrishna Mukherjee, *What Will It Be?: Explorations in Inductive Sociology*, Allied Publishers, New Delhi, 1979.

54 See Kinhide Mushakoji, 'A Non-Standard Model of the Future – The Limits to Future Modelling and Beyond', (a UNU-GPID working paper, January 1982); and see also Robert L. Bach, 'On the Holism of a World-system Perspective', *Political Economy of World-System Annuals*, 3, 1980, pp. 289–310, and the contributions by Chase-Dunn, Mukherjee and Hopkins in the same volume, pp. 311–318.

55 This quote from Stedman Jones will illustrate the point. 'The attitude of

early theory towards the worker was distant and paternalist. Both Owen and St. Simon before the late 1820s focus primarily upon their lack of education. It is the middle class (when not the sovereign himself) as the enlightened section of the population which is most likely to form the vanguard of progress towards socialism (because of its educational level). After 1830 the working class is seen in a more hopeful light. Working-class enthusiasm for cooperation could show them to be harbingers of a purer morality (in Owen's view); or more widely, workers and women as the most oppressed groups were likely to adopt the socialist cause, as slaves had led the movement towards Christianity. Since the coming of Christianity was the main allegorial model for the coming of socialism . . . a movement of the oppressed at the bottom of society did not exclude the possibility of its ultimate promulgation from the top (Emperor Constantine)' ('Utopian Socialism Reconsidered' in Samuel (ed.) op. cit. pp. 140–141.

56 See the concluding chapter of his *Unequal Development*.
57 This position is less preposterous than it is true, as unpleasant as it may be.
58 Jean-Paul Sartre, 'A Plea for Intellectuals' in *Between Existentialism and Marxism*, New Left Books, London, 1974, p. 231.
59 Sartre, op.cit., p. 263.
60 Ibid., p. 256.
61 Ibid., p. 249.
62 Ayi Kwei Armah, *The Healers*, Heinemann, London, 1979, p.176.
63 The term *maji*, as Armah uses it, expressed a sort of self-actualizing transformational philosophy.
64 There is a sort of pervading nervous ambiguity about the role(s) that scholars allot intellectuals and revolutionary leaders in the whole process of transforming societies. This nervousness shows clearly in Freire's work. But at least he concedes that they are allowed, as the maximum, to do the 'initial unveiling' for us all. See his *Pedagogy of the Oppressed*, p.169.
65 Ayi Kwei Armah, *Two Thousand Seasons*, Heinemann, London, 1979, p. xi.
66 Ibid., p. xvii.
67 Husserl, *The Crisis of the European Sciences*.
68 Ibid.
69 Sartre's *Critique of Dialectical Reason* is directed at precisely these problems.

2

A Reflection on Developmentalism: From Development to Transformation

George Aseniero

Introduction

Were Leibniz alive today perhaps even he would be hard pressed to find any hopeful signs in the present state of the world to confirm his doctrine of universal harmonies, in which everything is rational merely because it exists and everything happens for the best in the best of possible worlds. It appears, in any case, that today's Leibnizians – heirs to the successive economic transmutations of Leibniz's metaphysics, from Smith's harmony of interests doctrine to the contemporary marginalist theory of general economic equilibrium – find themselves increasingly powerless to explain, let alone solve, the global crisis that is upon us today.

In 1975 Dr Henry Kissinger could still claim that 'the present economic system has served the world well';[1] in a recent article he wrote for *Newsweek*, entitled 'Saving the World Economy', he now admits that

> No previous theory seems capable of explaining the current crisis of the world economy. Until recently it would have been thought impossible that prices could rise during a recession – that a system of relatively free trade and floating exchange rates could spur embryonic trade wars; that the developing nations, through defaulting on their debts, could threaten the economies of the industrial nations.

> When reality clashes fundamentally with expectations, a political crisis is inevitable. That condition is upon us today. Since World War I we have expected progress . . . This illusion of uninterrupted

progress was suddenly shattered in the middle '70s . . . Thirty million workers are now unemployed in the industrial democracies and their number continues to increase. The developing nations are crushed under the twin burden of debt and collapsing hopes of progress.[2]

This sober reappraisal of the world economy is now heard everywhere and the resonance is all the louder if it comes, as in this case, from spokesmen of the dominant institutions in the world. The World Bank, which for decades has been fostering a development strategy based on deeper integration of Third World countries into the world economy with the rationale that this would 'close the gap', now discards altogether the objective of gap-bridging as never having been 'realistic . . . in the first place'.[3] The Bank's shift of emphasis (at least in rhetoric) in the last decade – from promotion of growth in GNP to 'redistribution with growth' – is now apparently shifting back to the sobering thought that redistribution will have to wait indefinitely and even growth itself seems hardly a realistic goal any longer. The demands raised in the 1970s for a New International Economic Order fizzled out almost as soon as they found expression in United Nations resolutions; and when the UN launched its Third Development Decade three years ago, it did so with the unmitigated pessimism that the 1980s would be even more bleak and dismal than the preceding two development decades. The question that presently occupies the international organizations and conferences, such as the upcoming UNCTAD VI, is whether the development objective can still be seriously retained on the agenda, now that 'recovery from the crisis' has become the global priority concern.

The upshot of all this is that, to borrow Andre Gunder Frank's phrase, the development of the crisis has led to a crisis in development, not only in practice, which we have had all along, but now also in the theory as well. Hence the rush, since the mid-1970s, to 'rethink the development problematique'. A plethora of self-proclaimed 'alternative' development concepts and strategies has issued forth from universities, governmental think-tanks and international research institutions, the sheer quantity of the research output being in inverse proportion to what, in the jargon, are called 'developmental results' in the real world.

As reality and theory diverge further away from each other, current development debate comes to resemble more and more the scholastic debates that marked the transition from medieval philosophy to modern thought. Locke's criticism of the Schoolmen of his time could well be levelled against the 'development experts' of today: hiding behind an artificial language which resulted in the breakdown of communication, dogmatically upholding the primacy of essences and mystical substances over concrete reality, and reasoning only in endless syllogisms that never brought them to examine empirical facts, the Schoolmen 'covered their ignorance with a curious and inexplicable web of perplexed words'.[4] No doubt Locke, the theoretician of empiricism, would have found much of today's developmentalist language and mode of abstract reasoning, with little point of contact between theory and empirical reality, equally artificial, mystifying and perplexing.

There is more to the comparison. The Schoolmen had mastered all of medieval philosophy but they could say nothing new beyond that; the *world* they were living in was in the process of changing into something epochally new, but their *words* remained those of the old: knowledge of words thus became a substitute for knowledge of the world.[5] Current development thought, I shall venture to argue in this essay, is in a similar situation. When it emerged shortly after the Second World War, it came not as a new vision of the world nor as a vision of a new world, but as an extended elaboration and application of a comprehensive philosophy that had preceded it and shaped it and whose fundamental premises needed only to be reasserted in appropriately up-to-date terminology.

This philosophy I shall call *developmentalism*. As we shall see, it has come under different names before, but the *historical theme* and the *historical function* of the philosophy have remained essentially the same over the long period of its existence, continuous and dialectical evolution, and world-wide extension. If I have started this essay with an allusion to Leibniz, it is not to drag into the present a great thinker from the distant seventeenth century. It is rather to put forward the claim that, if we are to fully understand the central organizing concept of our time, which comes by the name of 'development' and which numerous contending theories purport to interpret and promote each in its own way, we must go back to its roots in history. It is in seventeenth century Europe that we find the philosophy of developmentalism in its embryonic form, it was in the eighteenth century that it was aggressively advanced against feudal reaction and was systematized into an all-embracing *Weltanschauung*, and in the nineteenth century that it reached maturity and began to be challenged in its foundations from within. The twentieth century is heir to both this philosophical totalization *and* the challenge posed to it: thus, while developmentalism continues to reign supreme today, it is already on the defensive.

The development theories that successively emerged after 1945 are bedevilled at the outset by this ambivalence. Either they uphold the philosophy, which however no longer expresses the world (the reality and persistence of underdevelopment); or they seek to transform the world (search for solutions to the problem of underdevelopment), only to be encumbered by the philosophy that now stands as an obstacle to the necessary theoretical reformulation. This means, either they remain developmentalist, and thus reduce change to a mere reproduction of the existing order, or they must break through the confines of developmentalism to become truly transformative. It is therefore necessary to come to grips with the philosophy of developmentalism in order to understand the objective necessity of this theoretical and political choice. This means, first and foremost, the necessity for contemporary development research to become aware of its theoretical premises, the historical and contemporary meaning and function of its inherited conceptual categories, and to work out the alternatives to them: in short, to be critical of the philosophy of developmentalism.

What, then, is this philosophy? The argument that I shall advance here is that *developmentalism is the philosophy of the modern world-system.* It is the world-system that engendered it because it objectively required it for its own development. Practical from the very beginning, as all philosophies are, the developmentalist philosophy evolved for the purpose of giving expression to the general movement of the world-system, whose logic, processes and demands it seeks to clarify, promote, rationalize and justify. To speak of developmentalism is to speak of the logic of the world-system. To examine the fundamental principles of this philosophy, its axiological, aetiological and praxeological presuppositions, is to refer to the dynamic constitutive processes and secular trends of this socio-historical system.

To speak of the one is to speak of the other. For this reason this essay is in two parts. Part One deals with some of the fundamental principles of developmentalism, which for present purposes I have chosen to organize around the following themes: the progressivist conception of history, the development of the concept of national economic development, and the developmentalist theory of stages. I shall try to trace schematically the evolution of these interlocking concepts and themes in relation to historical developments which gave rise to them, in order to arrive at a fuller understanding of their present significance. From these general principles, current development theories derive the whole thrust of their arguments: that development consists in the three combined processes of modernization, economic growth and nation-state building. Although development theories take the nation-state as the unit of analysis, our argument here is that the development problematique – its dynamics and dilemmas, the possibilities and constraints – can be understood only in the context of the whole, and this is the world-system. It is also within the same world-system problematique that we would question – although this would require a separate study – the so-called 'non-capitalist path to development' offered as an alternative by those states which claim to be 'socialist' and which nevertheless seek to be fully integrated in the world-system and do everything they can to participate in the global capital accumulation process. Do they still pose a transformative challenge to the world-system, or are they in fact equally developmentalist and thus supportive of the system?

The three processes of modernization, economic growth and nation-state building, posited now as the development goals of the underdeveloped countries, are historically the constitutive processes of the modern world-system, which we propose to consider elsewhere. We shall summarize what world-system theory[6] tells us about this social system, the only one existing today which encompasses within it an ongoing extensive and complete social divison of labour with an integrated set of production processes which relate to each other according to the capitalist law of value. The history and continuing dynamics of the system as a whole are essentially determined by the movement of capital, namely, the valorization and accumulation of capital on an ever-expanding scale. It is this process of valorization and accumulation of capital that lies behind the historical and contemporary development of the modern world-system, and it is this which developmentalism – as the philosophy of that system – expresses and subserves. The secular evolution of that system is characterized – and necessarily so, because inherent in the capital accumulation process – by unequal and uneven development, which explains the dialectical unity of the opposite processes of development and underdevelopment, as well as the recurring cycles of expansion and stagnation. In seeking to 'develop' themselves via developmentalist strategies, individual countries collectively promote capital accumulation on a world-scale, and hence also reproduce the contradictions inherent in the movement of capital, globally and within each of them. It is because developmentalism refuses or is unable to recognize these fundamental contradictions, which continue to intensify crisis after crisis, that it has reached an impasse. This impasse, in turn, is nothing else but the particular expression of the crisis of the world-system itself; the immobility of the philosophy is conditioned by the contradictions of the global society.

The essay concludes by arguing that contemporary development thinking must define itself in opposition to the philosophy of developmentalism and the world-system that it subserves. To challenge the one is to challenge the other; to do both is necessary, if we are to strive for a truly human and social development for all.

The philosophy of developmentalism

Unity in diversity

The diversity of meanings accorded to the concept of development by various mutually-critical theories effectively conceals what at bottom remains a consensus among them. This consensus remains largely unexplored and uncriticized, if it is noticed at all, primarily because it continues to enjoy the status of 'the obvious' to so many and for so long. As Laing reminds us, however, the obvious 'is literally that which stands in one's way, in front of or over against oneself'[7] (from the Latin ob viam, in the way). In the nature of things, the obvious is taken for granted and consensus is placed outside of debate – until the time comes in the development of a theory when that which has long been consensually presumed to be self-evident eventually becomes an obstacle in the way of the theory's further development. Hegel observed this paradox, which we ought to bear in mind: that a philosophy is fully developed only when its main principles have come to be taken for granted and, to that extent, have become retarded in their speculative development.[8]

The rapidly growing literature on the development of development theory almost invariably highlights the points of disagreement among diverging currents, as 'alternative' conceptual formulations and policy options emerge in quick succession to challenge preceding ones. As a consequence, one often gets the overall impression that development research is continually advancing, that each new phase is different, more progressive and perhaps has better chances of succeeding than the predecessors that failed.

It is easy enough to miss the wood for the trees. What is obscured by all this is that, underneath the alleged differences between contending theories, lies in fact an old and enduring, powerful and all-pervasive philosophy, which is the domain where all these theories are firmly planted, from whence they draw their nourishment, and which circumscribes the field of their investigations. It is in this philosophy that we find the fundamental principles and concepts that the various development theories hold in common and which they take for granted. And it is in terms of this philosophy that we can assess in fact how deep and thorough contemporary development debate really is, and to what extent self-proclaimed 'alternative' development models really are different after all.

Let us use current coinage and call this underlying totalizing thought the philosophy of developmentalism. But first, why 'philosophy'; and then, why 'developmentalism'?

A philosophy, says Sartre, is a totalizing activity;[9] developed, under well-defined circumstances, for the purpose of giving expression to the general movement of society, a philosophy is first of all a particular way in which the 'rising' class becomes conscious of itself, but this consciousness must consistently strive to present itself as the totalization of existing knowledge. A philosophy, in the course of its development, effects the unification of everything that is known – of nature; of society and individuals, past, present, future; their metaphysical reflections on themselves, their fellows, and their relationships to the infinite – following certain guiding schemata which express the attitudes and techniques of the rising class regarding its own period and the world. Born from the movement of society, it is itself movement and acts upon the future; its method is a social and political weapon. This concrete totalization (of existing knowledge) is at the same time the abstract project of pursuing the unification of the knowable up to its final limits, this through the chosen method of investigation and explication which confers on the philosophy its specific epistemological character.

The confidence which the philosophy has in itself and in its future development merely reproduces the certitudes of the class which supports it; the ideals it professes are the values of the social group that is enlightened by it. A philosophy remains efficacious so long as the praxis which has engendered it, which supports it, and which is clarified by it, is still alive. In this case, the 'living' philosophy continually adapts itself to the course of the world, posing new questions, debating the answers, stimulating internal controversy, and enriching itself in the process: it is one with the movement of society. In short, a 'living' philosophy is simultaneously a totalization of knowledge, a method of investigation and explication, a regulative and normative idea, a social weapon, a community of language and a vision of the world – but always from the point of view and always at the service of the class which brought it about.

If the philosophy also extends beyong the ruling classes to embrace the whole of society, as all hegemonic systems of thought do, this only demonstrates Marx's observation that the ideology of the dominant class is the dominant ideology. For this very reason, critique and demystification of the dominant philosophy is an indispensable part of revolutionary praxis.

If this is what a philosophy means and if this is what a philosophy does, then we can designate the totalizing thought that underlies current development theories as a specific and well-defined philosophy, whose basic principles can be identified, understood and questioned, in terms of the historical theme and the historical function of the philosophy, and in the light of contemporary reality. The question then is: is it still a 'living' philosophy? – which is not to be confused with its still being dominant, of which there is no doubt. Does it continue to move with history and society, acting upon the future; or has it become a defensive and reactionary dogma, evading criticism by losing itself in the obvious?

Why call it 'developmentalism'? Certainly it can be called by other names, as in fact it has been during various phases of its long period of maturation and world-wide extension. But is it appropriate to call it in this present stage developmentalism, because the language of the philosophy is now entirely cast in terms of the central organizing concept known today as 'development'. This is nevertheless a purely linguistic translation with no semantic change whatsoever. The fundamental concepts retain their original significance, and the philosophy remains essentially the same in all its aspects. We can see this continuity of a thought very clearly in, for instance, the developmentalist conception of history and the developmentalist unit of analysis, to which we now turn.

The developmentalist conception of history

There can be no doubt that development has become the central organizing concept in terms of which the historical movement and direction of social systems are analysed, evaluated and acted upon. It is at one and the same time a methodological principle, an analytical matrix for conceiving and interpreting social processes; a regulative idea in terms of which these processes, and the structures they give rise to, are compared, evaluated and given some sense of direction; and a praxeological notion for mobilizing and justifying social action in pursuit of policy objectives. It is also the dominant organizing myth of our epoch, taking over the role played by the concepts 'progress' in the Enlightenment and 'growth' in classical economics. To call it a myth is not to belittle its significance; on the contrary, it is to recognize its power. The essential thing to consider about a myth is not that it is a lie, but rather that it is a belief, a very profound one, and must be recognized as such. As Immanuel Wallerstein puts it convincingly:

> . . . Economic historians have built their work around *organizing myths* (more politely termed perspectives) which have informed, pervaded, underlain their work. An organizing myth is not a testable proposition. It is a tale, a metahistory, which seeks to provide a framework within which the structures, the cyclical patterns, and the events of a given historical social system may be interpreted. It can never be proven or disproven. It can only be propounded (and defended) as a heuristic device which explains more elegantly, coherently, and convincingly than some alternative myth the historical system under observation, and which leaves fewer puzzles unsolved or requires fewer *ad hoc* additional explanations to account for the empirical reality.[10]

Progress, growth, development – through these metaphors runs a basic theme that had its precise date of emergence in the history of thought, and which irreversibly altered our thought of history. As is well known, one of the great intellectual shifts that followed the emergence and consolidation of the 'Modern World' was the adoption of a view of societal change premissed on the idea of secular progress. This conception of history has become so deeply rooted in modern thought that it useful to remind ourselves how quintessentially *modern* it really is, and thus tied to its epoch – that is to say, to the concrete temporal-structural context which engendered it and whose logic, processes and demands it seeks to express, rationalize and justify. This context is the modern world-system. Emerging in Western Europe in the late fifteenth century, this system pursued a new logic – the valorization and accumulation of capital – which required a radically new conception of societal change, one that recognized the possibility, desirability, and even inevitability, of continuous growth and expansion of the system. Struggling initially against the inherited notions of the past, the idea of progress began to take shape in the seventeenth century and emerged full-blown and triumphant in the eighteenth.

How vast and profound this intellectual sea-change was can be gleaned from its stark contrast to the earlier conceptions of history that modern European thought was heir to and which it was to sweep away. A quick glance at some of these will also serve to rebut the claim, common to many cultural approaches to history (and which typically have no historical approach to culture), that the progressivist-developmentalist view is characteristically Western. It *is*, if what is meant is that it originated in Europe, as did the modern world-system too, and that, as an ideological dimension of that system, it spread along with it all over the globe. But to impute it as somehow being an essential attribute of the Western mind, as being immanent in the occidental civilization which only had to unfold and materialize itself, is to fall into idealism, to commit the fallacy of reifying cognitive structures and abstracting them from their concrete temporal-material context, and quite simply to misread history – if only because the Western world-view (if there is such a thing) has been changing along with the epochal transformations of the European world, just as any other civilization's world-view does in relation to its own historical development. We shall come back to this debate in the conclusion.

The classical Greek conception of history was essentially cyclical. The doctrine of Eternal Return, according to which cosmic history – in its general features if not in all its details – will recur an infinite number of times in the same way as it has already occurred an infinite number of times in the past, ran as a thread through much of Greek philosophy. Not even Aristotle challenged this idea of circularity of becoming, although he hesitated before the implied relativization of succession;[11] his theory, (as well as that of Plato's) of the way forms of government characteristically succeeded each other in the polis clearly bore the imprint of this doctrine. Human history, as the Greeks perceived it, displayed the same cosmic pattern of historical return, with a Golden Age degenerating to a Silver Age and thence to an Iron Age before the process started all over again.[12]

This cyclical conception was radically different from the Judaeo-Christian tradition, which instead saw the history of the world as bounded by two unique and unrepeatable events: the beginning (Creation) and the end (Last Judgment). Between these two points is the history of a lapse from an original perfect state, that of the Garden of Eden, and a search for salvation in the hereafter. For a thousand years through all of the Middle Ages, the Christian view of history, expressed most powerfully by St Augustine, was that of a movement – a pilgrimage – from the Earthly City to the Heavenly City. Although the good society, the City of God, lay ahead and was destined to triumph over *civitas terrena*, the Augustinian conception was not a progress theory as the term is understood now, because the goal of history was beyond history: historical telos was spiritual redemption, not secular amelioration.

The Renaissance humanists, as the name of the epoch clearly expresses, believed the past was superior to the present, and was only to be rediscovered. So did the humanists of the Reformation, including Erasmus, who wished to purify society and the church by returning to its primitive sources – the New Testament and the writings of the Fathers.

The alleged superiority of the ancient world eventually came to be questioned in the late seventeenth century, as contemporary thinkers became conscious of the important scientific, artistic and economic achievements of their own epoch, and, more importantly, of the *limits* imposed on these advances by the archaic world-view. Decades earlier, Francis Bacon had soared far into the future with a vision of a technocratic utopia, the scientifically conceived and economically flourishing New Atlantis, encouraged by his observation of the gathering momentum of scientific advance, from which came 'the Knowledge of Causes and secret motions of things, and the enlarging of the bounds of Human Empire, to the effecting of all things possible'.[13] Similarly, his contemporary Descartes propounded that the scientific method would make men 'the masters and possessors of nature', thereby contributing 'to the perfection of human life'.[14] That science, he reasoned, was 'to be desired . . . for the invention of an infinite number of devices that would enable us to enjoy without any labour the fruits of the earth and all its comforts'.[15] And Locke noted in his journal that there was a 'large field for knowledge proper for the use and advantage of men', and that this was to 'find out new inventions of dispatch to shorten or ease our labours, or applying sagaciously together several agents and patients to procure new and beneficial productions whereby our stock of riches (i.e. things useful for the convenience of our life) may be increased or better preserved . . . For such discoveries as these the mind of man is well fitted.'[16] The philosophic response to the material requirements of the epoch could hardly be better expressed than in these quotations from three of the greatest thinkers of the seventeenth century.

What were those socioeconomic requirements? The 'long sixteenth century' had seen the emergence and steady growth of capitalism in Western Europe as the centre of a 'worldwide' division of labour that encompassed Western and Eastern Europe, the Americas, and various parts of the Orient. Compared to this 150-year period of heady and highly inflationary expansion of the world-economy, the seventeenth century was a period of slowdown in economic development, and saw the intensification of competition among European states for commercial and economic dominance (which underlay, complemented, or reinforced their military struggles for continental supremacy, such as the Thirty Years' War); in this competition within a contractionary world-economy, the Low Countries gained and maintained hegemonic position for a good half of the century. This period of contraction presented the necessity and opportunity for consolidation of the European-dominated world-economy, for assimilation and systematization of all that had been achieved thus far and what was now to be done.[17] The *intellectual* response to this challenge took the form of the so-called Scientific Revolution, whose impact went far beyond the consequent technological advance and economic benefits, to lead to a total revision of man's understanding of the universe and society and of his place in the whole.

This was the material basis of what has been called 'the intellectual crisis of Western Europe' during the last decades of the seventeenth century and the beginning of the eighteenth. This crisis in European philosophy brought together *in a single totalizing movement* the various intellectual (and of course social) processes that had been undermining the *Ancien Régime* through the preceding two centuries: the Humanist objective of *desacralization* of every sphere of practical activity in the interest of nascent mercantile capitalism;[18] the Reformation which, in challenging the universalism of Church authority, provided a language for the process of nation-state building[19] and set down a tradition for critical confrontation with *all* established authority, religious and secular, moral, political and intellectual; the Scientific Revolution which revealed a rational and thoroughly mathematized universe that was analytically accessible and instrumentally useful to man. Each of these movements contributed to the gradual dissolution of the *Ancien Régime* and its supportive organizing myths, and each contributed constitutive elements to the emerging developmentalist philosophy.[20] The crisis consisted in a dialectical confrontation between, on the one hand, this emerging philosophical totalization, called upon to clarify and justify in secular and rational language the actions of the rising bourgeoisie, and, on the other, the philosophical totalization of the old feudal order, now recoiling on the defensive.

One of the forms that this confrontation took was the debate that broke out towards the close of the seventeenth century, known in France as 'la querelle des Anciens et des Modernes' and in England as the 'battle of the books'. Ostensibly a literary issue – can the contemporary writers equal, perhaps even surpass, the great writers of Classical Greece and Rome? – it really marked the turning-point in the ceaseless confrontation between the past and the present, and what it meant for the future. Around this issue emerged, throughout the course of the eighteenth century, successive arguments on the idea of Progress. At mid-point in the century the *philosophe* Turgot outlined a full-blown doctrine of progress, later completed and expressed most forcefully by his disciple Condorcet. All the great thinkers of the Enlightenment pronounced themselves on the idea,[21] and a new 'philosophy of history' – the expression was first used by Voltaire – came into being. History had become intelligible, purposive and linear, and now fitted into the seventeenth century Cartesian tradition of *l'esprit géométrique* and the Leibnizian comic optimism.[22] It also became secular: Divine Providence, thought Voltaire, could not be bothered with the affairs of men, so history could only be the affair of man. Vico, while acknowledging the hand of providence in history, virtually identified it with the laws of the historical process itself. The German idealist philosophers of the late eighteenth and early nineteenth centuries, heirs of the *Aufklärung* and the Romantic movement, pushed the theme further, and transmuted providence into an immanent historic force (Kant's 'unsocial sociability', Hegel's 'self-realization of the Absolute'). In the Hegelian system, historical progression was cast in a dialectical scheme: a new form of reason – dialectics – emerged as the only method appropriate to study a totalizing reality which itself was dialectical.

If history is continuous and inexorable progress, what is it that is supposed to progress, what is the locus of historical progression? Implicit at times, but becoming increasingly explicit through the successive elaborations, the answer was quite clear: whether one spoke of the 'wealth of nations', the *Volksgeist*, or the *contrat social*, the ultimate term of reference was the *state*. Some thinkers went further: not only was the state the situs of progress, but it was thanks to the state that progress was possible. Such was the lesson gained by Voltaire and Montesquieu from their studies of English liberal institutions; such was the Hegelian conception of Prussia – 'the march of God in the world, that is what the State is'.[23] If the existing state was not perfect (or not 'enlightened' enough) – hence the critical edge of the Enlightenment, and the reason for the frequent banishments of the *philosophes* – this only underscored the fact of its perfectibility. Reason would sooner or later triumph, paving the way for the inevitable march of progress; the earlier existing states recognized Reason, and reformed (modernized) themselves accordingly, the more meritorious the achievement of progress would be.

While progress was ineluctable, it was nevertheless also to be pursued consciously; there was a need for society to adopt a *programme of action*, argued Diderot and Bentham. What was open for discussion was the appropriate *form* of government, whether a given political system facilitated (or hindered) progress, whether the programme of action was to be implemented through 'enlightened despotism' or through democratic institutions *à l'anglaise*. The French Revolution was to settle this debate in very dramatic terms later. What was beyond debate, both before and after the Revolution, precisely because it had already acquired the status of the obvious even then, was that *progress was immanent in the state*.

Where they were strong enough – as in the Lowlands, England, and, by the end of the 18th century, also in France as well, then the so-called 'core' states of the world-system – the bourgeoisie had no need for despots, enlightened or otherwise, and guided the 'modernization process' themselves. Where the bourgeoisie was weak, as in the semi-peripheral areas of central, southern and eastern Europe, it fell on the monarchs to initiate the modernization from above. For this reason 'enlightened despotism' was in effect confined to the 'backward' areas desirous of imitating and catching up with the front-runners: Prussia under Frederick II, Russia under Catherine II, Austria under Joseph II.

The situation has remained basically similar, insofar as concerns the Third World Today. As 'development experts' were recommending back in the 1960s, effective implementation of their development pro- grammes called for 'strong' states. Frustrated with the self-debilitating politics of Third World multiparty systems, such as they were, and – where the electoral system did work – distrustful of the independence and mass appeal of popularly elected governments that were ultimately accountable to the people, many of these experts began to look alter- natively to autocratic-technocratic rule, and counted on the military as 'great modernizers' capable of maintaining internal order while pro- moting with martial efficiency social and economic development. The 1970s saw an even more rapid spread of authoritarian regimes led or backed by the military in Latin America, Asia and Africa. 'Emergency rule', 'corporatism', 'crisis government', 'constitutional authoritarian- ism' – euphemisms are not lacking to dress up the brute reality of oppressive state power in India, Chile, South Korea and the Philip- pines. Underlying these euphemisms is the common idea that develop- ment is to be pursued at all costs, and that the most heinous despotism can always be justified in the name of national development. Super- exploitation of labour, marginalization of the masses, neglect of basic needs in preference for world market exports, total disregard of the ecology, destruction of non-capitalist modes of production and indi- genous cultures, suspension of civil liberties, repression of dissent – no price is too high for progress, modernity and development.

National economic development and the ideology of capital- accumulation

While the *philosophes* ranged broadly in their interpretation of progress, seeing it in moral, civilizational and even somewhat mystical terms, the economists imbued it with a rigorous and precise meaning: progress is growth in the wealth of nations. The birth of economics as a science was itself a product of this progress, Adam Smith reminds us. 'The different progress of opulence in different ages and nations has given occasion to two different systems of political economy, with regard to enriching the people,' he noted: 'the system of commerce' or mercantilism, and 'the system of agriculture' or physiocracy.[24] These precursors ('imperfect approximations to the truth') of classical political economy addressed themselves to the themes – in effect, one combined theme – of *capital accumulation* and *national economic development*, which Smith was to adopt as his own, making it the very title of his magnum opus, *An*

Enquiry into the Nature and Causes of the Wealth of Nations.

Even if its methodological cohesiveness as an economic theory may be questionable, the seventeenth century doctrine of mercantilism can arguably be considered the first theory of national economic development conceived in the context of the emerging capitalist world-system. In the mercantilist conception the two processes of capital accumulation and nation-state building were one and inseparable. Smith was only half right when he saw mercantilism as having sprung from the 'spirit of monopoly' of merchants and manufacturers; it was rather a thoroughly integrated complex of processes where economic growth and strengthening of the Crown – both internally as against contending groups and externally as against foreign powers – were indispensable to each other. The mercantilist 'obsession' with the accumulation of bullion, which appeared so irrational to political economists a century and a half later, was in fact logical and necessary for the core countries of Western Europe in initially setting into motion the world-wide system of commercial exchanges at that time, since the precious metals that they squeezed from the colonies were all that they could offer in exchange for Baltic wheat and Oriental spices, textiles and all the other imported items for which no adequate substitutes could be produced at home.[25] The mercantilist insistence on a favourable balance of trade and a host of protectionist measures to guarantee it were designed not only as a defence of the weaker states against the stronger ones and of competitors against each other, but were intended to achieve the middle-run objective of increasing overall efficiency in the sphere of production.[26] The role of the state in this venture was clear: to protect home industries (the infant industry and import-substitution arguments of our time) and to create the conditions for the success of private enterprise (e.g. the creation of trading companies).[27]

The ability of the state to affect the developmental processes of the world-system for the benefit of its capitalists obviously depended on its strength (along military, bureaucratic/administrative, and financial dimensions), and, equally obviously, vice versa: the strength of the state was a function of the economic role of its capitalists in the world-economy. The state's *political* stake in the mercantilist enterprise thus went without saying: mercantilism was, firstly, the logical extension of the age-old notion that bullion supplied 'the sinews of war', and, secondly, it was the strategy of strengthening oneself by weakening the economic, and, by extension, military powers of neighbours. In an age of brutally competitive state-making, which also coincided with world-economic contraction, mercantilist policies were the continuation of war by other means. As Josiah Child observed then, 'all trade is a kind of warfare'.[28]

Even as they competed fiercely with each other, the mercantilist states strove to imitate the great model of their time, the Lowlands. As the hegemonic power for at least half a century, the Dutch were hated and admired, feared and envied. Mercantilism, in effect, was the attempt by other states – notably the English and the French – to duplicate the Dutch miracle, even as it also meant, in true mercantilist fashion, the objective to destroy that economic miracle. To quote Wallerstein:

> There came a point in the mid-seventeenth century when cumulative economic advantage seemed so incapable of being undercut that both England and France decided that the 'Dutch must be driven from the field by force'. In fact, of course, even in purely economic terms, hegemony cannot last in a capitalist system; but one cannot blame the English and the French for chafing at the bit. We contend, then, that the state was an essential instrument used by the Dutch bourgeoisie to consolidate an economic hegemony that they had won originally in the sphere of production and had then extended to commerce and finance. The states of competing core and semi-peripheral powers would be equally essential instruments in the later process of destroying this hegemony.[29]

If mercantilism was the continuation of war by other means, war was the continuation of mercantilism by all means.

It would be wrong to presume, as liberal economic theory wishes so hard to believe, that mercantilism is a thing of the past, that it never recovered from the devastating critique of it made by Smith in the name of free trade. The fact is that mercantilist *state policies* are not confined to the so-called Age of Mercantilism but have always been employed by some states or others throughout practically the entire history of the capitalist world-economy, even if the ideological justification might have differed from case to case. We only need to read today's newspaper to remind ourselves that 'beggar-my-neighbour' policies, 'la reconquête du marché intérieur', and the spectre of trade war, are very much the reality of the present. While it is true that capital never allows its operations to be circumscribed by nation-state configurations, since the capitalist economic system has been a global one from its inception, it is equally true that, whenever capitalists cannot maximize their profit via the normal operation of the world-market, they resort readily to their nation-state to affect the functioning of the economy in their favour. Moreover, while the state is certainly more than just an instrument for capital, it is nevertheless the case that the state and capital have their political and economic stakes intertwined in the vicissitudes of the world-system. On this rests their symbiosis, but from this also arise time and again discrepancies between 'national interests' and the imperatives of capital, because the latter have at all times been dictated by the pursuit of profit-maximization within the real economic market, that of the world-economy.

Thus it was the case with England that when classical mercantilism had outlived its usefulness and London had effectively undermined

Amsterdam's hegemonic position, English economic thought was ready for a new chapter – that of liberalism, to which we shall turn shortly. French economic thought, too, was ready for a profound change, to which the physiocrats would respond, but for different reasons. Adam Smith suggests that physiocracy should be understood as a reaction to the excesses and failures of Colbert's mercantilist policies during the reign of Louis XIV, and to the ravages inflicted on the economy as a consequence of the king's life-long waging of war against European rivals. Recent historiography casts doubt on this simplistic interpretation, which we shall not go into here.[30] It is clear, however, that the physiocrats' predominant emphasis on agricultural development (hence Smith's appellation of physiocracy as the 'system of agriculture') was intended to redress its neglect in France relative to Colbert's all-out drive for commercial and industrial growth, this at a time when the capitalist transformation of agriculture in England was proceeding at full pace and was laying down the necessary precondition for further balanced economic development. In this sense, the physiocratic programme was to emulate the much-admired 'agricultural revolution' in England: to eliminate the vestiges of medieval institutions in the countryside, to rationalize the fiscal system, to replace *petite* with *grande culture*, to free the corn trade from all mercantilist restrictions.[31]

The outstanding contribution of the physiocrats to economic theory and, beyond that, to the philosophy of developmentalism in general, was their understanding of *the economy as a natural system*, comprehensible because, just like nature, it was subject to laws. 'In nature everything is intertwined,' said Quesnay, 'everything runs through circular courses which are interlaced with one another'.[32] Du Pont put it very forcefully: 'A knowledge of order and of the natural and physical laws should serve as the basis of economics'; the science of economics, he wrote, 'is nothing but the application of the natural order of government to society'.[33] The closer a society obeys the laws of nature, the greater is the cumulative prosperity of society's interdependent sectors, the larger is its 'net product'. This fundamental truth of 'circular flow' thought Quesnay, was demonstrated in his *tableau économique*, which revealed the working of the economy during a given time period and demonstrated the interconnections between sectors and social groups in terms of a flow of goods and money. This Newtonian conception of the economy as a mechanical model laid the foundation of modern macroeconomic theory – the same model which today underlies Leontief's input-output matrix and other systems of GNP accounting.

In equating the capitalist economy with nature, the physiocrats laid down two principles which have remained fundamental to developmentalist philosophy. The first is that the existing socio-economic system is part of a larger and higher natural, harmonious and rational order – Leibniz's best of all possible worlds, where 'interdependence of parts' (the very same concept so dear to the NIEO declarations and the Brandt Reports) is inherently positive, rational, and benefical to all, because consonant with the dictates of nature; in this universe, exploitation and unequal exchange are inconceivable. The second principle is that the functioning of the economy is determined by natural laws, fixed and eternal and beyond human reach, like the law of gravitation. As Sartre notes:

> By extending the idea of *natural law* to the economic sphere – an inevitable but fundamental error – they [the thinkers of the Enlightenment] both secularized the economy and converted it into a domain external to man: a system of inflexible laws whose constraints permitted no modification. The economy was part of Nature – here too [as in the natural sciences] one could only command Nature by obeying it.[34]

Several propositions follow as a consequence. There is the ready-made ideological defence (an offence at that time *vis-à-vis* the *ancien régime*): since the capitalist system is sacrosanct, deviations from it (alternative systems or archaic orders) are aberrations.[35] There is the tradition of mechanistic materialism dating from this period which, to quote Samir Amin:

> . . . postulates a series of chains of specific causal determinations. The chief of these is that science and technology, by their (autonomous) progress, determine every sphere of social life, transforming social relations in the process. The class struggle is expelled from history and replaced by a mechanical determination imposing itself as an external force, as a law of nature. This primitive materialism, which is often regarded as opposed to idealism, is in fact its twin: they are two sides of the same coin. Whether it is said that humanity is guided on the path of progress by God (Providence) or that this function is fulfilled by science, it comes to exactly the same thing: conscious, nonalienated society and social classes disappear from the picture. That is why the ideological expression of this materialism is often religious (e.g. the Freemasons or the Supreme Being); that is why the two ideologies go easily hand in hand in the United States – primitive materialism governs social behaviour (and provides its 'scientific' explanation), while religious idealism remains intact 'in the soul'. Bourgeois 'science' has never transcended this primitive materialism because it conditions the reproduction of alienation, enabling capital to exploit labour.[36]

British liberalism restated all these propositions as verities, and added more to the developmentalist philosophy. Smith's elaboration of the economy as a natural harmonious system (the 'Invisible Hand' argument) incorporated the other main strand of English political thought, *individualism*, and saw them reconciled in the free market. The naturally self-regulating operations of the market, by giving free play to individual pursuit of self-interest, led to the benefit of all – this, according to Smith, was the 'simple principle of natural liberty'. Natural laws operated both at the macroeconomic as well as at the microeconomic levels, since general laws of human nature predisposed the individual towards specific behavioural patterns, argued the utilitarians since Hobbes. Defoe's Robinson Crusoe, as the literary symbol of liberal 'man', was rational, utilitarian, and hedonistic, that is, motivated by the calculus of 'pleasure and pain' to strive for personal happiness. From the distilled behaviour of abstract *homo oeconomicus*, the economists purported to construct an algebra of logical deductions, a 'pure' economic science which to this day remains the ambition of marginalist economics. Conceived on the basis of supposedly general laws of human nature, this 'pure' science pretended to do away with the specificities of history and society as altogether scientifically irrelevant, because, just like Newton's physics, economics was reducible to behavioural mechanics, constant patterns of thought and action irrespective of culture and epoch.

Naturally, these assumptions about human nature were carefully chosen, for they were meant to promote specific values required by the socio-economic conditions of the time; economics, then, as it is now, was a normative science, objectivist pretensions notwithstanding. In pre-industrial Britain, classical political economy was concerned with encouraging in the middle classes the virtues of thrift, saving, self-interest and material acquisitiveness, thanks to which a sufficient surplus of capital could be built up for the mobilization of the productive forces; similarly, it aimed to inculcate in the labouring classes a work ethic that would assure discipline and mechanical order in the changing production process. What better way to promote these values and attitudes, quite different from those held since time immemorial, than to present them as rooted in the nature of humanity and part of the structure of the universe? Thanks to humanity's natural 'propensity to truck, barter and exchange', the division of labour had come about, that principle of social organization 'from which so many advantages are derived', not least of which being the wealth of nations. Underlying the synergetic dynamics of it all was private capital.

> Capital has been silently and gradually accumulated by the private frugality and good conduct of individuals, by their universal, continual, and uninterrupted effort to better their own condition. It is this effort, protected by law and allowed by liberty to exert itself in the manner that is most advantageous, which has maintained the progress of England towards opulence and improvement in almost all former times, and which, it is to be hoped, will do so in all future times.[37]

Private capital for public good: Smith's formula for harmonizing individual and social interests was elegantly simple. By defining both in the same way, as growth in capital accumulation and increase in production, he necessarily arrived at the logical conclusion that the arithmetical sum, namely society as a whole, increased to the extent that the individual capital accumulations making it up increased.

> As every individual . . . endeavours as much as he can to employ his capital in the support of domestic industry, and so to direct that industry that its produce may be of the greatest value; every individual necessarily labours to render the annual revenue of society as great as he can . . . he intends his own security . . . only his own gain . . . and he is in this, as in many other cases, led by an invisible hand, to promote an end which was no part of his intention.[38]

Beyond these normative concerns of classical economics, Smith, and later on David Ricardo, proceeded to investigate, as Marx put it, 'the real internal framework (*Zusammenhang*) of bourgeois relations of production', such as the division of labour, the capital accumulation process, the laws of distribution of the national product, and the labour theory of value, which Marx was to develop further and turn into a critique of capitalism.[39] Marxist economic theory was one line of development proceeding from what was in effect a bifurcation of economic thought running down from classical political economy. The other line was marginalist or neo-classical economics. It is probably not too much of an exaggeration to sum up that bifurcation, for present purposes, this way: what Marx rejected in classical economics, the marginalists took over, and what he took over from Smith and Ricardo, they eschewed.[40]

Thus W. Stanley Jevons, Carl Menger and Léon Walras rejected, first of all, the classical labour theory of value (an 'objective' theory in the sense that the value of a good was based on something inherent in it, that is, the amount of labour used in its production), replacing it with a subjective theory of value ('subjective' because the value of a good was not intrinsic to it but was based on an extraneous yardstick, that is, the satisfaction derived by the consumer of the good, or its utility for the consumer, subjectively assessed). This subjective explanation of economic value based on utility took the form of the so-called marginal utility theory of value, which is the starting-point of modern microeconomics' explanation of relative prices.

The entire edifice of modern price theory rests on very powerful assumptions about human nature. Here again, these assumptions are very carefully chosen to advance specific purposes. The Puritan growth-inducing values of the classical economists were transformed in neo-classical economics into virtues of purposive rationalism, maximization of monetary or consumption gains, and rational efficiency. Robinson Crusoe the producer was analyzed this time as a consumer; he was found to allocate 'efficiently' his scarce resources between alternative uses, and he tended to 'equalize values at the margin' due to the law of diminishing marginal utility. Consumer behaviour was inferred to be maximizing and efficiency-oriented (allocation with maximum effect), and economic choice was presumed to take place at the highest attainable indifference curve.[41] If true for the individual, concluded Alfred Marshall, it was equally true for the firm, and indeed for the entire national economy as well. For this enormous system of logical deductions that was economics to remain consistent with itself, assumptions were piled upon assumptions – such as, that the economic agent (individual or firm) has sufficient information about the economic environment within which it is to make decisions, that the environment is a free competitive system in the first place, and so forth. At all points in this thoroughly rational universe, costs and benefits are measured, considered, traded off each other, and decisions taken in accordance with the same formal logic that inevitably led (unintended, of course, by the individual agents themselves) to a *collective* maximization point and equilibrium. Vilfredo Pareto and Walras saw, in the logical linkage between the microlevel concept of optimum allocation of resources and the macro-level concept of general equilibrium, the harmonization principle of the free market.[42]

The shift from an objective to a subjective value theory in the second half of the nineteenth century was related to major changes in the character of the economy, explains Walter A. Weisskopf:

The increase in capital equipment, the progress of technology and the increase in output created the problem of finding marketing outlets for a capital-rich economic system with a high productive capacity. This explains the change of emphasis away from the objective, production-mindedness of the classicists. The marginalist and neo-classical schools partly reflected and partly foreshadowed this trend by moving the subjective element of wants, desires, need satisfaction and demand into the centre of economic thought, thereby taking seriously the utilitarian hedonistic approach . . . It had to be demonstrated that rationality dominates all types of economic activity. The consumer, housewife, entrepreneur, industrial firm, saver etc., are all represented as people who consciously balance opposing forces, values, interests in such a fashion that they maximize the total of their advantages, utility, profits, and so forth and thus aim at and reach a point of equilibrium. In all these cases the existence of inner conflicts between goals, values and impulses and between what man wants to do and what the economic system permits him to do is ignored. Conflicting drives and inclinations of a qualitatively different nature are reduced to a common quantitative denominator, so that conscious comparison of relative quantities of gain and loss can show the way to a clear-cut decision, maximizing benefits and equilibriating opposing forces. Rational economic conduct, maximization of gains and equilibrium become symbols of economic harmony.[43]

After this neo-classical elaboration of microeconomics in consonance with the conditions of the time, it took yet another catastrophic down-turn of the world-economy to shift once more the central focus of economics. The so-called 'Keynesian revolution', an outcome of the Great Depression of the 1930s, brought to the fore the critical concerns of employment, production, growth in national income, the interplay of aggregate saving and investment, – macroeconomic problems that had been neglected by neo-classical economics with its central emphasis on consumption and price theory in a high-productivity economy. Challenging the most important assumption of the neo-classical economists that the economic system, left to itself, automatically tended to find its equilibrium at full employment (Say's Law), Keynes argued that unemployment was, on the contrary, a natural condition of the economy, and that fiscal policies by the government were needed to correct this normal tendency. The adjustment mechanism for equal-izing aggregate saving and investment, he argued, was not the rate of interest and the corrective movements of wages and prices, but the total output of the economy. Keynes saw his contribution to the modern theory of income analysis as the turning point in economic thought: for him 'classical economists' were all those from Smith to Pigou who fell victim to Say's Law – in a word, the pre-Keynesians. Except, how-ever, for the crucial points of disagreement, such as the one just men-tioned, the Keynesian synthesis incorporates and builds upon the contributions of the marginalists. All this is what constitutes, today, mainstream economics, including resurrected doctrines that come under the label of 'monetarism' (Milton Friedman and the Chicago school).

True to the tradition of its predecessors, mainstream economics enthrones the GNP as the measure of all things.[44] An ever-rising GNP per capita stands for many things at the same time: it is the concrete symbol of the solid harmony that is presumed to prevail in society; it is the measure of the wealth of the nation; it is the sign of strength, dynamism and well-being of the country; and it is the *socially accepted goal* of what at bottom is the untrammelled pursuit of self-interest, the accumulation of capital. It is the essence of capital to expand and to grow, and it does so in an inherently contradictory and conflictual way, as the last five hundred years of world-history amply demonstrates; however, once projected into the social sphere in aggregative terms as GNP-growth, the imperative of capital to expand becomes a collective desideratum and is valued in itself, not just for the owners of capital but for all, because everyone benefits from a rising GNP, like the sun that shines on all. As before, the conflict between social good and individual interest that is inherent in a capitalist system finds its ethical justification in a collective myth: from natural law and invisible hand to equilibrium and GNP.

Throughout this section of the essay we have stressed the *normative* function of economics as it evolved over the last three centuries. More specifically, we have tried to spell out this normative function as being geared, first and foremost, to the advancement of capital accumulation. If it has been necessary to emphasize this normative thrust of economics, it is because contemporary mainstream economists do everything possible to deny it. In this respect, and here alone, today's economists differ from their predecessors: not in their mode of reasoning, since this has remained the same – analytic, deductive and mathematical; nor in their fundamental concepts, for these have retained an essential continuity in meaning from their earlier adumbrations (e.g. from the physiocrats' 'net product' to today's 'GNP'); nor in their theoretical presuppositions over a wide range of phenomena (e.g. Ricardo's theory of comparative advantage to Heckscher-Ohlin's factor-proportions approach to international trade); they differ rather in their attitudes towards the values that they hold. Whereas the classical economists, who saw their field of knowledge as being part of moral philosophy, defined their intellectual tasks in terms of the values and processes that they wished to promote in society, today's economists are scandalized by normative concerns, seeing them as being incompatible with economics' pretensions as an 'objective, value-free science'. The early economists placed their values at the centre of their research, and created a science in order to promote them; today's economists think they have discovered a science, and conceal their values under the guise of this science. This is a difference between a rising philosophy and a defensive one.

As is fairly well known, the question of values in economic thought broke into a debate among economists themselves a decade or so ago. One consequence of this critical reappraisal of the philosophical foundations of economics was a calling into question of the scientific validity of current economic theory.[45] What is valid in economics is a question that continues to provoke controversy, and now more than ever, as the current global crisis and the phenomenon of 'stagflation' challenge the explicative and analytical – not to mention prescriptive and prognostic – power of dominant economic theory.[46]

If the scientific validity of mainstream economics for the Western developed countries, where it originated, is problematic enough as it is, it is all the more so when it is transplanted, by persuasion or compulsion, to the Third World. 'Development economics', as that specialized branch of modern economic theory, seeks to apply the same tenets, inculcate the same values, and promote the same processes of the centre in the periphery of the world-system. Thus growth in GNP per capita is posited as the central problem of development, and everything follows from that. This is seen to depend on the 'import' of capital, since domestic savings are inadequate for the required capital formation (the Harrod-Domar growth model's justification for international capital penetration), as well as on intensified trade with the rest of the world-economy (the gains from trade theory of the Heckscher-Ohlin and Samuelson-Lerner models). National economic growth is equally dependent on the ability of the developing countries to convert new capital effectively into higher levels of output, and this necessitates a whole range of institutional and attitudinal changes (the modernization theory and all its variants: the pattern variable approach, accultura-tion, diffusionist and dualist arguments, etc.) As can be logically expected, the attitudes and values propagated by modernization theories are the very same ones that Smith hoped to inculcate in his countrymen two centuries ago, and the same puritanical corollary is there as an easy excuse: if people are poor, they are to be blamed for their own misfortune, for not being 'enterprising' enough, for not responding to the dictates of human nature. To the extent that everyone does his or her share in the capital-formation and economic-growth processes, and the 'traditional' barriers to capital-expansion are one by one torn down by the modernization process, everyone eventually benefits (the 'trickle-down' effect of an expanding GNP). Under-development then is simply a stage which will eventually be left behind as the entire nation moves onward to development.

The developmentalist theory of stages, or the 'follow-the-leader' ideology

If history is progressive movement, there remains the question of the trajectory – movement from what, towards what? Implicitly or explic-itly, the developmentalist conception of history reposes on a *theory of stages* through which the social unit that is supposed to progress (and we have seen that this means primarily the nation-state) *must neces-sarily pass*. Now, here we must be aware of a crucial distinction. It is one thing to recognize distinct historical systems and periodicities as a matter of historical fact and as an analytical procedure, quite another to hypostatize a teleological scheme, typically dressed up in deterministic language, whose triumphalist hierarchical ordering ('backward – advanced', 'lower – higher') of supposedly universal validity serves as an ideological justification for the 'leaders' dominance over the 'laggards', and pretends to be a pre-determined path (read: 'development strategy') which the 'latecomers' need only to follow. It is the latter sense which characterizes the developmentalist theory of stages, even if in some cases this is made to appear as 'purely conceptual' constructs.

When the great thinkers of the past projected their visions of the historical trajectory, it was with a critical intent. Existing society was taken to task in terms of the historical *telos*, which lay ahead and was to be striven for, never mind that the course of history was believed to be inevitable all the same. The future judged the present; the goal provided at the same time the criterion of social critique. The world they were living in was a world-in-the-making, and it was for the bourgeoisie, which was beginning to see itself as the rising class and the agent of change, to assume this historic task. Voltaire saw the trajectory as the movement from the darkness of superstition toward the increasing light of Reason. Kant interpreted it as the unfolding of a 'secret plan' of Nature, humanity's 'unsociable sociability' driving him – almost against his will – towards building a rational and ethical civil order, both national and global. Turgot suggested a pattern of three stages – an animistic, a speculative, and a scientific stage – which Comte was to recast later as the theological, the metaphysical and the positive stages. Hegel saw this movement as the actualization of the Absolute through time, the self-development of Spirit itself, through the successive careers of world-historical peoples. When Marx outlined his historical stages in terms of successive modes of production, it was at the same time to announce in advance the eventual dialectical supersession of the present capitalist system by a more humane and rational social order; capitalism, in accomplishing its historic task, would bring into being the objective conditions for the emergence of the new social order.

Today's developmentalist theories of stages have none of the critical edge of their predecessors. On the contrary, they are meant to justify the *existing* order. The bourgeoisie, firmly entrenched in power for so long now, congratulates itself for the 'developed' capitalist society it has created, and triumphantly presents this as the *model* for the countries of the Third World to imitate. It takes the arrogance and the ignorance of a Walt Rostow (to take but the most famous of the modernization theorists) to proclaim the stages allegedly traversed by all developed capitalist societies as the development path for all other countries to follow. The absurdity of Rostow's stages of economic growth is matched only by the utter poverty of his down-to-earth teleological vision: for him, universal history is the passage from the initial stage of traditional society to the fifth and final stage of mass consumption – and he quite content to let history consummate itself at that.

The Rostovian 'non-communist manifesto' of historical development finds its response in (or is itself a response to) Soviet Marxism's 'non-capitalist path of development'. The latter is equally self-serving and self-congratulatory as the former; both are perfectly isomorphic. Unilinear economic determinism has resulted in a mechanistic scheme of Eurocentric modes of production, with the Soviet model as the vanguard for the others to follow. In terms of the social theory that they profess to uphold and realize in the concrete world, socialism ought to be transitional towards communism. Neither in word nor in deed do the present self-proclaimed 'socialist' states indicate that they are still interested in pursuing this transition. Rather they are more interested, in competition with the US model, that the world transform itself in their own image. The plight of the Third World offers fertile ground for superpower rivalry.

Stage theories do not only enjoin the latecomers to catch up with the leader, they also imply that the leader knows what is best for everyone else's own good – as Western governments, institutions and 'development experts' remind Third World countries from time to time. Not surprisingly, this sometimes leads to friction or distrust, as when ecological concerns and 'limits to growth' arguments are interpreted (correctly or incorrectly, as the case may be) to mean attempts and rationalizations by the Centre countries to discourage industrialization efforts in the Third World.

Neither is this presumption of 'knowing what's best for you' confined to 'establishment' development thinking; a certain 'big brother complex' is clearly visible in many 'alternative' development movements as well. The belief that the Centre of the world-system maintains its historic lead and prerogative even in the 'self-transformation' of that system is quite common to many (by no means all) counter-movements in the industrialized countries, which see themselves as pioneering the way towards 'another development' by adopting 'alternative ways of life'. The presumption is that they represent a 'post-materialist, post-industrial' wave whose dissatisfaction with the stultifying affluence of their societies provides them with an ethic and a vision of a transcendent social order. The initiative for the self-transformation of the system and the eventual 'Greening of the world' is seen as the historic prerogative – like the preceding global transformations – of the advanced Centre. Indeed, it can hardly be otherwise, since the perspective for 'another development' is a privilege exclusive to those who have actually tasted the fruits of 'over-development' and found it wanting; the developing countries are well advised to pay heed. Consider, as an illustration of this tendency, the following quotation, taken from a highly provocative study on the similarities between the Roman Empire and contemporary Western imperialism, and the reasons for their decline (the assumption being that imperialism is on the decline):

The cause of the decline and fall of western imperialism is western imperialism itself, or, in other words, its ever-expanding or at least never-contracting cosmology . . And the carriers of the new social formation are, of course, found in the centre of the Centre – not in any other group not yet through with the patterns set by western imperialism, only aching to get into better positions or to do it themselves. The routines of a cosmology [western cosmology being inherently expansionist, which explains the phenomenon of western imperialism itself] have to be run through – to express it in computer language – they have to be tried out before one is through and starts looking for a new programme, a new 'way of doing things'. Revolts may be made by the masses; transformations are made by the elite who understand how to make use of the revolts. Together they constitute revolutions . . .[47]

Where, indeed, lie the transformational possibilities in the world-system? This is one of the crucial questions to which the contributors to this book address themselves. As the present global crisis intensifies, and with it the inherent social contradictions of the system, what are the alternatives available to whom; which of these are functional, in effect if not in intent, for the continuous operation of the system; and which have the potential to be anti-systemic and therefore, cumulatively with other anti-systemic forces, possibly transformative in the long-run? These questions call for a thorough analysis of what is happening in the world today, in the various geographic and functional parts of the world-system, in terms of the contradictions of that system. In analysing contemporary developments, it is all the more necessary to learn as much as we can from history – in particular, the phenomenon of unequal development in the history of capitalism, which points out (in direct opposition to stage theories, including that of orthodox marxism) that systemic transformations take place sooner in the weak and underdeveloped links of the system and not in the fully developed and structurally rigid centre of that system.[48]

Contemporary or historical, the question of transformation dynamics admits of no easy answers; the mistake is to assume, as the developmentalist theory of stages does, that the answer is easy from the start.

Developmentalism and the modern world-system

Following Sartre's understanding of philosophy as totalizing thought developed for the purpose of giving expression to the general movement of society, we have tried to describe developmentalism as one such totalizing thought which historically evolved as the philosophical expression of the modern world-system, whose organizational logic, constitutive processes and spatio-temporal structures this philosophy seeks to promote, rationalize and justify.

We have said that the progressivist conception of history developed in conjunction with, and as the conceptual expression of, the expansion of capital; that the valorization and accumulation of capital required such a conception of societal change premised on the inevitability and desirability of continuous growth and expansion of the capitalist system, and that this also meant, transformatively, the dissolution of the *Ancien Régime*, along with its philosophical self-representations.

We have seen how, in the hands of the classical economists, progress was equated with economic growth in its capitalist form (viz. the self-expanding appropriation of abstract wealth in the form of money), thereby justifying private gain as public good in the hypostatized harmonious sphere of the market; and how economics emerged as the theoretical instrument for understanding and promoting the mechanics of capital accumulation, this being seen as the dynamic process underlying growth in the 'wealth of nations'.

Capital accumulation being an inherently uneven, competitive and contradictory process, some nations grew wealthier than others, indeed at the expense of others, and over time these discrepancies were structurally reinforced and perpetuated, economically through the operations of the market (unequal exchange), and politically through direct action by state power to affect the developmental processes of the world-system in their national interest (imperialism, hegemonic rivalry). The interstate system that formed in the context of the single, unified, capitalist world-economy was thus hierarchical, competitive, and inextricably tied up with the capital accumulation process from the very start: the international division of labour that constitutes the structure of the world-system necessarily takes a centre-periphery arrangement of nation-states, with capital tending to accrue to the centre and away from the periphery and thus making possible the creation of 'strong states' in the core of the world-system. Mercantilism, we have seen, provided the first theoretical expression for this impulse towards the formation of strong states in the core via protectionist policies, while liberalism was the policy of the strong to become even stronger by dismantling state restrictions on the movement of goods and capital across political boundaries.

The strongest of the strong, the hegemonic powers, paved the way and provided the 'model' for other states to follow;[49] the developmentalist theory of stages was simultaneously a programme of development by imitation of the model and a teleological evolutionist schema that justified the predominance of the 'front-runners' over the 'late-comers'. What is now called the 'development gap', long recognized in the developmentalist perspective, is therefore but the distance between a lower and a higher stage yet to be traversed by the lagging nation-state. Then, as now, the central problem of development was thought to revolve around the question of 'bridging the gap' and 'catching up'.

All told, developmentalism boils down to this, which remains its message to the Third World today: development consists in the three combined processes of modernization, economic growth and nation-state building, all three of them being understood in a very precise sense – as constitutive processes linked to and reproductive of the global accumulation of capital. Thus modernization is not just any social change, much less an endogenously induced transformation process, but the steady penetration of capital into all spheres of social life, the progressive submission of non-capitalist social formations and self-subsistent economies to the dictates of capital, the proletarianization of the work-force, the commodification of all realms of production and exchange so that no exploitable economic activity remains exogenous to and autonomous from the operation of the capitalist law of value, and the destruction and displacement of indigenous cultures and their subsumption under a capitalist life-style adopted by the local elites.

Similarly, economic growth is not just an abstract aggregative increase in society's productive capacity and total output, which theoretically provide the material basis for improving the economic well-being of society as a whole, but rather means concretely the continued expansion of capital. Technological innovation, improvement in productivity, increase in social overhead capital and growth of the productive forces are all subordinated and subservient to the dictates of the movement of capital, with, as always, its contradictory effects on society. Hence the phenomenon of 'growth without development', of growth with increasing social inequality and mass impoverishment, known only too well in the Third World.

Finally, for all the rhetoric about decolonization, juridical sovereignty, and national self-determination, the reality of nation-state building in the epoque of neo-colonialism and monopoly capital means the creation of an internationally dependent and subservient state-machinery – whose functions insofar as the world-system and the national ruling elites' own vested interests are concerned include guaranteeing the continuing integration of the nation-state into the international divison of labour, maintaining the existing capitalist social relations of production through contractual institutions and the control of labour, regulating economic processes within its frontiers according to the world-system's prescribed norms and techniques of adjustment, maintaining a 'favourable investment climate' for transnational capital, and, should the need arise, militarily wiping out opposition movements which reject the system and which strive for an alternative, non-capitalist social order. As logic would have it, the individual state's willingness and capability to perform such functions are the criteria by which the dominant powers of the world-system judge the acceptability of that particular state within the so-called 'Free World'. The sanction for non-acceptance by this 'Free World', as the ever-lengthening list of post-Second World War cases dramatically reveals, is military intervention, economic boycott and sabotage waged by these global powers and their local allies on recalcitrant movements and governments. If man, as they used to argue in the Enlightenment, can be forced to be free, today's 'young' nation-states are being forced to 'develop' and, whether their populations like it or not, are forced to do so within and according to the rules of the 'Free World'-system.

Unquestioned through all this, because it enjoys the status of 'the obvious' within the developmentalist philosophy, is the idea that states are the units of development, that it is within each of them that economic growth and modernization take place over time, that they are the entities which progress and move through evolutionary stages. Developmental discrepancies between them (the 'gaps') are thus explained in terms of factors endogenous to the states in question (dualism, historical lags, inadequate capital formation, etc.: in short, underdevelopment as the explanation for underdevelopment), and not in terms of the dynamics and contradictions of the world-system itself. Indeed, in the developmentalist perspective, the world-system is an entity with a derived, second-order status: as the outcome of interaction processes between states, as the complex of relations among states, while ontologically and epistemologically the individual states are taken as prior and fundamental. The conception, therefore, is of a composite *international* system, rather than of an organic, complete and irreducible *world*-system whose logic (viz. the capitalist law of value), processes (principally, the valorization and accumulation of capital) and structures (e.g. the international division of labour) can be comprehended only at the level of the whole. The developmentalist concept of the international system is, in fact, nothing more than the classical liberal conception of society writ large, and thus open to the same criticisms. That eighteenth century doctrine, it will be recalled, conceived of society as the contractual coming together of self-contained individual atoms, each of them being propelled by self-interest to maximize his satisfactions and economic gain, so that the societal whole is nothing more nor less than the sum of its parts which remain basic and primordial. To arrive at the global level, the only modification effected on this liberal theory of society has been to replace 'individuals' with 'nation-states' – everything else of the theory remaining unchanged.

This, of course, is perfectly consonant with state-centred ideologies. It is also what the social sciences – which evolved in the context of the totalizing philosophy of developmentalism – by and large teach us about social reality.[50] Society, economy, polity, history and culture are generally conceptualized and theorized in the various disciplines within the parameters of the state. These domains are identified in relation to the state, and in effect are treated as if they were attributes internal to and 'possessed' by the state.[51] Hence mainstream economics – whose theorization of economic phenomena is framed within the parameters of the 'national economy', epistemologically conceived as being distinct from 'the rest of the world' – assumes that the international economy is but a juxtaposition of all the existing 'national economies', each of them being conceived as an integrated, analytically self-contained and bounded system, set off against, although interacting with, other equally bounded system. Such a scenario fosters the illusion that it is for each individual nation-state to optimally manage 'its' national economy, to improve the international competitiveness of its industries, to maximize its gains and promote national economic growth within the global market. In a Leibnitzian world characterized by interdependence and harmony of interests, every one of the nation-states can benefit, prosper and develop.

To continue to hang on to such an illusion is to ignore totally what the 500-year-long history of the world-system demonstrates about the workings of this system.[52] To believe that the countries of the Third World can develop themselves via deeper integration into the capitalist world-system is to refuse to recognize that it was precisely because of their integration into the world-system – whether forced, through colonialism yesterday, or voluntary, in the present international division of labour – that they have become underdeveloped in the first place, that their lot in the necessarily polarizing global accumulation process has been the continuing 'development of underdevelopment'. To imagine that the beneficent functioning of an 'interdependent' global order holds the promise of development to the countries of the South is to forget that this 'interdependence' is characterized by unequal exchange, uneven development and relationships of domination and dependence between the centre and the periphery, which no amount of North-South negotiations and NIEO resolutions over the last decade has been able to alter because these characteristics derive from the basic dynamics of the system itself. To hold that development is a process that takes place within the nation-state which this basic unit can accelerate by pursuing appropriate developmental strategies is to fail to see that development is not an internal attribute of individual states of which some may have more than others, but refers rather to their structural and functional position and role in the global capital accumulation process. The objective to bridge the gap is, in structural terms, the competitive drive to move up the hierarchical structure of the world-system, while maintaining intact – and indeed reinforcing – the international division of labour. To the extent that a handful of states (say, the so-called 'new industrializing countries' or 'NICs') *may* be able to improve their relative position and role in the international division of labour in the present crisis-ridden conjuncture of the world-economy, this will simply have meant promotion into the ranks of the core of the system. The system itself will remain, globally and in each of the states, including the NICs, as exploitative and dehumanizing as ever.

If development is to mean obtaining and securing the bases of life for the mass of the world's population, if it is to aim at the increasing emancipation of oppressed peoples, classes and marginalized social groups, if it is to aspire to the creation of a just, non-exploitative and mutually beneficial social order where the free development of each individual is the condition for the free development of all, then clearly developmentalism cannot be the answer. Human and social development for all can only mean the necessary transformation of the world-system into a different social order, aimed at a different mode of production and a different form of society.

It is the world-system itself that must be transformed. To say this is not to throw in yet one more vapid moral exhortation. It is rather to reaffirm the fact that the global expansion of capital has always produced, in its turn, resistance to the dominant forces and processes of the world-system, and that this struggle between the forces sustaining the system and those seeking to transform it has dominated the history and ongoing politics of the capitalist world-system since the last century. This struggle takes many forms, assumes a variety of names, receives different theoretical formulations, pursues diverse goals through diverse means, and poses a multiplicity of meanings to those involved. But the fundamental principle underlying the great diversity of anti-systemic movements is the same: the refusal by the oppressed and the exploited to continue to suffer the injustice, inequality and degradation that define their social reality within the existing global order, and their struggle for an alternative social order.

Whatever form a particular contestatory social movement may take, at whatever level and wherever in the world-system, it necessarily involves the rejection of developmentalism. Whatever else the particular cases might be, the militant and in some cases fanatical revival of indigenous cultures, whether expressed in religious fundamentalism or in the reaffirmation of national identity, is essentially a resistance to the modernization process. The rejection of economic growth in its capitalist form finds direct expression in the resistance by the peasantry to the further encroachment of capital in the Third World, and in the continuing class struggle between the direct producers and the appropriators of surplus-value in both the centre and the periphery of the world-system; the damage done to the environment and to human beings caused by irrational over-production and, in the case of the elites, over-consumption, finds its response in the Green movements and in 'small is beautiful' arguments.[53] And the developmentalist regimes currently wielding power over the state-machineries fashioned to the requirements of the world-system are everywhere confronted by intensifying popular opposition to their rule and by national liberation movements that aim for authentic nationhood and real political and economic autonomy.

Nor is this all. The other great issues facing mankind – militarization and the constant threat of war,[54] sexism, racism – are all directly related to the basic functioning of the world-system as a violent and exploitative system, and therefore the peace movement, the feminist movement and the fight against racism are all of them anti-systemic movements as well. Each, in its own way, contributes to the secular, incremental and multidimensional transformation of a system which maintains itself through military power and for which indeed war is 'big business', which devalues while profiting from the work of women, and which has always used racial discrimination as a justification for the rapacity of colonialism and now for the extreme stratification of the work-force within and between nations. Finally, the fight for freedom and socialism being waged against the bureaucracies by men and women in those countries claiming to be 'socialist' but which in fact have installed and consolidated a statist mode of production that itself thrives in the present capitalist world-system,[55] forms part of the global transformation process.

There is no Archimedean point on which one can stand and change the world; only the developmentalist experts of 'social engineering' can delude themselves into thinking that they have the lever of social change in their hands. The transformation of the world-system can only be the cumulative and secular outcome of all these anti-systemic forces at work wherever and whenever men and women forge the political will to strive for a better social order.

Below the level of the whole and within the immediacy of the concrete objectives of those involved in them, the multifarious attempts to work for authentic human and social development taking place at different places and different times and under a wide variety of circumstances pose a great plurality of meanings which are not always understood by those involved in other struggles. This lack of understanding of the unicity of the development problematique can only serve the interests of the present system which keeps the world unified economically – in the interest of capital – but divided politically. *Divide et impera* was not a stratagem only of ancient empires; it is that of modern imperialism as well.

It is here where researchers working for human and social development must step in. Their task is to bring theory to the service of practice, to illuminate this process of transformation which remains much of it still in the dark, to grasp the totalizing meaning of all these dispersed efforts at making history. It is to continue what Marx had started: to lay bare the processes (the 'laws of motion', as they put it in the last century) which govern the origin, development and continuing dynamics of capitalism, to articulate the contradictions of the system and to disclose the possibilities and means of its social transformation. It is to wage a relentless critique of the present system *and* of the ongoing transformation process itself since, discarding the progressivist conception of history as now being nothing more than a self-serving ideology of those who do not wish History to progress, we have no guarantees that the transformed world – whenever that might be – will be necessarily a better world: there might be socialism, but there might be barbarism instead, or else the ultimate totalitarianism, be it statist or capitalist, of '1984', or there might be nothing, only nuclear wasteland; there is always, in other words, the danger of what Sartre called 'counter-finality' – the ever-present possibility that the end result of social action could turn out to be something completely unexpected, or worse, the opposite of what was originally intended. Critique, comprehension, reflection, elucidation of action, self-critique – the task of research is, finally, to assume a historic responsibility that is unique to our period of world-systemic transition. Sartre understood this responsibility, and posed it for us in these words:

> The plurality of *the meanings* of History can be discovered and posited for itself only upon the ground of a future totalization – in terms of the future totalization and in contradiction with it. It is our theoretical and practical duty to bring this totalization closer every day. All is still obscure, and yet everything is in full light. To tackle the theoretical aspect, we have the instruments; we can establish the method. Our historical task, at the heart of this polyvalent world, is to bring closer the moment when History will have *only one meaning*, when it will tend to be dissolved in the concrete men who will make it in common.[56]

Notes

1 Quoted in Andre Gunder Frank, *Crisis: In the World Economy*, Heinemann, London, 1980, p. 1
2 *Newsweek*, 24 January 1983, p. 16.
3 'It was simply not a feasible goal. Neither is it one today . . .' concluded World Bank President Robert McNamara in his 1977 address to the Bank's Board of Governors.
4 *The Encyclopaedia of Philosophy*, Vol. V, Macmillan, New York, 1972, p. 254.
5 When a Schoolman chided Francis Bacon, 'Ye know not what hurt you do to learning, that care not for words but for matter', Bacon shot back: 'Here therefore is the first distemper of learning, when men study words and not matter . . . For words are but the images of matter; and except they have life of reason and invention, to fall in love with them all one as to fall in love with a picture.' (Francis Bacon, *The Advancement of Learning*, 1605, Oxford University Press, Oxford, 1974, I.IV.3, p. 26. Nothing gives today's mainstream economists greater pleasure than to behold the perfect geometry of their growth models – never mind if reality is not like that.
6 'World-system theory' is a convenient expression for the kind of inquiry that could also be called alternatively the study of long-term and large-scale historical systems and change, or world-historical studies, or capitalist world-economy studies, or the study of capital accumulation on a world-scale, or the study of the international division of labour. We shall use this expression, both for its brevity and for the fact that it has now gained wide recognition as a distinct and coherent theory concerned with the types of problems just mentioned. For an introduction see, amongst others, Terence. K. Hopkins, 'The Study of the Capitalist World economy' in Terence K. Hopkins, Immanuel Wallerstein and Associates, *World-Systems Analysis: Theory and Methodology*, Sage, London, 1982; Samir Amin. *Accumulation on a World Scale*, Monthly Review Press, New York, 1974, (French original 1970), particularly the introductory chapter and afterword; Folker Fröbel, Jürgen Heinrichs and Otto

Kreye, *The New International Division of Labour*, Cambridge University Press, Cambridge, 1980, (German original 1977), particularly Chapter 2; Andre Gunder Frank, *World Accumulation, 1492–1789*, Monthly Review Press, New York, 1978. See also the special issue 'Images of World Society' of the UNESCO quarterly *International Social Science Journal*, XXXIV, 1, 1982.

7 R.D. Laing, 'The Obvious' in David Cooper (ed.), *The Dialectics of Liberation*, Penguin, Harmondsworth, 1968, p. 13.

8 See George H. Sabine and Thomas L. Thorson, *A History of Political Theory*, 4th edition, Dryden Press, Hinsdale, Illinois, 1973, p. 608.

9 Jean-Paul Sartre, *Question de méthode*, the prefatory essay in his *Critique de la raison dialectique*, Gallimard, Paris, 1960. My summary in the following paragraph is based on the English translation *Search for a Method*, Vintage, New York, 1968, pp. 3–8.

10 Immanuel Wallerstein, 'Economic Theories and Historical Disparities of Development', mimeo, Fernand Braudel Center for the Study of Economies, Historical Systems and Civilizations, 1982. We note in passing that back in the early eighteenth century, Giambattista Vico already criticized the 'social contract' theories of Grotius and Hobbes as 'pseudo-myths', as distorting frameworks and schemata imposed on historical research. And there is that famous Voltairean quip that defined history as tricks the living play upon the dead.

11 *The Encyclopaedia of Philosophy*, Macmillan, New York, 1972, Vol. 3, p. 61.

12 Ibid. Vol. 2, p. 521.

13 Francis Bacon, *New Atlantis*, 1624, Oxford University Press, Oxford, 1974, p. 239.

14 René Descartes, *Discours de la méthode*, 1637, quoted in Karl Marx, *Capital*, Vol. I, Penguin Books, Harmondsworth, 1976, p. 513. Marx's comments on Descartes and Bacon illustrate, through the case of political economy, the totalizing activity of a philosophy grounded on analytical and empirical reason: 'In the preface to Sir Dudley North's *Discourse upon Trade* (1691) it is stated that the method of Descartes, as applied to political economy, had begun to free it from the old fables and superstitious notions about money, trade, etc. On the whole, however, the early English economists sided with Bacon and Hobbes as their philosophers, while, at a later period, Locke became 'the philosopher' *par excellence* in England, France and Italy' (Ibid.).

15 René Descartes, *Discours de la méthode*, quoted in Peter Gay, *The Enlightenment, Vol. II: The Science of Freedom*, Wildwood House, London, 1979, p. 6.

16 Ibid.

17 This is Immanuel Wallerstein's thesis in *The Modern World-System, Vol. II: Mercantilism and the Consolidation of the European World-Economy 1600–1750*, Academic Press, New York, 1980. 'Politically and culturally the seventeenth century represented a search for stability in form and structure that was concomitant with the moment of slowdown in the rate of development of the world-economy. Without such a period, the next qualitative leap would not have been possible. This makes the seventeenth century not a "crisis" but a needed change of pace, not a disaster but an essential element in furthering the interests of those who benefited most

from a capitalist system. Because the period from 1600 to 1750 was so important in the *consolidation* of the European world-economy, it is worthwhile to make a careful analysis of why this was so. We will then be able to understand what mechanisms the capitalist strata use to cope in recurrent periods of contraction in the world-economy'. (Ibid. pp. 33–34.)

18   See Jean-Paul Sartre, *Plaidoyer pour des intellectuels*, Gallimard, Paris, 1965, pp 18–20.

19   'Religion is a sixteenth century word for nationalism', says Lewis Namier, quoted in Immanuel Wallerstein, *The Modern World-System, Vol. I: Capitalist Agriculture and the Origins of the European World-Economy in the Sixteenth Century 1450–1600*, Academic Press, New York, 1976, p. 137.

20   We can only mention these elements and those yet to come *en passant*, our present purpose being to focus on only one central feature of developmentalism, viz. its conception of history which, of course, is built upon these elements. What is essential is to see these elements in the high unity of the whole, how they are dialectically integrated in the vast enterprise that was mercantile capitalism. Contemporary development researchers who work in the analytic tradition fail to grasp this synthesis and its material basis, and thus feel constrained to insist that science *too* is to be blamed for maldevelopment, that the loss of transcendental and spiritual values effected by European humanism lies at the root of the modern predicament, that man's promethean ambition to dominate nature is the original sin, etc. Their insistence on one or the other – and everyone has their own favourite aversion – distorts more than clarifies the whole situation, and to this extent distracts attention and political action from the real thing.

21   To be sure, there were those who, like Rousseau, were poised uneasily and critically between the progressive and the anti-progressive, and who sought to express the paradox that while progress seemed ineluctable, it was also certain to destroy the original nature of humanity and the harmony of primeval society. What price progress if, the more civilization advances, the more corrupting is its impact on 'the duties of man and the needs of nature?' Without wishing to push the argument too far, I suggest that, insofar as he may have any bearing on contemporary development theory at all, the author of *Discours sur les sciences et les arts* can be considered as a precursor of the concept of *maldevelopment*.

22   The fact that some *philosophes* had their doubts about the beneficence of progress, anticipating that all progress exacted its price sooner or later (e.g. d'Alembert's refusal to equate it with happiness, Ferguson's misgivings with the division of labour, Kant's insistence that moral progress did not necessarily accompany socio-economic improvement), did not detract one bit from the fact that theirs was an age of optimism. The central choice for them was *for* or *against* progress, not whether progress was or was not possible.

23   G.W.F. Hegel, *The Philosophy of Right*, 1821, translated and edited by T.M. Knox, Oxford University Press, Oxford, 1942, Section 258.

24   Adam Smith, *The Wealth of Nations*, 1776, edited by E. Cannan, Modern Library, New York, 1904, Book IV, Chapter 1.

25   See the debate on this subject of economic history between Eli Heckscher and Charles Wilson in *Economic History Review*, II, 2, 1949, III, 2, 1950 and IV, 2, 1951, and Wallerstein's discussion of this debate and related issues in *The Modern World-System Vol. II*, Chapter 3: 'Struggle in the

Core – Phase I: 1651–1689'; see also Mark Blaug, *Economic Theory in Retrospect*, Irwin, Homewood, Illinois, 1968, Chapter 1: 'Pre-Adamite Economics'.

26 Wallerstein, ibid. p. 38.

27 There were even, added to these, Keynesian arguments for optimum employment and stimulation of investment, as Keynes himself wished to suggest in his chapter 'Notes on Mercantilism' in *The General Theory of Employment, Interest and Money*, 1936. See Blaug's comments on Keynes' appreciation of the 'element of scientific truth in mercantilist doctrine', in ibid. pp. 14–19.

28 Quoted in Peter Gay, op. cit. p. 346.

29 Wallerstein, *The Modern World-System, Vol. II*, p. 65.

30 There is for instance C. Wilson's thesis that, on the contrary, the French were not mercantilist *enough*, that their mercantilism, unlike England's, remained relatively incoherent and unformulated, even in Colbert's time, because France lacked 'that combination of expanding commercial capital and government influence represented by the Westminster-City axis in London'. See Wallerstein's discussion of this debate and his own interpretation of the differential impact of mercantilism on France and England in ibid., Chapters 3 and 6. See also Samir Amin, *Class and Nation, Historically and in the Current Crisis*, Monthly Review, New York 1980, Chapter 4, where he argues that the decisive element here, as always in history, is the nature of the class struggles and the hegemonic class blocs and their relation to the productive forces, which accounts for the different historical patterns of capitalist development.

31 Cf. Blaug, op. cit. p. 26, and E. J. Hobsbawm, *The Age of Revolution 1789–1848*, Mentor, New York, 1962, Chapter 8, 'Land'.

32 Quesnay, *Dialogues*, 1758, quoted in R.L. Meek, *Economics of Physiocracy*, London, 1962.

33 Quoted in Gay, op.cit. p. 350.

34 Jean-Paul Sartre, 'A plea for intellectuals', in J-P. Sartre, *Between Existentialism and Marxism*, New Left Books, London, 1974, p. 235.

35 As Marx put it: 'The economists have a singular way of proceeding. For them, there are only two kinds of institutions, artificial and natural. The institutions of feudalism are artificial institutions, those of the bourgeoisie are natural institutions. In this they resemble the theologians, who likewise establish two kinds of religion. Every religion which is not theirs is an invention of men, while their own is an emanation of God . . . thus there has been history, but there is no longer any' (*The Poverty of Philosophy*, 1847, Lawrence and Wishart, London, 1966, p. 105).

36 Samir Amin, *Imperialism and Unequal Development*, Monthly Review Books, New York, 1977, p. 91.

37 Adam Smith, *The Wealth of Nations*, Penguin Books, Harmondsworth, 1981, p. 446.

38 Smith, *Wealth of Nations*, ed. Cannan, Book IV, Chapter 2, p. 9.

39 Marx, *Capital*, Vol. I, p. 174. Marx coined the term 'classical political economists' to refer to these thinkers to whom he owed so much, and to distinguish them from the 'vulgar economists' who made no attempt to analyze capitalism except to sing its virtues, 'which is to them the best possible one'.

40 This is not to imply that marginalist theory *originated* as the bourgeois

response to Marxism, since in fact its pioneers developed their theories without having yet encountered Marx; it was different in the 1880s, when Böhm-Bawerk, Wicksteed, Pareto and Wieber deliberately employed marginal-utility theory as the bourgeois antithesis to Marxist economics.

41 It is interesting to note that the concept of 'indifference curve' was first introduced into economics by F.Y. Edgeworth in a book entitled *Mathematical Psychics*, 1881, – a nice reminder of economics as mathematized psychology, or more accurately, as quantified behaviouralism, since even the psyche disappears from all this formalized abstraction.

42 So pervasive is the Newtonian imagery up to now that twentieth century economists continue to hail each other as Newtons of the economic universe. Witness Schumpeter on Walras, as recounted by Samuelson: 'The late Joseph Schumpeter (1883–1950) used to say that, of all great economists, surely Walras was the greatest, since it was he who discovered general equilibrium. It was Lagrange, "the Shakespeare of mathematics", who said: "Of all scientists Newton was surely the greatest. For it was he who discovered the system of the world. And, alas, there is but one system of the world to be discovered." Schumpeter apparently felt that Walras was also lucky as well as great, since there is but one system of general economic equilibrium to be discovered' (Paul A. Samuelson, *Economics*, 10th edition, McGraw-Hill, New York, 1976, p. 843). One can only wonder why Einstein's Theory of Relativity has not had as much fascination for contemporary economists; or is it not the relativity of theories that is precisely what is anathema to the universalist pretensions of mainstream economics?

43 Walter A. Weisskopf, *Alienation and Economics*, Delta Books, New York, 1971, pp. 82, 83–4.

44 It should be clear that it is not the technical concept of GNP as such that is objectionable, since there can be no doubt about the need for national accounting systems; it is rather the *ideological use* of such a concept that must be demystified.

45 See Gunnar Myrdal, *Objectivity in Social Research*, Duckworth, London, 1970; Robert Heilbroner, 'Economics as a "Value-Free" Science', *Social Research*, 40, Spring 1973; N. Kaldor, 'The Irrelevance of Equilibrium Economics', and related essays in *Economic Journal*, 1972; W. Leontief, 'Theoretical Assumptions and Nonobserved Facts', in *American Economic Review*, March, 1971; J.K. Galbraith, 'Power and the Useful Economist', in *American Economic Review*, March, 1973; M. Hollis and E.J. Neil, *Rational Economic Man: A Philosophical Critique of Neo-Classical Economics*, Cambridge University Press, Cambridge, 1975.

46 Henry Kissinger, 'Saving the World Economy', *Newsweek*, 24 January 1983; Andre Gunder Frank, *Reflections on the World Economic Crisis*, Hutchinson, London, 1981.

47 Johan Galtung, Tore Heiestad and Eric Ruge, 'On the Decline and Fall of Empires: The Roman Empire and Western Imperialism Compared', *Working Paper* HSDRGPID-1/United Nations University, Tokyo, 1979, p. 38. *Cosmology* is defined by Galtung as a cognitive structure, a sort of social grammar, or a cognitive map of the world, organized in terms of key categories, such as the structure of social space, the composition of social time, the nature of knowledge, the relation between individuals, and the relation between humanity and nature. Cf. his discussion on Western

cosmology in, among other papers, *Development, Environment and Technology*, UNCTAD, New York, 1979, pp. 6–8

48 Samir Amin argues: 'In the system's centre, where the relations of production are most firmly established, the development of the productive forces as directed by these relations reinforces the system's cohesion. However, in the periphery, insufficient development of the productive forces results in greater flexibility; this explains why revolutions occur sooner in the periphery' (*Class and Nation*, op. cit. pp. 14–15). Cf. also his *Unequal Development* and *Imperialism and Unequal Development*, Monthly Review Press, New York, 1976 and 1977 respectively, for a full exposition of the theory.

49 Hence the French fascination with England in the first half of the eighteenth century, to give an example. 'Learn from England and catch up with England' may be said to have been the developmentalist slogan of the Frenchbourgeoisie during that period, with Voltaire, Montesquieu and the physiocrats among the most fervent advocates. Voltaire's *Lettres philosophiques* (1734), written whilst in exile in England and which was to become to the chief inspiration for the rise of liberal thought on the Continent (the book was the first bomb hurled at the *Ancien Régime*, as Gustave Lanson put it), was a critique of French society via comparison and contrast with England's economic, political, philosophical, and cultural achievements. So pervasive was the English influence over the *philosophes* that Enlightenment thought was initially called in France 'la philosophie anglaise'.

50 Cf. Eric R. Wolf, *Europe and the People without History*, University of California, Berkeley and Los Angeles, 1982, pp. 7–23; Immanuel Wallerstein, 'The Development of the Concept of Development' (mimeo), 1981.

51 There are, of course, exceptions, but they remain precisely that. In historiography, for instance, the *Annales* school provides a powerful counterthrust to traditional, even focused, nation-centred, political and diplomatic history, but clearly the dominant tradition remains overwhelmingly dominant. Cf. Fernand Braudel, *Ecrits sur l'histoire*, Flammarion, Paris, 1969; Geoffrey Barraclough, *Tendances actuelles de l'histoire*, Flammarion, Paris, 1980. Recall also Herb Addo's critical remarks on 'history as celebration' in Chapter 1 of this volume.

52 See note 6 above for the bibliography where the ideas summarized in this section are fully developed.

53 See the contributions by Björn Hettne and Mats Friberg, and Samir Amin in this volume.

54 See Hiroharu Seki's contribution in this volume.

55 Cf. Andre Gunder Frank, *Crisis: In the World Economy*, Heinemann, London, 1980, Chap. 4, 'Long Live Transideological Enterprise! The Socialist Economies in the Capitalist International Division of Labour and West-East-South Political Economic Relations'.

56 Jean-Paul Sartre, *Question de méthode*, Gallimard, 1960 (English translation *Search for a Method*, Vintage, New York, 1968, p. 90).

3

Dead End: Western Economic Responses to the Global Economic Crisis*

Folker Fröbel, Jürgen Heinrichs, Otto Kreye

Introduction

For the industrialized countries the 1980s will be a decade in which the question of war and peace will take on a new and threatening urgency. The primacy of this question should not, however, blind us to the presence of the *social* and *economic crisis* of the capitalist world. Whereas the developing countries have long since felt the crippling impact of this crisis in its chronic form, since the early 1970s it has also reasserted itself in its periodic form as a moving force in the world economy in general and in the industrial countries in particular. The intimate connection between the problems of war and peace, and economy and society is once again pointedly revealed in the present US Administration's programmatic intent to restore the USA to the position of world Number One in military and economic terms, via a political strategy which is yet one further step along the path towards delivering up the entire planet to the totalitarian exigencies of the military-industrial complex.

The project of a resurgent America was able to feed off the obvious and easily denounced helplessness of previous administrations in tackling the symptoms of US weakness internationally: the humiliation of military impotence despite military strength in Vietnam and Iran, the erosion of US hegemony in the world capitalist system, the persisting economic crisis. Based on its continued economic superiority, and prepared for with deliberate advances in weapons' technology, the USA is

*Translated by Pete Burgess.

embarking on a strategy for the attainment of a new, politically exploitable, military superiority over the Soviet Union with its 'defensive yet threatening weaponry',[1] in the clear knowledge that this will unleash a new and dangerous round in the arms race, and in the less explicit hope that in the course of this arms race the Soviet Union will 'arm itself to extinction' at least in economic terms. Toying with the possibility of a limited 'theatre' nuclear war, possibly in the Middle East or Europe, is one element in this strategy. In the economic sphere the current dominant American bloc, together with its allies abroad, are determined to exploit the achievement of such a position of politically utilizable military power to fend off encroachments on US hegemony within the capitalist world-system, and to revive their economies through massive redistributions of income (tax cuts for the haves, welfare cuts for the have-nots), and where it can be financed, a massive arms programme. As a complement to this, any attempts to develop independent, let alone divergent, reponses to the periodic-cumulative crisis of the system, either within America or overseas, will be uncompromisingly suppressed in favour of an imperial strategy, in which the world is to be reshaped in accordance with conservative conceptions of development – a Sunbelt Model on a world scale.

In particular, success for this strategy would make the countries of Western Europe, and especially West Germany, all the more susceptible to military and political blackmail (one reason being the proposed deployment of land-based medium-range nuclear-armed missiles), and would overwhelm the narrow scope for independent Western European economic and social politics and for an independent structuring of Western European relations towards the countries of the East and South, which have been laboriously carved out of the capitalist world-system. It goes without saying that such a strategy could also imply the final closing off of any space for political reforms in Eastern Europe. The alliance between the US centred military-industrial complex and the forces of the political right can also be expected to strangle any attempts at reform in the developing countries. Considered as a whole, the result would be the re-establishment of a global confrontation between two monolithic, military, economic and ideological blocs.

Moreover, success for this imperial conservative strategy over its political opposition, including that located within the USA itself, would imply a massive set-back for all those attempts to identify alternative paths, which have intensified in step with the growing economic, social and environmental crisis and the acute awareness of the dangers of war – and which have now begun to mobilize and organize major sections of the population in the industrial countries in opposition to the 'system': that is, those alternatives which have sought to formulate, and progressively implement, long-term sustainable policies on such matters as security, the environment etc., examples of which can already be seen in the field of defence.[2]

Within this broad frame of reference we want to concentrate attention on three particular questions. *Firstly*: what caused the current economic crisis? *Secondly*: how should we judge the main political responses to the crisis which have either been implemented or proposed in the industrial-capitalist countries, and what are the implications of these responses for the developing countries? And *thirdly* (and solely as a subject for future research and policy, and not as a question which can be answered here and now): is it possible to parallel those initiatives taken towards the formulation of an alternative *defence policy* in Western Europe by formulating some of the premisses of an alternative *economic* and *social policy*, which without any false optimism, and consistent with the premisses sketched out for other areas, might at least hold open the possibility of avoiding the identifiably ominous tendencies inherent in current developments and political strategies, and create the space for steps, or pathways, in a less potentially calamitous direction?

The causes of the economic crisis

What caused the current economic crisis?

In the early 1970s, after twenty-five years of unprecedented – and seemingly continuing – boom in the world economy, the 'discovery' of a world market for labour-power led us to forecast imminent mass unemployment in the western industrial nations.[3] Our 'discovery' and forecast found little response at that time. Only a small number of writers, such as György Ádám, Giovanni Arrighi, Andre Gunder Frank, Andrew Glyn and Bob Sutcliffe, André Granou, Stephen Hymer and Ernest Mandel, recognized that the capitalist world-economy was beginning to show signs of structural changes or transformations which bore the mark of a crisis.[4]

And even as late as the late-1970s, our initial explanation of these structural changes or transformations – which is still essentially valid – and our analysis of the tendency towards a new international division of labour leading to structural unemployment in the industrialized countries and partial industrialization in the developing countries, still ran into the criticism that we far overestimated the effects on the western industrialized countries of either relocation in general, or 'special cases' such as Hong Kong or the garment industry, in particular. The incontrovertible evidence of economic problems in the western industrialized countries which had accumulated by then was regarded as nothing more serious than the transient phenomena accompanying economic adjustment to new market conditions in the wake of increased oil and energy prices. Claims that these problems might represent deep structural changes in the world-economy, an enforced global reorganization of capitalist production by means of rationalization and relocation, and a crisis which impinged on the basic institutional and political structure of (post-war) capitalism were dismissed as insane economic romanticism. However, these critics could not themselves produce a convincing explanation for the return, let alone the persistence, of mass unemployment in the western industrial countries – and are still unable to do so.

Confronted now with the reality of almost a decade of high and rising unemployment in the industrialized countries – the OECD estimates 31.7 million registered unemployed for 1985 in the western industrialized countries, equal to 8.5 per cent of the economically active population, and over three times the 1970 figure[5] – no one can now seriously dispute that an entire era of capitalist development has finally come to an end. Nor is it possible to overlook the total failure, and sometimes quite deliberate disinterest, of governments and their appointed experts to find ways to rapidly reduce unemployment in the industrialized countries – let alone strategies for alleviating the chronic underdevelopment of the Third World. The model of accumulation of the golden years of the 1950s and 1960s has clearly run into a cul-de-sac without any conclusive political decision as to a viable replacement, or any indication of who will bear the costs of resolving the industrialized world's economic crisis.

There is now broad agreement as to the *outward manifestations* of the crisis, and consequently no necessity to repeat them once again here. However this consensus does not, surprisingly, extend to the politically more explosive issue of the *causes* of the crisis. To set the scene for subsequent discussion of rival paths out of the crisis, we therefore propose initially to summarize the most recent formulation of our own approach (Fröbel 1982), which in turn owes a debt to a number of contributions which have not, as yet, received their due recognition.[6]

The post-war 'growth and partnership' model in the industrialized countries

Before considering the tendencies inherent in the post-war model of accumulation which have begun to undermine its quasi-stability, we first have to explain how and why this model was able to function successfully, and with a degree of stability, over a number of years.

In the initial phases of industrial capitalism, capitalists keep wages as low as possible in order to maximize their own rates of profit – the limits being set by the resistance, or collaboration, of their workers. This policy is made possible by the existence of a 'non-capitalist milieu'[7] which – whether simply encountered or deliberately and calculatedly created and maintained – serves to subsidize the reproduction of labour-power for industrial-capitalist production, and hence enables capitalists to suppress the level of wages paid to industrial workers. As a

consequence, labour costs in the industrial-capitalist sub-system feature essentially as a cost-factor, and only incidentally as a factor in
demand.[8]

The long-term price exacted by this strategy consists in the risk of
realization crises, unmitigated by the stabilizing influence of sufficient
effective demand for the mass consumer goods produced by capitalist
industry. These crises are progressively deepened by the 'spontaneous'
creation of a high level of monopolization through concentration, and
cartellization, which inhibits price-competition, the intensification of
inter-imperialist antagonisms (scramble for Africa, 'a place in the sun',
Griff nach der Weltmacht, struggle for world hegemonic power,
Lebensraum and so forth), together with the hesitancy, or plain refusal,
of pro-business governments in the principal capitalist countries to
implement internationally coordinated (anti-) cyclical and employment
policies. The end-results are a drastic decline in international economic
links, high and persistent unemployment – and, as a further consequence, the provision of a fertile soil for radical political solutions
within national confines.

The reality and the gravity of this risk was finally exposed in the
crisis-ridden period extending from 1914 to 1945. With the very existence of the capitalist system itself under threat, the resolution of the
crisis within the basic parameters of the system demanded drastic
steps – the First World War, *Burgfrieden*, crushing of revolutionary
movements, the obstruction of economic democracy, inflation, political repression of the workers movement and its internationalist
aspirations, fascism, national-socialism, job-creation through
rearmament, the war economy, and finally, a Second World War – all
instruments paid for in terms of uncounted sacrifices by the vast mass
of the population.

The model of accumulation installed in the post-Second World War
period has been analysed by Michel Aglietta, Giovanni Arrighi, Fred
Block, Robert Boyer, Andre Gunder Frank, David Gordon, André
Granou, Eric Hobsbawm, Stephen Hymer, Ernest Mandel, James
O'Connor, Christian Palloix, Thomas Weisskopf and others. It was
dominated by the fact of US hegemony in the world capitalist
system – a fact conclusively established by the outcome of the war
itself. This hegemony enabled the USA to impose a new model of
accumulation, in which the tendencies towards international and
internal conflict inherent in the pre-war system were to be counteracted
by two major departures from the preceding model: *firstly*: an extensive – including international – freedom for corporate activity; and
secondly: the systematic extension of the market for mass consumer
goods in the industrialized countries. By inducing a high rate of capitalist growth against the background of these new preconditions, it was
hoped that a course could be steered between the Scylla of realization
crises (the fatal 'flaw' in the previous system) and the Charybdis of

valorization crises. Such a strategy would simultaneously facilitate the political integration of the workers' movement(s), which despite its exhaustion and decimation through war and crisis, still represented a serious oppositional factor in view of the collapse in the credibility of the capitalist economic and social system following the events of the previous three decades.

The central role in this model of accumulation was played by the progressive capitalization of all areas of life in the industrial countries, including the family and leisure, in a process which step by step eliminated traditional or alternative options for the reproduction of labour-power, and created an expanding market for mass consumer goods in line with wage increases. After an initial 'starting-up' period, the linking of wage increases to increases in productivity in the industrial countries was intended to ensure that overall profits and wages would be neither 'too high' nor 'too low'.[9] The accumulation of capital was therefore to be achieved through the steady increase in the industrial-capitalist production of mass consumer goods (with a corresponding increase in the production of investment goods).

Relations between the (Western) industrial countries and towards the developing countries were determined by a policy of closer international, in fact, transnational economic links: for example, the dissolution of the old colonial empires with their systems of preferences (for the old colonial powers), and their replacement by an open-door policy for foreign corporations. It was clearly no accident that, under the circumstances following the Second World War, this policy implied a very one-sided boost to the overseas expansion of US capital into the industrialized and developing countries.

Despite the various forms and degrees of resistance encountered in the immediate post-war years (to which we cannot do adequate justice here), the USA succeeded in exerting the required political and economic pressure to install the new model of accumulation in Western Europe, and to a more limited extent in Japan. Once established the model was able to generate precisely those features which rendered its continued functioning an increasingly attractive proposition to the hard core of the organized working class (typified at this time by the trade-union organized, male, middle-aged, skilled worker), and which further enabled it to determine capitalist development in the western industrialized countries and the world-economy as a whole over the subsequent two and a half decades: that is, high rates of growth (although fluctuating according to 'growth cycles'), expanding mass incomes (even if to a large extent the necessary corollary of the increasing commodification, and even capitalization, of the sphere of reproduction and leisure – without any proportionate increase in 'welfare'), a trend towards full-employment, and in Western Europe, primarily as a result of the success of trade union organization (and as a method of combating the challenge of the social welfare systems of the socialist countries), a 'womb to tomb' system of social provisions of growing comprehensiveness. The political expression of this was the hegemony of reformist labour parties in the industrial countries in determining the framework of political consensus in the post-war period (the social-democratic welfare state) even though these parties may not themselves have directly held national power.

The perceptible increase in alienating commercialization, the loss of individual control over everyday life, and the pressure for more productivity and achievement in the factory, office, school, within the family and in leisure, which occurred in the course of the development of this model, were accepted either in the confidence that humanizing 'reform policies' would soon follow, or by being translated into monetary compensation. The whole issue of the extent to which capitalist growth was being paid for through the destruction of the natural basis of human life was more or less totally neglected.

The cul-de-sac of the 'growth and partnership' model

It is hardly surprising that the United States began to question the virtue of the 'growth and partnership' model as soon as the economic recovery of Western Europe and Japan, which the model had facilitated, started to threaten US hegemony within the capitalist world-system. The modification of the Bretton Woods system and the crisis, although obviously and chiefly indicators of the erosion of US hegemony, should also be seen as mechanism or attempts to re-establish this endangered hegemonial status, long before the most recent political shifts in US policy.

However, what was of more immediate and enduring impact was the fact that as far as individual units of capital were concerned – and in contrast to the position of the organized workforce – the 'growth and partnership' model could be jettisoned at any time should changed circumstances require it. And during the late 1960s and early 1970s the model was indeed undermined by economic and political mechanisms or formulae which represented corporate responses to problems which were the inevitable end-result of the model's very success.

Beginning around the mid-1960s, and subject to modification on the one hand by the dissolution of traditional agriculture, the increased employment of women and the addition of labour-power from abroad (refugees, *Gastarbeiter*) more or less up to their 'natural' or political limits, and on the other by the extension of the tertiary sector, reductions in working time, and similar developments, the long period of growth in the industrialized countries began to generate changes in the model's variables which, although initially apparently purely quantitative, were in fact assuming a cumulative, and disruptive quality capable of threatening the continued functioning of the model. For example: the standardization and commercialization, or actual capitalization of the social conditions for the reproduction of labour-power, with rising costs which had to be met from the industrial-capitalist sub-system (amongst other things because of the gradual exhaustion of the 'non-capitalist milieu'); the rising costs incurred in the utilization of a natural environment subject to constantly increasing pollution and despolia-tion; noticeable decrease in unemployment; and a strengthening of the bargaining position of organized and unorganized labour (itself an integral element of the model as far as the level of wages was con-cerned), in some areas taking the form of a degree of disillusionment and aggression which in its questioning of the capitalist organization of work and social life led beyond the acknowledged limits of the system. All these, and similar factors, made it increasingly difficult for firms to sustain their long-standing ideological and political hegemony, and eventually impinged on their most delicate nerve, their accustomed, and as far as the functioning of the 'growth and partnership' model was concerned, necessary, rates of profit within the industrialized coun-tries. Needless to say, this threat to rates of profit simultaneously jeopardized the further progress of accumulation as a whole.

The corporate response: rationalization and relocation

Confronted with such a situation, firms could fall back on two com-plementary and combinable mechanisms or formulae, the enforced application of which held out the hope that the supply of disposable labour-power and the conditions under which this supply was forth-coming could be restored to a measure compatible with an adequate level of profit. In the words of the *New York Times*, 4 March 1982: AUTOMATE, EMIGRATE OR EVAPORATE!

The first mechanism, the first formula ('rationalization') consists in the temporary reduction in the overall volume of investment in the industrial countries (the 'investment gap' since 1970!), with a simulta-neous shift towards an increased share of investment in rationalization at the cost of investment for expansion. Where possible this strategy will be supplemented by political measures intended to weaken organized labour. The direct result of this mechanism or formula: increased displacement of labour in the industrialized countries without any parallel creation of an adequate number of new jobs matched to those made unemployed. It seemed reasonable to hope (a belief theo-retically grounded in Goodwin's model of the growth cycle, [10] and given political and propagandist support by governments, the academic high priests of economic and trade-union leaderships) that with a commensurable degree of 'moderation' on the part of workers over wages, aggregate profits could be restored to a level which would guar-antee the continued functioning of the model both relatively rapidly and without too many problems. Against all these expectations or promises, this hope was spectacularly dashed by events. Why?

The explanation lies in a second mechanism, a second formula ('relocation'), which threatens an enormous lowering of the overall level of wages in the industrialized countries, together with the final overpowering of working class resistance in these countries to the reorganization of capitalist production, the burden of which they will inevitably have to bear. This mechanism, or formula, consists in the global reorganization of industrial production through an intensified cost-reducing redistribution of individual fragments of the fragmented production process to sites with cheaper and more disciplined labour forces, either in the 'informal' sector in the industrialized countries (outside the extensive scope of the 'social state'), or in the developing countries. This mechanism reverses the trend of the previous twenty-five years, in which the reproduction of labour-power had increasingly been brought under capitalist supervision via the commercialization of the welfare state (especially in Western Europe) though never actually superseding the key role of the 'non-capitalist milieu' in the process of accumulation (as in housework and childcare).

Although firms may have been desperate to put such a strategy of partial relocation into operation, its actual implementation required that certain preconditions be met. These can be divided into two basic groupings. Firstly, the preceding development had to have left or created a sufficient reserve of unemployed work-seekers in the informal sector or in the developing countries. And secondly, the calculations made by firms had to indicate that, for a significant number of (sub-) processes, the specific cost-advantages (such as access to skilled labour) derived from locations in the industrialized countries, or from using labour-power from the formal, welfare state-overseen, sector no longer outweighed the different cost-advantages (such as low wages) which could be derived from locations in the developing countries, or from the use of labour-power from the informal sector. Such calculations and investment decisions were not, of course, based merely on those items which featured in the company's profit and loss account but encompassed all those factors which influenced costs: availability, skill and discipline of the labour-force, wage-levels, labour-productivity, infrastructure, availability of background services, taxes and subsidies, transport costs, terms of credit, trade union organization, political stability, and so on.

Of these, the level of wages emerges as a factor of strategic significance – not simply because it represents the principal cost element in many industrial processes, but also – in fact primarily – because the steady increase in wages in the industrial countries (or formal sector) in the post-war model of accumulation, together with the concurrent stagnation in the developing countries (and to some extent in the informal sector) played a key role in the systematic widening of what were initially much less marked differences between the two spheres.

A number of indicators testify both to the existence and effectiveness of this mechanism, or formula, for a partial shift of labour-power out of the formal sector and into the informal sector (or the developing countries), with its associated increase in the degree of externalization of the reproduction costs of labour-power: for example, world-market factories and free production zones, agribusiness, the tourist industry, international contract-labour in the developing countries, and the placing of contracts with middlemen, moonlighting, 'do-it-yourself', short-term contracts of employment, 'women back to the hearth' in the industrialized countries, and many more. For example, the share of world exports of manufactured goods accounted for by the developing countries doubled to c. 9 per cent during the 1970s after many years of stagnation (with less than ten countries dominating the figures). The share of developing country exports accounted for by manufactured goods is now virtually equal to that accounted for by primary products (excluding fuels).[11]

Considered in terms of the relationship between the industrialized countries and the developing countries, this process signifies the transition from the classical international division of labour (in which the developing countries essentially merely figured as suppliers of primary products, markets and occasionally as providers of cheap labour-power) to a new international division of labour, in which the developing countries are increasingly integrated as sites for world-market competitive production in the sphere of manufacturing industry, agribusiness, and tourism. Considered at the level of the individual firm this process signifies the increasing subdivision of the production process of a commodity into different sub-processes at different sites scattered around the globe, with the result, amongst others, that a considerable and growing portion of world trade is becoming essentially the international movement of goods (or bits of goods) between different plants of the same company.

The direct result of this second mechanism or formula: additional displacement of employees in the industrialized countries or out of the formal sector; regional decentralization and social diversification of material production and the reproduction of labour-power; dispersion and division of the labour force with simultaneous centralized control of a growing share of production and employment of globally operating companies.

The crisis of accumulation

The decline in the profitability and international competitiveness of industrial production in the industrialized countries (or of labour-power from the formal sector), together with the disciplinary effects of mass unemployment, has necessitated a change of outlook on the part of trade unions and other employee organizations. Instead of wage increases being linked to increases in productivity, those (still) in employment will have to resign themselves to wage levels set by what is 'acceptable for the economy as a whole' – which may entail noticeable decreases in real incomes. Those workers displaced by unemployment are expected to become regionally and occupationally mobile and search for new jobs, or join those already dependent on the social security system for an income. The financial problems encountered by the state in maintaining social spending levels precisely because of the twin mechanisms of rationalization and relocation will force increasing numbers of people in the industrialized countries back into the 'non-capitalist milieu' (the family, neighbourhood, communes etc.), either as preserved or reactivated by deliberate social policy or possibly in forms struggled for by those concerned. Under present circumstances, however, this cannot amount to an effective withdrawal from the broader social dynamic of the industrial-capitalist sub-system.

The end-result of all these restructuring processes has been a drastic reduction in rates of growth, not only in individual industrialized countries, but worldwide. No identifiable substitute has yet emerged to step into the vacuum left by the breakdown of the two former engines of growth – rising profits productively reinvested in the industrialized countries in the solid expectation of satisfactory or 'sufficient' future profits, and rising mass incomes in the industrialized countries. Any putative increase in luxury consumption would certainly not be 'sufficient'; quick and sustainable opportunities for profit-making in the industrialized countries are unlikely as long as the resistance of the organized labour force obstructs the enforcement of a solution purely and simply on the backs of the employed population; and no 'sufficient' expansion in effective demand in and from the developing countries (including the oil producers) is feasible since, looking at the history of previous development and underdevelopment in the Third World taken as a whole, and despite several 'decades of development', there are still evidently too many social obstacles to a 'sufficiently' rapid and extensive penetration both by industrial capital in particular, and by capitalist relations into social life generally – for example, through world-market oriented production (new international division of labour) – to induce a 'sufficient' increase in the production and export of investment goods from the industrialized countries. And as long as the subsidizing effect of the 'non-capitalist milieu' and mutual competition between developing countries for industrial sites under the prevailing conditions of capitalist production continues to keep wages in the new industries in the developing countries to a mere average of 10 per cent of the values for corresponding processes in the formal sector of the industrialized world, there is no likelihood of any substantial increases in mass purchasing power in the developing countries.

The stark necessity of reorganizing capitalist production and reproduction of labour-power on a world scale on the one hand, and the inevitable difficulties faced by such a reorganization on the other:

this dilemma, recognized and diagnosed by Giovanni Arrighi in the early 1970s,[12] constitutes the central causal nexus for the current economic crisis, central because it derives from the conditions for the functioning of the old model of accumulation based on economic growth and social partnership.

There are of course other factors which either mitigate or sharpen the crisis – for example, uncertainty as to the future development of the crisis leading to investment in financial or speculative assets rather than productive-capitalist investment; the ability of large transnational corporations to displace the crisis into the medium and small firm sector; rising if not yet deterrent, costs in the use of a natural environment increasingly plundered, polluted and robbed of its vital diversity and wildness; or the refusal of many young people simply to be swallowed up and 'productively consumed' by a system which holds out no prospect for the future.

Responses to the crisis

How should we judge the main political responses to the crisis, either implemented or suggested in the industrial-capitalist countries, and what are the implications of these responses for the developing countries?

Although apparently paradoxical, the current crisis is, as we showed, a necessary outcome of the long period of success enjoyed by the 'growth and partnership' model in the post-war period. A crisis is not, however, a terminal breakdown. Despite the enormous cost in life and suffering, the last world economic crisis, which peaked in the years 1929–1932, was ultimately resolved within the basic parameters of the capitalist system. The current crisis must also be regarded as potentially containing the seeds of a new model of accumulation with the capacity to carve a way out of the cul-de-sac into which the old model has run, end the stagnation induced through rationalization and relocation, bring a measure of resolution to the political uncertainty and indecision accompanying the new round of struggles between capital and labour in the present depressed phase, and consequently create the preconditions for a new 'stable' period of vigorous capitalist growth, perhaps again lasting two or three decades.

It must be said, however, that such a model is unlikely to emerge spontaneously as a result of simple, pragmatic 'muddling through', or via the 'laws of the market place'. The current stalemate, together with the awareness of the magnitude of what is at stake, generates conflicts between social groups and classes – and between nations and blocs – which, in all probability, will culminate in a decision, irreversible in the medium-term, as to who is going to bear the costs of those measures considered essential to resolve the crisis, and as a consequence, what type of model will be installed.[13]

So far two main candidates have emerged in the Western industrial countries: the conservative and the social-democratic. In the developing countries the conservative programme is strongly advocated and frequently imposed by the IMF, whilst the social-democratic programme appears in the form of the global Keynesianism advocated for example by the Brandt Report or more modestly in the New International Economic Order.

The conservative programme for resolving the crisis

The only part of the industrialized world in which the conservative model was practised in the more immediate post-war period was Japan – and then not in its fully-blown form. As long as the 'growth and partnership' model was adding to wage-levels and social benefits in competing industrialized countries, in particular in Western Europe, this model was able to confer increasing international competitiveness on the Japanese economy. The conservative model is currently being implemented in Great Britain, and spiced with 'military Keynesianism' (subject to the constraints of the fiscal crisis of the state and internal opposition to an unrestricted arms build-up) in the United States. As a consequence of an accumulation of homeopathic doses of policies inspired or induced by this model, the conservative programme may well soon become dominant in other Western industrial countries: the need to respond to the 'Japanese challenge' is already finding an echo in West Germany, for example.

The central features of the conservative model both in the industrialized countries, and in the developing countries (where it appears as the IMF programme) are: suppression of wages to as low a level as possible; dismantling or drastic reduction of the welfare-state (under such mystifying slogans as 'individual responsibility versus bureaucratic control'); push for higher productivity and effort, either through 'civilised' methods such as unemployment, wider wage differentials, the encouragement and sponsorship of ideologies and structures designed to invoke greater individual or national effort, or through more 'barbaric' methods, such as the daily use of naked violence in the developing countries, and its occasional use – 'where necessary' – in the industrialized countries. The aim of the programme is to raise profits; improve international competitiveness, and finally, or more accurately possibly, reduce unemployment. To repeat former Chancellor Schmidt's classic formulation: 'Today's profits are tomorrow's investments: and tomorrow's investments are the jobs of the day after tomorrow'.

The costs of resolving the crisis by the means of the conservative model will fall almost exclusively on members of the working class: the ubiquitous 'little man' in general, but disproportionately on 'marginal' social groups of all types, and in particular on working women, who are being forced into the position of a target for a variety of regressive prejudices, whose activation is designed precisely to appease, and thereby control, the 'little man' (or 'little patriarch'!), and where possible, the trade unions. The diffuse political support which the conservative programme can muster is primarily based on the fact that the crisis of the 'growth and partnership' model – and with it the crisis of the social-democratic welfare state – has allowed the conservative position to acquire credibility through the common fallacy, or 'political syllogism' as Carl Friedrich von Weizsäcker has termed it, that 'My opponent is wrong, therefore I am right'.[14]

It is entirely foreseeable that the conservative model will not only continue to be practised in many, if not most, developing countries (the IMF model), but will spread from its current fortresses in Japan, the United Kingdom, and the United States to embrace the whole of the western industrialized world. The political fate of the current US administration will clearly have a decisive bearing on this issue. A victory for the conservative model – which in Western Europe is essentially at the stage of mounting a rapidly escalating attack on the largely still intact bases of the welfare state – could well imply a virtual return to the previous antediluvian model of accumulation which more than adequately revealed its propensity to degenerate into crisis in the 1914–1945 period, with all that that entailed in human sacrifice. And in view of what did take place during that period, it is a chilling experience to reflect on what type of social developments the conservative model might lead to in its efforts to resolve the politically most explosive problem – explosive because of its acute impact on the bulk of the population – namely, unemployment.

Advocates of the conservative position are not entirely wrong in arguing that lower wages, a smaller welfare state etc, could, in the short-term at least, raise international competitiveness and allow profits to recover. However, the crucial question is whether rising investments of the appropriate type will be forthcoming, either at the level of the individual economy, or the international economy, in sufficient volume to create enough jobs at appropriate wage levels for those seeking work. The blunt answer to this question is, no.

If the last decade represents any kind of a precedent, a continuation of the considerable 'wage restraint' of the last few years will simply be accompanied by the devotion of a noticeable portion of profits to luxury consumption, financial investment and speculation; any remainder finding its way into productive investment will be disproportionately directed into rationalization and relocation. A further drive to hold down wages and undertake a more fundamental dismantling of the welfare state in the industrial countries would not make any fundamental difference to this prognosis: in the short-term, there would still be uncertainty as to whether the conservative model is destined to become a permanent fixture; in the medium-term, there would be the obvious risk of social disorder if the model was installed in the industrialized countries. Either way, domestic effective demand would fall. Most crucially, the desperate (or merely declared) hope that wage-reductions, cuts in welfare spending, and other measures to cut production costs will lead to increased international competitiveness and trade surpluses – with a subsequent export-led revival, a push forward in domestic investment, and a reduction in unemployment – would be utterly dashed if other countries pursued the same course. In fact, the sole outcome of such a heightened form of international competition would be a downward spiral, at the end of which workers in the industrialized countries might be faced with wages, conditions, and a degree of political repression not too different from that currently prevailing in countries such as Singapore, South Korea, South Africa, and Brazil.

To expect the conservative model to make any contribution to the revival of economic growth in the industrialized countries under such circumstances – let alone to make any decisive impact on unemployment – demands a considerable, if not dangerous, degree of blind faith in the 'self-healing powers' of the economy, which is neither justified by present circumstances nor by past history. Recent British experience provides a clear negative answer to the question as to whether a few years of a strict regime of the 'pure' conservative model are sufficient to influence the overall distribution of incomes, create a climate for investment of long-term advantage to firms, and improve international competitiveness to such an extent that a vigorous revival of capitalist growth and a long-term reduction in unemployment becomes possible. And there certainly is no evidence to confirm the vague forecasts of some social-democratic advocates of the conservative model that a resumption of the abandoned 'growth and partnership' model will be possible after a few years of the current 'medicine'.

If we now shift our gaze from the 'pure' conservative model, with its usually unstated assumption of extensive international freedom of corporate activity, to the 'imperfect competition' of the real world, we can draw up a more accurate picture of what the conservative model might actually bring about.

Both the USA and Japan each possess a wage structure and social structure which remains comparatively advantageous in terms of the model's requirements. Both have a large and relatively protected, or protectable, internal market which can continue to attract both local and foreign capital. In addition, Japan possesses a substantial 'historic' international competitive advantage (relatively undeveloped social-welfare state, giant corporations receiving almost unconditional state support) whilst the United States is proposing an implicitly expansionary arms programme on a massive scale financed through large increases in public indebtedness (or, more cautiously, expansionary as long as the increase in public borrowing is not translated into high interest rates which might choke off any economic revival). The modifications which these factors exercise on the conservative model mean that a modest revival or continuation of industrial-capitalist growth is conceivable in these two particular sets of circumstances. Nevertheless, this in itself may be insufficient to bring about any long-term reduction in unemployment.

In contrast, despite the sacrifices already demanded from the working population under the 'normal' workings of the conservative model, the advantages built into the Japanese and US economies mean that any sustained revival of economic growth, let alone a steady fall in unemployment in Western Europe, will have to be paid for by an even more rigorous application of the model – including drastic political repression designed to weaken working class organisations, a considerable tightening of protectionist policies across-the-board, and a massive state-financed job-creation programme, possibly through arms manufacture. It is unlikely that such a programme could be politically implemented.

The overall effects of the installation of the conservative model can be summarized as follows: in the western industrial countries, high material and non-material sacrifices by the bulk of the population, and in particular 'marginal' groups, mass unemployment, and the deliberate stimulation of nationalism, racism and other types of chauvinism, a noticeable increase in political repression intended to weaken the organized labour-force and head off the inevitable increase in social tensions (recent developments in Great Britain give a clear indication of what form this might take), reduction in the welfare state, retraction or weakening of measures to protect the environment, and a consequent widening of opportunities for such spheres as nuclear power, genetic engineering, and the creation of cable networks (always accompanied by the mendacious appeal to the need to create or retain jobs). In the developing countries the model will reaffirm the domination of the 'Chicago boys' and IMF – whose ideal-typical economic development is post-Allende Chile – and, in particular, encourage the forced development of world-market oriented (part-) industrialization, solely in the interests of private profitability, and without any priority to whether this will in fact yield any improvements in the living, or working, conditions of the mass of the population. In the international field there will be a gradual increase in protectionism, which one day might unwittingly backfire in the disintegration of the world economy – despite the 'liberal' pretensions of the conservatives – together with a revival of international and inter-imperialist aggression, despite the temporary stabilization of US hegemony in the capitalist world system: at the end of the day, the unrestrained pursuit of 'business as usual' at all costs and on all fronts, but in all probability more massively, more wantonly, more dangerous to both human and natural life than before, and, more seriously, without the slightest indication of a long-term perspective on how to tackle the grave problems confronting humanity – war and peace, hunger and poverty, the urgent need to establish just and dignified social relations, and a non-predatory relationship to nature.

Three variants of the social-democratic programme for resolving the crisis

The mere desire to avoid the evident and distasteful consequences of the liberal-conservative model guarantees the general social-democratic model a certain amount of political support. What all three variants have in common is firstly, the aspiration to maintain as much of the welfare state as possible during 'difficult times', and subsequently to extend it as soon and as much as circumstances permit, and secondly to spread the burden of any necessary sacrifices as evenly as possible across all social groups and classes. The capitalist economic and social system is explicitly *not* placed in question. The issue is, of course, whether the old social-democratic 'growth and partnership' model can be made to function economically in its new form, and consequently be politically realizable – and, above and beyond that, whether as a model of capitalist growth it can offer a long-term prospect for human life (and human survival).

Modernization of the economy The first variant of the social-democratic approach trades in West Germany under the rubric 'modernization of the economy'[15] or 'Modell Deutschland'. In the USA it is advocated in the form of 'reindustrialization'; in Great Britain it is proposed by the SDP and the Labour Party; and in France it determined the policy of the decade preceding the election of Mitterrand.

According to this variant, the feat of maintaining or achieving sufficient international competitiveness and stimulating adequate domestic investment – to create the 'jobs of the day after tomorrow' – can be accomplished through an active reshaping both of the economy and of society. Within this reshaping, the state has the particular role of furthering, and to a certain extent actually directing, restructuring through the promotion of suitable research and development, and through retraining the workforce. The cooperation of the trade unions is to be obtained in exchange for assurances that the victims of restructuring will be granted state help. Restructuring is intended to concentrate economic activity in those areas of production and processes in which the national site is particularly internationally competitive, and for which an adequate world demand can be identified even during periods of world economic crisis. International competitiveness may rest on access to leading technologies, quality of manufacture, reliability of delivery dates, and the capacity to offer entire 'problem-solving packages': investment goods, which continue to have a market during crises because of the pressure to rationalize, and which are not subject to such vigorous price competition, are especially favoured. An economy which manages to be successful in such a specialized field can – at least according to the theory – continue to afford high wages and welfare benefits. In West Germany, for example, greatest confidence is placed in mechanical engineering, construction of plant, nuclear power and the pharmaceuticals industry.

This cunningly seductive strategy has to overcome two major snags however: firstly, other countries will have also come across the same idea and will no doubt attempt the same policy – with the result that the world market will soon prove too small for the number of competitors. And secondly, the 'modernization of the economy' in fact requires a 'healthy contraction' of entire economic branches, with the result that large numbers of unemployed, equipped only with outmoded skills, will have to brace themselves for the physical and psychological rigours of retraining for 'redeployment' into other branches – with no certainty as to which skills will be in demand in the future. In West Germany, for example, it is quite clear that all the leading sectors added together, even given a high degree of international competitiveness and high (obligatory) occupational mobility, do not – and will not – have sufficient capacity to absorb labour in quantities capable of reducing the high – and rising – level of unemployment. This apparent contradiction between new sales and export successes and high unemployment is, to a great extent, explicable by the fact that full order books do not necessarily mean the full utilization of all domestic manufacturing capacity. For example, a DM 100 million order for a turnkey plant would only generate DM 20 million of manufacture within West Germany, with a further DM 30 million for domestic engineering services and assembly: the remainder is accounted for by manufacture carried out abroad.[16]

Such a strategy of individual national salvation also represents an even greater obstacle to coordinated international efforts to resolve the crisis (such as at EEC or OECD level, let alone the ambitions of the North-South dialogue) than either the conservative model or the second variant of the social-democratic model, and threatens to ruin the last vestiges of the internationalism within the working class movement.

National Keynesianism A second variant of the social-democratic model, national Keynesianism, as advocated in West Germany for example by the study group 'Alternativen der Wirtschaftspolitik'[17] proposes the application of pump-priming policies to boost demand at a national level. The consequent increases in real wages, leading to more demand from households, and increases in state-spending to stimulate employment, are intended, or hoped, to bring about the momentum needed to revive investment and create a sufficient number of new jobs. However, because of anxieties that increased consumer demand will culminate either in price-increases by domestic producers and/or increased imports from cheaper producers abroad, rather than expansionary investment at domestic sites whose international competitiveness is not fully established, this model requires urgent buttressing with protectionist measures, price controls and possibly extensive nationalization.

The measures proposed are clearly all of dubious effectiveness, beginning with campaigns to 'Buy British', 'Buy American', 'Achetez Francais', which have a mere propaganda value, and extending to the well-intended, but illusionary plans for a social clause in GATT treaties, which aims to ensure certain minimum standards of wages and working conditions in low-wage countries, and concomitantly reinforce the competitive position of the industrialized countries. Even the nationalization of large industrial and commercial concerns with the intention of strengthening governmental influence on the level, structure, timing and location of investment (cf. the programme of the Left Alliance in France – Projet socialiste) will yield only meagre results if state undertakings remain as subject to the imperatives of the world capitalist system as their private enterprise predecessors – and, in the absence of a fundamental challenge to the priorities of the capitalist system or a rigorous and comprehensive system of protection, are consequently obliged to come to much the same investment decisions.

Keynes himself was in no doubt that Keynesian policies at a national level would be ineffective as long as individual economies remained heavily integrated into the capitalist world economy.[18] In view of what is advocated in the name of Keynes, one sometimes wonders whether the disciples are actually aware of the advice of their mentor:

> I sympathize, therefore, with those who would minimize, rather than with those who would maximize, economic entanglement among nations. Ideas, knowledge, science, hospitality, travel – these are the things which should of their nature be international. But let goods be homespun whenever it is reasonably and conveniently possible, and, above all, let finance be primarily national . . . We do not wish . . . to be at the mercy of world forces working out, or trying to work out, some uniform equilibrium according to ideal principles, if they can be called such, of *laissez-faire* capitalism . . . We wish – for the time at least and so long as the present transitional, experimental phase endures – to be our own masters, and to be as free as we can make ourselves from the interferences of the outside world.

Historical experience seems to indicate that it is, in fact, extremely difficult for individual capitalist economies to extract themselves from the capitalist world-economy without abandoning their essential capitalist character. It is therefore inevitable that at some point the logic of a social-democratic approach which does not envisage a break with capitalism (as a precondition for withdrawal from the world-economy) will bring it face to face with the notion that the only Keynesian pathway out of the crisis consistent with the basic parameters of the capitalist system is a Keynesianism practised on a world scale.

Global Keynesianism The notion of a 'global Keynesianism'[19] is a central element in the report of the North-South Commission.[20] It constitutes the third variant of the social-democratic model for resolving the crisis.

According to the illusion eagerly nourished by employers' organizations and widespread in trade union circles, the classic formula for combating rising labour-costs – an absolute drop in investment but relative increase in the share devoted to rationalization – combined with a policy of 'pay restraint', or under more serious circumstances 'pay pause', should have produced a reasonably rapid return to the 'growth path' of the industrialized economies. Leaving aside the dramatic empirical refutation of this perspective by experience in Great Britain, our analysis of the crisis has already shown why this is necessarily an illusion. The promised, relatively painless readjustment of the overall share of wages in gross national product through a few years of pay restraint, which should have led back to the 'growth path' has been subverted by that second mechanism – the partial relocation of production into the informal sector and developing countries. Although this may yield a short-run increase in profitability for individual companies, its main effect may actually reduce world effective demand: mass incomes will fall, but the possible eventual increases in profitability will not lead to a sufficiently large, or sufficiently rapid increase in investment to compensate – and there is no guarantee that any investment which is forthcoming will have a positive impact on employment.

The North-South Commission's answer is that measures have to be designed to siphon off high profits and transfer them to the Third World where they can boost world effective demand, resolve the crisis of the world capitalist economy 'in the common interest of both industrialized and developing countries', and thus 'secure survival'. This conclusion presupposes, irrespective of how realistic one feels it to be, that those Western industrialized states who have just had to abandon a revival of the internationalist non-Keynesian social-democratic 'growth and partnership' model of the 1950s and 1960s, and who are not attempting a solo voyage through the world economy, will be able to combine their efforts and introduce Keynesianism on a world scale.

However, the Achilles heel of global Keynesianism is not so much a lack of political will on the part of individual governments as the fact that the international competitiveness of world-market oriented production in the informal sector and developing countries has not yet reached a level – despite all efforts at overcoming the political and social resistance of the 'non-capitalist milieu' and despite some notable increase over the last decades – sufficient to mobilize and tie-up adequate volumes of capital. Given these circumstances, a massive transfer of idle or mobilizable capital would only be feasible under the totally unrealistic assumption of a globally centrally-planned economy, in which a 'modernizing' and 'civilizing' use of force on an unprecedented scale would be needed to compel the 'non-capitalist' sector to yield up free wage labourers.

Perspectives

The nature of the current economic crisis and the problems inherent in the various attempts to resolve or overcome it which we have considered above, suggest that the development of the industrialized countries is likely to be determined by the continuation or ascendancy of the conservative model, together with its IMF variant in the developing countries: this does not, however, mean that this model will emerge as *the* model of accumulation for the next few decades. But irrespective of whether this does in fact take place, or whether the conservative model manages to prove itself in the medium-term in capitalist terms, the mere fact that it is being attempted will mean the realization and intensification of all those developments cited at the end of the section on p. 95 – from persisting and probably increasing unemployment, the aggressive exclusion of 'marginal groups', and political repression of the labour movement in the industrialized countries to the continuing imposition of the IMF model, with its associated austerity, world-market oriented private-profit maximising industrialization, and 'stabilizing' pro-business regimes in the developing countries. International relations will take on an increasingly aggressive edge, at least as a well-tried means of diverting domestic attention away from local problems to the alleged guilty parties or villains abroad.

The advance of the liberal-conservative model has meant that no one – not even the hard-core of organized labour – is now spared the experience of being pushed out of the (real or imaginary) security of the social-welfare state and into the wilderness of the capitalist market. And the more that workers cannot find the means to reproduce their labour-power in the market, the more they will be forced to make increasing reliance on the 'non-capitalist milieu', though at the same time remaining available for wage labour – thus enabling labour-costs to fall and international competitiveness to rise. Moreover, those affected are actually expected to regard, and applaud, their fate as an extension of freedom and a strengthening of 'individual responsibility'. Beyond these crude obsessions, the conservative model offers no additional perspective, and in particular no perspective for mitigating or solving any of the pressing problems of humanity.

The task of an alternative strategy

The purpose of this study was firstly to indicate the causal nexus behind the present crisis, and secondly, with these causes in mind, to test whether any of the current proposals for resolving the crisis are either plausible or realizable.

Although possessing differences which should not be minimized, both the conservative and the various variants of the social-democratic model have one thing in common: they all strive for an accommodation with the 'functional dictates' (*Sachzwänge*) demanded by economic growth in the capitalist world system, on the assumption that no free alternative exists.

One of these 'dictates' is that in order to induce them to invest at all, any state-policy directed at creating jobs has to offer companies various incentives – be they in the form of measures to reduce labour-costs, increasing guaranteed demand through public expenditure, or others. But not only do firms require these incentives; additional steps have to taken to ensure that this hard-won investment actually creates jobs – and is not directed abroad or into rationalization.

In view of the fact that the current economic crisis, although undeniably real, is not about to spill over into a total breakdown of the world capitalist economic and social system, the invocation of these 'functional dictates', and the appeal to an ill-defined new 'freedom' has so far proved sufficient to obstruct any deliberate and systematic steps towards reducing the danger of nuclear war, minimizing the damage which might be expected from a technological catastrophe, mitigating physical and psychological misery and establishing a sustainable relationship with nature – let alone achieving the necessary revolutionary 'radical change in consciousness and organizational forms' which are needed.[21]

The socialist alternative, the counter-model to the capitalist programmes, which possesses the theoretical capacity to guide such steps, precisely because it is more than a mere negation of capitalism, is now so irreparably discredited in practice in the industrialized countries – on the one hand because of the historically explicable, but no less real, grim realities of 'actually existing socialism', and on the other through its systematic defamation by its enemies – that it is no longer able to function as a serious point around which resistance to the onward march of capitalism's 'dictates' can crystallize.

What is to be done? Carl Friedrich von Weizsäcker writes:

Steps *within* the present danger are steps which an individual, a party, a nation or an imperial leadership can actually make today. They must meet three conditions. Firstly, they must offer a safe way around the visible perils of the moment. Secondly, they must allow the current state of the world to continue and to be developed – in other words, they must change the world without catastrophes. And thirdly, they must lead towards a major, radical change in consciousness and organizational forms. To achieve all this they must be recognizably rational according to the standards of a rationality which although not presently realizable, nevertheless exists in the mind of the rational: rational – that is, facilitating and not obstructing the realization of reason, and recognizably rational – that is, clearly indicating the way ahead.[22]

What might such steps, or indications, look like? Steps to establish internal and external peace, to overcome hunger and poverty, to restore a measure of control into the life of the individual (and relax the grip of alien control – wage labour, patriarchy, the relation between the First and the Third World), to preserve the natural basis of human existence?

Although the exigencies of the present crisis may stand in the way of the ideas of such thinkers as Carl Friedrich von Weizsäcker and Erhard Eppler,[23] we would nonetheless be foolish to close our ears to the voices of those who, because of their knowledge or experience of the power, potency and workings of the capitalist system, warn against political conceptions or programmes which, in their ignorance of the history or operation of the capitalist system, represent a naive and potentially dangerous political trend; for example, the notion that the mere aggregation of small non-capitalist cooperatives or niches (the 'non-capitalist milieu' of family, neighbourhood and commune) within the broader system is capable of solving humanity's problems – as if these forms were not first and foremost forms for the organization of labour and social life which industrial capitalism has repeatedly exploited, if not actively created, and will continue to exploit and create in step with its own systematic requirements – even if always subject to the rhythm of the resistance and cooperation of those it has tried to subordinate.

It would be sheer wishful thinking to imagine that it is possible to trace pathways out of, or within, the present danger without heeding and avoiding such pitfalls. We therefore return to the question we asked at the outset: is it possible to formulate some of the premises of an alternative economic and social policy, which without any false optimism and consistent with the premises outlined for other areas, might at least hold open the possibility of avoiding the identifiably ominous tendencies inherent in current developments and political strategies and create the space for steps, or pathways, in a less potentially calamitous direction?

This question remains as yet unanswered.

Notes

1 Carl Friedrich von Weizsäcker, *Der bedrohte Friede*, Hanser, Munich, 1981, p. 491.
2 Cf. Horst Afheldt, *Verteidigung und Frieden*, Hanser, Munich, 1976; Emil Spannocchi and Guy Brossollet, *Verteidigung ohne Schlacht*, Hanser, Munich, 1976.
3 Folker Fröbel, Jürgen Heinrichs, Otto Kreye and Osvaldo Sunkel, 'Internationalisierung von Kapital und Arbeitskraft', *Leviathan*, IV, 1973, pp. 429–454.
4 Cf. György Ádám, 'New Trends in International Business: Worldwide Sourcing and Dedomiciling', *Acta Oeconomica*, 7, 1971, pp. 349–367; Giovanni Arrighi, 'Una nuova crisis generale', *Rassenna Communista*, 2, 3, 4, & 7, 1972; shortened English version 'Towards a Theory of Capitalist Crisis', *New Left Review*, 111, 1978, pp. 3–24; Andre Gunder Frank, 'Reflections on the World Economic Crisis' (1972), in Frank, *Reflections on the World Economic Crisis*, Monthly Review Press, New York, 1981, pp. 7–16; Andrew Glyn and Bob Sutcliffe, *British Capitalism, Workers and the Profits Squeeze*, Penguin Books, Harmondsworth, 1972; André Granou, 'La nouvelle crise du capitalisme', *Les Temps Modernes*, 328, 1973, pp. 808–831; 329, 1973, pp. 998–1025; Stephen Hymer, 'International Politics and International Economics: A Radical Approach' (1973) in Hymer, *The Multinational Corporation: A Radical Approach*, CUP, Cambridge, 1979, pp. 256–272; Ernest Mandel, *Late Capitalism*, NLB, London, 1975 (first published in German, 1972).
5 OECD, *Employment Outlook*, Sept. 1984, 3 million more than at the original time of writing.
6 Cf. for our own approach Folker Fröbel, 'The Current Development of the World-economy: Reproduction of Labor and Accumulation of Capital on a World Scale', *Review*, V, 4, 1982, pp. 507–555. See too, Giovanni Arrighi, op. cit. and 'Hypotheses on the Current Global Crisis', manuscript, 1980; Robert Boyer, 'La crise actuelle; une mise en perspective historique', *Critique de l'économie politique. Nouvelle serie*, 7/8, 1979, pp. 5–113; André Granou, Yves Baron and Bernard Billaudout, *Croissance et crise*, Maspero, Paris, 1979; Thomas Weisskopf, 'The Current Economic Crisis in Historial Perspective', *Socialist Review*, 57, 1981, pp. 9–53.
7 Rosa Luxemburg, *The Accumulation of Capital*, Routledge & Kegan Paul, London, 1963.
8 Cf. Max Weber, 'Die ländliche Arbeitsverfassung' (1893) and 'Entwicklungstendenzen in der Lage der ostelbischen Landarbeiter' (1894), in Weber, *Gesammelte Aufsätze zur Sozial - und Wirtschaftsgeschichte*, Mohr (Siebeck), Tübingen, 1924; Luxemburg, op. cit.' Henry Ford, *My Life and Work*, Doubleday, Page, Garden City, 1922; Pierre-Philippe Rey, 'Introduction théorique' in Emile Le Bris, Pierre-Philippe Rey and Michel Samuel, *Capitalisme negrier*, Maspero, Paris, 1976, pp. 39–67.

9 Arrighi, 1978, op. cit.
10 R.M. Goodwin, 'A Growth Cycle', in C.H. Feinstein (ed.), *Capitalism and Economic Growth*, CUP, Cambridge, 1967, pp. 54–58; a revised version is published in E.K. Hunt and Jesse G. Schwartz (eds.), *A Critique of Economic Theory*, Penguin Books, Harmondsworth, 1972, pp. 442–449.
11 Starnberger Studien 4, *Strukturveränderungen in der kapitalistischen Weltwirtschaft*, Suhrkamp, Frankfurt, 1980.
12 Arrighi, op. cit.
13 Weisskopf, op. cit.
14 Carl Friedrich von Weizsäcker, *Möglichkeiten und Probleme auf dem Weg zu einer vernünftigen Weltfriedensordnung*, Hanser, Munich, 1982, p. 23.
15 Volker Hauff and Fritz W. Scharpf, *Modernisierung der Volkswirtschaft*, Europäische Verlagsanstalt, 1975.
16 See *Handelsblatt*, 26 June 1982, p. 13.
17 Memorandum '81, Arbeitsgruppe 'Alternative Wirtschafts-politik', *Demokratische Wirtschaftspolitik gegen Markmacht und Sparmassnahmen*, Pahl-Rugenstein, Cologne, 1981.
18 John Maynard Keynes, 'National Self-Sufficiency', *The Yale Review*, 22, 1933, 755–769.
19 Andre Gunder Frank, 'North-South and East-West Paradoxes in the Brandt Report' in Friedrich Ebert Foundation (ed.), *Towards One World? International Responses to the Brandt Report*, Temple Smith, London, 1981, pp. 329–343.
20 Brandt Report, Independent Commission on International Development Issues, *North-South: A Programme for Survival*, Pan Books, London, 1980.
21 Von Weizsäcker, 1981, op. cit. p. 593.
22 Ibid.
23 Cf. von Weizsäcker, op. cit. and *Wege in der Gefahr*, Hanser, Munich, 1976; Erhard Eppler, *Wege aus der Gefahr*, Rowohlt, Reinbek bei Hamburg, 1981.

4

The Global Crisis and Developing Countries*

Folker Fröbel, Jürgen Heinrichs, Otto Kreye**

The current crisis of the capitalist world-system

The capitalist world-system is in the grip of a crisis: its symptoms and its consequences are clearly visible. But a proper understanding of the current international developments and their effects requires an inquiry into the origins of the crisis.[1]

Although the crisis has its familiar economic, political, social, and ecological aspects in the Western industrialized countries, it is in fact a crisis of the world capitalist system as a whole, including much of the Third World too. The socialist countries have not been spared, the extent to which they are affected depending on how far they have become integrated into the capitalist world-system.

Two closely linked processes have contributed to the crisis: first, the gradual erosion of United States global hegemony, and second, internal contradictions within the industrialized countries.

At the end of the Second World War, the dominance of the United States seemed assured. It provided the context within which free international – in fact transnational – mobility of capital could be guaranteed, evidenced most clearly in the progressive global spread of United States corporations, later followed by Western European and Japanese firms. The growing economic and political strength of Western Europe and Japan gradually eroded the dominance of the United States, which was further weakened by political changes in the periphery.

---

*Translated by Pete Burgess
**A shorter version of this text has been published under the same title in *Trade and Development* (5, 1984), the review of the United Nations Conference on Trade and Development.

In addition, transnational corporations achieved a level of economic and political power to a large degree independent of their home governments. This power was sufficiently strong in some cases to override the authority of many states or even powerful supra-national institutions.

The model of capital accumulation that came into being in the period after the Second World War has been analysed by Michel Aglietta, Giovanni Arrighi, Robert Boyer, Andre Gunder Frank, David Gordon, André Granou, Eric Hobsbawm, Stephen Hymer, Ernest Mandel, James O'Connor, Christian Palloix, Thomas Weisskopf and others.[2] Hegemony enabled the USA to impose a new model of accumulation, in which the tendencies towards international and internal conflict inherent in the pre-war system were to be counteracted by two major departures from the preceding model: *firstly*, an extensive – including international – freedom for corporate activity, and *secondly*, the systematic extension of the market for mass consumer goods in the industrialized countries. By inducing a high rate of capitalist growth against the background of these new preconditions, it was hoped that a course could be steered between the Scylla of realization crises (the fatal 'flaw' in the previous system) and the Charybdis of valorization crises. Such a strategy would simultaneously facilitate the political integration of the workers' movement(s), which despite its exhaustion and decimation through war and crisis, still represented a serious oppositional factor in view of the collapse in the credibility of the capitalist economic and social system following the events of the previous three decades.

Relations between developed market-economy countries and developing countries were fostered by a policy of closer international, in fact transnational, links: for example, the dissolution of the old colonial systems of preferences and their replacement by a free trade policy. In the circumstances following the Second World War, this policy implied a great overseas expansion of United States capital into the industrialized and developing countries.

Despite the various forms and degrees of resistance encountered in the immediate post-war years, the USA succeeded in exerting political and economic pressure to install the new model of accumulation in Western Europe, and to a more limited extent in Japan. Once established the model was able to generate precisely those features which rendered its continued functioning an increasingly attractive proposition to the organized working class, and which further enabled it to determine capitalist development in the Western industrialized countries and the world-economy as a whole over the subsequent two and a half decades: that is, high rates of growth, expanding mass incomes, a trend towards full-employment and the expansion of the social welfare system.

The very success of the model led to shortages of labour, despite large-scale labour migration into the industrialized countries. As a consequence, profit margins were squeezed and the dominance of capital was threatened. The corporate response took two forms. The first was the method of economizing on labour power by cutting back investment and introducing labour-saving technologies. The second was the method of relocating plants in cheaper and/or more profitable alternative sites, specifically in developing countries.

The combination of these two methods had the effect that the period of labour shortage in the industrial countries was followed by large-scale unemployment, a fall in real wages and measures for curbing the size of the welfare state. The consequential decline in mass purchasing power reinforced the tendency towards the under-utilization of capacities and growing unemployment; opportunities for profitable productive investment declined.

After functioning successfully for 25 years, the post-war capitalist economy has now run into serious difficulties, and there is little prospect of an improvement in the situation. The doctrines of conservative economics, which dominate policy in most of the large industrialized countries, assume that capital accumulation can be revived simply by further cheapening labour as a factor of production, despite continuing mass unemployment and diminishing mass purchasing power.

The transnational corporations have an obvious interest in maintaining the present world market system. In this they are supported by institutions, such as the World Bank and in particular the IMF, which are forcing more and more countries, especially in the Third World, to adopt measures that are inconsistent with the interests of the bulk of their populations and that are intended to intensify integration into the capitalist world-system.

How the crisis will end is still unclear. Those conservative forces seeking to preserve the essentials of the existing system, in fact to use the crisis as a mean of saving it, undeniably have the upper hand at present. Eric Hobsbawm has observed at this point 'capitalism lived with [slumps], capitalism lived through them, capitalism survived them'.[3] Nevertheless, as the crisis persists, and as the failure of conservative policy becomes evident, new political forces will perhaps come to the fore and work for the establishment of an entirely different social system.

Against this background, we now consider the effects of the crisis on the Third World.

The crisis and the periphery

The experience of the early 1980s has shown more than ever before that the developing countries of Asia, Africa and Latin America which are

integrated into the capitalist world market have little prospect of bene-
fiting from an independent and self-reliant path of development.
Owing to the social and political crisis of the capitalist world system, it
would be a fallacy to think that underdevelopment can be overcome
within the present system.

Social and economic conditions for the majority of the population in
many if not most nations of the capitalist periphery steadily worsened
in the course of the immediate post-war decades. In the last few years
their situation has become parlous. A number of countries are now on
the brink of default.

The economic crisis is not reflected directly in altered, or reversed,
growth rates for industrial and agricultural production, and foreign
trade – in fact, these have not fallen as dramatically in the developing
countries as in some industrialized countries – but rather in unbalanced
sectoral and regional growth, increasing dependency, and their social
effects. The evidence includes:

– Stagnation and drop in industrial, agricultural and service output
  intended for consumption by the population, in particular food-
  stuffs. Simultaneously, an increase in capital-intensive agricultural,
  industrial, and service output for mostly foreign markets – controlled by transnational corporations – including the production of
  food. The consequence is an accentuation of the disequilibria
  between domestically-oriented and world market-oriented production to the detriment of output for domestic consumption.
– Indebtedness of the developing countries to the public and private
  international financial institutions, and a consequential external
  dependency amounting to subordination to the international financial system. Indebtedness has now reached such heights – $810 bil-
  lion at the end of 1983[4] – that debt service now absorbs a large share
  of the economic surplus of these countries.
– Further encroachments on and destruction of the rural subsistence
  economy, that is, that part of the economy in which the bulk of the
  rural population of the developing countries produces what it
  needs for subsistence or has been able to do so up until now. The
  rapidly advancing destruction of this sector by capital-intensive
  export-agriculture explains the emigration of large numbers of the
  rural population.[5]
– Extensive damage to the environment in the countries of the periphery, often exceeding the environmental damage in the industrialized
  countries.

Most of these indicators relate to manifestations of underdevelopment which look more like a continuation of the trends and
processes known only too well in the developing countries, rather than
anything startlingly new. But the fact that they have come virtually to
dominate social and economic development, at the expense of an independent or alternative development in individual countries, regions and

branches, puts them in a new light. In addition, almost all the countries and regions of the periphery which once appeared to demonstrate the possibility of capitalist prosperity even in the periphery – at least in the individual cases of what are variously described as threshold countries, semi-periphery, economic miracle countries, newly industrializing countries – are now compelled to abandon any idea of a nationally determined economic policy.

The main cause of this state of affairs is not difficult to spot: compared with the two post-war decades of boom in the capitalist centres, the crisis-ridden 1970s offered far fewer obstacles to the integration of the peripheral countries into the world market, and in particular to the opening-up of countries for investment-seeking international capital.

The levers which enabled this accelerated opening-up and integration to take place, and continue to do so, are both numerous and diverse, ranging from management contracts to military pressure. Amongst the most important of these levers are private foreign investment, export and import credits, technology transfer, weapons transfer, development advice and consultancy, the Green Revolution, infrastructural investments and petro-dollar recycling. The actors were, and are, primarily transnational corporations in co-operation with the World Bank and the IMF, and in collaboration with the respective national bourgeoisies. The fields of investment were, and are, high-price domestic markets and production for export. Production structures have become overwhelmingly oriented to the world market; these are paralleled by consumption structures heavily dependent on imports.

The world market orientation of developing countries has also made them more vulnerable to fluctuations in world demand. The crisis-induced drastic fall in world demand is also impinging on those areas of production and services that operate within the ambit of transnational capital. Increases in exports of manufactured goods are heavily concentrated in a few developing countries. The drop in demand and the collapse in commodity prices have brought about a corresponding fall in the developing countries' export earnings. The situation is aggravated by the general absence of any effective state control and the widespread practice of transfer pricing.

Never before in the history of the capitalist mode of production has the contrast between the enormous unmet needs of the vast bulk of humanity, living in poverty, and an enormous unused productive capacity – unused because its use is not profitable – been so glaring as in the periphery today. And never before has the capitalist mode of production been shown to be so irrational as in the current crisis.

The political crisis

The economic crisis and the threat of economic bankruptcy of entire states find a counterpart in the political crisis of both the bourgeois-democratic state – where it has survived – and the bourgeois-military state. A series of coups, putschs and external interventions have more or less ousted bourgeois-democratic state forms and other reform-oriented regimes in the third world.

The political crisis of the *bourgeois-democratic* state in the periphery is scarcely surprising. The replacement of bourgeois-democratic forms by bourgeois-military state forms seems to have acquired a certain inevitability. The existing structures of the capitalist world-system and the imperatives of capital accumulation prevent the bourgeois state of the periphery from fulfilling the promise of development, conceived as an improvement in living standards. The strategy of the bourgeoisies of the periphery, who chose integration into the world market to maintain their own rule, can prevent neither growing social inequality and impoverishment nor economic bankruptcy. Social peace under such circumstances means simply the repression of labour and peasant movements and of any other movements for reform. The continued rule of the bourgeoisie depends in the final analysis on the support of the military.

But nor will the *bourgeois-military* state solve the economic crisis. On the contrary, unproductive military expenditure imposes a growing burden on foreign capital in return for external military support. The bourgeois-military state of the periphery – as it has evolved in recent years and decades – is characterized by certain indicators of *political crisis*, viz.:

- The continuing and expanding diversion of resources to military purposes,[6] particularly in the Middle East.
- The maintenance and intensification of a state of emergency over a number of years, the suspension of freedoms, the maintenance of bans on trade unions and political parties for many years, the use of torture as a routine political instrument.
- Progressive surrender of national political and economic sovereignty in return for external political, military, and economic support. This includes the establishment of foreign military bases on national territory, the abandonment of protectionist economic policies, and the creation of enclaves for foreign capital in which the operation of national labour legislation is suspended (free zones, etc.).
- Exacerbation of class antagonisms to such a degree that even the bourgeois and petit bourgeois middle classes, frequently willing aides and auxiliaries of the bourgeois-military State, are deprived of political power and threatened in their economic existence.
- Loss of political, economic, social and military control over entire

areas, provinces, regions, with the growth of separatist and seces-
sionist movements.

In its efforts to regain control over the conflicts generated by the
economic and political crisis, the bourgeois-military state of the
periphery seeks salvation through collaboration with imperialism. The
price to be paid for this 'assistance' is virtually the eclipse of the state in
the economy. In handing over control of economic activity to transnational corporations, their economies become effectively fully subordinated to the dictates and vagaries of the valorization of capital.

The current intensification of the economic and political crisis in
certain countries exemplifies how the ruling bourgeois-military class of
the periphery has very rapidly created its own crisis by stepping up the
exploitation of the working population by both internal and external
forces.[7]

Although Hobsbawm's observation that crisis is the constant accompaniment of capital applies both to the capitalism of the centre and to
that of the periphery, nevertheless, the undisguised and growing inability of the peripheral bourgeoisies to guarantee even a minimum of
economic, political, and social stability creates conditions in which
resistance to bourgeois-military rule can become so widespread that
peasant and proletarian movements *and* certain strata of the middle
classes may form alliances to oppose the prevailing system.

The intensification of the crisis

The period since 1945 has seen the integration of most countries of the
periphery into the world capitalist market. There are, however, exceptions. Power relations in a small group of countries have changed
sufficiently for them to be able to resist successfully further integration,
withdraw from it, or, at least, bring the scale and nature of their integration into the world market gradually under national control. This
group comprises, among others, certain developing countries.

The advance of socialist developing countries shows that it is feasible
to create, within the time-span of a generation if not less, the foundations of an agricultural and industrial economy capable of satisfying
the basic needs of the mass of the population. This presupposes a
fundamental change in the relations of production and distribution,
and in the nature of the country's incorporation into the international
division of labour.[8] No doubt, it is the intensification of the conflict
over fundamental change in the relation of production and distribution, and in the incorporation of the developing countries into the
capitalist international division of labour, which gives a special character to the class struggles of the present.

We would venture the thesis that all political movements seeking fundamental change as the prerequisite for overcoming under-development would always attempt to follow the path of change through parliamentary and non-violent means if such a path held out any likelihood of success. Historical experience suggests, however, that almost any attempt to change the structures of the capitalist world system by parliamentary democratic means meets resistance.[9]

Historical experience also shows that any change in power structures, as constituted in the relations of production and distribution in the capitalist world system, is only possible through the growth and appli-cation of power. For the exploited classes the most potent source of power lies in their political will to overcome exploitation. As develop-ment in the post-war period illustrated, this political will can be a force for changing power relations if the resolution to do so grips a majority of the people of a social class, a nation, a region or a group of states. Success naturally requires more: both the prevailing conditions for accumulation on a world-scale, and the balance of power between the superpowers have to be conducive too.

Conversely, it was the lack of political will for change in the Western industrialized countries which allowed these countries – including their socialist and social-democratic parties and trade union organizations – to become the conservative bastion of the global capitalist system during the two or three post-war decades. As Samir Amin once observed: 'Nothing is happening in the North'.[10] Whether this will remain the case in the present period of deepening crisis is a matter for speculation. Given its position as the power house of world capitalism, it is necessary, if not sufficient, that far-reaching changes have to be made in the North before fundamental changes can occur in the capital-ist world system.

The critical factor in turning the potential political will of the exploited classes into an effective transforming force is their capacity and preparedness for forming an alliance. The stars on the Chinese national flag still symbolize the alliance of peasants, proletariat and bourgeoisie which Mao Tse Tung regarded as a crucial prerequisite for the success of the Chinese war of liberation in the 1930s. Mao regarded this alliance as possible since all these classes suffered, albeit in differing degrees.[11] Though of a different character, the alliance of peasants, urban proletariat, middle class, and rural and urban marginalized groups was important in certain developing countries in that it facili-tated revolutionary changes in national and international power structures.

In many countries and regions of the Third World, the economic crisis of the capitalist world system is not only giving renewed impetus to new alliances between and within the urban and rural proletariat; these alliances are also extending to the middle classes. Where this happens it is possible that the crisis may engender political forces strong enough to make further changes in international power structures, and push ahead with the delinking of the countries of the periphery from their present, all too unequal, incorporation into the international division of labour. It remains to be seen whether this possibility will crystallize in political action.

The present time of crisis is, of course, also a period in which conservative politics in the Western industrialized countries aim not only at entrenching the status quo of international relations of production and distribution, but also at changing the capitalist world-system so that both obstacles to the valorization of capital and – more importantly – the relative independence of a number of countries in the periphery are removed.

The United States has placed itself in the vanguard of the conservative politics of restoration – with the added intention of returning the USA to its former position of undisputed hegemonial power in the capitalist world-system. Official American doctrine envisages a policy along the following lines:

- Firstly, retention of existing political and economic structures throughout the world in so far as they facilitate the unlimited pursuit and maintenance of American political, economic, and military interests.
- Secondly, regaining lost spheres of influence in the Third World and recapturing American control of those regions in which limits are currently placed on the maintenance of American political, economic, and military interests.
- Thirdly, the prevention of any development in the Third World which could imply a change in global power relations to the detriment of the United States.

The revitalization of the military is given first priority in the implementation of this policy. What the inner dynamics of the capitalist mode of production cannot achieve, namely stable economic and political structures, and what political control cannot successfully execute, namely the prevention of anti-capitalist movements in the periphery, is to be carried out using military means.

The International Monetary Fund has had a leading role in advocating conservative policies for some considerable time. The IMF exerts its influence on the countries of the periphery through its ability to grant or withhold vital stand-by credits, thus negating any pretensions to truly independent policies or development.

The reason why the mere control over credit enables the IMF to render such effective support to conservative policies for controlling the periphery is not difficult to find. It lies in the consequences of the accelerated integration of many countries of the periphery into the world market in the post-war period. The exploitation of the periphery, on the one hand, and even more so, the unbalanced sectoral and regional export-oriented and import-dependent economic structures of the periphery, on the other, have forced increasing numbers of countries to tread the humiliating path to the IMF and apply for stand-by credits. If a country's economy is on the verge of breakdown, if vital goods cannot be imported, if economic bankruptcy is threatening, credit-seeking countries have little choice but to accept the IMF's terms and conditions, which correspond to the main criteria of conservative economic policy.[12]

In recent years more than 100 countries have been forced to approach the IMF for stand-by credits. The conditions which the IMF attaches to the granting of credits, requiring in essence the application of liberal-conservative policies in the credit-seeking countries, hardly vary from one country to another, and pay scant regard to specific national economic circumstances. Under the guise of stabilization programmes, the IMF regularly demands the abandonment of any national economic policy, and in particular any self-reliant policy for agriculture, industry, trade, finance, or social welfare geared to the needs of the population. In place of such policies the IMF requires the establishment of economic and social conditions which impose few if any limitations on the operations of transnational corporations. Almost without exception the conditions call for:

- The liberalization of external trade and payments, and in particular the removal of import controls, foreign exchange controls and other protectionist instruments.
- The removal of restrictions on the activities of foreign capital, such as discrimination against foreign capital, in particular branches and sectors, and limitations on the transfer of profits.
- The devaluation of national currencies (frequently, the payment of individual tranches of loans already granted is made dependent on additional devaluations).
- The reduction of state subsidies for food, health and transportation which shelter the low-income groups.
- Changes in budgetary policy intended to reduce direct and indirect taxes on companies and to increase direct or indirect subsidies for companies (e.g. provision of investment finance, infrastructure, and industrial inputs).
- A reorientation of national economic policy and development towards increased promotion of production for export, with the concomitant neglect of areas producing for domestic demand and consumption, and an eventual increased dependency on imports.
- State intervention in the determination of wages and other incomes, whereby – notwithstanding the free market principles otherwise propagated by the IMF – the state is assigned the role of guaranteeing low wage levels.

In reality, the IMF's policy of 'conditionality', or the withholding of a loan, portrayed as a policy of financial stabilization, ignores the prerequisites for stable trade and payments;[13] it is in fact a policy designed to perpetuate the integration of the developing countries in the capitalist world market.

The insistence on the uninhibited transfer of profits has a destabilizing effect on trade and payments, since it renders a considerable portion of foreign currency earnings unavailable for meeting payment obligations. The insistence on devaluation, allegedly to boost exports and limit imports, in combination with the liberalization of trade and payments, exercises a destabilizing effect since, with declining demand on world markets, it can only lead to a fall in export earnings and an increase in the price of vital imports. The insistence on cutting state subsidies which benefit the poorest sections of the population has a directly destabilizing effect. 'Its inevitable result is to turn the population against the government and to dismember social alliances supporting regimes embarking on a course of internal reforms and economic independence, often resulting in the demise of the government and the installation of authoritarian regimes.'[14]

The policies of the IMF have so far fallen short of their goal of stabilization. The IMF is now itself on the brink of a liquidity crisis and finds itself confronted with a series of debtors teetering on the verge of default.

The implementation of the IMF's policy aimed at maintaining the existing structures of capitalism does not relieve the poverty of the Third World. Sooner or later the costs of maintaining a minimum of political stability in the face of the disruptions wrought by the crisis will exceed the gains which this stability is intended to guarantee. Even some conservative voices are now being raised about the course of the present crisis. Kissinger – one of the architects of conservative global politics – seems to have started doubting the wisdom of a policy 'forcing developing countries to reduce their standard of living drastically over a long period (which) is likely to weaken precisely those moderate governments that are the most likely to accept Western advice'.[15]

Against pessimism

The struggles for or against the imperatives of global capital are certain to intensify in the coming years. It is equally certain that at present the champions of conservative economics are on the offensive given the proven incapacity of reformist social-democratic policies to manage the crisis. But there should also be no doubt that the political, economic, social and ecological effects of these policies will strengthen the resistance to the imperatives of capital accumulation on a world scale, not only in the countries of the periphery, but also in the Western industrialized countries and the socialist countries.

As far as this latter group is concerned, it should not be overlooked that conservative policies, especially the revival of the military, serve to reinforce the populations' rejection of the capitalist system and its corollaries.

In a few years' time the conservative policies, currently followed in the majority of Western industrialized countries, will be found incapable of dealing with any of their pressing economic, ecological and social problems (as they have already been found wanting in the periphery). Resistance to world capitalism will grow in the Western industrialized countries with the support of many heterogeneous movements.

There is hope, therefore, that resistance to further and greater exploitation and plunder in the countries of the periphery, to the imperatives of capital accumulation on a world-scale, will find allies amongst a growing number of people in the Western industrialized countries, and – in defiance of any anti-socialist offensive – in the socialist countries too.

There seems to be a certain pessimism, according to which the possibility of a transformation of the capitalist world-system into a truly humanized system is not viewed as possible since even non-capitalist countries seem incapable of disentangling themselves from the imperatives of accumulation in a largely capitalist world. This pessimism feeds off the fact that countries whose declared development perspectives are non-capitalist, and in fact socialist relations of production and distribution have only made small advances along their intended paths. However, such pessimism and resignation are not justified.

Delinking from the world market system and a transformation of the system itself do not take place through individual regions and countries suddenly replacing capitalism by socialism.

Delinking from the system, and the transformation of the system itself, are a process which cannot be governed by a single strategy. The heterogeneous anti-capitalist movements worldwide will have to shape their own strategies in the light of the existing conditions.

Notes

1 For a more elaborated discussion of the causes of the crisis, see the previous chapter.
2 Michel Aglietta, *Régulation et crises du capitalisme*, Calmann-Lévy, Paris, 1976; Giovanni Arrighi, 'Towards a Theory of Capitalist Crisis', *New Left Review*, No. 111, September-October 1978; Robert Boyer, 'La crise actuelle: une mise en perspective historique', *Critiques de l'économie politique*, Nouvelle série, No. 7–8, April-September 1979; Andre Gunder Frank, 'Reflections on the World Economic Crisis', in Frank, *Reflections on the World Economic Crisis*, Monthly Review Press, New York, 1981; David Gordon, 'Stages of Accumulation and Long Economic Cycles', in *Processes of the World-System*, edited by Terence K. Hopkins and Immanuel Wallerstein, Sage, Beverley Hills, London, 1980; André Granou, 'La nouvelle crise du capitalisme', *Les Temps Moderne*, No. 328, 1973; Eric J. Hobsbawm, 'The Crisis of Capitalism in Historical Perspective', *Socialist Revolution*, No. 30. 1976; Stephen Hymer, 'International

Politics and International Economics: A Radical Approach', in Hymer, *The Multinational Corporation: A Radical Approach*, Cambridge University Press, Cambridge, 1979, pp. 256–272; Ernest Mandel, *Late Capitalism*, New Left Books, London, 1975; James O'Connor, *Accumulation Crisis* Blackwell, New York, 1984; Christian Palloix, *Travail & Production*, Maspero, Paris, 1978; Thomas Weisskopf, 'The Current Economic Crisis in Historical Perspective', *Socialist Review*, No. 57, 1981, pp. 9–53.

3 Eric Hobsbawm, op. cit., p. 78.

4 World Bank estimate (*Neue Zürcher Zeitung*, 11 February 1984).

5 For a recent study on this subject, see Ernest Feder, *Perverse Development*, Foundation for Nationalist Studies, Quezon City, 1983.

6 The growth of military spending of developing countries over the period 1972–1981 was about twice as high as that of their gross domestic product. See *Trade and Development Report 1982*, (UNCTAD/TDR/2/Rev. 1), United Nations publication, Sales No. E. 82.II.D.12, paras. 536–550.

7 The bourgeois-military class still ruling in a certain country once justified the liquidation of a bourgeois-democratic government on the grounds that it would install an exemplary model of stable economic, social and political development for the periphery as prescribed by neo-classical economics.

8 For a contribution to this debate, see Samir Amin, 'Crisis, Nationalism, and Socialism' in Samir Amin, Giovanni Arrighi, Andre Gunder Frank, and Immanuel Wallerstein, *Dynamics of Global Crisis*, Monthly Review Press, New York and London, 1982, p. 218; see also Samir Amin, 'After the New International Economic Order: The Future of International Economic Relations', *Trade and Development*, No. 4, 1982 United Nations publication, Sales No. E.83.II.D.1.

9 See Herbert Marcuse, *Counterrevolution and Revolt*, Beacon Press, Boston, 1972: 'The Western World has reached a new stage of development: now, the defence of the capitalist system requires the organization of counterrevolution at home and abroad . . . The counterrevolution is largely preventive and, in the Western World, altogether preventive' (pp. 1–2).

10 Cf. Samir Amin, 'La vocation africaine et asiatique du Marxisme'. Project 'Strategies for the Future of Africa', Dakar, 1983 (mimeo).

11 Mao Tse Tung, 'On the Tactics in the Struggle Against Japanese Imperialism' (27 September, 1935), *Selected Works*, Vol. I, Foreign Languages Press, Peking, 1968, pp. 153–178.

12 We cannot broach the question here whether this explanation, which certainly applies in cases like Brazil, fully accounts for cases like Zaire. Owing to Brazil's high level of integration into the world capitalist market economy, it dare not risk being unable to import the inputs indispensable for its economy, in particular petroleum and food for its huge urban masses, who lack access to direct subsistence. By contrast, a country like Zaire, with a relatively low degree of capitalist market integration, could (as Tanzania has done) risk being unable to pay for his imports, since its population could still, if necessary, resort to national sources of food and other vital materials.

13 Sally A. Shelton, Vice President of International Business Government Counsellors and from 1979 to 1981 US Ambassador in the Caribbean, puts it this way in an article contributed (together with Richard Nuccio) to the *New York Times*: 'This year's crisis will develop because, not in spite of,

the negotiation of their debt' (*International Herald Tribune*, 28–29 January 1984).

14 'The Terra Nova Statement on the International Monetary System and the Third World' (a working group to consider the nature of the international monetary system and its impact on Third World countries was convened at the Terra Nova Hotel, Kingston, Jamaica, 5–7 October 1979: the meeting was sponsored by the Dag Hammarskjöld Foundation, the Institute for Policy Studies (IPS), the International Foundation for Development Alternatives (IFDA), the Latin American Institute for Transnational Studies (ILET) and the Third World Forum, and organized with the collaboration of the National Planning Agency of Jamaica).

15 Henry A. Kissinger, 'Saving the World Economy', *Newsweek*, 24 January 1983.

5

From Atlantic Alliance to Pan-European Entente: Political Economic Alternatives*

Andre Gunder Frank

The days of the old 'Atlantic' system are over.
> Four Western Foreign Policy Institutes

The Alliance as it was is no longer.
> *International Herald Tribune*

A major crack in the Soviet bloc has become the occasion for nearly as big a crack in the West.
> *The Guardian*

Security in the West, Business in the East.
> *Neue Zürcher Zeitung*

Introduction

President Reagan's June 1982 decision to prohibit European subsidiaries and licencees of American firms from delivering components for the Soviet-European gas pipeline brought long-simmering conflicts within the Atlantic Alliance to a head and into the headlines. America's European allies were especially angered by the fact that the pipeline decision was taken only days after American implicit promises not to do so at the June 1982 Western economic summit at Versailles and NATO summit in Bonn, and it provoked the resignation of Secretary of State Alexander Haig in protest. The Europeans sent several ministerial delegations to the United States to protest against the violation of their sovereignty and, on his American tour, West German

*Revised and extended versions of this chapter have been published separately by the author in book form under the title *The European Challenge: From Atlantic Alliance to Pan-European Entente for Peace and Jobs*, (Nottingham, Spokeman Books, 1983 and Westport, Conn., USA, Lawrence Hill & Co., 1984). The author and the present publisher wish to thank these publishers for their permission to include this earlier – and now summary – version in the present volume.

Chancellor Schmidt demanded the retraction of the decision and the limitation of the damage already done to Atlantic Alliance relations.

The *Financial Times* (30 June, 1982) editorialized under the title 'Europe at odds with Reagan':

> It is a measure of the perturbed state of the Western world that the leaders of the European Community at an EEC summit . . . should have drafted communiques concerned predominantly with external affairs. The theme which united both main statements – on the crisis in Lebanon and on US-Common Market relations – is the rift which has suddenly re-opened between the American and the European halves of the NATO alliance. The virtuous-sounding undertakings of the Versailles summit are now shown up to have been little more than a papering-over of that rift.

> Painful developments have taken place since they were made. The US has turned a blind eye to an Israeli invasion of Lebanon. Mr. Alexander Haig, an unsatisfactory US Secretary of State, who, nevertheless, provided a link between Europe and the Reagan Administration, has resigned. The US has attacked European sales of steel to America with anti-dumping levies. The US has abruptly blocked European subsidiaries and licensees of US companies from participating in the Russian gas pipeline project. And in the background, the US monetary squeeze has re-asserted itself, driving dollar interest rates and the dollar exchange rate upwards. In Europe there is not only anger about these developments in themselves but also a mounting disquiet about the US administration which has unleashed them.

The West German Minister of Economics, Otto Graf Lambsdorff, warned in the *Washington Post* that 'the West European reaction to the embargo decision, however, should give the White House cause to reconsider . . . The West Europeans are in agreement . . . The principle of extra-territoriality in US government decisions is unacceptable to us. It violates our sovereignty. Therefore, we have to reject it . . . Above all, the harsh words of President Reagan's closest ally, British Prime Minister Margaret Thatcher, are an alarming signal of discontent within the alliance' (reprinted in *International Herald Tribune*, 1 August, 1982).

This essay examines this growing disarray and discontent within the Atlantic Alliance and the transformation of the balance of power between Europe and America, especially in the economic field. This is followed by a review of the growing political-economic conflicts in the Soviet Union and Eastern Europe and by an examination of the economic basis that they offer for Pan European political economic and strategic alternatives and possibilities for the world peace movement and a European de-nuclearized zone, which could help avert nuclear war in Europe.

In early 1981 the growing rift in the Atlantic Alliance was the subject of an important study issued jointly by the four most influential American, British, German and French foreign policy institutes, entitled *Western Security: What has changed? What should be done*.[1]

The days of the old 'Atlantic' system, based on US predominance and its corollary, European reluctance to take wider responsibilities are over (p. 17).

It is particularly striking to note that the prevailing debate over the future of American-European relations (as well as East-West relations) revolves around two opposite nostalgias: on the European side, it is the nostalgia for the far-reaching detente hoped for in the early 1970s . . . A similar phenomenon is at work in the United States. Here, a growing aspiration is to return to the era of US supremacy and absolute leadership in world affairs. This is translated in the resurgent tendency to consider every event in the world in purely East-West terms, and the use of force as the panacea for most such issues (p. 18).

The common denominator is the relative decline of US power over the past decade and a half (in political and economic terms in the first instance, in military terms in the second) . . . The transformation of the balance of power between Europe and America has been most spectacular in the economic field. Here the American supremacy of the immediate post-war period has been replaced by a situation in which the European Community as a whole has become as rich as the US and often more competitive on the world market. As a result, the ability of the United States to influence European policy in accordance with its own interests has sharply declined. Conversely, the Europeans have shown a greater willingness and ability to defend their own interests against those of the United States, where these have diverged. Examples are the German-American quarrel over the 'locomotive theory' and the European-American controversy over nuclear energy and non-proliferation. In the monetary field, the creation of the European Monetary System was aimed to a large extent at shielding Europe from the consequences of the decline of the dollar-based international monetary system (p. 12).

Militarily, Europe as a whole remains dependent on the nuclear guarantee provided by the United States . . . Nonetheless despite the decision laboriously reached by NATO in December 1979, the modernization of long range theatre nuclear forces (LRTNF) in Europe remains in doubt . . . Similarly, disagreements over the Middle East and policy towards Iran also sharpened (p. 8).

Divergences bear not just on isolated problems, but on a whole spectrum of issues, ranging from defence to economics and basic foreign policy . . . Because of the magnitude of these disagreements and divisions, actual and potential . . . the authors have decided jointly to write this Report (p. 9).

This increasing tension in and threat to the Atlantic Alliance is widely echoed elsewhere. For instance the American magazine *Newsweek* and the *International Herald Tribune* (25 January, 1982) editorialized under the title 'The Alliance as It Was Is No Longer' and suggests that 'perhaps it was always doomed . . . We could have been living in a nuclear-armed fool's paradise all these years. But that was then. The question now is what variation on the alliance or substitution for it can fill the void?' The *Financial Times* (14 April, 1982) informs that 'Professor Hedley Bull, a prominent international affairs specialist, argued that the countries of Western Europe are now perfectly capable of providing for their own defence, and that they must do so because of the underlying divergence of interests between them and the United States. In particular . . . over the Soviet Union'. *The Guardian* (23 December, 1981) commented on military rule in Poland and observed that 'the trouble with East-West crises, is that they all too rapidly turn into West-West crises. So it is again'. Another aspect of the situation is that 'trade problems between Japan and the West are much worse than most people realise and could . . . lead to a breakdown of free trade between Japan and the US and Japan and Europe' (*Financial Times*, 26 January, 1982). The *International Herald Tribune* quotes an OECD official's evaluation of the 'wave of protectionism spreading among Western industrial nations': 'we are facing a situation potentially as dangerous as the 1930s' and the *Financial Times* (23 December, 1981) editorializes under the title 'Sick patient, no cure': 'the most depressing aspect of the latest (OECD) report is the virtual absence of all economic prescription . . . The need for economic co-ordination and guidance is much greater today than it was then, yet the OECD is apparently much less able to provide them'. On the contrary, as the *International Herald Tribune* (11 May, 1982) headlines 'Divided on Tactics in Recession, OECD Nations Take Separate Paths'. *The Guardian* (19 February, 1982) quotes the then West German Chancellor Helmut Schmidt: 'For my taste, there is too much talk about so-called strategic questions in the military and political field, and too little talk and too little co-operation in the economic field. We have not seen a world economic recession of this degree since the 1930s. One could easily turn this into a general depression of the Western world'. (Subsequently, President Reagan's ban on foreign gas pipeline component deliveries to the Soviet Union led to a storm of European protest and the US Secretary of State's resignation.)

The above quotations and expressions of serious concern reflect world developments that cannot be brushed off lightly as accidental or momentary aberrations in an otherwise harmonious development. The background and causes of these recent and prospective developments should be sought in the long run development of the world economy, with its apparently regular long waves of economic growth alternating with relative stagnation or crisis, the tendency of hegemonic powers to decline first relatively and then absolutely – economically, politically, militarily and financially more or less in that order – in the course of successive crises, and their replacement by others who are more success- ful in adjusting to the exigencies and opportunities presented by renewed world economic crisis. Although this long run structure and development of the world economic and political system is beyond the immediate scope of this paper it is useful to keep it in mind as a back- drop to the recent development.

A related fundamental background, if not cause of these shifts in world political economic power and international relations that are the centre of attention in this essay, is the current world economic crisis, which must remain beyond our scope here but which the present author has examined in recent books and articles.[2] Briefly, it appears that, since about 1967, the world capitalist economy – but with very far-reaching repercussions also in the socialist ones – has entered another of its periodically recurrent major crises, of over-accumulation of capital. In such crises, profits, investment and economic and produc- tivity growth rates decline or even turn negative and the most far- reaching economic, political and social transformations must occur to lay the basis for a possible renewed period of expansion, such as that of the two post Second World War decades. The last such crisis period lasted from 1914 to 1945 and included two world wars, two major socialist revolutions, the intervening Great Depression of the 1930s (but whose roots began earlier), the rise of fascism, and the final replace- ment of British by American hegemony. The analogous crisis of a century ago started in 1873 and was accompanied by the rise of monopoly capitalism, classical imperialism and renewed colonialism. In each of these – and also earlier – major crises, capitalist competition became more acute as the growth of the world economic pie slowed down and political relations sharpened, leading for instance to renewed colonialism and major war in the last two crises respectively. Analogous convulsions during the present crisis should not be unexpected.

It is not necessary to share this author's interpretation of the nature of the world economic crisis to observe its all too visible manifestations, such as low growth rates, high unemployment, and changing competi- tion and division of labour as well as distribution of political power. For instance, one of the most unpleasant manifestations of the current crisis, unemployment as officially registered but actually under- estimated in the Western industrialized countries, more than doubled from less than 7 million in the 1967 recession to 15 million in the 1973–75 recession and then more than doubled again to 32 million at the time of writing in the 1979–82 recession, and it is certain to continue rising even further and by some predictions even to double once again.

The growth rates of production (or real output) and of productivity (or output per unit of labour input) in each of the major Western economies from 1960 to 1981 are summarized in Table 5.1 below, which also distinguishes between the periods before and after 1973, which marked the beginning for the first major post-war recession. The table shows that growth rates of output in the period since 1973 have fallen to half or less (excepting for the nearly half in the United States) of their averages for 14 years before 1973. Growth rates of labour productivity have fallen even more drastically in some economies to a third or a fourth (in Canada even a tenth) and in Germany and France to about 60 per cent of their previous averages. Productivity in the United States even declined absolutely during the three years 1978, 1979 and 1980, which overlapped with the renewed recession that began in 1979 (*Economic Report of the President*, February 1983, p. 279).

Table 5.1 *Growth rates of real output, 1960–81* (per cent)

| | Total | | Per capita | | Per unit of labour input | |
	1960–73	*1973–81*	*1960–73*	*1973–81*	*1960–73*	*1973–81*
	(1)	*(2)*	*(3)*	*(4)*	*(5)*	*(6)*
United States	4.2	2.3	3.0	1.2	3.1	0.9
Japan	10.5	3.8	9.3	2.9	9.9	3.6
Germany	4.8	1.9	3.9	2.0	5.8	3.3
France	5.7	2.5	4.6	2.2	5.9	3.4
United Kingdom	3.2	0.5	2.7	0.5	3.8	1.8
Italy	5.2	2.4	4.4	2.0	7.8	1.4
Canada	5.4	2.4	3.7	1.7	4.2	0.4

Note: Data for France, Italy, and the United Kingdom are based on gross domestic product. Data for the other countries are based on gross national product.
Source: Cols. 1, 2, 3, 4: International Monetary Fund, *International Financial Statistics*, various issues. 1981 partly estimated by the American Enterprise Institute. Cols. 5 and 6, 1973–1979: John W. Kendrick, 'International Comparisons of Recent Productivity Trends' in *Essays in Contemporary Economic Problems*, ed. William Fellner, 1981–82 edition (Washington, DC: American Enterprise Institute, 1981), p. 128. Col. 6, 1979–81: Organization for Economic Cooperation and Development, *Economic Outlook*, December, 1981, p. 46.
Source: The AEI Economist, 1 May, 1982.

The balance of power and the competitive rivalries within the West, however, are even more affected by the *difference* in growth rates of output and especially of productivity among the major Western economies. Over the entire period, the strongest and oldest economies, the United States and Britain, have held the lowest growth rates of both output and productivity. Until 1973, productivity in the major Continental European economies grew at nearly 6 per cent or almost twice as fast as the c. 3 per cent annual growth in the United States (and 3.8 per cent in Britain); and in Japan productivity rose at 10 per cent per year, or nearly twice as fast as the United States. When all the growth rates of output and productivity declined after 1973, Japan experienced the greatest absolute decline to 3.6 per cent and the United States the greatest relative decline to less than 1 per cent per year in productivity growth rates; while European rates only declined by less than half to over 3 per cent (and 1.8 per cent in Britain). Thus, as all the economies slowed down, the Japanese, who still lag absolutely behind in the pro- ductivity race, were catching up more slowly with the Europeans, although both of them were still running faster than the United States. (For a discussion of relative productivity changes, see Kendrick 1981 and UNECE 1982, pp. 73–97.)[3] On the other hand, a recent European Economic Commission study suggests that this European productivity is concentrated in medium-technology industrial products, while Euro- pean productivity and exports in the most advanced high-technology fields is seriously lagging – or comparatively declining – compared with both Japan and the United States over the past decade (*Business International*, 30 April, 1982; *Financial Times*, 6 December 1982).

These absolute and relative changes in growth rates of output and productivity have been the basis of substantial modifications of relative competitiveness in the world economy and in the balance of power and the degree of competition on the world market (as the foreign policy institutes observed); the devaluation of the dollar especially relative to the German mark and Japanese yen; the consequent relative changes in the 1970s of labour costs and earnings, which have risen particularly in Europe and declined relatively and in some cases absolutely to lower levels in the United States; the shift in the direction of foreign invest- ment across the Atlantic and of the shares in the Third World, and the transformation of the international balance of power and interests generally. A vivid manifestation of these transformations in the world economy is that at the end of the 1970s West Germany had overtaken the United States as the world's largest exporter, with Japan coming up fast behind.

The recent and prospective developments in the Atlantic Alliance and East-West and trilateral relations with Japan as well as North-South relations derive most immediately from recent changes in growth rates of economic, and especially industrial, production and productivity both over time and relatively as between different (country or regional) parts of the world economy. It is these economic changes which form the basis of 'the transformation of the balance of power between Europe and America' as the four foreign policy institutes rightly observe. Since this shift has been from America to Europe and particu- larly to Germany, it is not surprising that the view of the West German Chancellor is that economic matters should receive more attention and strategic ones, where America retains greater dominance, should be de-emphasized in international affairs.

Economic crisis and increasingly conflictual political relations are, however, also very manifest in and between the Soviet Union and Eastern Europe, China and Vietnam and within the Third World and particularly Western relations and all these regions. All of these are generating or aggravating conflicts of interest and new disputes about different alternatives for their resolution. We will examine some of these conflicts and alternatives with regard particularly to emerging strains within the Atlantic Alliance and Western Europe, difficulties within the Soviet Bloc and Eastern Europe, and European political economic policy alternatives particularly in Western Europe in the face of the world economic and political crisis.

West-West conflict

As the four foreign policy institutes observe, the increasing divergences within the Atlantic Alliance bear not just on isolated problems but on a whole spectrum of issues, through which they are interlinked. For the sake of convenience, we may classify these issues, conflicts of interest and disagreements over policy in the Atlantic into three major groups: *firstly*, economic policy, primarily in the United States and secondarily in Europe and Japan; *secondly*, trade relations and policy, with regard to each other and to third parties, especially Japan and the Third World with particular emphasis on the Middle East; and *thirdly*, East-West relations.

Western conflicts over economic policy

Conflicts of interest and disagreements over economic policy grew in the 1960s as the United States engaged in and increasingly abused inflationary finance of the Vietnam war, which flooded the world with dollars that Europe was obliged to accept and hold because the dollar was 'as good as gold' as the only international reserve currency, even though its value increasingly declined and the Americans used newly printed and devalued dollars to buy up European industry virtually free of charge through what was still called 'American foreign investment'. De Gaulle reacted by cashing French held dollars at the US Treasury for gold. As the American ability to back the dollar with gold declined at the same time as the competitiveness of its exports did (as observed above) and the 1969–70 recession aggravated matters further, President Nixon took the dollar off gold on 15 August, 1971 and began effectively to devalue the dollar. This measure laid the basis for a major American drive to increase exports, especially of agricultural products and military hardward, in order to restore at once US companies' balance sheets

and the US balance of trade and payments, which had seriously deteriorated. These measures were quite successful particularly in 1972 and to
varying degrees later in the 1970s.

However, this American economic offensive was undertaken at the
expense of the Japanese (who called its initiation 'Nixon shokku' especially inasmuch as they were initially penalized by a discriminatory 10
per cent export surtax) and the Europeans. Despite some adjustments,
their exchange rates remained effectively pegged to the dollar by the
Bretton Woods (1944) and Smithsonian (1972) agreements, which
exposed their economies to the vicissitudes of the American economy
and dollar, and especially to speculation with their currencies, which
their central banks were obliged to try – unsuccessfully – to counteract
by buying and selling these currencies on the open market. Therefore,
on 19 March, 1973 the post-war system of fixed exchange rates was
abandoned and replaced by one of flexible exchange rates in which all
the currencies floated up and down against each other in response to
supply and demand. It was hoped that this floating flexibility would
take the wind out of speculator's sails, but it only made speculation
steadier and reduced sudden runs on the banks. Changes in the now
flexible exchange rates helped to act as shock absorbers in the
international transmission of waves of inflation and deflation, which
mostly originate in the United States. However, this partial protection
of the national economies has been bought at the cost of fluctuations
that render all price and cost calculations insecure. Accordingly, West
Germany sought to dilute the effects of these shocks and uncertainties
on itself by spreading them wider over her European trading partners'
economies. The solution, which Germany bought at the cost of other
economic guarantees to her major trading partners, was first the
'snake' (1972) and then the EMS or European Monetary System (in
1979) in which the French, Benelux later, the Italian and some other
currencies fluctuate within a maximum and minimum band of rates and
wiggle in unison against the dollar like a snake. The EMS is designed
essentially to protect Germany and France from fluctuations in the
dollar, the vagaries of the American economy, and US economic
policy. Britain has steadfastly refused to join in Germany's snake and
EMS embrace.

The devaluation of the dollar, to which many other currencies elsewhere in the world remained pegged in fact if not in law, did much to
restore US competitiveness in Europe and third markets and to raise the
cost of European and Japanese exports in the US. On the other hand, it
cheapened the purchase price of US assets for the Europeans and the
Japanese. These complementary factors plus the elevation of wage
rates in Europe/decline of wage costs in America relative to each other
tended to reverse the flow of foreign investment across the Atlantic and
to a lesser degree across the Pacific, so that foreign investment in the
United States rose significantly during the 1970s, while some American

investment was repatriated from abroad. The manufacture of German Volkswagens and Japanese TV sets in the US are well known examples of the former and the divestiture of Chrysler subsidiaries in Europe of the latter.

The common recession in 1973–75 and the weak recovery, especially in much of Europe, from 1975–79, the continuing inflation throughout, and the renewed recession and American policy since then have served to generate or strengthen other major conflicts of interest and policy disagreements. Some of these have been more out in the open than others. Among the latter is perhaps that of the price of oil. It has been suggested that the American response to European economic challenge was deliberately to penalize and weaken the Europeans and Japanese again by obliging them to pay more for the oil on whose import they (and the Japanese for nearly 100 per cent) are much more dependent than the US. American oil production maintained the domestic price at about half the level to which it was elevated in 1973–74 and again in 1979 by OPEC and other oil producers – and mostly American-owned Seven Sister major oil companies, whose profits rose spectacularly – and, it is sometimes claimed, by American government connivance or agreement. What is a matter of public record is that the then US Secretary of State, Henry Kissinger, was the first to propose a floor price for oil, under which it should not be allowed to sink again. It is also a matter of public knowledge that during the mid-1970s European and Japanese resistance to American pressures weakened again in public international conferences and apparently in negotiations behind closed doors.

Nonetheless, and counter to the expectations of many – and hopes of some? – American dependence on oil imports and their balance of payments costs was not quickly reduced but rather the opposite; and Germany and Japan weathered the oil price storm by increasing their exports despite strong currencies, particularly to the OPEC Middle East and socialist countries. As a result, they achieved a large balance of trade and some balance of payments surpluses in the mid 1970s. The Americans were pursuing relatively deflationary monetary and fiscal policies, supposedly to combat inflation during and after the 1973–75 recession. Since these policies put a brake on the recovery of the world economy, the Americans began to argue that the countries with a balance of payments surplus and a lower rate of inflation should prime the economic pump through reflation – which the Americans themselves refused to do – and become the 'locomotive' to pull the world economy out of the doldrums. This American locomotive theory and its subsequent elongation into a convoy theory became major issues at the 1977 and 1978 economic summit meetings. The Germans and Japanese resisted the American pressure and rebutted their argument with the contention that their economies were too small to serve as locomotives for the world and that any effort to do so would only lead to domestic inflation. That is, reflation in these smaller national economies would price them out of the competitive world market and destroy their balance of payments. The size and relative isolation from foreign trade and the American economy (although even there exports doubled from 5 to 10 per cent of GNP while they rose from 7 to 15 per cent in Japan over the decade of the 70s) and the still relatively dominant dollar reserve currency, allows the US to pursue its own economic policies to a considerable extent without too much regard for any repercussions at home of its effects abroad – and the devil take the hindmost elsewhere. But the smaller more trade-dependent European and Japanese economies, whose currencies are only beginning to rival the dollar, still lack this degree of economic independence. (This fact of life is illustrated by the opposite but common negative international boomerang repercussions on their own economies of Mrs Thatcher's domestic deflation with a high North Sea petropound in Britain and President Mitterrand's reflation with a twice devalued franc in France in the early 1980s and will form part of the basis of our discussion of European economic policy below.)

The continued relative economic independence of the United States and its damned if they do, damned if they don't repercussions on Europe and Japan (not to mention the still weaker Third World economies) also made itself felt through the increasingly serious conflicts of interest and policy disagreements first over American balance of payments deficits and then over skyhigh American interest rates. In the late 1970s, the growing American balance of payments deficit drove down the dollar to the increasing annoyance of the Europeans, whose competitiveness was thereby weakened. On both sides of the Atlantic, much of the reason for the American trade and payments deficit was attributed to growing and increasing costly oil imports. The Europeans and Japanese began to demand effective restrictions of American consumption and importation of oil, while President Carter claimed that he was quite unable to force his national energy (saving and alternative synfuels) programme on an unwilling Congress and public, not to mention on the uncooperative oil companies and their powerful allies. In fact Carter's programme was a total failure as American oil dependence increased rather than decreased; and the Europeans vainly cried in the wind.

The turnaround on the US balance of payments and the effects of US economic policy on Europe and Japan came not as a change of policy but from a downturn of the underlying economic cycle. In mid-1979 the long awaited recession arrived in America. After a partial and brief recovery during late 1980 and early 1981, the recession became much deeper again in the United States and spread to Europe, Japan, and the rest of the world in 1981 and 1982. One result was that the consumption, import, price, and purchase cost of oil plummeted as a worldwide oil glut replaced its supposed scarcity. The American balance of payments deficits declined through lower import demand and expenditures on oil and other commodities (with raw materials in mid-1982 at so far rockbottom prices). The new American administration instituted its so-called new Reaganomic monetarist and supply-side policies, which (like Thatcherism in the UK) simply carried to their logical conclusion the policies begun during the preceding administration. However, Reagonomics – also like Thatcherism before it – has not succeeded[4] particularly in reducing government budget deficits, which have instead grown to over $100 billion in the US and obliged the government to borrow money on the open market to fill up this hole in its pocket, thereby helping to drive up the interest rate cost of the money borrowed by itself – and everybody else. The American shift from negative interest rates (that were lower than the rate of inflation for most of the 1970s) to real interest rates of 6, 7 and up to 10 per cent has attracted a flood of money into the dollar, whose value rose again on most foreign exchange markets; and it has obliged everybody else either to let their own currencies fall through the floor thereby feeding inflation or to follow the American suit in raising interest rates and the cost of borrowing, thereby choking off investment in an already very recessive national and world economy.

The Europeans and Japanese are objecting, again, this time because the American dollar and the rate of interest are too high. This issue has replaced the previous ones as the major bone of contention between the Europeans and Japanese (who witnessed an unexpected massive capital flight from the therefore weak yen to higher interest currencies) and the Americans at the 1981 Ottawa and 1982 Versailles summits and numerous confrontations in between. However, this new conflict has become meshed with a whole spectrum of others with regard to issues of international trade policy between West and West, West and South, and finally West and East, which we may examine under these titles. One of the real but rarely mentioned links is that, if interest rates are elevated by the budget conflict, that deficit in turn is elevated by increased defence spending in the American cold and economic war against the Soviet Union.

Western conflicts over international trade

West-West political economic conflicts of interest and policy disagreements or even battles are seriously shaking the Atlantic Alliance and Pacific relations. Indeed, the press headlines 'US faces up to "real threat" of trade war with Europe' (*Financial Times*, 14 June, 1982) and 'US-European Trade "Shooting War" Feared' (*International Herald Tribune*, 26 January, 1982) and speak of an impeding 'breakdown of free trade' with Japan (*Financial Times*, 26 January, 1982).

The large Japanese trade surplus with the United States and Europe, and the repeated failures so far to eliminate or significantly reduce it, are well publicized in the West. What is not usually mentioned, however, is that Japan absolutely needs such a surplus in its American and European trade to cover its unavoidably huge deficits with its Middle Eastern and Asian suppliers of oil and raw materials, on which Japan is nearly 100 per cent import dependent; these oil supply economies could not possibly absorb an equivalent sum of industrial imports from Japan in exchange. Therefore, the maintenance of this triangular trade relationship of deficit with the South and surplus with the West is literally a matter of life or death for Japan. No wonder then that Japanese officials and business regard Western pressures to reduce the trade gap with them as the threat of a 'trade war' in which they have no choice but to defend themselves at all costs.

The penetration of the American market by Japanese automobiles, TV sets, photographic equipment, and a myriad of other consumer products as well as steel and now even the threat from advancing Japanese high technology in electronic components and other producer goods is well known. So is the American insistence that Japan open its markets to imports of Western industrial goods and services, including banking. Less well known, except in Japan itself, are the huge Japanese imports of American agricultural products and the Japanese threats of consumer boycotts against American beef and oranges in retaliation against American pressures and complaints. However, when forced to choose among unpalatable alternatives, Japan is likely to prefer its economic and political alliance with the United States and the latter is increasingly leaning to a Pacific Rim strategy (to be examined below). In any event, the first option of United States policy with regard to its economic conflict with Japan has been to try to shift the burden of adjustment onto the back of Europe. If the Americans want to reduce their take of Japanese exports, let the Japanese sell them in Europe and elsewhere. The former French Ambassador to Japan observed that Japan needs the United States but believes it can do without Europe, a view confirmed by Japanese officials who privately regard Europe as a declining power whose national markets can be picked off one by one (*International Herald Tribune*, 27 May, 1982).

In the face of the increasing gravity of the economic crisis in Western Europe, both absolutely and relatively to the US, (which recovered more in 1975–79 and again briefly in 1981), the Japanese export offensive in Europe is anything but welcome. On the contrary, the Vice-president of the European Economic Commission suggests that 'trade problems between Japan and the West . . . could lead Europe to impose a total ban on Japanese imports', while in the Commission itself 'Japan [is] seen as 'most vulnerable' to trade pressures . . . [and] liable to become the first victim of EEC trade curbs' (*Financial Times*, 26 January and 8 February 1982). Thus, the immediate economic basis for a major West-West economic conflict between Europe and Japan already exists. A longer historical perspective should lead us to expect the most serious rivalry to develop between the principal contenders for the hegemony of the declining economic power in the world with a tactical alliance between the latter and one of the major contenders. Thus, previously Germany and America fought for the mantle of Great Britain, which took the side of the ultimate winner in the conflict. Since similar situations had also developed earlier in world history, it would not be surprising if an analogous struggle and even the eventual victory of Japan in alliance with the declining America should develop in the future.

Other serious economic conflicts of interest and policy have developed between the United States and Western Europe over trade, particularly in petrochemical products, steel, and agricultural products and policy. The conflict about American oil consumption based on low domestic prices was not only about the American balance of payments and its effects on the dollar, but also about the European balance of payments and industrial profits in the face of American exports. Cheap oil in the US also subsidizes American petrochemical products, which are either exported to Europe at prices with which European high oil cost producers cannot compete during a time of crisis in the world petrochemical industry; or the cheaper petrochemicals are converted into synthetic fibres for the textile and other industries that compete with European ones that are in an even deeper crisis. Understandably, European producers have raised alarmed cries of unfair competition from America and have used the Multifibre Arrangement (MFA) to turn against more defenceless low labour cost textile exporters in Asia and Brazil to restrict their penetration of the European (and American) markets. Only the high dollar has reduced the American petrochemical/textile offensive.

Another major and growing conflict turns around steel. The world steel industry has been in the doldrums since 1973, and lagging or declining industrial investment and construction have sharply reduced steel demand and prices. Even after numerous steel mill shutdowns and/or labour dismissals, which have caused widespread social and political uproar all over Britain, Germany's Ruhr region, France's Lorraine, Belgium's Wallonia, Youngstown, Ohio in the US and elsewhere, much of the Western world's steel industry is working to only 60 to 80 per cent of capacity. In June 1982, capacity utilization in the American steel industry dropped to 42 per cent, the lowest since 1938. Productivity in modern Japanese steel mills is over twice as high and labour costs less than half of the United States, with West European producers (except the British) in between. Accordingly, both Japanese and European steelmakers have been increasingly able to penetrate the American market to compensate a bit for the weakness of their own (and the Europeans to cushion the effects of the necessary reorganization of their steel industry through intra-EEC cartel-like export quotas) but to the increasing chagrin and fury of American steel producers and workers. American steel consumption declined from about 120 million tons in 1973 to 100 million tons in 1975 and again in 1981. In the meantime, imports increased from 15 to 20 million tons, of which 6 million originated in Western Europe and raised their share of American consumption from 13 to 20 per cent (*Financial Times*, 10th June, 1982, citing the American Iron and Steel Institute and the US Department of Commerce). The Americans charge that, beyond productivity advantages, the European exporters enjoy cost advantages from European government subsidies rangling from $50 to $300 for a ton of steel that sells in the US for $500. To counteract this foreign steel invasion, the US government proposed so-called trigger prices based on estimated Japanese and European costs of production below which it would restrict imports. The never very satisfactory measure went on and off and on again, until the present recession depressed the American domestic steel price itself below the trigger price, and the high dollar cheapened the American price of European steel, which then made the whole scheme increasingly inoperative. The American steel companies took matters in their own hands and pressed a whole series of cases before the American courts and the US Department of Commerce to enjoin European producers from dumping, as the Americans claim, steel on their market. With the June 1982 American rulings in favour of the American steel companies and the imposition of US countervailing duties against them, the steel war between Europe and America was on. Moreover, the new American steel duties deliberately hit at the weaker and more subsidized British, French and Belgian producers than at the stronger German ones and were designed to sow discord among the Europeans and to impede their effort at EEC common agreement on the necessary restructuring of the European steel industry and the multilateral sharing of the apparently obligatory reduction of their steel export to the United States. Indeed, in the event West Germany did hold out against a common EEC agreement in Brussels until literally the eleventh hour of the American deadline for a settlement. The significance of these decisions and measures, 'goes well beyond the steel industry . . . and could well be applied to other products which benefit from government subsidies . . . [and] many set a precedent for other countries wishing to take action against subsidized imports' (*Financial Times*, 14 June, 1982).The European Economic Commission and its member governments sought countermeasures against the Americans. One of these was to take the dispute to GATT but at the very real risk of breaking the organization, or least its effectiveness in safeguarding international trade as well in other goods, if they cannot reach mutual agreement on steel. Another major field in which to look for them is agriculture – which by itself has been developing as an even more acrimonious Euro-American field of combat.

One of the paradoxes of world economic development is that the industrial capitalist economies are the most efficient producers of the major agricultural commodities, especially wheat and meat, but also other grains and dairy products. In addition, both the United States and Western Europe have been heavily subsidizing their farmers for decades, who respond with huge food surpluses that either accumulate as mountains of wheat and butter or are exported at below market prices, or both. Although another world food shortage (not so much physically as because of high prices that the poor cannot afford) even deeper and longer than that of 1972–74 is looming for the later 1980s, the early 1980s have witnessed a massive increase of agricultural market surpluses, plummeting prices; and American farmers, who suffer from sky-high interest rates to boot, saw their incomes fall by more than one-third, signifying their worst crisis since the one of the 1930s, which was so dramatically depicted in John Steinbeck's *Grapes of Wrath*.

Throughout the 1970s and spurred on by the devaluations since 1971 and the conversion of 'Food for Peace' (Public Law 480) to 'Food is a Weapon' (US Secretary of Agriculture Earl Butz) and 'Food is Power' (US Senator Hubert Humphrey), American commercial exports of agricultural products have soared. The Soviet 'great grain robbery' and the increasing import dependence of much of the Third World on American wheat have received wide publicity, but less so the equally significant Japanese imports and West European dependence on American soybean and corn-gluten feedstuffs to maintain their intensive feedlot livestock and the surplus-producing European meat and dairy industries. Moreover, Brazil is challenging the American soybean supremacy. Therefore, the Europeans are set to reduce their dependence on American feedstuffs. To the fury of the Americans, the Europeans have also launched their own export drive in a weak international market, partly to bolster their own balance of payments and mostly to rid themselves of their own expensive agricultural surpluses and thereby to reduce the costs of the Common Agricultural Policy, contributions to which have become politically increasingly divisive and difficult to squeeze out among member states. Therefore, the Reagan administration has begun to 'read the riot act' to the Europeans. It charges that the EEC share of world agricultural imports declined from 25 to 20 per cent, while EEC exports rose from 9 to 11 per cent between 1973 to 1980 (*Financial Times*, 8 February, 1982). The Reagan administration is gunning for EEC agricultural exports to Third World markets in the Middle East and Latin America and charging that these exports, like those of steel, are unfairly and illegally subsidized by the EEC. The US Secretary of Agriculture told Congress that 'we fear that the (EEC) is seeking to solve its internal agricultural overproduction and budget problems by converting CAP into a Common Export Policy based on extensive subsidies' (*International Herald Tribune*, 26 January, 1982).

In early 1982 warnings appeared that 'Washington has gone on the offensive in this now major US-EEC dispute' (*Financial Times*, 8 February, 1982). Then, the press warned that agricultural products, which are the major US export today, may prove to be the most serious trade conflict yet with Western Europe after the latter had successfully resisted the American demands for reduced European agricultural subsidies and protection at the November 1982 GATT ministerial meetings and immediately afterwards. The US Secretary of Agriculture John Block threatened, 'We have only one alternative. The alternative to deviate temporarily from our free-market stance and engage in costly short-run trade wars. If that is what it takes to achieve the principles of free markets, then we will have to start looking more seriously in that direction' and massively dump $3 billion worth of the greater American stockpiles of agricultural products on the world market until the Europeans give up (*Financial Times*, 23 November, 1982). The imminent threat of this new trade war by the US Secretary of Agriculture was only defused until March 1983 by the conciliatory quiet diplomacy of US Secretary of State George Schultz and the intervention of the US Secretary of the Treasury with his European and Japanese Finance Minister colleagues. They want to try and work out a multilateral multi-issue settlement and possibly a new institutional world financial set-up in the attempt to ward off a world financial crash and international trade breakdown in the wake of the inability of the world's three largest foreign debtor countries, Argentina, Mexico and Brazil, to pay their over $200 billion of debts. Indeed, Reaganomic ideology and US intransigence, which were still manifest in American opposition to increasing the IMF leading capacity at the IMF and World Bank meeting in Toronto in September 1982 and continued American pursuit of economic policy without regard to its effects on the rest of the world – bloody-minded unilateralism the *Financial Times* (11 December, 1982) called it – gave way by the end of 1982 to world reality and a more pragmatically universalist American realism. In face of the very real threat of total world economic collapse, the American administration opted for a perhaps last attempt to lead its allies to hang together economically on pain of hanging separately if the financial trap door under them crashes open.

West-West conflict over North-South trade

Transatlantic conflicts of interest and policy over international trade and foreign policy issues have increasingly shaped the North-South debates and negotiations in which the Americans and Europeans appear as competitors as often as allies. Through the late-1970s the American were joined and sometimes even outdone by the Germans in their hardline opposition to any concessions to Third World demands for a New International Economic Order (NIEO) at the many conferences and negotiations at the World Bank and International Monetary Fund and the 1977 International Finance Conference in Jamaica, the United Nations, FAO and Law of the Sea conferences, the

Paris North-South Dialogue, and elsewhere. The smaller European countries and especially the Scandinavian ones and Holland were always more conciliatory to Third World demands for bending, or, as the recalcitrant opponents claimed abrogating the sacred law of the market, in which the smaller European industries and countries also found themselves at a disadvantage second only to the Third World. More recently, however, Germany has also softened its line towards the Third World, and the American government has sought to impose its Reaganomic marketeering on the South almost alone, except for the loyal political support of Mrs Thatcher's Britain, while the Third World view has found its loudest northern echo in Mitterrand's Socialist Party government of France (which has not hesitated to continue pushing its arms exports to the Third World right behind the US and the USSR). For instance, the US unilaterally torpedoed the laboriously negotiated compromise on the UN Law of the Sea and dragged its feet alone on Global Negotiations (the new euphemism for the ill-fated NIEO) until Canada and France in particular elicited a grudging provisional go-ahead for the talks from Reagan only in return for concessions to the Americans' hardline on financial matters at the summits in Cancun, Mexico and Versailles.

The developments underlying these shifts in interest and policy seem to be that the Europeans have become much more competitive and competition-minded on Third World markets. An early manifestation of this development was the German proposal to sell nuclear power plants and fuels to Brazil and the French one to Pakistan in a very depressed international market on which the United States and the Soviet Union had previously had a virtual monopoly. The Americans immediately raised a storm of protest against the dangers of nuclear proliferation to Third World powers that might convert this technology and material into atomic bombs. In the meantime, the much more threatening development of the bomb by Israel and South Africa proceeded much more quietly, while the Brazilian and Pakistani projects were put on ice under American pressure.

European and American competition also noticeably increased in each others' economic backyards and political spheres of interest in the Third World. The Europeans and the Japanese increased their penetration of traditionally US markets in Latin America in everything from automobiles, equipment and machinery, to agricultural products. The Third World magazine *South* (February 1982) reported that the EEC, 'is planning closer trade and economic links with Central America, including a cooperation agreement and increased financial assistance for eight states'. This initiative is backed by France and Germany, but 'the United States will consider any 'special relationship' with these eight states an intrusion into its own sphere of influence. There has been speculation that the US may retaliate by making inroads into the southern Mediterranean states, the EEC's "backyard".' The political accompaniment to this eagerly pursued incipient and fervently hoped for penetration of previously private American economic hunting preserves has been the increasingly vocal overtures and political-economic support of social democratic Second International parties and even armed political movements in Latin America by European and especially German social democracy, under the leadership of Willy Brandt, while the Americans back the military dictatorships and at best Christian Democratic civilian alternatives in Latin America. The resulting political conflict became most visible through European social democratic support for the Sandinista movement and then government in Nicaragua and for the opposition to the American-backed government in El Salvador. Ironically (but as we may observe in the review of East-West relations below, not so uncharacteristically) the Reagan administration White Paper on El Salvador in early 1981 called the opposition a typically Soviet communist plot when the Soviet Union or Cuba had sent no material support to the rebels but the West German Social Democrats had! The French competed with the US for Mexican oil while it was still scarce and then underlined the continuing transatlantic conflict of interest and policy over Central America by selling arms to the Sandinista government in Nicaragua.

Only over the war in the Falklands/Malvinas Islands have the Americans and Europeans lined up on the same side with Britain, though the West Germans have done so very halfheartedly to protect their NATO interests and collaboration with Britain, while the French Socialist Government has lent Britain its fullest support, possibly with a view to receiving the same when her own remaining colonial possessions may be threatened.

The opposite is happening in Africa, where the Americans seek to penetrate French and British markets, inherited from the latter's colonial empires and then consecrated through the Lomé Convention between the EEC and the ACP (Africa, Caribbean, Pacific) countries, which inevitably also opened the door to West Germany. This treaty provides for preferential trade and some price support for trade between ACP countries and the EEC. United States policy is trying to mobilize opposition to the Lomé Convention amongst the countries who are supposedly discriminated against through their exclusion from this arrangement by virtue of their not having been French or British colonies! The US is also encouraging ACP objections to EEC extension of trade agreements to non-member states in Central America. The *New York Times* (7 March, 1982) quotes David Rockefeller as recently telling Africans that his Chase Manhattan Bank 'has found that we can deal with almost any kind of government as long as it is methodical and responsible . . . The more African countries I see who call themselves marxist, the more it seems to me that this is a matter of labels and ornaments, and not of realities', adding that therefore he does not regard African marxism to be a threat to the United States or to the interests of its firms (retranslated from the Spanish in *Comercio Exterior*, May 1982). At the same time, the United States is courting the still predominantly British South Africa for its raw materials, lucrative market and strategic position.

East Asia and increasingly Australia have been left substantially to Japan, and India to the Soviet Union, but both the Americans and the Europeans are making some efforts to reassert their economic and political influence in the region generally and especially in and in part through China. However, the more Japan is excluded by European or American competition elsewhere, the greater will its dependence be on Asia. There is a possible revival of the Japanese 'Greater East Asian Co-Prosperity Sphere' of the 1930s through the creation of a new Japan-Asia bloc in the 1980s or 1990s. The possible collaboration by China and the United States in a Pacific Basin and Rim strategy remains to be seen.

The main bone of contention between the Americans and Europeans, however, is the Middle East. Europe is highly dependent on oil imports from the Middle East and on exports to pay for them. Exports to the Middle East OPEC countries and the Socialist countries provided an essential safety net for the West, and especially for European heavy industry, during the slump of Western demand in the 1973–75 recession and its subsequent faltering recovery. The inability of both market areas to pay for similar imports and increases of Western exports during the 1979–1982 recession is a major reason for the failure of the European economies, which are much more dependent on them than the American, to weather the last recession as well as the previous one. Moreover, although the Europeans have a payments surplus with the Socialist and non-oil exporting Third World countries, the Europeans have a significant trade and payments deficit with the USA, Japan and of course OPEC. In view of the already reviewed trilateral conflict among the industrial capitalist regions of the West, it is all the more important for Europe to redress its deficit with the Middle East as much as possible by exporting there in return – and driving the Americans and Japanese out of these lucrative markets. This is the economic background for the European political disagreements with the United States about foreign policy with regard to Iran and the American embargo sparked by the US Tehran embassy 'hostage' crisis as well as with regard to the Israeli-Arab conflict and especially the Palestine issue. The Americans sponsored the Camp David accords between Israel and Egypt, for which the latter was isolated by other Arabs as a traitor to their cause. The Europeans, especially at their 1980 declaration in Venice, instead lent some support to the PLO and the formation of a separate Palestinian state (which are anathema to the Begin government in Israel, but are contemplated by its Peres Labour Party, and recommended by far-sighted Americans such as the former Under-Secretary of State, George Ball, who tirelessly insists that a settlement of the Israeli-Arab conflict and the Palestine issue on terms more favourable to the latter is essential to guard American interests in what he and others regard as the focal point of Western interests).

In this context, it is revealing that the above-cited four Western foreign policy institutes recognize this West-West conflict of interests and write in their chapter on 'The Security Situation in the Third World':

> We can also agree to take a relatively relaxed view about a number of so-called 'marxist' regimes in the Third World whose relationship with the Soviet Union is tenuous and cynical. Speaking merely in ideological terms, the Soviet drive in the Third World has been unsuccessful . . . and there are many countries whose political label as such does not hurt Western interests.

> *Where Western interests are at stake, Europe and the United States should agree on the need for a Western capacity to intervene and should take steps to improve their capacity for doing so.*

> At present the main region in the category is that of the Middle East and the Gulf . . . The threats to this supply [of oil] come from four main directions. *The menace of Soviet military power . . . National and ethnic rivalries . . . Revolution or internal disruption . . . A new Arab-Israel war . . .* The failure to solve the Palestinian problem is a permanent contribution to the instability of the whole area . . .

> These considerations point to active European military participation on the ground and at sea in the Middle East . . . [and] *the main burden of putting together a rapid deployment force falls on the United States, but the Europeans make some contribution in terms of men and material* (pp. 35–38, all emphasis in the original).

To organize the same, the report proposes seven-nation summits 'devoted at least as much to political and security concerns as to economic ones' and the formation of 'principal nations groups . . . [for] crisis management and joint assessments'. 'The first such group to be formed immediately should be on the Gulf/South West Asian region' (pp. 44–48). Nonetheless, in the face of a new Arab-Israeli war, timed by the latter's invasion of Lebanon to coincide with the Versailles economic and Bonn NATO summit meetings in June 1982, the assembled leaders of the West failed even to agree on a joint NATO statement, let alone action, to respond to the occasion, as the *Financial Times* (11 June 1982) observed in its editorial. But the European heads of state assembled at an EEC summit a couple of weeks later issued a joint communique demanding Israeli withdrawal from Lebanon, although without even hinting at an embargo on Israel, such as they imposed on Argentina over the conflict with Britain.

Western conflicts over East-West trade

Soviet armed intervention in Afghanistan in December 1979 is widely claimed to have undermined the East-West detente of the 1970s and to have ushered in the beginnings of a new cold war. But the Soviet Union had reason to believe that detente and especially its relations with the United States were deteriorating anyway, independently of Soviet policy: it had after all offered to defuse tension in Europe by pulling some of its troops out of East Germany. The United States, to the contrary, had in fact been blowing an increasingly cold war wind in the Soviet face for some time. The US Senate had been dragging its feet against ratifying the SALT II arms control treaty, so laboriously negotiated in good faith by the USSR with the US, while the latter was preparing and then announced a new programme to install intercontinental MX missiles in its Western states (whose vulnerability would only make them adequate for first-strike purposes). To add insult to injury, the US increasingly used its 'China card' against the Soviet Union. The Carter administration also pledged to increase real military expenditure by 3 per cent per year and elicited promises from its NATO partners to do the same (in an economic climate in which consumer investment and export demand were unstable or lagging). Most significantly, NATO had already taken its 'Two Track' decision to install new Pershing and Cruise missiles directed toward the Soviet Union from European soil by 1983 and in the meantime to use this track and threat to provide new arms control agreement with the Soviet Union on another track, that Carter's successor Reagan would baptize START. That is, the Carter administration had already been blowing very cool air on detente before the events in Afghanistan, which the US then used to justify even colder blows (and Carter himself used to take the wind out of the Kennedy challenge to his Democratic nomination) before Reagan defeated him and made the cold war wind even icier.

The new Reagan administration, in the throes of a nostalgia to make America No. 1 again, certainly developed what the four foreign policy institutes termed 'the tendency to consider every event in the world in purely East-West terms' to the nth degree. Among other things, it immediately set out to despatch Carter's modest 3 per cent annual increase of military expenditures to the garbage heap and to escalate the arms race several fold. Apart from the hoped for salutary economic effects of arms spending in the United States (which Reagan soon found to be dampened by their unsalutary effects on the budget deficit and Congress) the *Washington Post* editorialized, 'There is a crucial economic dimension to the Reagan strategy for dealing with Soviet power. It is that the Soviet Union, although a superpower, is relatively backward and cannot keep up in arms-building competition without suffering even harsher internal strains. This has been, of course, a familiar element in Western thinking about the Soviet Union since 1917 . . . It is being asked now, however, whether this time around the Soviet Union may not be near a bending point – some observers say a breaking point – after all' (*International Herald Tribune*, 19 November, 1981).

On the occasion of the dispute about the gas pipeline, the US Ambassador to France officially clarified: 'I welcome this opportunity to explain our actions. This is the background. The Soviet economy is in trouble . . . One is serious shortage of [foreign] currency in relation to ambitious five-year plans . . . Their foreign cash flow is down because of a drop in prices of oil' etc., and the United States wants to keep it down. The Ambassador goes on to explain that:

> I do not see the pipeline issue as primarily one of European dependence . . . The central point is that the Russians are in economic trouble . . . [and] the United States is perfectly justified in refusing actively to facilitate the quantum leap forward that will come from the Russians' expanded use of gas . . . [of which] 85 per cent is to be used to fuel Soviet internal industry . . . [and] provide the basis for further industrial expansion, which would otherwise be impossible . . . (and which) would have a profound beneficial effect on Soviet industrial, and subsequently Soviet military, capability . . . This view is the primary basis of the American measures against the Siberian pipeline' (*International Herald Tribune*, 24–25 July, 1982).

Of course, this new American economic offensive strategy against the Soviet Union also includes other moves. The Carter administration had used the Afghanistan issue to impose a grain embargo against the Soviet Union, which was broken by the Argentine military junta and never totally enforced even in North America and which the far right Republican candidate Reagan promised to annul, which he finally did. The US also lengthened the list of prohibited 'strategic' exports to the Soviet Union. The Americans boycotted the Moscow Olympics in the summer of 1980 and twisted as many allied arms as possible to do the same – with varying success in Europe in the face of their allies' responses, which varied from recalcitrance to grudging support (except from Mrs Thatcher, whose British athletes went to Moscow anyway). More seriously, the United States started trying to infuse the cold war Co-Com(mittee) with new life to procure agreement from its NATO allies to increase the list of industrial items whose export or licencing to the Soviet Union is embargoed for 'strategic' reasons. Since exports to the Soviet Union and Eastern Europe – except for grain – are small potatoes to the United States, it could well afford to press for such export prohibition. Its implementation would, however, impose a significant absolute loss of markets, profits and jobs on some European economies, and thereby help to weaken them relative to the United States to boot. Exports to the East account for 6 per cent of Western Europe, and 6 to 9 per cent of the exports and 1.5 per cent of the GNP of West Germany. But several hundred thousand jobs and untold profits depend directly on these exports from Germany and France and a small number of very large heavy industrial equipment firms and their banking connections would face serious losses from the reduction of trade with the Soviet Union and Eastern Europe. Some medium-sized German companies depend for 30 to 40 per cent of their trade with the East and would face bankruptcy by its elimination. Not surprisingly, therefore, the Europeans have steadfastly rejected most of the American proposals and the hypocrisy of their political justification in the face of renewed US grain exports to the Soviet Union. The American 'red alert' about technology transfer with subsidized credit to the Soviet Union and Eastern Europe awoke some Europeans but failed to move them.

This increasingly serious conflict of economic interest and acrimonious political disagreement over foreign policy came to a head over the crisis, martial law declaration, and debt management in Poland. The Americans sought to blame all of the events in Poland on the Soviet Union and to cut off trade and credits to both of them as much as possible. The American Secretary of Defence Weinberger even went so far as to propose that the West refuse all further credit rollover or refinancing of the US$27 billion Polish debt in order to force Poland into default and to oblige the Soviet Union to pick up the pieces and carry the burden. Secretary of State Haig replied that a Polish default could 'bring the ruin of East-West trade and mean the collapse of the West German economy' and other far-reaching and unpredictable effects and that 'had we followed the advice of some, we'd be in a hole . . . [and] have the Europeans side with the Russians' (*The Guardian*, 20 February, 1982). Wiser counsels in the Department of State and among virtually all Europeans involved prevailed to quash the Weinberger idea, whose implementation would also have seriously exposed several major European banks to failure and thereby threatened to start a chain reaction throughout the entire Western banking system, which could bring its already exceedingly unstable financial house of cards crashing down. Already before the 13 of December 1981, the *Financial Times* (22 June, 1981) quoted the explanation of an international banker: 'In essence the problem is simple. They've got our money and can't repay: either we agree to wait, or we write it off. With so much money at stake no one wants to take the loss. So we agree to wait – we have no choice.' The declaration of martial law and military rule in Poland – as an alternative to Soviet intervention – in no way increased the range of choice. Rather the contrary, it undermined the 'umbrella' theory according to which the Soviet Union would eventually (especially after any Soviet military intervention) be willing or obliged – as a sort of lender of last resort – to bail Poland and other East European debtor countries out of their inability to pay. Soviet inaction in this regard left the entire East European trade and financial situation temporarily a bit confused.

In 1981, West Germany's trade with the East went into deficit for the first time as the economic and debt crisis in East and West undermined business. Then the Polish crisis was followed soon after by Romania's inability to service her debt, which also had to be rescheduled. Western bankers suffered a severe crisis of confidence in Eastern Europe's formerly good as gold ability to pay and in the supposed umbrella insurance of Soviet gold as a last resort. Suddenly all of Eastern Europe suffered a liquidity crisis, as even the miracle economies of Hungary and East Germany found themselves unable to raise syndicated loans through regular Western financial channels (which also observed that precisely these two countries already had the highest debt/population or GNP ratios). German industrialists feared that the fat years of sustained East-West trade expansion were over, and bankers sought to avoid any further unnecessary risks (*Der Spiegel*, No. 5, 1982). Both inclined to lend a more attentive ear than before to the American advocacy of economic sanctions against the East. But only with uncertainty.

The *Business International* newsletter for multinational executives advised its readers that 'the US-USSR face-off over martial law in Poland will sorely test the Atlantic Community, already severely taxed by several other strains. Europeans felt that many headaches are being thrust upon them by the US: high interest rates, recession, nuclear weaponry and now, economic sanctions against the USSR' (8 January, 1982). It examined 'Beyond Poland: Broader Implications for World Business . . . Delay for Western European recovery . . . Disruption of East-West trade . . . The Soviet-West European pipeline . . . Further energy distortions . . . The debt debacle . . . Soviet burden' to keep Poland afloat (18 December, 1981).

Other headlines in *Business International* (BI) and its affiliates *Business Europe*(BE) and *Business Eastern Europe* (BEE) in early and mid-1982 were revealing:

'Confusion Follows Reagan Trade Ban' (BEE, 25 June, 1982); 'Summits Underline Soviet Role in Trade' (BEE, 18 June, 1982); 'Trade War Threats to US Exports' (BE, 18 June, 1982); 'US Business opposes Reagan Sanctions' (BEE, 26 February, 1982); 'Western Imports Vital to Polish Economy' (BEE, 19 February, 1982).

Confirmation of the last one came from the Polish Deputy Minister of Foreign Trade (quoted by the *Financial Times*, 26 March, 1982): 'We must realize that demands that our imports from the West be replaced by imports from the Socialist countries is out of tune with economic reality. For the moment such large scale changes are not possible.' At the same time, the size and membership of the West German official business and government delegations to the Leipzig Trade Fair in East Germany led the *Financial Times* (22 March, 1982) to observe that 'there appears to be no drop in West German interest to revive East-West trade which, it is hoped, is only temporarily in the doldrums' and West German Chancellor 'Schmidt opposes Soviet trade war . . . Despite concern over the US attitude, the West German government feels all European Community countries are agreed in their desire to avoid a trade war with the East' (*Financial Times*, 1 April, 1982). On 31 May *The International Herald Tribune* observed that Eastern Europe's creditworthiness was again starting to improve, and since then Hungary and Romania have received new credits while Poland's balance of trade registered significant improvements.

As a counter to European resistance to sanctions over Poland and to their objections to Cocom reclassification of items for export embargo, the Americans tried another tack: the reclassification of the countries in the East into the richer country categories, which do not merit concessional credit terms or guarantees for suppliers from Western governments. The European governments have again resisted the American pressures, while individual firms and/or their banks have been absorbing the difference between the officially supported interest rates on supplier credits and the even lower real interest that they charge Eastern buyers under the table to secure the contracts. The United States pressed its allies on this matter at the Versailles summit and received a grudging but vague commitment from them which led to an agreement a few weeks later to reclassify the credit eligibility of all countries and therefore to increase the official credit costs to the East (until interest rates fall).

Another issue of East-West trade that brought Europe into conflict with the United States is the construction and finance of the gas pipeline and the export of gas from the Soviet Union through Eastern Europe to Western Europe. The Americans have claimed to be concerned that Western European dependence on some energy from the Soviet Union would endanger the security of the West Europeans, who do not share this concern or even believe the concern of the Americans, who have offered to sell Europe surplus American coal instead! The Europeans argue that they plan to derive only a small part of about 6 per cent of their energy supplies from the Soviet Union, in fact reducing European dependence on Middle Eastern oil, and that the construction of the pipeline provides much needed outlets for European steel and equipment. Moreover the eventual Western European purchase of more Soviet gas will provide the Soviet Union with a steady stream of hard currency with which to buy industrial and agricultural imports from the West, from which Europe of course hopes to benefit more than the United States. The Americans argue that 'we' cannot afford to underwrite Soviet economic development with Western business finance and government guarantees; while the Europeans argue that they cannot afford not to guarantee their own economic growth through business with the East. In other terms, while an American Senator argues that the US should pull its troops out of Europe if Europeans insist on 'business and life as usual' with the East, the French Minister of Trade replied to the American emissary sent to plead for credit restrictions against the East that our 'principle is that trade is life. If you don't have trade you could have, as the end result, war' (*The Guardian*, 4 March, 1982).

The gas pipeline issue, after building up in combination with American pressure on Europe to restrict export credits to the East and the US decision to impose countervailing duties on European steel, suddenly brought on American and European political explosions after the June 1982 Versailles summit (and after the bulk of this essay was written). The summit had produced an uneasy compromise involving European acceptance of some (undefined) concessions on export credits and American ones on the gas pipeline. A week later, apparent shifts in the balance of power within the Reagan administration led the President of the United States to order the prohibition of pipeline component deliveries also by extra-territorial holders of US licenses for technology in Europe and elsewhere. Secretary of State Alexander Haig resigned in protest against this decision (which was taken in his absence against his known opposition to it) and others including support for Israel after the invasion of Lebanon, over which he was in conflict with Secretary of Defence Weinberger and National Security Advisor Clark. The political wisdom of both the American pipeline decision and US support for Israel in Lebanon was editorially questioned by the *New York Times* and the *Washington Post*. The shaky legality of 'Reagan's March Toward Economic War' through American prohibitions to non-American firms on foreign soil was highly questioned even in the US, and the Europeans threatened to take the matter to the International Court of Justice.

The European reaction was unprecedented in post-war history. The EEC Commission demanded that the US rescind its pipeline decision. The EEC foreign ministers 'denounced US actions in firm and menacing terms'; the EEC heads of state summit meeting issued a joint declaration against the US decision and also called for the withdrawal from Lebanon of Israel, which enjoys US support. The Vice-President and Industry Commissioner of the EEC declared, 'We are in a state of extreme political and economic tension with Washington' (*International Herald Tribune*, 23 June, 1982).

National protests in Germany, France, Britain, Japan and elsewhere were even stronger. The governing Social Democratic Party in Germany accused the US of 'interference in internal European affairs' and the German Finance Minister of failing to observe the sovereignty of other states, which would seriously affect the credibility of US companies abroad; the head of the German industrial association predicted major new tensions between Europe and America; the head of Germany's biggest union referred to American 'insolence'; and Chancellor Schmidt announced that the pipeline and gas deal would proceed as contracted. The already tottering German electric industry giant AEG faced immediate bankruptcy had its AEG-Kanis division been unable to proceed with its gas turbine deliveries order, worth about $300 million. A number of French and Italian firms were also liable to suffer severely (*Financial Times*, 21, 22, 24, 28, June, 1982). French President Mitterand, who has lent Reagan's political anti-Soviet line substantial support, 'delivered a wide-ranging attack on US economic and financial policy' and his government prepared for an 'uncompromising fight against the US decision'. The Japanese Premier Suzuki and his International Trade and Industry Minister also protested and asked for exemption of the offshore Siberian Sakhalin gas project, in which Japan has a direct interest. The British Minister of Trade denounced 'an attempt to export unemployment from the US to Europe', and President Reagan's most faithful ally and anti-Soviet ideologue, Prime Minister Thatcher announced in Parliament that any British firm that observed this American ruling would be violating British law and would be prohibited by her government from complying with the American prohibition to sell to the Soviet Union! (*Financial Times*, 29 and 30 June, and 1 July, 1982). The Italian government concretely signified its rejection of the Reagan decision by having its state-owned engineering company supply turbines in fulfilment of its contract despite the American prohibition to do so. (*Financial Times*, 8 July, 1982). Then, all of these major European governments declared that the American pipeline ban should be defied and that their firms would fulfil their delivery contract.

The newly-named EEC ambassador to Washington declared in response to all this that, 'our trade relations with the United States are the worst I have ever seen since the end of the war . . . [and] I am not excluding that the situation with the [Reagan] administration will get worse' (*International Herald Tribune*, 2 July, 1982). The situation did get worse throughout the summer and autumn of 1982 as the pipeline dispute became increasingly acrimonious until President Reagan was forced to backtrack in the face of united European opposition and increasing divisions within his own ranks. Reagan finally lifted the pipeline ban in return for a, for him, face-saving but vague agreement by the Europeans to limit the list of exportable items and the state subsidized export credits to the Soviet Union and Eastern Europe that the Americans had long been demanding, as observed above. Nonetheless, France hastened to deny that it had been party to any such agreement about East-West trade and that it rejects any 'economic NATO' that might dictate allied commercial policy (*International Herald Tribune*, 16 December, 1982). However, no sooner was the pipeline dispute patched up than European relations with the Reagan administration took another turn for the worse over the threatened agricultural trade war and American demands at the November 1982 GATT ministerial conference and elsewhere that the Europeans reduce agricultural subsidies and protection. The problem is that each of these disputes about trade policy, no matter how it is papered over or resolved, is a recurrent manifestation of an inevitably deepening structural political economic conflict of interests between American and European capital and capitals.

Nato Alliance conflicts over strategic issues

Paralleling these political economic conflicts over trade policy is the growing dispute over military expenditures and the stationing of new nuclear weapons in Europe with which the United States opened its new cold war offensive. Anti-nuclear and peace movements throughout Western Europe (except France) and opposition parties especially in the parliaments of the smaller countries and Britain, but even strong opposition within the left-wing of the Social Democratic Party in West Germany, have rapidly grown in popular strength and in political influence. Two hundred to four hundred thousand people – a million within a single month – demonstrated against the stationing on their soil of new nuclear missiles in each of several countries. German Chancellor Helmut Schmidt told the United Nations that it is necessary to listen to these people who cannot all be wrong, but at home threatened to resign if they got their way. President Reagan and Secretary of State Haig first dismissed these European demonstrations of opposition to new American weapons as insignificant mass manipulations by Moscow and poured fuel on the fire of European fury and insecurity by declaring that Europe might become a theatre of nuclear war without direct American-Soviet nuclear engagement. The European response and the sudden development of a movement for local nuclear free zones and an arms freeze in the United States, however, obliged Reagan to alter his tactical stance. To take his own cold war wind out of the sails of these peace movement initiatives, Reagan proposed a 'zero option', according to which the US offered to desist from placing the new missiles in Europe if the Soviet Union would dismantle or withdraw existing ones.

Moreover, political-economic conflicts about strategic issues in East-West relations are weakening the NATO alliance itself as political disagreements grow wider and deeper between European and American allies and within Western Europe and the United States themselves. Debates have grown increasingly acrimonious about the burden of increasing military expenditures and the distribution of its shares, the related question of the costly stationing of American troops on European soil, the American proposal to increase NATO reliance on conventional weapons in Europe, and of course over the deployment of new generations of MX missiles in the US and Cruise and Pershing II missiles in Europe as well as about the related Soviet-American negotiations on arms control.

The growing burden of military expenditures and their contributions to budget deficits have become increasingly onerous on both sides of the Atlantic and have fired up the long-simmering trans-Atlantic dispute about 'burden sharing'. At a recent NATO ministers meeting, the British Secretary for Defence declared that none of the European members had any more money to spend on strengthened conventional forces beyond the 3 per cent annual increase to which they are already committed (*The Guardian*, 3 December, 1982). American politicians and propagandists for their part are voicing louder and louder complaints that the Europeans are not paying enough for their own defence – and incidentally not buying enough American weapons for the same – and that if the ungrateful Europeans are not interested enough in their own defence to pay for it, the Americans should consider abandoning them to their fate and start by bringing the costly American troops home from Europe. 'Is the US Congress an Ally of NATO?' asks a former Under-Secretary of Defence in the *International Herald Tribune* (10 December, 1982). He was commenting on Congressional proposals to cut American military spending in Europe, which 'reflect a strain of neo-isolationism that is never far from the surface on Capitol Hill'. The American NATO Commander-in-Chief, General Bernard Rogers, has poured further fuel on this debate through his recent 'air-land battle' proposals to increase the absolute and relative reliance on new generations of highly accurate conventional weapons in Europe. Among the implications of this proposal are to increase the flexibility of response by the possibility of abandoning the forward defence of part of West Germany against any invading ground forces (which is politically unacceptable in Bonn), increasing European military expenditures for conventional weapons (which is politically unacceptable in most European capitals), and a looser relationship between the US and Europe (which is problematical if it is to be loosened on American terms).

American terms both to their European NATO allies and to the Soviet Union at the Geneva arms limitation talks have been turning on the proposals to deploy new generations of intercontinental MX missiles in the Western United States and of intermediate range Cruise and Pershing II missiles in Western Europe. The December 1979 'Two Track' decision to threaten to place the latter missiles in five West European countries by the end of 1983 and in the meantime to use this threat as a bargaining counter in Soviet-American arms talks has fuelled the fires of the peace movement and the debates of the governments in Western Europe. Parliaments in Holland and Belgium have evidenced strong reluctance to the stationing of these new missiles on their soil. The Labour Party has rejected them for Britain. Even the most strongly Atlanticist French President Mitterand has turned to ask for a solution somewhere between Reagan's zero option and the Soviet proposals. In West Germany, the environmental Greens have made political inroads on this issue, which has also split the Social Democratic Party. Christian Democratic commitment to go ahead with the missile placement was a major issue in the March 1983 elections not only for the Germans but for the Soviet-American arms negotiations in

Geneva, since firm German government commitment to the missile placement is essential for the strength of the US negotiating position in Geneva. On the other hand, in the face of their own peace movements at home, West European government leaders must press the reluctant Americans to demonstrate serious negotiation of arms limitations in Geneva instead of playing for time until the new missiles can be installed on both sides of the Atlantic. This disagreement about approach also manifested itself with regard to the re-opening of the Helsinki conference in Madrid in late 1982, where the Americans wanted to pursue an intransigent tough line against the Soviet Union, while the Europeans insisted on using the Madrid conference to lay the basis for an East-West European security conference on 'confidence building measures'. However, challenges to the Reagan administration military policy of build-up and to its attempted justification through charges of Soviet military superiority have also grown stronger in the United States itself. The nuclear freeze movement won referenda in nine states and several major cities, indeed everywhere that it was on the ballot except in Arizona, in the November 1982 elections. The House of Representatives voted down Reagan's 'dense pack' MX missile siting proposal by a large majority. Reagan's military stance and propaganda have been publicly criticized by former President Carter and his ex-national security advisor Brzezinski, by former Secretaries of Defence McNamara and Schlesinger, and in less severe tones by Henry Kissinger, all of whom deny Reagan's supposed justification for his military policy. In a major article in *Newsweek* (29 November, 1982) Kissinger also denies the supposed success of Soviet foreign policy (and notes that 'it has been said, and not only as a joke, that the Soviet Union is the only country in the world entirely surrounded by hostile communist states') and observes that the war in Lebanon demonstrated the 'near irrelevance of Soviet power in the Arab-Israel conflict' and the near impotence of its tanks and planes in Syrian hands against those of Israel.

The Soviet Union for its part has repeatedly offered to withdraw missiles to beyond the Urals in return for some concessions and lesser threats from the Americans, and in June 1982 Brezhnev gave a Soviet pledge to the United Nations not to be the first to use nuclear weapons in the hope that the United States might make the same pledge, as proposed in an important *Foreign Affairs* article by McNamara, Bundy and others. In his subsequent United Nations speech, President Reagan failed to respond positively, while other American officials responded quite negatively. To commemorate the 60th anniversay of the founding of the Soviet Union, Brezhnev's successor, Yuri Andropov, again offered to withdraw further Soviet SS-20 missiles from European soil and to reduce them to the number of British and French missiles in place.

This offer was followed in January 1983 by a Warsaw Pact proposal to NATO to sign a non-aggression pact, reminiscent of the Rapacki Plan of a quarter century earlier, which at the time was rejected by the West. The characteristically cool first response to both proposals by the United States was to call them 'nothing new'. The British and French disliked the first proposal to link arms reductions to their own stocks of nuclear weapons, which they like to regard as not part of NATO. But otherwise, the more forthcoming official responses, especially to the second proposal, in continental Europe and even in Britain, was to call the Soviet and Warsaw Pact proposals 'worth studying'. The reason for this difference in American and European responses is explained by the growing political strength of the peace movement in Europe, which is making insistence on the American 'zero option' increasingly unrealistic. Thus, this new Soviet peace offensive found an important echo in the European peace movement and served, perhaps designedly so, to drive the NATO allies further apart on this issue as well.

In view of the consistently conciliatory Soviet stance on these nuclear issues and the fact, which is repeatedly emphasized in Washington, that the only Soviet strength lies in the military field since they are extremely and increasingly weak in the economic, political and ideological ones, the question arises as to why the West Europeans and Americans should consider the Soviet Union such a threat to their security. One answer is that, according to the opinion surveys, the younger generation in particular in Europe no longer feels any such Soviet threat. The Americans continue to insist on it (although the youngest there also seem to feel more threatened by the bomb than by the Soviets).

Perhaps another answer to the question of the supposed threat by the Soviet Union is that not only it, but also the United States, is increasingly economically and politically weak relative to Western Europe, and that both superpowers can only rely on their nuclear arms and troops to exercise any decisive influence on and sway economic and trade policy in Western Europe! That is, in view of the shift in the economic and political balance of power from the United States to Europe, observed by their four foreign policy institutes, the only remaining ace in the American bargaining hand with the European powers is the American nuclear umbrella and the associated American troops on European soil that are supposed to make the American nuclear commitment to Europe credible. But of course, the United States can only maintain a nuclear ace up its sleeve if there *is* a corresponding Soviet threat against Europe from which the United States can protect – or threaten no longer to protect – the Europeans. Therefore, the Americans are obliged to and repeatedly do play up the Soviet nuclear and conventional arms threat to Western Europe for all it is worth. But it is worth less and less to more and more Europeans, especially as the Soviet Union is increasingly less able to keep its own and its East European neighbours' houses in economic and political order and could hardly be expected to intervene effectively let alone militarily in Western Europe. The real value of the supposed Soviet threat to Western Europe, which the Americans repeatedly try to conjure up by reference to and transference from real or supposed Soviet relations with Vietnam, the Middle East and Iran, Angola, Ethiopia, Afghanistan, Nicaragua and now El Salvador, is to the United States and its economic and political interests itself. For if Western Europeans once liberated themselves from the objectively unnecessary trauma of the supposed threat of a Russian bear embrace, the American bald eagle would find its wings very much clipped down to size. The American use of the nuclear ace to blackmail Western Europe (and Japan) on matters of conflicting economic and trade policy would become a useless joker, whose further attempted use by the Americans would render them ridiculous.

Economic crisis and political crisis in Eastern Europe

The Soviet Union and Eastern Europe also demonstrate 'increasing participation . . . in the international division of labour, at levels and tempos normal for countries at their stage of economic development and fully in line with their economic strategies and plan objectives'.[5]

East-West trade, primarily with Western Europe, has consistently grown faster than intra-socialist trade since the death of Stalin in 1953. By the late 1970s trade with the West accounted for up to half of some East European countries' total foreign trade, although for Western Europe as a whole exports to the East accounted for only 6 per cent of total exports. However, 30 per cent and 40 per cent annual increases of Western exports to the East, concentrated in machinery and agricultural products, during the 1973–75 recession provided an important safety net for falling intra-Western exports and deteriorating balance of payments after the oil price increase. During the 1975–79 recovery, Eastern exports to the West were able to increase again, albeit not as much as Eastern Europe had hoped for. During the 1979–82 recession, Western trade with the Soviet Union continued to grow, but trade with Eastern Europe failed to do so in view of the economic and political problems reviewed below. Nonetheless, the United Nations Economic Commission for Europe writes, 'Recent developments in the West have intensified Western governments and enterprise interest in maintaining, and if possible, even enlarging Western exports to the East'.[6] This interest is also manifest in the continued increase in East-West intergovernmental economic and interfirm industrial cooperation agreements. Their number, concentrated in the metal-using and machinery sectors, grew from 200 in 1971 to 600 in 1973 and over 1,000 in 1975; and they have continued to increase since then to include the major German, French and Italian 1981–82 agreements with the Soviet

Union about pipeline construction and delivery for gas. The over 500 tripartite agreements, through which a Western and an Eastern enterprise collaborate in a third country, and especially in major Third World energy-generating projects, have also continued to grow.[7]

Especially in view of these growing East-West economic relations, the Soviet and East European economies have also been substantially affected by the world capitalist economic crisis, and their growth rates of output and productivity have declined for both internal reasons and those connected with their increasing integration into a crisis-ridden world economy.[8] Growth rates of output and productivity fell noticeably during the 1976–80 five-year plan period, but their deceleration is part of a long-term trend that appears to have begun a decade earlier. Annual growth rates of net material product declined in the Soviet Union from 7.8 per cent for 1966–70, to 5.7 per cent for 1971–75, to 4.2 per cent for 1976–80 and 3.2 per cent in 1981. In Eastern Europe the corresponding growth rates were 6.5 per cent for the first five-year period, 7.8 per cent for the second in which Poland significantly elevated the rate and average, and 5.0 per cent for the last period, but excluding Poland whose absolute decline of output in 1979 would distort the average downward, and 2.8 per cent in 1981 excluding Poland or a decline of 1.3 per cent including Poland. Growth rates of labour productivity also declined during 1976–80 to rates often two-thirds and half of those of 1971–75, and most spectacularly so in the Soviet Union where the overall average declined from 6 per cent to 3 per cent and in particular branches of industry from 5–7 per cent to 1 per cent and even lower.

In nearly every case actual growth rates of output and productivity have been lower, and often significantly so, than planned rates for both plan periods in the 1970s and again in 1981. In the Soviet Union no single output plan target was achieved in any year, and actual labour productivity in both industry and agriculture was barely half that planned. Yearly plan targets had to be repeatedly reduced when it became clear that they would not be achieved, which led Mr Brezhnev to complain about the further disorganization of the economy through this procedure. Production of coal, steel, cement and agricultural commodities actually declined between 1977–78 and 1980 (*Economic and Political Weekly*, 5, December 1981, and *Der Spiegel*, No. 4, 1982). In the face of similar circumstances everywhere, planned rates for 1981–85 in the Soviet Union and Eastern Europe have for the most part been significantly reduced even below the actual ones for 1976–80.[9] Nonetheless, it already appears yet again that many of these plans will not be fulfilled during the present plan period.

A confidential study prepared for the Soviet leadership has outlined a near-disastrous decline in the Soviet Union's ability to feed itself . . . Figures showed a tenfold increase in Soviet imports over the past decade . . . For the period 1966 to 1970, the Soviet Union had to import 15 million tons of food, mainly grain and meat. From 1976 to 1980, food imports rose to 80 million tons . . . One-fifth of the grain harvest is lost because it is harvested too late or left to rot . . . One-third of the potato crop is left to rot . . . About half of potato production . . . is lost each year because of a chaotic distribution system and lack of storage facilities . . . The Commission . . . concluded that the 'existing economic mechanism does not provide necessary economic incentives for production increases and fuller use of the potentially available land'. The study has provided the basis for an internal debate leading to a special Central Committee meeting on agriculture, to be held Monday (*International Herald Tribune*, 24 May, 1982).

A few days later, the press reported some of the decisions taken at this meeting in which President Brezhnev outlined 'a new food programme: further encouragement of private plots and small-scale cooperative farming, significant decentralization of the organization of the farming system, and substantial new incentive payment schemes for farm managers and workers' (*Financial Times*, 27 May, 1982). However, new agricultural programmes and improved organization have had to follow each other with alarming regularity since Krushchev took over in 1953, and despite the large-scale expansion, especially in Siberia, and the massive improvements West of the Urals, another reorganization of agriculture is due now – and still another will be necessary again. For much of the problem of Soviet agriculture must, in fact, be traced to the inefficiency of Soviet industry and distribution as well: poor quality, shortages and maldistribution of spare parts, and the consequent perpetual breakdown of agricultural machinery places about half of it out of commission at each harvest time; and ploughing, sowing and fertilizing for the next crop are further hampered by recurrent shortages of inputs from the industrial sector. Meat consumption in the Soviet Union has increased significantly over the past decade or more; but coincidentally as in Western Europe, much of the fodder for the livestock has to be imported in the form of grain from North America, for which the Soviet Union is less and less able to afford the foreign exchange earned primarily through exports of fuel to Western Europe.
Another press reports examines:

The Soviet Economy, Why something has to give: The Soviet economy has been sending out a series of unmistakable distress signals in the shape of forced sales of key hard-currency earners such as gold, diamonds, timber and oil products . . . It is also quietly running down its deposits with Western banks and borrowing more to pay for the Western equipment going into the Siberia-West Europe gas pipeline . . . What is more, the terms of trade have now also moved against the Soviet Union. . . On the other hand, the Soviet Union itself has reduced by 10 per cent, or 8m tonnes annually, the amount of oil it is prepared to sell to its Comecon partners on concessionary terms (*Financial Times*, 5 February, 1982).

This development is one of several that also suggest that the Soviet Union finds it increasingly difficult, if not impossible, to continue supporting its allied economies in Eastern Europe through raw materials at prices that have risen significantly during the 1970s but still lag behind those on the world market. These circumstances, of course, place the economies of Eastern Europe in a scissors crisis: whilst import prices for raw materials from the Soviet Union to the East have risen, they suffer lower earnings from trade with the West due to inflated import prices for technology and reduced export prices and opportunities because of recession reduced demand in the West.

For Eastern Europe the result is imported inflation, reduced income, and an accumulation of debts to both the Soviet Union and the West. Between 1971 and 1981, the total Soviet Bloc debt to the West grew ten-fold from US$8 billion to $80 billion, of which $20 billion is owed by the large Soviet Union and $60 billion by the small East European countries, $27 billion by Poland alone. 'The economic crisis facing Eastern European countries has become so severe that governments have reached a turning point where leadership must decide between reforms or a period of brutal austerity' (*International Herald Tribune*, 17 May, 1982). The background, briefly, is as follows.

In 1968–1970 far-reaching economic reforms were introduced in Hungary, which intentionally opened the economy to large-scale trade with the West, linked the internal price system to that of the world market, extended and intensified the use of the market mechanism to income incentives, production and distribution, and permitted the development of a parallel grey market economy that is now estimated to account for over 30 per cent of Hungarian production and income. Though the economic reforms were slowed down again in the mid-1970s, they worked to increase income and consumer satisfaction without unduly offending the vital foreign sensibilities of the Soviet Union, whose staunch ally Hungary remained within the Warsaw Pact and in international affairs.

Czechoslovakia also tried to introduce similar economic reforms through 'socialism with a human face' in 1968, but failed to allay the fears of the Soviet Union, which invaded and quashed all of the reform initiatives. Under pressure of mass political revolt in 1969 and 1970, Poland also introduced some economic and agricultural reforms in 1970, and with spectacular success in terms of income, but reversed them again in the mid-1970s. Romania went on an industrialization and industrial export drive but without any organizational reforms or an adequate agricultural infrastructure, which Bulgaria built up instead.

Beginning 1971–72 all of the East European countries (as well as the

Soviet Union, China and North Korea) almost simultaneously went on a concerted drive to import Western technology. They hoped to digest it economically, to use it to generate a surplus of industrial exports, and in the meantime to export raw materials to the West to pay for the imported technology. All of them miscalculated drastically, literally banking on continued Western prosperity: when this evaporated with the coming of the 1973–75 recession and the subsequent faltering 1975–79 recovery, not to mention the renewed 1979–82 recession, the economic rug was pulled out from under their calculations. Their import costs rose; their export possibilities shrank; their debts to finance the, by then, necessary component imports piled up; and then with sky-high Western interest rates, their costs to service this debt grew to the unsustainable proportions of often over 50 per cent – and for Poland over 100 per cent – of annual foreign exchange earnings.

So now 'Eastern Europe has arrived at its moment of economic truth . . . The small East European countries – with the possible exception of Poland – have hardly any resources with which to pay off their massive . . . debt to the West . . . They are locked into a vicious circle of central planning commissions issuing directives which soon become out of date, fictitious costs and prices, along with an economic structure which has been severely distorted over the past 37 years' (*Financial Times*, 9 February, 1982). In the 1970s, internal economic organization and management – except in Hungary, although even it is beginning to feel the external crunch – have not been sufficiently flexible to permit adequate adaptation to the enormous technological, economic, social, cultural, political and ideological influences and changes imported from the West, not to mention the accumulated indigenous problems and their strained economic relations with the Soviet Union. The question arises whether the East European economies have reached or even passed the point of no return in this headlong plunge into extensive external economic relations with the West without concomitant internal reorganization and intensive domestic growth. Now the East European economies certainly must reorganize their economies internally.

But there is also increasing evidence that the East European and to a lesser extent Soviet economies have indeed passed this point of no return and that only a flight forward to further integration and not a renewed involution is economically and politically possible. Beyond their now already built-in economic dependence on the West – illustrated by the above quoted observation by the Polish Deputy Minister of Foreign Trade that replacing imports from the West by others from the Socialist countries is for the moment out of tune with reality – there are internal economic constraints connected to this externally related reality. In general, the slowdown in growth and productivity in the Soviet Union and Eastern Europe can be traced to the growing maturity of their economies, the increasing scarcity of labour as demographic changes and reduced urban-rural migration militate against supply-constrained growth; the difficulties, often bordering on impossibility, of making the transition from mobilizing resources for extensive growth to increasing their productivity for intensive growth; the rigidity of economic planning, organization and incentive motivation that militate against technological change; the simultaneous opening of their economies to technological imports, exports and world market prices to overcome this limitation externally and the increasingly far-reaching privatization of economic incentives, rewards and decisions in a more extensive market economy internally.

The turning point to reforms or brutal austerity, or more likely a mixture of both, has been brought on by the moment of economic truth in the most dramatic way in Poland. Spectacular rates of economic growth and growth in incomes through the mid-1970s, brought on in large part through the opening to the West and partly through internal agricultural reform, turned out to be unsustainable, especially without accompanying organizational reform of the economy and continuation of the agricultural reform. Growth slowed down again after the mid-1970s, and in 1979 total output actually fell by 2 per cent. In 1980 the drop in output accelerated to 4 per cent and obliged the government to impose austerity measures (already attempted in 1976 but retracted in the face of popular unrest), which included the increases in the price of meat that sparked off the strike wave that began in August 1980 and developed into the 10-million-strong Solidarity movement. In 1981, output declined a massive 14 per cent, only secondarily as a result of Solidarity work stoppages and disorganization, but primarily because of shortages of domestic and foreign inputs derived from the malfunctioning of the economy in general. Further austerity measures were demanded by the West (the banks, the IMF and others), the Soviets and the Polish government, but were politically unenforceable. These economic and political problems led to the imposition of martial law on 13 December, 1982. Solidarity has been legally suppressed, interest payment on the Polish debt has been rescheduled despite Western reservations and arguments for sanctions, imports have been drastically reduced, output especially of foreign exchange earning coal has been revived; and according to a spokesman for the new military government, the sweeping price rises, often tripling and quadrupling the prices of basic necessities, were the start of the, 'biggest upheaval in post-war history of a socialist country' whose economic reforms would now go further even than those of Hungary (*Financial Times*, 2 February, 1982). Soon Poland began to cut state subsidized bank credits to enterprises making losses and to permit or even encourage the unemployment of workers.

However, the same day's press also reports 'Czechs stunned by steepest food price rises in 30 years . . . [and] the authorities are preparing for other austerity measures . . . and the official media have launched a campaign to explain that without price increases and other savings, the country would find itself heading for a catastropic financial crisis' (*Financial Times*, 2 February, 1982). In Hungary itself, where income declined by 1 per cent and investment by 8 per cent, an economist member of the Party Central Committee observed that 'continuation of reforms is not just an alternative as it was in 1968. It is . . . a necessity'. And the head of the Hungarian Institute for World Economics observes that 'we have been running too egalitarian a wage and salary system . . . We must increase the flexibility of the Hungarian economy and introduce more incentives', including the sale to private entrepreneurs of state-owned restaurants and small shops, and of course some ways to finance the foreign debt, which relative to the size of the economy is Eastern Europe's highest, at a time when Hungary's balance of payments is seriously deteriorating (*International Herald Tribune*, 27 and 14 May, 1982).

The other highest per capita debt economy, East Germany, demonstrated substantial strength and development during the 1970s, but has not escaped the world, Western, East European, and Soviet (to which it supplied industrial products whose makeup is to be changed) economies' several and common economic crises. Romania still resists economic reforms, which the government may feel are still too dangerous to introduce while its head is physically assaulted by angry mobs in the streets and factories; but it must nonetheless impose severe austerity measures in the face of the near bankruptcy of its economy and its intermittent incapacity to pay even the interest on its foreign debt in response to which the IMF, of which Romania is a member, has recommended its usual belt-tightening remedies. The continued success of agriculture in Bulgaria (as in Hungary and East Germany) absolves it of similar belt-tightening, but not from the introduction of a 'new economic mechanism' to achieve greater cost effectiveness.

The political events in Poland and the foreign debt crisis there and in Romania produced a short-run setback to East-West political *détente* (or at least to West German and European efforts to safeguard it) as the Americans pressed for 'sanctions' and to the further extension of Western credits to Eastern Europe as the banks came to fear for the safety of their money. In Eastern Europe, and particularly Poland and Romania themselves, an initial reaction was also to look to Comecon for more economic ties and to turn to the Soviet Union for more political support. However, there are important economic and political reasons why this East European step backwards toward political economic involution may be a short one and why these events, paradoxically, could lay the basis for a longer term further flight forward to more extensive political economic ties between Eastern Europe and the West. For such an involution would further increase the Soviet economic burden and political responsibility for supporting the East European austerity measures and their political unpopularity in the supply-constrained Comecon economies. Paradoxically, the political economic crisis of Poland could pave the way for more stable long-term economic relations with Western Europe and especially Germany, which could help ease the Soviet and East European supply constraints, reduce their need for austerity and therefore permit greater political liberalization, while at the same time combating Western Europe's own demand and cost constraints.

In the face of this deepening economic crisis in Eastern Europe and the economic and political transformations occurring and impending in each of the countries, in their relations to each other, and in their relations to both the Soviet Union and the West, the political room for maneouvre or margin of choice may often be tight and/or the problem of timing may be delicate. However, this room could be enlarged and the time lengthened through appropriate political economic relations with both the Soviet Union and Western Europe, which could be in the interest of important economic interests and influential political forces in each of these three regions. Smoother progress of economic reforms, and a minimization of austerity in Eastern Europe, as well as a reduction of the economic burden or responsibility for the Soviet Union could be in the interest of many groups in these countries themselves – and in Western Europe also. Such a decline in the economic burden to the Soviet Union and of the burden of austerity in Eastern Europe itself could be facilitated through appropriate economic – and political – cooperation between Western and Eastern Europe, or even a sort of West European 'Marshall Plan' in Eastern Europe, such as was proposed for Poland from someone in its Foreign Trade Ministry after martial law (*Financial Times*, 3 April, 1982). For a Western European economy beset by low profits and high unemployment in industry as well as by agricultural surpluses, such an arrangement could offer some attraction to influential economic and political interest groups. The important underlying political economic opportunities for both Eastern and Western Europe through the export of Western agricultural surpluses to the East have been highlighted by the recurrent Soviet 'great grain robbery' from the United States and President Reagan's offer of increased grain sales to the Soviet Union during his pipeline ban, as well as by the West European 'butter mountain' and the political pressures surrounding its subsidized sale to the East, where these purchases help relieve economic and social tensions. *Business International* (12 February, 1982) and its division *Business Eastern Europe* (21 May 1982) look forward to the next five years of 'prospects for profits (in) Comecon' by emphasizing 'planning chaos, energy/agriculture key, creative financing needed' and observe that the Soviet Union and Poland have 'left Comecon countries convinced that they must strive for economic independence . . . and greater emphasis in each member nation on developing its own industrial sectors in competition with those of its bloc trading partners . . . (and plant managers) greater freedom to make both import and export decisions . . . Western firms will want to take note of this' and keep or develop their sales organizations in Eastern Europe accordingly. But perhaps the very crisis in Eastern and Western Europe can generate conditions for joint 'creative financing' of their crisis management strategies beyond those of Western firms and embrace their associated banks and states to a greater extent than they already do.

Commenting on the succession of Yuri Andropov to leadership in the Kremlin, the Western press frequently noted that since his days as Soviet Ambassador to Budapest during the intervention in 1956, he has maintained a special expertise in East European affairs and lent strong support to the Hungarian economic reforms. At the same time, the press also observed that Andropov's first major speech as Premier was on the need for economic reform in the Soviet Union, that, 'thus, to forestall further unrest at a time when he is facing major problems at home, Mr Andropov may be willing to tolerate a greater degree of economic experimentation and reform in Eastern Europe, as long as this remains carefully circumscribed and controlled by the party' as in Hungary (*International Herald Tribune*, 10 December, 1982) and that, 'the counterpart to greater assertion by Moscow of Soviet economic interests is greater freedom for its allies to work out their own economic salvation' (*Financial Times*, 24 November, 1982). These possibilities may offer new political economic policy alternatives in both Eastern and Western Europe.

Political economic alternatives

Striving for economic independence and the greater emphasis on national industrial development are, of course, not limited to Eastern Europe, but are important tendencies in the West on both sides of the Atlantic. In the West, however, these defensive economic and offensive political nationalist tendencies will appear less profitable and thus less welcome to important sectors especially of multinational business. Instead, this resurgent political economic nationalism appeals to and is furthered by strange bedfellows from the right and the left of the political spectrum. Such *de facto* political agreement on economic nationalism is clearly visible, for instance, in France and Britain. In France, the nationalism of the Gaullists now led by Jacques Chirac is rivalled – or perhaps even excelled – only by the Communists 'à la couleur de France' led by Georges Marchais, although one of the main planks in the Socialist economic programme of President Mitterrand also is 'to reconquer the French market' for French industry. In Britain, the proposal to abandon the Common Market has become official Labour Party policy after having long been the flag of the nationalist right wing of the Conservative Party. Indeed, political economic nationalism is also shared by the far right and the far left in various countries, if only because both share the view that the Common Market and other

Western international ties and NATO not the least among them are an international obstacle to the revolution or counter-revolution that they seek to promote, and more easily so at home than in a large political economic region.

This narrowing nationalist tendency on the right and left also extends to the United States ('America first' at both ends of the political spectrum) and to various regions and ethnic movements throughout Europe, such as in Basque Euzcadi, Bretagne, Wallonia, and Kosivo.

The domestic political economic response to the economic crisis in the West has been to abandon Keynesian demand management and to bid welfare farewell[10] and in the East to question Soviet-style economic planning and introduce increasing privatization of the economy. On both sides of the Elbe, and of course elsewhere as well, the economic crisis has placed all kinds of economic austerity measures on the order of the day. More often than not the implementation of economic austerity has required an increased measure of political repression, which in Europe has reached its most dramatic forms in Poland and Turkey. In Western Europe, now excepting (temporarily?) France, and of course in the United States, these political economic adjustments to the economic crisis have been accompanied by a marked shift of the political and ideological centre of gravity to the right.[11] This political shift exacerbates the economic polarization already engendered by the crisis and further shifts the economic burden of the crisis onto the poor who can least afford to bear it. Though this domestic class struggle has led to some outbursts of labour militancy and ethnic/race rebellions, the former is undermined by the weakened bargaining power of labour through unemployment and the latter (as well as in part the former) are countered through increased legal and police repression. Often the militant and political protest movements are deflected, or sought to be deflected from and by their class targets, through appeals to nationalism. This was most vividly the case in the war over the Falkland/ Malvinas Islands, but nationalist appeals also take many less belligerent forms of beclouding the class struggle.

In the face of heightening economic competition for markets, mounting or recurrent balance of trade and payments deficits, and growing unemployment in the West and some of the same and other problems in the East, existing governments in Europe and America are also falling prey to increasing pressures to rely on protectionist and other nationalist measures. In Eastern Europe, various countries have imposed export restrictions on each others citizens and tourists, while CMEA (Comecon) industrial divisions of labour are increasingly difficult to agree upon and implement. In Western Europe, the EEC Common Market and especially its Common Agricultural Policy (CAP) is subjected to recurrent and increasing strains as Britain and Germany object to the contributions they are obliged to make to sustain agricultural subsidies, especially in France, which wages wine wars with Italy, and mutton and apple battles with Britain. The EEC steel war with the United States is in part the internationalization of the intra-EEC battles over steel export and import quotas within the Common Market. National labelling, packaging, 'safety' and other regulations are increasingly used to protect not so much the domestic consumer as the national producer against EEC and EFTA partners.[12] The European Monetary System (EMS) has not expanded to include the British pound and other currencies and is itself under the threat of breakdown through the chronic weakness of the French and Belgian francs. The expansion of the Common Market to incorporate more of Southern Europe is stalled and has become the source of additional strain within the EEC itself, while the European Parliament fulfils largely decorative functions. The exacerbation of these political economic nationalist pressures and tendencies in response to deepening world economic and domestic political crisis is a real possibility and could lead to the *de facto* or even *de jure* breakdown of the EEC and/or the CMEA and heightened international conflict in Europe.

Indeed, a worldwide financial crash and breakdown of the international trade system are real possibilities, both separately and even more so together. Despite their far-reaching implications for the problematique and policy alternatives considered in this essay, a detailed analysis of this threat is beyond our scope here. Therefore, we confine ourselves to the review of a few newspaper headlines that reveal some of the circumstances and opinions at issue.

The first GATT ministerial level conference in a decade took place in Geneva in November 1982 amid sharpening disputes about trade policy among the giants of the world economy, the United States, the European Economic Commission, and Japan about 'safeguard' protectionist measures against each other, American attempts to destroy the sacrosanct West European Common Agricultural Policy, and American-led North-South disputes about whether or not to bring the increasingly lucrative banking and other service sectors under GATT rules. The press speculated: 'Heading for a Trade War? A GATT meeting this week may be the last chance to slow the worst protectionist wave since the 1930s' (*Newsweek*, 29 November, 1982); 'A last stand against the forces of protectionism' (*The Guardian*, 16 November, 1982); 'GATT's finger in the dam against rising world protectionism' (*Financial Times*, 15 November, 1982).

The mid-conference verdicts, as it was repeatedly prolonged to avoid a deadlock, and the post-mortems were: 'GATT conference faces collapse' (*Financial Times*, 27 November, 1982), 'Participants Are Sceptical of Effect on Protectionism' (*International Herald Tribune*, 30 November, 1982). The next day, the *International Herald Tribune* (1 December, 1982) ran an eight-column banner headline announcing 'GATT Meeting on Liberalizing Trade May Have Helped Launch a Trade War'. *The Guardian* (30 November, 1982) pronounced a dict: death by slow strangulation'. Others opined that, 'It is difficult to overstate the degree to which . . . [it] was a bust . . . perhaps the chief victims at Geneva . . . are the developing nations' (*International Herald Tribune*, 4–5 December, 1982). The relative losers were the United States and the 'winners' who sacrificed the least were the Europeans. Therefore, 'Protectionist pressures are likely to increase in US Congress as a result of the GATT ministerial conference' (*Financial Times*, 2 December, 1982).

A related problem, which threatens to accelerate or exacerbate the breakdown of the post-war international trade system, is the growing financial crunch, especially on the major Third World and East European debtor economies, and the increasing possibility of a financial crash with worldwide repercussions. Next to such a crash, the 1929 Wall Street Crash and the 1931 collapse of the Kreditanstalt in Vienna could appear as a storm in a teacup. The reasons for the growing financial crunch and the immediate causes of a possible crash might be any one or a combination of many. The ones that have received most recent attention are related to Third World debt, particularly since, first, Argentina during the Malvinas/Falklands War, then Mexico since August 1982 and finally Brazil in late 1982 became unable to service their foreign debts as scheduled. The press headlines observe: 'Fear of Widening World Debt Load Slows Down 2 Decades of Tumultous Growth! (*International Herald Tribune*, 29 November, 1982, special report on Euromarkets); 'Trouble for world banking. Frail economies of Poland, Mexico provoke fear of chain-reaction failures' (*Minneapolis Star and Tribune*, 8 September, 1982); 'Bank Lending Cuts: Third World growth rates threatened' (*Financial Times*, 11 October 1982); 'Former IMF Chief gives warning amid flurry of reassurances by bankers: Bank crisis could lead to real slump' (*The Guardian*, 6 October, 1982); 'International Banking: The illusions are stripped away', 'Holes in the supervisory net'; 'Bankers meet in private summit on liquidity crisis' (*Financial Times*, 15, 17, and 27 October, 1982); 'International debt crisis 'will hit industrial growth', US banker warns' (*The Guardian*, 9 October, 1982). In short, the scenario is that the new debt crisis is reducing the banks' willingness to continue lending to Peter to enable him to pay Paul and for Mexico and Brazil to import industrial goods from each other and for both of them to pay for exports from the United States and Western Europe, whose own growth rates are thereby put in check. The inability of one of these countries to pay, especially through the New York interbank clearing house CHIPS, and the inability or delay in launching a rescue operation internationally could launch a domino-effect chain reaction of bank liquidity crises, defaults or failures around the world that could bring the whole world financial system crashing down like a house of cards – with incalculable effects on world trade and production, except that they too would break down and the first efforts to contain or to remedy the impact throughout the world would likely be further protectionist measures and attempts at economic bloc formation.

In the face of aggravation of the world economic crisis and the apparent bankruptcy of post-war Keynesian demand management remedies in the West, a succession and mix(up) of alternative political economic policies have been tried and/or proposed in the West, which may be roughly classified as follows: *firstly*, national and/or regional and enterprise monopolistic competitive policies, often at beggar-my-neighbour expense, which have generated or aggravated the West-West conflicts of interest and policy disagreements reviewed above; *secondly*, national monetarist policies of (largely unsuccessful) restrictive management of the national (but not international) money supply and government expenditure in virtually all Western countries, which have failed to achieve their stated objectives anywhere and have encouraged the de-industrialization of the United States under Presidents Carter and Reagan and nearly achieved it in Britain under Prime Ministers Callaghan and Thatcher; *thirdly*, anti-state interventionist supply-side policies of tax reductions to stimulate private investment and productivity, which under their Reaganomic guise in the United States have contributed to monstrous budget deficits and significant upward redistribution of income, but no visible stimulation of business investment or effort; *fourthly*, interventionist supply-side macroindustrial state investment controls, proposed for the 're-industrialization of America' by some Democratic Party 'neoliberals' like Senator Gary Hart and economist Lester Thurow, also found in *Business Week*, and Felix Rohatyn's proposal to revive the Reconstruction Finance Corporation (RFC) of the 1930s as an 'investor of last resort', and attempted in France by President Mitterrand's government intervention and nationalization to upgrade the technological level of French industry, and in the special circumstances of Canada by Pierre Trudeau's constitutional reform efforts to capture Alberta's and some American oil companies' fortunes and funnel them through the federal government to Ontario and other industries and in general encouraged perhaps by the attractiveness of the 'Japan, Inc.' model; *fifthly*, neo-Keynesian government pump-priming proposals for social wage spending and employment creation on the national level, combined with support for national industry, as proposed by the Schmidt government in Germany in early 1982, or also combined with import controls as in the British Labour Left's alternative economic strategy (AES) supported by Tony Benn, and sometimes supplemented by macroindustrial investment controls as in the AES proposals and Mitterrand France, and/or increased arms expenditures as virtually everywhere; and *sixthly*, global Keynesianism à la Brandt Report and other proposals to create and/or transfer Marshall Plan type purchasing power to the Third World so that it might be spent in and revive industrial development in the West. The prospects for these policy options individually or in combination are not brilliant. The past and foreseeable consequences of the first three approaches to crisis management (beggar-my-neigbour, monetarist and anti-interventionist supply side policies) are visible throughout the West, including Giscard France and Schmidt Germany, Frazer Australia and Muldoon New Zealand, and elsewhere, but of course most vividly in and through the economies of the prime exponents of Reaganomics and Thatcherism.[13]

The fourth and fifth policy options are presently being put to the acid test by France under the presidency of Mitterrand. In particular, the short-term policy and prospects of the fifth policy, neo-Keynesianism are anything but encouraging. An early *Financial Times Survey* (25 November, 1982) observed: 'President Mitterrand was elected to carry out the almost impossible task of restoring France to full employment in the midst of world recession. Six months into his term of office his administration is not unexpectedly floundering in its bid to achieve higher rates of growth without exacerbating inflation'. Soon thereafter, with its seat in Paris the 'OECD warns France . . . with carefully worded scepticism about the likely results of France's current economic strategy . . . One of the main reservations . . . is that the international economic environment is unlikely to help . . . A policy leading to an expansion of domestic demand would merely exacerbate an already serious balance of trade and payments situation . . . Other hurdles which have to be overcome include a possible acceleration in inflation and a persistence of private industry's reluctance to invest' (*Financial Times*, 2 February, 1982). Another half-year later, 'France is now having to face up to the painful consequences of having pursued last year an expansionary economic policy at a time when her major trading partners were deflating. The unexpected (*sic*) extent to which France is out of step . . . has badly thrown out the Government's economic calculation . . . The scale on which there has been a haemorrhaging of France's foreign exchange reserves has greatly limited his room for manoeuvre' (*Financial Times*, 9 June, 1982). The 'increase in imports sucked in by the continued buoyancy of French consumer demand' forced the government into two major devaluations of the French franc; and the inflation in excess of its EEC partners (which reduces the competitiveness of French exports and which is also fed by higher import prices after devaluation) led to the imposition of a four-month government freeze on wages and prices and the renewed cutback on social expenditures, the employers' contribution to which reduced their firms' competitiveness and investment. The *Financial Times* (21 June, 1982) commented again on 'France after Devaluation: Socialism with an austere face':

> For the Socialist hierarchy (not to mention the Communist) it has been a bitter pill to find that the hopes of 12 months ago of charting an 'alternative' economic strategy towards higher growth and full

employment have been so humiliatingly swallowed up by a second devaluation, expenditure cuts and prices and wages freeze.

But the only other alternative to these painful internal economic measures would have been the external one of withdrawing from the European Monetary System (EMS), which was recommended by some cabinet ministers but was rejected – so far – by President Mitterrand, who fears the Common Market and other international repercussions of such a step, but warned that he did not have a 'religious attachment' to the EMS. Nonetheless, the following observations about Mitterrandomics Mark II 1982 vintage appear realistic: 'Keynesianism in a new guise: "We put our money not into demand, but into the supply side" . . . (moving) away from grants and subsidies towards tax incentives . . . which could have come out of a Conservative Party manifesto' (*Financial Times*, 28 September, 1982). A 'French union chief who believes wages must fall . . . says "The loss of salary is the only possible serious position if you want to keep industry competitive" even in nationalized industry, which still practices the same capitalist-style management as before' (*Financial Times*, 2 December, 1982). 'Now the socialists are taking on a different task. The consumer is being held down with a new austerity programme and industry is being force-fed funds to invest. The strategy, with its focus on nationalization and planning, sounds new, enlightened and socialist – and, for Mr Mitterrand it is. But in a fundamental way, the policy is old, very French and liable to prove dangerously protectionist '(*International Herald Tribune*, 1 December, 1982). The ruling that each imported Japanese video recorder must be individually inspected to clear customs in the small inland town of Poitiers is a vivid illustration of this protectionist stance.

This French experience with short-term neo-Keynesian demand stimulation against the international economic and EEC tide need not have been unexpected in France or elsewhere. It does, however, vividly illustrate the severe limitations of Keynesianism today, and especially of *national* attempts to implement it alone. If this fact of life so severely limits the room for manoeuvre of relatively strong and prosperous France, what greater ills would it bode for a smaller and economically still more foreign trade dependent and industrially much weaker Britain, even if the Labour Party took it out of the Common Market or the Labour Left (an unlikely event indeed) were to attempt implementation of its AES. Did Chancellor Schmidt not warn that Germany alone (or even with Japan) is not a strong enough locomotive to pull the world economy out of doldrums? Would a far weaker national economy be strong enough to pull even itself out of the doldrums – or in the case of Britain out of an industrial depression that exceeds even that of 1932?

To answer this question it is necessary to examine the prospects of the other longer leg of French economic policy, which is also a pillar of the British AES and is gaining more adherents in the United States the more Reaganomics fails to deliver the goods: a 'macroindustrial' policy of state support for ailing industries and regions, for technological innovation, for domestic capital flows with foreign protection at home and competition abroad, and with suitable collaboration from business and labour etc., as proposed in a study of *US Industrial Competitiveness*, published in July 1981 by the Office of Technology Assessment of the US Congress, and perhaps mediated by a sort of RFC. The official in charge of this industrial policy in the Elysée Palace in Paris remarked on the 'shift from an economy led by demand to one in which costs and quality have become all-important . . . To this extent, the French Socialists are supply-siders . . . investment is the central element in this process' under Socialist guidance (*Financial Times*, 8 January, 1982). It is, of course, still too early to know what the outcome of this dirigiste supply-side policy will be in France which, after Japan, has pioneered it, or what will happen later in America or Britain and Germany. The new link of the French research and industries ministries has been dubbed an incipient French version of the Japanese MITI superministry. However, even the relative success of Japan so far and the relative size of the American domestic economy leave ample room for caution about the extent to which it will be possible to go very far with macroindustrial policy on a strictly *national* political economic basis in an international economy. This limitation on national policy would obtain even more so in Europe and especially in its smaller countries and weaker economies. Indeed, the apparently increasingly stringent limitations on socialist economic and technological development in the Soviet Union and Eastern Europe, in each of their economies individually as well as through Comecon, jointly suggest the rationality of examining this alternative for its flaws and considering other political economic alternatives as well.

A sixth alternative political economic strategy has, of course, been proposed by the Brandt Commission and others: a sort of global Keynesianism through a North-South – and in that case, why not, West-East – Marshall Plan on a global scale. Apart from the implausibility of getting political economic support for global Keynesianism worldwide at a time when national Keynesianism is being abandoned in one country after another and protectionism is spreading like wildfire, there are other serious problems with this proposal.[14] The United States was able to administer the Marshall Plan in Western Europe after the war when American hegemony was unparalleled and unchallenged. But who would or could administer a global Marshall Plan today, when American hegemony is increasingly eroded and challenged? Indeed, the vary malfunctioning of the Atlantic Alliance and the challenge of Japan, not to mention the East-West tensions, are an essential part of the crisis and of the inability so far to prevent it from deepening. How, then could this disharmony or market-anarchy – as Arrighi calls it[15] – be transformed from being the problem or at least its manifestation to becoming the reason for its own solution? Through a strengthened and expanded International Monetary Fund – World Bank Group with Security Council police powers? That seems hardly realistic for the foreseeable future. Too many powerful political economic forces would be unwilling to play along in this ball game according to still non-existent rules (the United States even torpedoed the modest Law of the Sea Authority), and there would be no arbiter to blow the whistle on anyone who broke the rules or even refused to play at all and oblige them to comply. Potential recourse to force and war is too widespread.

Beyond the recourse to major war and/or the total breakdown of the international economic system, are there no alternatives that might be both plausible in their appeal and practical in their interest and possible implementability? Is there no political economic strategy that avoids the Scylla of the present impracticability of a really alternative economic political and military international order and the Charybdis of ultimately impracticable national (ist) political economic policies which moreover enhance the danger of nuclear war? There may be some that could perhaps emerge out of the conflicts of interests and disagreements over economic and strategic policy reviewed above.

One such proposal is the creation of a 'Fortress (Western) Europe' behind external tariff barriers. This seems to be the strategy recommended by the European Research Associates in their study of growing protectionism in the EEC and elsewhere, which threatens to break up the Common Market. But if growing protectionism is inevitable in the present economic climate, as they argue, then they suggest that it would be far more preferable to direct it outward from the EEC and EFTA, that is from all of Western Europe, to the rest of the world and maintain free trade within that region. In that case, the ERA proposal could also be extended to attempt the application of Mitterrand and Benn type economic nationalism (theoretically supported by the Cambridge Economic Policy Group's import and investment control proposals for the UK) not on the national levels that almost certainly condemn them to failure, but on a West European wide level.

The press reports some straws in the wind that indicate further thinking and possible moves in this direction. The *Financial Times* (30 November, 1982) carried an article by David Lea, the assistant general secretary of the British Trade Union Congress and joint secretary of its liaison committee with the Labour Party, entitled 'Economic planning – there is no alternative', which stresses that planning has become economically and socially necessary because of the world economic crisis and 'cannot and should not be confined to national economic blocs'. Stuart Holland, British Labour MP and author of *Beyond Capitalist Planning*, sets out a 'New Strategy for Europe' in the *New*

Socialist (November/December, 1982) based on 'planning by agreement: the European convergence' and joint 'better-my-neighbour ' reflation through which participating economies 'could certainly go much farther before running into major financial constraints'. Holland reports on a joint European economic project under elaboration by members of the executives of the socialist parties of Portugal, Spain, Italy, Greece, France, Belgium, the Netherlands, Sweden and Britain's Labour Party.[16]

Interest is not confined, however, to individuals from parties of the left but extends to governments of the right and the EEC Commission itself. John Palmer, the European editor of *The Guardian*, reports (3 December, 1982) that, 'the European Community is well down the road towards economic 'Fortress Europe' and may soon follow by asserting its autonomy in political and even security policy. The strains within this week's meeting of NATO defence ministers could not be hidden from view. And the Copenhagen summit discusses a German/Italian plan encouraging ultimate European union which, stripped of its pious symbolism, will result in the EEC governments including security and disarmament within the ambit of Common Market political cooperation.' Commenting on the same EEC Copenhagen summit, the *Financial Times* (6 December, 1982) observed, 'External pressures coupled with a persistently gloomy economic outlook are moulding a new unity on commerical issues among the Ten . . . There is growing support in Europe for the combination of protectionism at the EEC level and unrestricted free trade within the Community. This is thought to be the only practical way of coping with competition from Japan and the newly industrialized countries.'

The same sentiment is reflected among some European government leaders and officials.

> President François Mitterrand's Government, in a bid to arrange strategic marriages with eligible foreign consorts for state-owned enterprises in high-technology sectors is playing the European card for all it is worth . . . French officials believe that the extended world recession has made the EEC more amenable to the idea of European co-operation to fend off US and Japanese competition. The plan adopted at the EEC summit in Copenhagen to boost European industry is seen in Paris as proof of this. The programme includes the formula, officials admit, of greater trade liberalism within the Community, but a more protectionist policy externally. When President Mitterrand put forward similar ideas in the autumn of 1981, they recall, he was cold-shouldered (*Financial Times*, 15 December, 1982).

> EEC governments reached a remarkable degree of agreement in Brussels yesterday that the only viable means of halting, and eventually reducing, unemployment lies in a sustained attack on public

deficits, inflation and excessive production costs . . . Yesterday's consensus on macro-economic policy was a remarkable change of opinion for Sir Geoffrey Howe (then British Chancellor of the Exchequer) who was alone in arguing the case against coordinated reflation at a similar meeting 18 months ago. But the move to austerity in France, changes of political complexion in the governments of Belgium, the Netherlands and Denmark, together with deepening economic crisis elsewhere, has swung the balance of economic orthodoxy within the EEC closer to the British position (*Financial Times*, 17 November, 1982).

Chancellor Helmut Kohl recently stood on the steps of the European Parliament building here and declared his belief in 'a united states of Europe'. This went further than the ritual declarations of belief in building the community . . . His predecessor, Helmut Schmidt, was never so expansive (*Financial Times*, 12 October, 1982).

The EEC Commissioner for Industry, Viscount Etienne Davignon, argues for a movement 'Towards a more united Europe' which must 'wage battles on the world market' over the next 20 years in the new fields of information technology and biotechnology, but which nonetheless should not pin its hopes on export-led revival but on opening up Europe's internal market through the following keys: discouraging national protectionist measures; European specifications and standards to ensure preference to European goods; company law, taxation systems and community action to encourage the creation of European industrial companies; taking account of the European market as a whole and not just national markets; a European pool of telecommunications systems to replace existing state monopolies; and a European-wide research and development strategy. 'Without a European response the Commission believes that the Community is threatened with extinction. The important thing is to ensure that public money is injected into the national economies in accord with a coherent European strategy', Davignon writes (*Financial Times*, 13 December, 1982).

For the moment, not only at the EEC Commission but also in government cabinets and the board-rooms of industrial companies that include privately and state-owned firms, the emphasis is on European cooperation in the micro-electronic and information advanced technology fields.

Arriving at a common industrial policy that would relaunch the EEC's stagnating micro-electronics sector is an agreed priority of all member governments, but it is proving fraught with political difficulty. Yet the EEC governments are well aware that to leave the field open to the present market leaders of Japan and the US will ultimately cost more in economic slowdown and lost employment than would the depredations of the new 'smart' machinery on factory floor jobs (*Financial Times*, 13 December, 1982).

Accordingly, a dozen of Europe's leading electronic groups have felt compelled to join together in a still pilot venture called ESPRIT, which stands for European Strategic Programme of Research in Information Technology, which is angling for some $2 billion from the EEC Commission support, or about 2 per cent of the Community's budget. The companies include GEC, ICL and Plessey from Britain; Siemens, AES and Nixdorf from West Germany; Thompson-CSF, Honeywell-Bull, and CIT-Alcatel from France. Olivetti and STET from Italy, and Philips from the Netherlands (*Financial Times*, 1 August, 1982). Though, as one of the participants warns, 'there are plenty of hurdles before ESPRIT becomes a reality', some of the firms involved are also trying to proceed with research and production-sharing that involve fewer of them.

Of course, in the absence of a single European state (whose creation is not yet on the horizon at a time of resurging nationalism), the achievement of such West European-wide economic cooperation would pose considerable difficulties, even if there are mutual interests in hanging together in order to avoid hanging separately. In addition to the intra-West European problems, the construction of this Fortress (Western) Europe would generate or exacerbate economic and political conflict: Western Europe would be increasingly cut off from its Third World and particularly Middle Eastern sources of supply and markets both by its own action and by the resultant enhanced competition from the US and Japan, who might be led to undertake a new political economic offensive in the Third World. Such a likelihood lends all the more weight to the argument for extending any possible such West European economic integration to embrace enhanced economic and political rapprochement with Eastern Europe and to some extent the Soviet Union, which from both the supply and demand side would offer the opportunity to construct an economically much more viable – and politically more stable? – All-European Fortress or Pan-European Entente.

The very increasing West-West dissension within the Atlantic Alliance and NATO and the, no doubt different but complementary, economic and political difficulties emerging in Comecon and the Warsaw Pact countries combined with the potentially common European interest in a stable solution to the Middle East crisis – ensuring the steady flow of oil to all of Europe – not to mention the desire for peace and arms limitations in Europe, could perhaps provide the political economic basis for a major international and national political realignment and an alternative regional or economic bloc strategy, which might offer a realistic path between the impractical whole world harmonious political economic order and the impracticable disharmony of and dangers of national political economic competition. A Pan-European economic strategy or even bloc with ties to the Middle East and perhaps Africa could possibly provide the basis of sufficient mutual economic interest in enough economic and political class and national segments in both Western and Eastern Europe to reduce the tension between the two areas and be coupled with the denuclearization of the region through the revival or modernization of the Rapacki Plan that called for the latter a generation ago.

The political economic rapprochement of Western and Eastern Europe that proved to be beyond reach then may be more possible to grasp now that there are many real common (that is, same) or at least mutual (that is, parallel) economic and some political interests among powerful political economic class and national segments on both sides of the Elbe and particularly in Germany itself. Moreover, the growing conflicts within both the Atlantic Alliance and the Eastern Bloc and the underlying economic and political weakening of both of the American and Soviet 'superpowers' relative to their respective economic and political allies on either side of the Elbe could enable important political and economic forces in each of the present four major regional groupings, Western Europe, Eastern Europe, and their no longer so big respective brothers in the United States and the Soviet Union to consider an alternative East-West European economic and political rapprochement. Such a solution might perhaps not be ideally the most desirable, but it could become the practically second best and certainly the lesser evil solution to either the prolongation of the increasingly economically and politically untenable present trends within the various economies, societies and states; or to the other alternative political economic policies that range from totally impossible to construct in practice towards practically certain to totally destruct altogether.

As long as far-reaching global Keynesian demand management and supply-side *dirigisme* remain quite impracticable, and limited national Keynesian demand management and supply-side policies turn out to be impractical in a world economy, there is perhaps some practical room and plausible reason for a major regionally-based European-wide macroindustrial effort at combining state intervention in investment finance and decision for sale of output on a regional preference market in an international economy and some coordination of credit creation and the distribution of effective demand on a similar regional basis.

By cutting the Gordian knots of their separate political economic limitations both CMEA and EEC might be able to overcome their separate limitations through a more perfect West and East European economic union and political alliance. Expanding the boundaries of systems that can no longer operate within the confines of their old boundaries offers no guarantee of salvation but is at least as practical as breaking the systems down into little pieces. And when there is a real basis in mutual economic interest for the amalgamation or at least rapprochement of the two systems, as there is between the EEC and CMEA, and the alternative is the possible nuclear destruction of both, there is more than enough reason to make the political effort. Significantly, this political effort also opens the door for important economic and political interest groups and the peace movements within Western Europe to join in a common cause or at least to forge a tactical alliance with (rather than as heretofore a strategic one against) each other. Of course, mutual economic interests do not provide or guarantee political agreement. But the replacement of economic conflict by some economic agreement of interests certainly removes some obstacles to and facilitates political rapprochement between East and West and collaboration in the West between the peace movement and some business as well as state interests. Moreover, within Eastern Europe some interests in favour of economic and political liberalization, not to mention any peace movements there, could perhaps collaborate in this direction without thereby threatening the vital security interests of the Soviet Union (that is, through extension elsewhere of the Hungarian reform model). A favourable straw in the wind may be that French President Mitterrand who, excepting Britain's Mrs Thatcher, has been the vocally most anti-Soviet European leader and who comes from the country with the least developed peace movement, 'is seen as feeling its way towards a new relationship with the Eastern bloc during the current visit to Hungary . . . [which he] deliberately picked . . . His aim is to demonstrate that coolness towards the Soviet Union does not exclude developing relations with other Communist states. The visit is inevitably seen as opening the door to the resumption of more normal relations with Moscow. The difficulties over the gas pipeline . . . are also on the agenda' (*Financial Times*, 8 July, 1982).

Most significant is the important priority that the Social Democratic Brandt and Schmidt governments in West Germany have given to the 'Ostpolitik' toward each Germany, and the continuation of this emphasis by the Christian Democratic government under Helmut Kohl (and von Weizsäcker in West Berlin). Schmidt observed after leaving the government that both East Berlin and Bonn are aware of the parallels of interest in economic cooperation and peacekeeping, and the East German leader Erik Honecker suggested that for the West 'trade between East and West is the best job-creation programme there is' (*Financial Times*, 16 December and 25 October, 1982).

Each of the present allies of Eastern and Western Europe may have at the very least lesser evil reasons to acquiesce in such a political economic realignment, especially if their vital interests are safeguarded in the process. The Soviet Union, for whom prolongation of the present is very costly, could find the economic burden of its support of Eastern Europe and of its military expenditures very much lightened by a European rapprochement, which would also reduce some of the sources of political tension within the USSR. The mere weakening or breakup of

NATO should offer the Soviet Union a significant enticement to go along with such a European rapprochement and could compensate for what might be a sort of political Finlandization of Eastern Europe, which need not threaten vital Soviet interests by turning against her.

The United States would find the apparently inevitable loss of its hegemony in Europe increasingly confirmed, but would be freed to shift its economic and political attention increasingly to the Pacific, including parts of Latin America and Asia in whose direction powerful forces are drawing or leading important American political economic interests anyway. Moreover, the Americans would be liberated from a major basis of their all-consuming obsession with Soviet power and its supposed threat. To the extent that this Soviet threat were to persist, it would also be turned more towards Asia and the Pacific, where it would also be checked through a further development of the Washington-Tokyo-Peking axis and their possible political economic collaboration in the Asia Pacific region.

Important economic and political interests in the United States, especially in newer technologically more advanced industries and the expanding 'sunbelt' states in the South and West of the country, have for some time been pushing for a Pacific Rim strategy to replace the old transatlantic European ties. At the same time, Jacques Attali, Mitterrand's principal economic adviser and the organizer of the Versailles summit, suggests that in the course of the present world economic crisis the centre of the world system will shift from the Atlantic to the Pacific. Other emerging sentiment in the United States is reflected by former Under-Secretary of State George Ball writing in the *Washington Post* who criticizes 'the doctrine-according-to-Reagan . . . that the Soviet Union is to blame for all major world ills' and who argues that, 'if many Europeans now regard United States' policy as erratic and unpredictable . . . [and] no longer trust American judgement and good sense . . . they are right' (*International Herald Tribune*, 20–31 January, 1982). On the other hand, in the United States W.W. Rostow, who was former National Security Adviser to Presidents Kennedy and Johnson (and whose brother Eugene was handling arms control for President Reagan), writing in the *New York Times*, reflects the apparent readiness of influential circles in the United States to contemplate a significant change in 'Dealing with Russia after Poland's Coup: A Plan for Entente in Europe':

> Four historical processes make the continued acceptance of the division of Europe unwise, not merely for the West but also for the Soviet Union. First, the coming to maturity and responsibility of the generation in Eastern Europe born after World War II, to whom the present arrangement makes little sense . . . Second, powerful decelerating economic forces at work in the Soviet Union and Eastern Europe . . . Remedy requires, among other things, wider and

more harmonious economic relation with the West, including increased flows of capital and technology . . . Third, the economic forces at work in the West as well as in the East dictate efforts of the highest seriousness to reduce defence spending. Fourth, there is a new generation in the West . . . Young people in Western Europe and the United States are asking perfectly fair and understandable questions: Why should Germany not be unified? Why should the European continent be littered with American and Soviet nuclear weapons? Why should American and Soviet forces be stationed in Europe more than 37 years after the end of World War II? . . . The question must be answered. What is needed now . . . is to allow Europeans, in both East and West, to organize themselves more as Europeans; to ensure continued security for the Soviet Union and the United States, with reduced but not totally eliminated involvement in the military affairs of Europe . . . that would reduce the level of the European armed forces in both NATO and the Warsaw Pact countries; . . . strategically balanced US and Soviet military force withdrawals from Europe . . . provisions for heightened multilateral economic cooperation within Europe. This would ensure, among other things, that a powerful united Germany would not seek to establish hegemony on the Continent . . . Others in the Soviet Union would seize on the prospect . . . to achieve the abiding Soviet dream of a Western Europe cut off from the military support of the United States. They would be supported by a few Americans who have long hankered to cut Western Europe loose . . . But without such an agreed vision and plan, Western policies are unlikely to be stable, patient and effective (*New York Times/International Herald Tribune*, 26 January, 1982).

In conclusion, it appears that the natural course of world capitalist development and its renewed structural crisis are undermining the economic basis of and generating ever sharper political conflict within the Atlantic Alliance. Increasingly this dissent also covers strategic issues of relations with the Soviet Union and its allies in Eastern Europe. This area is also facing increasing economic and political problems in part because of the world economic crisis.

The combination of these Western and Eastern political economic problems poses serious dangers for the stability and peace of the world based on the bi-polar Mutual Assured Destruction (MAD) and nuclear parity face-off between NATO and the Warsaw Pact. But the same political economic forces that pose this danger also offer the opportunity – the Chinese ideographs for crisis are a combination of those for danger and for opportunity – to forge a new multi-polar balance of power including a possible Pan European political economic entente to stabilize the strategic balance at least in the European theatre. Moreover, this possibility can become a more practical proposition insofar as the combination of the economic crisis in the West and in the East and their effects of undermining the economic basis of the Atlantic and Soviet-East European Alliance also provide a new economic basis for the tactical if not strategic cooperation of the peace movement and powerful political economic interests (and therefore the, at least, grudging acceptance or even support of the former by the latter) in Europe, West and East, and even the acquiescence in the same by influential forces in the United States and the Soviet Union. The implementation of such global political economic realignments would not eliminate East European and Third World dependence any more than alternative realistic proposals would. Compared to the, in any case, untenable status quo and other alternative policies, however, the proposed world realignment centring on a Pan-European entente would offer greater hope for the achievement of important and widely shared desires: maintenance of world peace or a least avoidance of nuclear war, greater possibilities for economic growth in Western Europe, wider opportunities for national independence and political liberalization in Eastern Europe, and increased political bargaining power and room for manoeuvre for socialist and nationalist liberation movements in the Third World South.

Notes

1 Karl Kaiser, Winston Lord, Therry de Montbrial, David Watt, *Western Security: What has changed? What should be done?* A Report prepared by the Directors of Forschungs Institut der Deutschen Gesellschaft für Auswärtige Politik (Bonn), Council on Foreign Relations (New York), Institut Français des Relations Internationales (Paris), Royal Institute of International Affairs (London) with the assistance of an Advisory Group, New York and London, Council of Foreign Relations and Royal Institute of International Affairs, 1981.

2 See Andre Gunder Frank, *Crisis: In the World Economy*, Heinemann, London, and Holmes & Meier, New York, 1980; *Crisis: In the Third World*, Heinemann, London, and Holmes & Meier, New York, 1981; *Reflections on the World Economic Crisis*, Hutchinson, London and Monthly Review Press, New York, 1981.

3 John W. Kendrick, 'International Comparisons of Recent Productivity Trends' in William Fellner (ed.) *Essays in Contemporary Economic Problems, Demand Productivity and Population*, American Enterprise Institute, Washington D.C.; United Nations Economic Commission for Europe, 'Economic Survey of Europe in 1981', Prepublication Text of Chapter 3, ECE (XXXV/II/1 Add.1.), Geneva, 1982.

4 See Andre Gunder Frank, 'After Reaganomics and Thatcherism, What? From Keynesian demand management via supply-side economics to corporate state planning and 1984', *Contemporary Marxism* (San Francisco), No. 4. Winter, also *Thesis Eleven*, (Monash University), No. 4, both 1982.

5 UN Economic Commission for Europe, op. cit., p. 6.
6 Ibid., p. 292.
7 For details see Frank, *Crisis: In the World Economy*, Chapter 4.
8 Ibid.
9 UN Economic Commission for Europe, *passim*.
10 See Frank, *Crisis: In the World Economy* and 'After Reaganomics', op. cit.
11 Frank, *Crisis: In the World Economy*, Chapter 3.
12 See *European Research Associates, EEC Protectionism: Present Trends and Future Practice*, ERA, 29 Boulevard Clovis, Brussels, 1981.
13 Frank, 'After Reaganomics'.
14 See Frank, *Reflections on the World Economic Crisis*.
15 See Samir Amin and Giovanni Arrighi, Andre Gunder Frank and Immanuel Wallerstein, *Dynamics of Global Crisis*, Macmillan, London, and Monthly Review Press, New York, 1982.
16 Published March 1983, Spokesman, under the title *Out of Crisis: A Project for European Recovery*.

6

Militarization and Development

Hiroharu Seki

Militarization – a crucial element in the global problematique

Ever since the Club of Rome published its highly pessimistic *The Limits to Growth*[1] the concept of the global problematique has slowly become accepted by a considerable number of attentive scholars interested in this type of clinical diagnosis of the future world. However, the global problematique has mainly been categorized as a long-term issue of human survival in terms of population, food, energy, resources and environment. Other micro-human problems related to this long-term perspective were also included, of course, and the problem of war and conflict figured amongst these. Nevertheless, war and conflict were considered not so much a problem of immediate urgency but rather as one problem amongst many and a subject for systematic classification. The efforts of the Goals, Processes, and Indicators of Development Programme (GPID) may well have been typical of such classificatory efforts. The collapse of detente, accelerated by the mutually worst-case learning of the, ironically cooperative, leaderships of Reagan and Brezhnev in pursuing a further nuclear build-up, have now made this conventional way of classifying the global problematique obsolete: the process of global militarization, centred on the nuclear arms race between the superpowers, and disseminated via arms transfers from the First and Second to the Third World, is now *the* most urgent and imminent issue for survival.

Since military strategists in the United States are already predicting attaining the capability for winning a limited nuclear war, and a group of strategists including Defence Secretary Weinberger have informally referred to the possibility of fighting a protracted nuclear war, the avoidance of such disasters urgently demands a thorough analysis of these eventualities, and of the various predictions of nuclear catastrophe. Such an analysis is the real prerequisite for avoiding nuclear war, and considered formally is also certainly one intellectual prerequirement for opening the way to remedying the global problematique. In this sense the global problematique is not simply a global set of disturbing situations, but also represents the lack of a deep understanding of the imminent crisis – a crisis which will not be resolved without the creative and fresh institutionalization of an alternative information order counterposed to the present power-structure, in which the nation-state system occupies one of the core parts of the set of relations in the process of global transformation.

The first prediction of nuclear catastrophe is based on a very simple diagram of the statistical distribution of the relationship between frequencies of different scales of wars measured against time.[2] According to this diagram a limited nuclear war appears inevitable within this century, and in the first part of the next century; not only is it inevitable that two instances of war on this limited scale will occur, but a total nuclear war, killing 3.6 billion people, is also inevitable. This type of analysis is also validated by the waiting-hour type of approach, derived from the original statistical distribution.[3] In this diagram, as well as in the original, the most significant issue is whether the parameter value for predicting the future trend should be extrapolated continuously (in a linear or non-linear form) or not. However, it is evident that without a sudden creative change taking place in the global situation the parameter values seem to be constant in both linear and non-linear extrapolations.

The second prediction of nuclear catastrophe is based on a more detailed analysis of statistical correlations between the same categories of wars, and the probability that war of the same category will be repeated in the future. According to David Singer's work, the probability of war between the US and USSR is nearly 60–70% based on an extrapolation of historical data of wars between great powers,[4] and nearly 90% if present US-USSR relations are categorized as the superpower relation which should be extrapolated further within this model to reflect the change-of-scale-effect occasioned by the size of these great powers *vis-à-vis* former great powers.[5]

The third prediction is based on the more substantial development of strategic interaction and a deep analysis of its effects. This type of prediction is formulated on the basis of the increasing accuracy of missiles, and the chances of success of a pre-emptive counter-force strategy. Because of this possibility, and the mutual fear that the opposition will seek to implement it, the nuclear arms race has accelerated through the increased militarization of science and technology, and resulted in the vicious circle illustrated in the collapse of detente.[6]

The fourth prediction is based on the various phenomenological data directly or indirectly related to the social process itself. This is a more ambiguous, and in a certain sense, intuitive area, akin to a fortune-teller's prophecy. However, such an approach could possibly by transformed into the formulation of alternative indicators offering the detection of early warning symptoms. *Kenzaburo Oe*, a well-known Japanese literary critic, has offered the suggestion that a literary individual might function as a kind of human canary, sensitized to the signs of impending disaster. This idea is not based merely on the personal experience of an individual critic, but on empirical evidence of the past keen sense of the canary.[7] Thus, a set of empirical facts about past wars would, if collected, provide good early warning indicators for the prediction of future wars. It might also be possible to develop a theory of early warning indicators based on more substantive alternative international conflict theory.

The fifth prediction is based on a more fundamental mathematical theory, an approach which does not necessarily require any empirical facts at all. Mathematical games theory tells us of the existence of plural discontinuous solutions for a multi-person game.[8] Within this framework, it is possible to predict the inherent instability of multi-person games, and develop a deep understanding of the causes of the collapse of *détente*. Such a method is particularly necessary in the social sciences, since it could open up an alternative creativity through an understanding of the reality which might culminate in nuclear catastrophe.

Above and beyond these five predictions, militarization has generated grave problems within the overall process of global transformation, initially illustrated in the development of competitive industrial nation-states. This pattern of competition has passed through a number of profound changes. Increasing military expenditure has now not only followed the generalized depression of the world economy, intensifying bankruptcy and unemployment, but at the beginning of the 1980s has also been a specific product of the economic crisis in the Third World in particular, where numerous regimes are becoming increasingly militarized via the transfer of arms from the USA, USSR, France and others. Some of these weapons are intended for the suppression of political opposition, and some for the pursuit of armed struggle.

That type of militarization symbolized in the nuclear arms race at the top level of the current global structure, and that type symbolized in arms transfers to the Third World, at the resultant intensification of oppression at the lowest level, are not independent and isolated phenomena. Each is closely interwoven with the other through the initiatives of top-level rivalry. The militarization of the contemporary world is therefore the most serious global problematique for human survival, in both the long and short-term. The global problematique is a global political-military crisis exposed to the hazard of acceleration by the world economic crisis: it should also be defined as a total political, military, economic, and social crisis in the global transformation process of the present interdependent world.

The task of developing a system of early warning indicators for predicting catastrophe is a very arduous one. More intuitive indicators for warning symptoms might be developed, in addition to the five types of prediction noted above, even though such an approach remains, as yet, not fully adequately theorized. Such indicators offering alternatives to those generated by nation-centred statistics might include: the acceleration of world military expenditure relative to public spending on education and health, the diversion of resources for military purposes compared with the number of adults who cannot read and write, the number of people who have no job or are less than fully employed, the number of children who cannot attend even a primary school, the number of people suffering from hunger or malnutrition, the number of babies who die every year before their first birthday, the number of people who do not have safe water to drink, and the number of people who live in urban slums or shantytowns. Although tentative, such indicators can form the basis for symbolic comparisons: for example, the lack of $100 for each of the poorest young children and mothers meant that 17 million children lost their lives in 1981 alone. The sum of $1.7 billion needed to combat this emergency is what the world spends in only one day on military arms. The cost of eradicating malaria – the most serious disease in the tropical Third World – is put at $450 million, less than half what the world spends each day for military purposes. Three out of five people in the developing countries do not have easy access to safe drinking water, and three out of four have no kind of sanitary facilities. The $60 billion required annually for a ten-year plan to provide such facilities is what the world spends in forty-three days on arms. To reduce the absolute number of undernourished people in the world from 420 million to 230 million by the year 2000 is estimated by the FAO to require a total investment of $21.9 billion, equivalent to 16 days spending on arms. Finally, an aggregate total of the contributions needed to rescue all the world's refugees in 1980 is equivalent to 8 hours' military spending. What do such comparative figures mean? As far as conventional theories of international relations are concerned, they possess no serious meaning. However, once we recognize the necessity for developing an alternative theory of global militarization, and its remedy, such figures would be important in developing an alternative system of indicators. The problem here is concerned with whether militarization is recognized as one of the most imminent and significant elements in the global problematique.[9]

Alternatively, one can consider this question in terms of the destructiveness of nuclear weapons: the combined explosive power of the, at the least, 40,000–50,000 nuclear weapons currently in existence is estimated at more than one million Hiroshima bombs; or some 13 billion tons of TNT – more than 3 tons for every man, woman, and child on earth. The situation appears more serious, and more obvious, if we reflect on the fact that more than one million Hiroshima bombs could kill 200 billion people, or about 50 times the total world population of 4.2 billion. Even if those equivalent calculations are based on simple assumptions, it should be emphasized over and over again that the total explosive power of the current stock of nuclear weapons is estimated at 20,000 megatons, and that strategic interaction between the two superpowers is expected to become increasingly unstable through the accelerated militarization of science and technology.

Causes of the arms race and global militarization

As we have already explained in the preceding section, the process of global militarization has now become the most imminent issue for survival. And since this process centres around the nuclear arms race, the first step towards achieving any remedy must involve an exploration of the causes of the nuclear arms race. These, of course, constitute a specific subset of the more general causes of the arms race. However, since such complex processes often preclude a separate analysis of causes, we treat both sets here as being interrelated.

Firstly, the nuclear arms race is the product of the increasing international tension between rival nation-states in the current nuclear setting of the global transformation process. Of course, international tension is externally oriented, at least at the outset. But because of the feedback processes set in train via the responses of rival states, this tension easily becomes transformed into a *combination* of the products of both external and internal stimuli. This positive feedback mechanism means that the external stimuli always produce internal stimuli in the opponent, and via the feedback loop in turn accelerate external and internal stimuli.

Secondly, the nuclear arms race is a product of the increase in international conflicts which develop relatively independently of each individual nation-state, particularly in the age of a multi-polarized, diversified world. In the peripheral area of world politics, moreover, so-called structural violence has emerged as a new source of conflicts, characteristic of a different, incongruent phase of the cultural matrix in the given political, military, economic, and social structures and illustrated in such instances as Indo-China, Iran, Afghanistan and El Salvador. The see-saw of severe conflicts in the contemporary international environment demands a tough security policy on the part of each nation-state, even though any individual state may not have a direct relationship to the various causes of conflicts. In this sense, international conflicts in the environment of any given state have become external elements in the arms build-up of all states. Depending on the overall structures of the configurations of power, such stimuli can easily increase international tensions. In the case of the nuclear arms race, conflicts in the international environment are unlikely to be independent of the two nuclear superpowers, inasmuch as these have exercised a profound influence over the operation of the international system in which new conflicts are constantly generated, and old conflicts exacerbated. If we include such kinds of international conflicts, the increasing number of international conflicts will act as a cause of the arms race, as a consequence of the 'rational' national security policies governed by traditional means-ends rationality.

Thirdly, once a process of military build-up is semi-permanently internalized within a given nation-state, the internal demands of the arms race automatically increase, independently of the external stimuli. Because of this internalization, the internal motivations specific to organizational dynamics – such as those of the military-industrial-bureaucratic-academic-labour complex within certain industrialized nation-states – may sometimes, intentionally or otherwise, manipulate these external stimuli. Where this happens the internal stimuli themselves are a major cause of the arms race.

However, the development of an international network between sovereign states creates a new political situation in which the above clarification is not so manifest nor so easily applicable. Given this quite recent development in the transnational political situation, internal stimuli themselves take on international characteristics, in the sense that the armers in one country have close contact with the armers in others. These phenomena themselves constitute the *fourth* cause of the general arms race, in which the *nuclear* component cannot be neglected since it occupies the uppermost stratum within the arms race's hierarchical structure. This was well illustrated in the formation of the alliance between NATO, and the Japan-US security pact – that is the adoption of a tough strategic posture, especially in the late 1970s – in which a global linkage of hawks in the different blocs played an initiating role. The causes of the arms race are structural in such a context, in the sense that they can no longer be explained through a so-called billiard ball type of model of national interaction; the real causes of the nuclear arms race have to be sought using global functional theory.

The structural causes of the arms race may be classified into two main categories: marginal causes and internally structured causes. As we have already explained, the latter are undeniably growing in importance with the diminishing validity of the billiard approach. Although such a model might still retain some limited validity in explaining the reopening of the Cold War, internally structured causes are now more significant: marginal causes could only subsume internal causes in the classical theory of international politics, in which states encounter each other horizontally, so to speak. Vertical causes, acting throughout the social structure, are more appropriate when we turn to the phenomenon of *global militarization*, rather than the arms race *per se*. This does not mean that we should abandon any explanation based on balance of power theory, but rather reflects the fact that the internal-external dichotomy of international relations has now become extremely sterile, and that a new type of mixed vertical and horizontal explanation is needed given that the current international system is participating in the global transformation process.

The concept of the *process of global militarization* has therefore emerged at the forefront of our analysis. In one sense, global militarization can be termed a pathological process, one which has brought humanity to an acute crisis of survival through the nuclear arms race, and its accompanying global oppression. The process is symbolized by the militarization of science and technology, which is illustrated in the scale of nuclear weapons – the accumulation of the equivalent of one million Hiroshima-sized bombs – and the increasing accuracy of long and medium range missiles. It is also symbolized by the pathological evolution of rational military strategy – from MAD to NUTS – around which serious disputes have developed in the US and Europe, which is faced directly with the deployment of theatre nuclear forces (so-called TNF problems).

The theory of global militarization focuses on an aspect of the international power structure in which superpower rivalry still prevails as a form of horizontal and vertical struggle among states, and spreads to the intermediate as well as to the peripheral part of the world. The process of militarization thus develops at the level of the superpowers, the level of intermediate areas, and the level of dependent areas. The entanglement of the three levels produces $_3C_2$ plus $_3C_3$ relationships in addition to $_3C_1$ interrelations between each level.[10]

Moreover, the theory of global militarization focuses on various aspects of the functional transnational order of the global structure, not only re-examining the political, military, and economic orders, but also the cultural, informational, scientific, technological, and educational orders in terms of their contribution to stimulating militarization in the global transformation process. Within this framework of analysis, it becomes relatively easy to distinguish between the marginal causes of global militarization and its internally structured causes, even when applied to the explanation of militarization based on the central dynamics of power relations between nation-states. The marginal causes of global militarization are well illustrated in the contemporary militarization of science and technology, in the sense that this is the most significant factor in the present nuclear arms race, and an indispensable element in the collapse of *détente*. This does not mean that there were no internally structured causes already present, but which have not contributed to the current acceleration of the nuclear arms race: such causes have not ceased to be of explanatory relevance. However, the current prevalence of the militarization of science and technology has pushed such causes into the background, and whether such internally structured causes might become marginal once again remains an open question.

In my paper 'Global Militarization and Its Remedy'[11] I offered a design for creating overall peace under six categories: the reduction of international tension, the demilitarization of science and technology policy, active participation (of science and technology) in peace-building via university reform, creation of new integrated disciplines through re-examining goals of development, re-evaluation of various institutions as actors in global politics, and the formation of alternative networks to create a new learning process. Each of these categories can be seen to correspond to the causes of militarization. Hence, the more diverse these causes, the greater the need for diversity in the strategy for peace.

This section has highlighted increasing international tension, an increase in internal conflicts, and internal motivation rooted in organizational dynamics as the causes of global militarization. It should be pointed out here that the second cause was added to my original six categories, and that the third category could be broken down into many sub-categories, as illustrated in my previous paper.[12] New additions could be made to those sub-categories, such as the financial weakness of institutions such as the United Nations University, and related institutions, the lack of autonomy or weakness of provincial and local government in supporting peace-building institutions (and the fact of the qualitative underdevelopment of such governments *per se*).

Disarmament theory and global strategy for demilitarization

The causes of global militarization are more structural than the causes of the arms race inasmuch as global militarization constitutes a total societal phenomenon, and is a product of the global transformation process. The neglect of disarmament by decision-makers in the super-powers is deeply rooted in the ideological framework in which balance-of-power politics and principles, and sovereignty structurally dominate the present international setting. Sheer neglect of disarmament is not, however, the whole story. An intensive disarmament effort was made by a *minority* of decision-makers. But these efforts were not successful, despite the fact that predictions of a coming nuclear showdown promoted arms control negotiations between the superpowers (the Partial Test-Ban Treaty, Nuclear Non-Proliferation Treaty and SALT) which resulted in *détente*, at least during the mid-1970s. Nevertheless, the combined effects of breakthroughs in military technology, illustrated by the marked improvements in missile accuracy, and sudden unstable political changes in pivotal areas inside the existing balance-of-power system inflicted serious damage on *détente* and resulted in the opening of the second Cold War in the late 1970s. What has to be emphasized here is that the failure of disarmament is not only the result of the collapse of *détente*, but also one of the most significant causes of the collapse of *détente*.[13]

Previous theories of disarmament, if any, were deficient in their failure to establish a correspondence between the causes of the arms race and their proposed path towards disarmament. Of course, given the complex nature of the causes of the arms race, interrelations between different causes are often very significant, and it is consequently virtually impossible to remove any individual causes without influencing other causes. One strong argument for the pursuit of more indirect methods of removing the causes of the arms race would be establishing that such methods would encounter relatively meagre structural resistance from the power-establishment. This approach necessitates the formation of alternative networks in close proximity to power relations. Within this framework, the causes of global militarization which are located in the global setting, such as the reinforcement of worst-case learning, might be surmountable at a higher level within the hierarchy of an alternative network formation and/or in terms of future perspectives for an alternative institutionalization to control the global transformation process.

However, before taking up such an integrated strategy for disarmament and demilitarization, we consider the more substantial correspondence of causes of the arms race and opportunities for disarmament. We first have to consider the causes of the increasing international tension within the framework of the collapse of *détente*. This requires a phenomenological analysis of why Kissinger's attempt to form 3 or 2.5 poles between the US, USSR and China – 'a floating peace structure' – failed. According to the position which sees the current development as a revival of the Cold War – although some disagreements as to the definition of the Cold War remain – the collapse of *détente* was produced by the balance-of-power type of global rivalry: if this was indeed so, N-persons games theory could easily predict the instability of alliance patterns by using the Pareto-optimum cores. Anatol Rapoport's 'N-persons game theory' is a good illustration of a successful application of this approach for predicting stable or unstable balance-of-power relations between the US, USSR, and China. Rapoport severely criticized the use of N-persons games theory for strategic purposes since military strategists apply it to achieve their narrow, national interest rather than, as intended, as a means for mutual peaceful accommodation by arriving at a deeper understanding of the fundamental characteristics of the structure of the game.[14] The grey area in the SALT negotiations suddenly enlarged after the concept of parity moved from US-USSR relations to US + China + USSR triangular relations. NATO's theatre strategy also faces increasing uncertainty regarding the concept of parity in the same 3-person game theory logic. Nevertheless, it should be pointed out that the above explanation for the revival of the Cold War considers only one of several causes. However, in our view it was the most significant marginal cause of the revival of the Cold War in the sense that it operated as a *necessary* condition: naturally, once internalized into the present international structure, it ceases to be a marginal cause.

Different marginal causes would appear successively as the situation deteriorated further. Within this framework of analysis, indirect remedies will probably be the most effective means of weakening or eliminating identifiable causes, once the various successive structures of linkage between the causes in the revival of the Cold War are identified. Indirect methods often do not attract strong reactionary responses from the hawkish group.

Actual decision-makers did not listen to the advice of scientific peace research when N-persons games theory successfully predicted the unstable outcome of Kissinger's tri-polar structure: they will also probably ignore its advice in the future too. Nevertheless, such applications of peace research do make a positive contribution to raising the level of consciousness within the general population. At some point, this higher consciousness within the population at large will have an impact on the inner circle of decision-makers. This would therefore appear to be an effective indirect strategy for remedying a number of current global maladies.

When looking at the role of increasing international conflicts in causing the arms race and militarization, it is also necessary to make a distinction between short and long-term remedies. These correspond to the marginal causes of the arms race, in the first instance, and the internally structured causes of the arms race and militarization in the second. Great power intervention in regional conflicts via arms transfers also inevitably aggravates these conflicts, and therefore acts as the most salient marginal cause of the intensification of such conflicts.

Tetra-structural relations between the US-USSR-Afghanistan-Iran could offer the most demonstrative proof of this: it is easy to see how the policies of the superpowers represent the marginal cause of the intensification of international conflict, despite the prevalent, stereotypical, view that conflicts in the Third World are increasingly independent of the industrialized world. Within the framework of conflict formation in the global transformation process, each superpower tends to compete with its opponent in further aggravating the situation simply by shifting the responsibility onto the opponent. There are, of course, other types of marginal cause behind the increase in conflicts: for example, the overlapping effect of economic, religious, educational, linguistic, and ethnic discrimination in the peripheral region (sometimes as a significant marginal cause). However, in general these causes are internally structured and mostly static within the context of a given conflict. It should also be recognized that identifying the salient marginal cause of the increase in conflict is more amenable to phenomenological judgement than computerized calculation. Once the salient marginal cause of a given conflict is established, the strategy for resolving the conflict becomes apparent. If the conflict is relatively isolated, intervention by neutral forces might be possible, such as the activities of the UN Peacekeeping Operation in Cyprus, or by a number of neutral countries, as in the Middle East. However, if the conflict in question is not isolated from the actors who wish to intervene in it – that is, if the actor is a partner in the process of conflict formation – any intervention by such an actor would naturally aggravate the situation. In such an instance, indirect methods would be required. First and foremost, phenomenological identification of the given conflict is always the prerequisite for diagnosis, prognosis, and so-called clinical treatment of the conflict. It should be noted that the superpowers are not in general free from the process of the formation of conflicts. This has also been identified historically and phenomenologically.

As far as the militarization of science and technology as a cause of the arms build-up and militarization is concerned, the *differences* in the phase reached by the development of science and technology between countries have become the immediate marginal cause – although the overall phase attained constitutes a salient marginal cause of global militarization. This situation throws the concept of nation-centred science and technology into question. Of course, in the formulation of alternatives for any stage of science and technology, it is necessary to consider the steps in sequence. However, the total structural reform of science and technology policy based on alternative human values would clearly be more important as a long-term indirect method of achieving demilitarization and disarmament.

The role played by inactive or militarized universities in global militarization raises not only the specific issue of the militarization of universities, but additionally the general issue of these institutions' conservative character. Addressing the latter involves discussion of how to set about removing the internalized structural causes of global militarization. University reform is therefore closely linked to the total structural reform of science and technology policy, since both are interrelated in the process by which scientists and engineers are reproduced. The establishment of the UNU, related peace research organizations, related academic societies, including the International Peace Research Association, are extremely significant in this context, since the development of such an alternative academic network holds out the hope of university reform. This possibility also rests on the indirect strategy for global militarization.

As far as over-specialization in disciplines, and their associated loss of any integrative perspective for analyzing the real world as an implicit cause of global militarization is concerned, the required remedy not only involves innovation in each specialized discipline, oriented towards solving the global problematique, but also the urgent creation of more integrative alternative theories for peace-building. The research activities of the GPID project were the first effort to create such a theory amongst UNU research projects. However, this project faced tremendous difficulties in conducting analytical research in a coordinated effort at global network formation involving, originally, twenty-six units. The UNU is proposing to begin a new project on peace and conflict-resolution, and alternative security as one of five medium-term research subjects. The GPID will therefore become the strong base for the further development of alternative integrative global theory, provided that the GPID's original scheme of alternative categorization can be revived in the field of attempts to develop theories of global demilitarization.

Under normal circumstances in contemporary society, it is virtually impossible to overcome the negative inertia of organisations and actors which never contribute to the peace-building process. However, it is possible initially to develop instead an indirect alternative network which can be interpenetrated into conventional power relations. Such a strategy is also based on identifying each salient and marginal organiza-tion, together with the more internalized and structures pattern of organization. An assessment of various actors in terms of their peace-building capacity is an urgent task for a creative global intellectual strategy.

As far as the strengthened feedback mechanism of the worst-case learning network is concerned, the direct formation of alternative net-works for generating best-case learning will inevitably appear to be a frontal assault on older, established networks. However, here too the indirect method of alternative network formation seems to be more effective because the contemporary social structure exhibits a con-tinuous gradation between the worst-case and the best-case. An assessment of the various characteristics of different actors could easily be applied to this purpose. One factor of importance is the interrelated-ness and mutual reinforcement of the various causes of global mili-tarization; as a result, global demilitarization strategies should also be interrelated and mutually supportive, depending on the complicated relationship between the various causes of militarization.

The fundamental question when confronted with the financial weak-ness of the UNU and related institutions is simply how to bolster the financial basis of such bodies. The UNU's 1982 budget amounted to US$ 17.5 million; in contrast the annual budget of the University of Tokyo totals US$360 million – more than twenty times more. Of course, the University of Tokyo is not a militarized university, having removed the suffix 'Imperial' and adapted its development to that of the economic and political climate of post-war Japan under the Japa-nese 'Peace Constitution'. However, it did not develop any active insti-tutionalization for the study of peace-building. The University's various new institutions were developed exclusively within the framework of the exigencies of Japan's industrial advancement – in fact, with somewhat of a lag compared with the country's business class. This was not a mistake for the Japan of the 1950s, 1960s, and 1970s. However, the Japan of the 1980s has reached the stage at which the advancement of high technology has to be combined and integrated with active peace-building. The University of Tokyo does not possess the capacity to inaugurate such a new era since it could not generate the appropriate spirit within the university community, and is still very conservative on issues such as university reform. In contrast, in its short seven-year history – compared with the University of Tokyo's hundred – the UNU has been able to inspire such a spirit. Many universities in other countries are in an even worse position than the University of Tokyo inasmuch as they have direct involvements in military research via funds provided by military agencies. The UNU's alternative network is, in this sense, very creative from the perspective of establishing a New International Information Order.

As far as the weakness of autonomous provincial governments is concerned, two aspects stand out: the budgetary powers of provincial and local government vis-à-vis central government, and the increasing significance of the *quality* of provincial budget allocations. In Japan, examples of local government activities can be seen in the progressive role played by the Kanagawa prefecture in organizing international peace-oriented conferences in Yokohama, with the close cooperation of the City of Yokohama, the UNU, and several peace research societies. The City of Hiroshima is also expanding the scope of its activities beyond its own, inwardly oriented, profound experience of being an atomic-bomb victim.

Turning to the qualitative underdevelopment of autonomous provincial units is concerned, several stages of strengthening autonomy can be considered as steps towards accelerating the process of global transformation through the formation of alternative networks. The first stage would appear to be the formation of a network of sister-cities across national boundaries. The second stage is the promotion of transnational exchange between these cities. During this stage, the qualitative improvement of exchange and the further development of the network are always a significant factor in catalyzing the peace-building process. In the third stage, some of the provincial units would declare themselves as units in the world federation network. Creative intellectual exchange could continue to improve the contribution of this network. In the fourth state, some of the provincial units would declare themselves as nuclear-free zones, or demilitarized zones: such a development is already occurring even before this stage. If those tendencies were to be reinforced still further, some provincial units could enter the new era in which they would want to declare themselves independent of their mother-country. The European Community developed via the integration of many different nation-states in Western Europe. The alternative movement for peace-building could follow a different path: if, within some large nation-states, an alternative community at the stage of overall development but emerging from opposite forces and aspirations to present nation-states could be created by the independence of provincial units from the mother-country/centralized state, the character of the international system would be further transformed into a peaceful one.

Development and demilitarization

Disarmament theory was explained above in terms of a close relationship with the theory of the causes of global militarization and the arms race. In general, the order of presentation was successively from marginal causes to internally structured causes – although some exceptions may have crept in unintentionally. The significance of internally structured causes makes it increasingly evident that the theory of global disarmament and demilitarization is in fact equivalent to an alternative theory of development. Any development theory which accelerates militarization must therefore represent a *pseudo*-theory of development.

In his famous 1968 Montreal speech, Robert A. McNamara stressed the importance of development over military security, emphasizing that security *is* development, and that without development there can be no security. A developing nation that does not in fact develop simply cannot remain secure for the intractable reason that its own citizenry cannot shed its human nature. If security implies anything, it implies a minimum measure of order and stability. Without internal development of at least a minimal degree, order and stability are impossible. McNamara continued:

> As development progresses, security progresses and when people of a nation have organized their own human and natural resources to provide themselves with what they need and expect out of life, and have learned to compromise peacefully among competing demands in the larger national interest, then their resistance to disorder and violence will enormously increase. Conversely, the tragic need of desperate men to resort to force to achieve the inner imperatives of human decency will diminish.

Although located in the framework of conventional development thinking, McNamara's speech was attempting to highlight the importance of development over military security. He subsequently departed from Johnson's Vietnam strategy and became the President of the World Bank. The GPID programme's research perspectives identified conventional development – centred on the nation-state – as a cause of current global militarization. The programme therefore began working with an alternative conception of development from the outset. This was later developed a step further into the concept of transformational capability for solving the global problematique. The development of a higher level of hierarchical control should promote an alternative path of development via demilitarization. The deeper content of this claim is that if alternative development and demilitarization were to form a cyclical feedback loop, capable of promoting demilitarization and alternative development through the transformation capabilities of new networks and the fresh potentialities of newly created peace-oriented institutions, this would indeed represent the successful attainment of the transformation of transformational responsibility.

The concept of development is now, therefore, the most significant issue in the framework of disarmament and global demilitarization. Even the conventional concept of economic development now has to confront the question of whether disarmament and demilitarization are possible solely via the conventional strategy of the nation-state. The most vivid example of a response to this question is Japan's choice of whether to assume more military responsibility from the United States or not. Japan's choice also involves choices as to its contribution to alternative peace-building objectives, totally different to those of military security. At present the Japanese government is pursuing a double-track strategy, in the sense that, although strong pressure from the Reagan administration has forced it to increase its military budget, it is nonetheless developing alternative institutions, such as the UNU and its related organizations, by providing some financial support. With the globalization of the Japanese economy and Japanese technology, Japan as a nation-state is now faced with a serious dilemma. Historically, any nation-state which has become a big economic power has had a natural tendency to become a big military power too. There have, of course, been various variations in individual instances. Some nation-states hurried to become big military powers, without a commensurate economic basis. The best example of this was the pre-war development of Japan. Some nation-states have been hesitant to become military powers, even after becoming giants economically – as in the case of post-war Japan. And some nations which could not become giants economically because of geographical and other factors – such as Sweden – decided very early on in their history not to become big military powers. We cannot neglect the existence of many such peaceful neutral countries, which have an entirely different diplomatic logic to the big powers.

However, the intrinsic logic of central power dynamics in the Westphalian international system still operates in the global transformation process. It is here that the conventional development of the nation-state would be open to question on the issue of whether it is able to overcome the restrictions imposed on the ability to remain a disarmed nation-state, once having become an economic giant. According to Takashi Inoguchi's classification scheme of security policies, the policies of nation-states can be tabulated along three dimensions: the focus of attention, level of activity, and level of strength. The following table shows his classification of the eight categories of security policy.[15]

Level of Strength	Level of Activity	Outward Looking	Inward Looking
Strong	Active	Conquest	Revolution
Weak	Active	Hegemony	Finland Model
Strong	Passive	Manipulation	Seclusion
Weak	Passive	Manoeuvring	Submission
		Focus of attention	

The historical dynamics of Japan's security policy can be seen to be accommodable within this framework. The development of modern Japan started from seclusion in the Tokugawa era, and developed to conquest during the period of the Pacific War via manoeuvring, manipulation and hegemony, in step-by-step correspondence with Japan's international development as a nation-state (in the conventional sense of development). By contrast, post-Second World War Japan began from submission to the US Occupation Forces and developed to economic hegemony, mainly through manoeuvring. It must be emphasized here that Japan's Peace Constitution has the potentiality to transform Japan into a Finland Model. However, this process was not realized, and the interpretation of the Japanese constitution remains a major issue. It should be noted here that the Finland Model was originally termed Finlandization, intended in a perjorative sense, by some hawkish strategists. However, nation-states such as Switzerland, Austria, and Sweden, are more or less oriented to the Finland Model of national security. In this sense, the Finland Model should be re-examined in the light of alternative theories of international security policies. In the global transformation process, the capability of the nation-state system *per se* is radically diminishing in relation to the mounting pressure of the global problematique. The nuclear arms race and global militarization are amongst the most significant elements of the global problematique, inasmuch as they involve the survival of both small states as well as the big powers. If we look at other categories of security policy, the Finland model is the only possible alternative for a nation-state to survive in the age of global conflict formation between the two superpowers. It might be true that military strategists in the superpowers still believe in their capacity to win a nuclear showdown. However, this is surely no longer true for the people of other countries.

The Finland Model is therefore the only alternative for other nation-states to survive. But the basic concept goes even further.

It offers the only way out of the intrinsic properties of the Westphalian international system, in which the central dynamics of power relations tend to determine the whole process of the transformation of the system. It should, however, be re-emphasized, that the Westphalian system itself is also currently involved in the global transformation process – not in the sense of the successive rising and falling of empires, but through the gradual dissolution of the system based on billiard-ball type of nation-state relations. The process is not symmetrical through time, since the rise and fall of empires cannot be repeated in the global transformation process. A symbolic proof of this would be Japan's refraining from becoming a big military power despite becoming the number one economic power, and skilfully transforming its economic capacities for the creative purpose of peace-building. The crucial question here is how to put Japan's economic capability at the disposal of the common intellectual effort of the global academic community. The concept of alternative development is crystallized in this creative process of intellectual institutionalization.

The strong relationship between development and demilitarization – development first, demilitarization second – would be well illustrated in the case of Japan were it to successfully resist the Pentagon's pressure to increase its military budget. In the previous economic development of Japan, Japanese economists in the main subscribed to a conventional understanding of development. Political and military problems were outside the scope of their consideration. However, it is undeniable that post-war Japan's concentration on economic development involved a transformation of the pre-war military spirit to a commercial merchant spirit. The difference in the international environment was clearly crucial in post-war Japan being able to develop so fast through a concentration solely on economic development. However, the conventional concept of development of a nation-state even in the field of economic growth is faced with a serious dilemma within the conventional framework of the theory of international politics, since this theory demands that a big economic power take on a commensurate financial burden towards its own security. This demand is based on empirical, historical reality. But it is a very superficial argument. An alternative normative argument can be developed through the application of an alternative theory of the global transformation process to the analysis of the process of the development of the nation-state.

In the process of Japan's development, the marginal factor in development varied depending on the stage of development reached. Educational variables were very significant in the sense that they operated over a considerably longer period of time than other variables, such as transportation, communication, or production.

As space precludes a detailed empirical study here I propose to summarize the study undertaken by Johan Galtung and myself in another context. In the early period of Meiji Japan, between 1875–1895, the increase in the number of primary school students and teachers was the most significant factor in subsequent economic growth, with a lag of five years. Between 1895 and 1915, the increase in the number of students in vocational middle school was the most significant marginal factor for later economic growth, with a 10-year time lag. Between 1915 and 1932, the most significant marginal factor for time-lagged economic growth shifted from vocational middle school to vocational college (producing a very elegant shift in the map of the computer output based on time-series time-lag correlation analysis). The shift in the marginal factor from the pre-war period to the post-war period is more significant in the sense that the number of university graduates has become the most salient factor in time-lagged economic growth. The lag is seven years for graduating undergraduates, and five years for graduating graduates (taking higher degrees). These correlations were calculated up until the mid-1960s. In the 1970s such a strong and salient correlation disappears as far as university students as a whole are concerned. There might be another shift of marginal effect from universities to think tanks. Or a specific university specialism might exercise a salient effect on the growth of the economy. No economist is currently undertaking empirical research of this type in Japan. However, the pioneer diagnosis of the present-day Japanese economy is moving towards emphasizing the importance of high technology and the internationalization of the Japanese economy.

An intuitive diagnosis of the contemporary world would suggest that the globalization of the Japanese economy should be developed further, in the sense that Japan's high technology should contribute to the demilitarization of the world and facilitate further development. It should be noted here that the present issue for Japanese technology centres around the Pentagon's demand for Japan to contribute to the development of US military technology. In the context of the development of this issue between the US and Japan, scientists and engineers who work in the field of high technology should be mobilized for an alternative dialogue and multi-sided discussion in which they could play a creative role in peace-building. The demilitarization of high technology is the most significant marginal factor for the further development of the global community, as well as for Japan itself.

Alternative political science in alliance with peace research could follow the example of Professor Glenn Paige, who is attempting to systematize non-violent political science. According to Professor Paige, the social role of political science will shift from the relatively passive, peripheral role of a 'pro-violent service station' to the more active role of a central institution for the creation and application of non-violent political knowledge. It will seek to change the environment, rather than 'trouble shoot' its defects.[16]

This might be the same task required of scientists and engineers who wish to develop high technology. The difference between them is that the latter have tended to conceive their task within the narrow context of conventional national security, whilst the former tries to conceive its task for human survival in the global transformation process. However, the accomplishment of this shift in social role is a very difficult task, even for political science. Professor Paige himself emphasizes that to accomplish such a shift, political science will have to detach itself from its present dependent relationship towards institutions which accept violence, and create non-violent institutions which it can wholeheartedly support. This task would be more difficult in the case of scientists and engineers because of big science and technology, which tend to rely on the traditional nation-state for their financial support.

What is the salient marginal factor for the next phase of development? This question should be posed in a creative way. Development and demilitarization cannot be dissociated, since development *means* alternative global development.

Notes

1 Donella H. Meadows, Dennis L. Meadows, Jorgen Randers, William W. Behrens III, *The Limits to Growth. A Report for the Club of Rome's Project on the Predicament of Mankind*, Universe Books, New York, 1972.
2 Ivan A. Getting, 'Halting the Inflationary Spiral of Death' in *Air Force/ Space Digest*, April 1963, cited by Robin Clarke, *The Science of War and Peace*, McGraw-Hill, 1972, p. 4.

Casualties per war	1820–1859	1860–1899	1900–1949	1950–1999	2000–2050
500–5,000	100,000 killed in 63 wars	100,000 killed in 75 wars	100,000 killed in 71 wars	100,000 killed in 64 wars	100,000 killed in 57 wars
5,000–50,000	300,000 killed in 25 wars	200,000 killed in 21 wars	300,000 killed in 25 wars	300,000 killed in 25 wars	300,000 killed in 25 wars
50,000–1 million	400,000 killed in 4 wars	700,000 killed in 7 wars	1.5 million killed in 15 wars	2.2 million killed in 22 wars	2.5 million killed in 25 wars
1 million–5 million	—	3.6 million killed in 3 wars	4.6 million killed in 4 wars	5 million killed in 5 wars	6 million killed in 6 wars
5 million–50 million	—	—	36 million killed in 2 wars	38 million killed in 3 wars	40 million killed in 4 wars
50 million–500 million	—	—	—	360 million killed in 1 war	400 million killed in 2 wars
500 million–5,000 million	—	—	—	—	3,600 million killed in 1 war
TOTAL	800,000 killed in 92 wars	4.6 million killed in 106 wars	42 million killed in 117 wars	406 million killed in 120 wars	4,050 million killed in 120 wars
World Population	1,000 million	1,300 million	2,000 million	4,000 million	10,000 million
Per Cent Population Killed in War	0.1	0.4	2.1	10.1	40.5

3 Carl Sagan, *Cosmos*, Random House, 1980, p. 327.

The Richardson diagram. The horizontal axis shows the magnitude of a war (M = 5 means 10^5 people killed; M = 10 means 10^{10}, i.e. every human on the planet). The vertical axis shows the time to wait until a war of magnitude M erupts. The curve is based on Richardson's data for wars between 1820 and 1945. Simple extrapolation suggests that M = 10 will not be reached for about a thousand years (1820 + 1,000 = 2820). But the proliferation of nuclear weapons has probably moved the curve into the shaded area, and the waiting time to Doomsday may be ominously short. The shape of the Richardson curve is within our control, but only if humans are willing to embrace nuclear disarmament and restructure dramatically the planetary community.

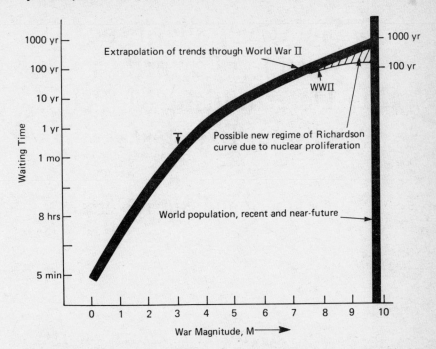

4 David Singer (ed.), *The Correlates of War: II Testing Some Realpolitik Models*, The Free Press, 1980, pp. 68–82; David Singer and Associates, *Explaining War, Selected Papers from the Correlates of War Project*, Sage, 1979, pp. 240–252.
5 Cf. Singer, *Explaining War*, pp. 199–229.
6 Rober Sheer, *Enough Shovels*, 1982.
7 Yoshikazu Sakamoto (ed.), *Boryoku to Heiwa* (Violence and Peace), Asahi Newspaper Co., 1982.
8 Anatol Rapoport, N-Persons Game Theory.
9 The Dept. of Public Information, The United Nations, 'The Nuclear Threat to Our World: An Exhibition', pp. 90–105.
10 Hiroharu Seki, 'From a Theory of Disarmament to a Theory of Demilitarization', mimeo, presented at Yokohama Asian Peace Research Association Meeting, 1979.
11 Hiroharu Seki, 'Global Militarization and its Remedy', IPSHU Research Report Series No. 3, August 1979.
12 Ibid.
13 Hiroharu Seki, 'Re-opening of the Cold War and the Crisis of the World Order', in Hans-Henrik Holm and Eric Rudeng (eds.), *Festschrift for Johan Galtung*, Universitetsforlaget, Oslo 1980, pp. 122–138.
14 Rapoport, op. cit.
15 Takashi Inoguchi, 'Political Security: Towards its Broad Conceptualization', mimeo, 1978.
16 Glenn Paige, 'On the Possibility of Nonviolent Political Science', IPSHU Research Report No. 4, 1980.

7

The Greening of the World – Towards a Non-Deterministic Model of Global Processes*

Mats Friberg and Björn Hettne

Prologue

Thus the attitudes engendered by our guiding perspective are some-what different from those that move either the establishment intellec-tuals committed to modernizing the world in the image of Western technological civilization or the anti-establishment intellectuals from the same centres who are roaming the world after the fashion of new missionaries and preaching revolution. Both these sets of propagan-dists are moved by theories of predetermined change that provide little scope for alternative futures based on autonomous choices and diverse perspective. We are motivated, on the contrary, to building autonomy, freedom, well-being, and justice at a number of levels so that ordinary men and women can realize these values. Neither the vision of an overriding world government in the image of some transcendental ideology nor the hope that a once-and-for-all smash-ing operation can do away with all encumberances holds any attrac-

Authors' note: The title of this chapter alludes to the title of an important book by Charles Reich, *The Greening of America* (Random House, New York, 1970), which has been a main source of inspiration for all of us who want to understand the cultural revolution we are in the midst of. The paper is one product of an ongoing research project at the Dept. of Peace and Conflict Research, Gothenburg University, which deals with processes of penetration and mobilization in different parts of the world. The paper has been discussed at various places. We are particularly grateful for detailed comments by Samin Amin (Dakar), Dag Poleszynski (Oslo), Folker Fröbel (Starnberg) and Edmund Dahlström (Gothenburg).

tion for us. Perhaps our approach comes from an ancient civilization seeking to reorder its elements on the basis of a new consciousness, seeking actively to realize preferred values through a series of challenges and encounters in the real world. (Rajni Kothari, 'World politics and world order: The issue of autonomy' in Mendlovitz (ed.), *On the Creation of a Just World Order*, Free Press, New York, 1975).

Introduction: The Red, Blue and Green dimensions in development thinking

The purpose of this study is to clarify the intellectual content and political relevance of what has come to be called the 'Green' alternative in world development. This task is far from easy due to the fact that this alternative is much less articulated, discussed and politically organized compared to the 'Blue' (market, liberal, capitalist) and 'Red' (state, 'socialist', planning) options. It is our contention that the Blue and the Red can be seen as varieties of a dominant Western development paradigm, whereas Green development thinking represents a fundamental opposition to this paradigm and that the sources of this opposition are to be found both within the West and in Third World countries, economically and intellectually penetrated by the West. In this context, the socialist industrialized countries of Eastern Europe are included in the concept of the West. By 'socialism' in this context we refer to what Bahro has called 'actually existing socialism', not the whole socialist tradition, which contains several different orientations, including Green ones.

Mainstream development thinking can be analysed along a continuum running between two ideological antipoles, Red socialism versus Blue capitalism. Much of the political debate in the West has been concerned with State versus Market, and the relative merits of these supposedly antagonistic institutions, in the context of economic development.[1]

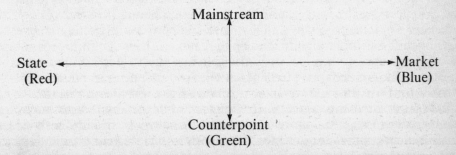

Along the horizontal Red-Blue dimension it is possible to identify several more or less distinct development strategies within the mainstream Western tradition: the liberal model, the state capitalist strategy, the Soviet model, Keynesianism and neo-liberalism. The liberal market-oriented model has historically been the most important one, but in twentieth century capitalism Keynesianism, expressing the increased role of state power, has become predominant. The other development strategies are varieties of the basic paradigm, expressing different historical possibilities and constraints. They differ mainly with regard to means (i.e. the relative role of state and market) but as far as ends are concerned (the Western concept of modernity), they are basically all similar. The differences as regards means can largely be explained by the specific circumstances in which the strategies emerged. Keynesianism is thus a compromise between the Red and the Blue. Since the 1930s it has been the dominant development ideology in the industrialized capitalist world, particularly in countries with strong social-democratic parties. Today, however, state-fostered growth is less popular and Keynesian orthodoxy has been challenged by a *neo-liberal* Blue wave in the industrialized countries, looking for ways out of the present impasse. It is not especially surprising that the capitalist industrialized countries find it hard to accept this message and abandon a well-established economic doctrine, but in the absence of any real alternative many are now moving towards the Market pole of the Mainstream axis.

The alternatives along the horizontal axis indicate the scope of action permitted by the dominant paradigm. This rigidity is also reflected in various analyses of and strategies for the global system. The idea of a 'non-capitalist path' explicitly stated that socialist development was possible without going through the stage of capitalism and revolution if, and this was the main requisite, the Soviet Union gave its support to the country embarking upon the non-capitalist path. Apart from this, the strategy implied in this theory or ideology (it has served both functions) basically conformed to the Soviet model. The Brandt Commission Report articulated a Keynesian solution to world poverty by proposing a Massive Resource Transfer (MRT). According to this theory, the poor peoples of the world are to function as the unemployed in Keynes' system. In using these financial resources to buy goods produced by the industrial countries, the economic problems of the latter would be solved as well. The rich and poor countries are to move forward together rather than the poor countries being given benefits at the expense of the rich world, which was the strategy of the New International Economic Order (NIEO). At the Cancun summit (October 1981) on global development problems the neo-liberal philosophy was translated into 'global Reaganomics', while the Keynesian strategy contained in the Brandt Report (which originally was meant to provide a framework for the discussion) was tacitly buried. Instead the developing countries were advised to liberalize their economies, encourage their entrepreneurs and find out their competitive advantages. That is, they are *also* required to move towards the market pole of the axis. This recommendation implies a return to the *ideal model* of capitalist development from which *actual* development in the industrial countries themselves has deviated substantially.

Opposed and dialectically related to the predominant development paradigm, there has been a Green Counterpoint, articulating diverse interests in varying historical contexts. The Counterpoint protest has increasingly been reduced to a more or less ideological phenomenon, as the modern complex was institutionalized in structures such as the state and the bureaucracy, the industrial system, the urban system, the market system, the techno-scientific system, and the military-industrial complex. These structures dominate both Red and Blue industrial societies, and the vested interests in them are, of course, immense. What the Green position at present can hope for is therefore a gradual weakening of the modern complex as its maintenance costs increase, and the economic growth it is supposed to guarantee fails to come about. A society organized according to Green ideals would, in negating the modern complex, be *physiocratic*, in the sense that the earth and the natural resources constitute the ultimate precondition for human existence, *ultrademocratic*, in the sense that people exercise control over their own situation, and *structurally undifferentiated*, in the sense that the division of labour will be located within rather than between individuals.

This counterpoint may be traced back to premodern structures, but should not be interpreted simply as nostalgic conservatism, even if this is one of its manifestations. We may find typical expressions in romanticism, anarchism, utopian socialism, and other ideologies reacting against 'modernity'. It should be pointed out that the marxist tradition is broad and complex enough to contain its own mainstream-counterpoint contradiction. As is well-known, 'the young Marx' criticized industrial capitalism in terms not too different from the romantic critique – the problem of alienation. However, the old Marx also tended to support the narodnik or Russian populist view on the possibilities of skipping over capitalism and building socialism on the traditional agrarian commune in opposition to the more 'orthodox' or 'mainstream' interpretation of the Russian marxists. Perhaps the clearest manifestation of the Counterpoint is the *populist* tradition, where Russian narodism is the classical case. Its most interesting contribution to the Counterpoint was the criticism of the idea of the division of labour. The narodniks would not accept the sacrifices in terms of human personality (recognized but considered necessary by both Adam Smith and Emile Durkheim) to achieve a more differentiated, complex and efficient society. Mikhailovskij's law of progress is a good example of this:

Progress is the gradual approach to the integral individual, to the fullest possible and the most diversified division of labour among man's organs and the least possible division of labour among men. Everything that diminishes the heterogeneity of society and thereby increases the heterogeneity of its members is moral, just, reasonable, and beneficial.[2]

By *neo-populism* we refer to the revival of populist ideas, which bear a certain resemblance to the classical populism, for example in their urge for community (*Gemeinschaft*) and moral distaste towards industrial civilization. However, there are also significant new elements of which the most prominent are an ecological consciousness (encompassing the total global ecological system) and a strong commitment to a just world order. Thus, modern Green ideas have achieved a global relevance, whereas the historical populist movements were parochial. However, the Green alternative posed at a global level is even less articulated in terms of analytical framework and development strategy than is the case at the national level. On the other hand, we would assert that Green ideas are more widespread and have a stronger potential than Red and Blue ideas.

In fact, Russian populism, Third World populism and the present upsurge of neo-populism in the West may be seen as an example of a constructive intellectual interaction between 'developed' and 'developing' societies. It is significant that there exists one intellectual trend which is rooted both in Western and Non-Western traditions, and that this type of development thinking is drawing on contributions from both Western and Third World thinkers. This can be seen in Johan Galtung's and Ignacy Sach's references to Gandhi, Schumacher's attempt at articulating what he called 'Buddhist economics', the impact of maoism on the new left, and the emerging interest in oriental religions in the industrial countries. What all this amounts to is, in our view, a Greening of the world, even if the Red and Blue options are still dominating the debate. In the sections that follow we will go somewhat deeper into this war of colours, both in terms of development theory and political praxis.

The persistence of evolutionism in development theory

'Development is one of the oldest and most powerful of all Western ideas.'[3] The central element of this perspective is the idea of evolution, which implies that development is conceived as firstly, directional and cumulative, secondly, predetermined and irreversible, thirdly, progressive, and fourthly, immanent with reference to the nation state.

Certainly, the emphasis within this perspective shifted as new elements were added during the history of Western civilization. Thus, the emergence of capitalism, the bourgeoisie as a ruling class and the industrial system all gave a certain shape to Western developmentalism.

The most significant shift in emphasis was the identification of growth with the modern idea of progress which was a novel emergent in the Western mind.[4] Growth in Greek and Roman civilization was a cyclical process, whereas medieval authorities conceived growth in terms of degeneration, decay, and with a sense of doom. The modern idea of progress, in contrast, implied that 'civilization has moved, is moving and will move in a desirable direction'.

This idea has its roots in the scientific movement at the beginning of the modern age. The pioneers of science maintained that all natural phenomena can be explained on the basis of the operation of mechanical laws upon material bodies. Nature is nothing but a machine which can be manipulated by humanity to its own advantage. The scientific method of controlled experiments and deductive reasoning guarantees the infinite growth of valid knowledge about the mechanisms of nature and this knowledge will lay the foundation of a technological society marked by material abundance. This optimistic mechanical worldview was later extended to include humanity and society. The Enlightenment thinkers made the individual into an object, just as nature had been objectified in the new sciences. The dynamics of society follow natural laws. Infinite human progress is assured by the application of scientific knowledge about these laws in the governance and regulation of society. The most explicit articulations of this perspective may be found in the works of Comte and Saint-Simon.

The father of sociology, August Comte, maintained that the 'progressive march of civilization follows a natural and unavoidable course, which flows from the law of human organization'. All societies develop from the theological and the metaphysical stages to the positive and industrial stage with the successive growth of scientific knowledge. His teacher Henri Saint-Simon predicted that future society would be an industrial society governed by industrial magnates and technical experts whose skills were grounded in 'positive' knowledge. Certainly different dimensions of 'progress' were emphasized by different social thinkers. Condorcet, Saint-Simon and Comte focused on the knowledge of humanity and society, whereas Marx, in contract, stressed the progressive movement of the productive forces and stated that new 'higher' relations of production (i.e. socialism) could not appear 'before the material conditions of their existence have matured in the womb of the old society'. Herbert Spencer, using an organic metaphor, saw the development of society as a process of increasing complexity, increasing differentiation and increasing division of labour between the differentiated parts. Later thinkers have emphasized a number of dimensions such as economic growth, technological development, the capacity to mobilize energy and information, industrialization or socioeconomic modernization in general.

Whatever their differences, evolutionist thinkers tend to agree on four basic axioms:

A1 *Direction* The general change of history is directed and cumulative. It can be described as a process of growth, expansion or evolution with respect to some particular linear dimension.

A2 *Determinism* The evolutionary process is predetermined and irreversible. It is not possible for humanity to influence the course of history except for minor details.

A3 *Progress* Evolution means progress in the normative sense of the word. We are moving towards a better world.

A4 *Immanence* The evolutionary process is immanent in every society, which in practice means in the nation-state.

In what follows we shall try to demonstrate how this mainstream perspective, albeit modified, lingers on in a succession of schools in development theory. As will become clear we see the emergence of the Green view as a reaction against this perspective.

The Modernization Paradigm

The intellectual climate after World War Two was confident and optimistic and theories of social change with their roots in the Victorian Age reappeared. Modernization Theory can thus in a way be seen as a revival of Western Development Thinking as described above, only more optimistic. After all, the classical preoccupation with the transition was fraught with some misgivings about future progress.

Modernization Theory is thus only the most recent manifestation of central tradition in Western social thought: evolutionism. This implies among other things that modernization is a basically endogenous process, the realization of a potential that lay dormant in all societies. Often there is a need for external factors in order to initiate the process, but the process in nevertheless immanent.[5]

For all practical purposes Modernization is equivalent to Westernization, since the Western countries first reached modernity and therefore have served as models for the rest of the world. Thus, development in the 50s and 60s was seen as an imitative process.

The Modernization Paradigm can be summarized as follows:

- Development is a spontaneous, irreversible process inherent in every single society.
- Development implies structural differentiation and functional specialization.
- The process of development can be divided into distinct stages showing the level of development achieved by each society.
- Develement can be stimulated by external competition or military threat and by internal measures that support modern sectors and modernize traditional sectors.

The idea of dualism was also central to the modernizers engaged in the problems of underdeveloped-countries. It may appear as if this idea signified the abandoning of the unilinear, evolutionistic framework, but this is not in fact the case. Rather, the two sectors, the traditional and the modern, were conceived of as two stages of development, co-existing in time, and in due course the differences between them were to disappear because of a natural urge towards equilibrium.

Modernization policies were thus regarded as a development strategy through support for universal historical forces, analogous to the transition from feudalism to capitalism in Western economic history. Among the modernizers there were fundamentalists who believed in development as a basically repetitive and endogenous process, realizing the potential inherent in more or less embryonic form in all societies.

The dependency school

The 'dependency school' was very critical of modernization theory, but, as we shall argue, not so fundamentally different in its conception of development. It was never a uniform doctrine shared by all the *dependenistas*: Cardoso, dos Santos, Sunkel, Marini, etc. It is, therefore, necessary to analyse their works in relation to different theoretical dimensions.[6] Certain ideas are, however, common to most of the *dependentistas*:

- The most important obstacles to development were not lack of capital or entrepreneurial skills. They were external to the underdeveloped economy – not internal.
- The international division of labour was analyzed in terms of relations between regions, of which two kinds – centre and periphery – assumed particular importance.
- Due to the fact that the periphery was deprived of its surplus, development in the centre somehow implied underdevelopment in the periphery. Thus development and underdevelopment could be described as two aspects of a single global process. All regions participating in the process were capitalist, but a distinction between central and peripheral capitalism was made.
- Since the periphery was doomed to underdevelopment because of its linkage to the centre, it was considered necessary for a peripheral country to disassociate itself from the world market and strive for self-reliance.

Dependencia was not strictly a theory, rather a new perspective. Therefore there was a basic agreement on a high level of abstraction, while theories differed in emphasis when it came to more concrete issues. As soon as this perspective was accepted, many previous approaches in social science drastically lost relevance. With respect to the *content* of development, however, the difference between the dependency theory and modernization approaches was slight. *Dependencia* was basically a paradigm of underdevelopment and as far as development is concerned the approach was fairly conventional. The persistence of evolutionism is revealed in attempts at applying dependency theory at the level of praxis.

On the national level regimes influenced by the dependency perspective include Chile under Allende, Jamaica under Manley, and Tanzania under Nyerere. Significantly only one of these regimes survived (but modified its development strategy substantially), which indicates that self-reliance is a difficult option in the context of the present world order. So much stress was put on the external obstacles to development that the problem of how to initiate a development process, once these obstacles were removed, was rather neglected. In fact, one gets the impression that the development perspective implied in dependency theory was the endogenous growth and modernization paradigm.

On the global level, the dependency paradigm stimulated the debate on the NIEO and provided the critics of the old international order with a relevant belief system, many good arguments and an appropriate language. Some of the weaknesses and biases of the dependency approach also crept into this debate, e.g. economic nationalism, the stress on external factors and lack of concrete development strategy. It is therefore natural that the radical dependency theorists consider this as a case of conservative reabsorption. To Amin the NIEO is 'a consistent and logical program for getting out of the crisis, that reflects the interests and views of the bourgeoisies of the South'.[7]

According to Frank, 'dependence has now completed the cycle of its natural life'.[8] The reason is the crisis of the 1970s. Amin also devotes most of his interest to the current crisis.

A new situation calls for new theoretical approaches and the abandonment of old.

The world-system approach

The criticism of dependency theory is to a large extent related to its over-emphasis on external factors. On the other hand, the *dependentistas* attacked the modernization theorists because of their obsession with internal factors. Thus, there are two kinds of bias in development theory: endogenism and exogenism. Both approaches are, if carried to their extremes, equally misleading. The obvious remedy is to transcend this dichotomy and find the synthesis. There are in fact no countries that are completely autonomous and self-reliant, and no countries that develop (or underdevelop) merely as a reflection of what goes on beyond their national borders. The world-system approach maintains some of the most disputed tenets of dependency theory, for example that the world is capitalist, and that part of it has been so since the sixteenth century. From this time onwards there emerged a world-

system, incorporating a growing number of previously more or less isolated and self-sufficient societies into a complex system of functional
relations.[9] The result of this expansion was that a small number of
core-states transformed a huge *external* arena into a *periphery*.
Between these core-states and the periphery, the world-system theorists
identify *semi-peripheries*.

The world-system is a social system which, according to Wallerstein,
is characterized by the fact that its dynamics are *internal*. This proposition implies an internalization of the external factor. Thus, the problem
of the external versus the internal, which caused the dependency
theorists a great deal of trouble, has, ostensibly, been solved. Like the
dependentistas, Wallerstein describes the world-system as *capitalist*.
However, he does not make the distinction between development and
underdevelopment, or central and peripheral capitalism. Thus, there is
only *one* kind of capitalism, namely that of the world-system, although
its various branches may manifest themselves differently. By avoiding
the prerequisite polarization between centre and periphery, Wallerstein
circumvents another of the pitfalls of the dependency school: the idea
of two different sorts of capitalism.

As the recent cases of Chile and Jamaica suggest, it is not easy to
break the chains of dependency and initiate a process of self-reliant
development. In fact, the experiences of these countries give credence
to the thesis that all countries are part of the 'system' whether they like
it or not, and that there are 'limited possibilities of transformation
within the capitalist world-economy'.[10] According to the world-system
theorists, it is a matter of changing the structural position from a
peripheral to a semi-peripheral one, a possibility that is open only to a
few. A genuine change would necessitate a transformation of the
world-system into a socialist world government – a very distant prospect indeed!

> Everywhere, the reality has been that the fact that a movement pro-
> claims the unlinking of a state's productive processes from the inte-
> grated world-economy has never in fact accomplished the unlinking.
> It may have accomplished temporary withdrawals which, by
> strengthening internal production and political structures, enabled
> the state to improve its relative position in the world-economy.[11]

Considering the limited possibilities of transformation within the capitalist world-economy, there are, according to world-system theorists,
three strategies open for development: the *strategy of seizing the
chance*, the *strategy of promotion by invitation*, and the *strategy of
self-reliance*. The first solution is a classical one, roughly identical with
what was above termed the state capitalist strategy, since it involves
aggressive state action to transform the structure of comparative
advantages for the country in question. Of course, not all countries can
seize the chance. Development by invitation is based on existing

comparative advantages, such as low wage level and a general hospitality (the liberal strategy). Of course, not all countries will be found hospitable enough. Self-reliance deviates from both of these strategies by its inward orientation but in the context of the present world-system it is the strategy most unlikely to succeed, if we believe the world-system theorists. As will be argued, we think that this option has been prematurely ruled out.

Several of the post-dependency approaches, such as the marxist analysis of the internationalization of capital, neo-structuralism and the world-system analysis, are all marked by the ambition to grasp the dynamics of world development. This interest in global theories can be regarded as an effort to go beyond dependency to create a framework in which *both* centre *and* periphery, as well as the relations between them, are considered. Several manifestations of a new global consciousness could be noted during the 1970s, when the world increasingly came to be seen as *one* system. However, the *globalization* of development theory has not only been extremely structuralistic and deterministic, but also marked by a neglect of cultural dimensions. World-system analysis will have to account for the cultural implications of shifts in the geographical location of centres, as well as the mobilization potential of cultural systems only partially penetrated by Western values. The future of the world-system cannot simply be derived from historic trends or some revealed inner logic. By internalizing external factors, world-system analysis in a way returns to endogenism of a more grand scale, the endogenism of the world-system rather than the endogenism of the national state.

Thus, the repeated attempts at transcending endogenism have not quite succeeded in getting us out of the teleological trap. Early development theory took development for granted as a more or less automatic process and was interested in barriers to this process rather than in the mechanisms behind it. To some extent this bias has been overcome, but still it needs to be stressed that development is a result of human action and that any development process consequently can be reoriented through human action. Thus development theory has to move beyond evolutionism of both the Red and the Blue kind. Green thinking seems for some reason to be less deterministic. What happens if one tries to apply that in analysing world-system dynamics?

Beyond evolutionism: the essence of Green development thinking

A new stream of thought has emerged in the development debate in the 1970s. All over the world there are advocates of 'another development', 'indigenous alternatives', the 'Green wave', 'populism'. Alternatives which were considered as utopian not more than a decade ago are now taken seriously, even by members of the establishment. The reason is that more and more people are beginning to realize that it is the development process itself which engenders most of our problems. Of the four axioms of evolutionism discussed above, *progress* is the first to be rejected. If we have all been floating along the stream of evolution, we are now starting to doubt whether it will carry us to the promised land. Instead we hear the roaring from the approaching waterfall. Almost all the traditional indicators of development have changed their emotional loading from plus to minus. What were once regarded as forces of production are now, with greater justification, described as forces of destruction.[12]

The conventional idea that the capitalist mode of production stimulates the development of the productive forces in such a way that they will provide the technological means for a better world seems to be completely unfounded. Modern technology is not asked to solve our ecological or social problems, but to deliver war machines, control-oriented data and information systems, centralized energy-producing systems, and new consumer gadgets for those who have purchasing power. Complex advanced technology requires technical expertise and a centralized social organization. Thus it is *per se* incompatible with a system of self-management.[13]

The next assumption to be doubted is the second axiom – the idea of a predetermined and irreversible process. Western man has long been told: 'You cannot stop the development process. You cannot go against the forces of evolution.' The instinct of self-preservation, however, does not listen to such reassurances. Having a presentiment of an approaching catastrophe we simply try to swim against the stream. Is perhaps the very idea of evolution itself the main obstacle preventing us from taking, 'the future in our hands'? Technology is not an inexorable force which develops independently of human will. It is not a politically neutral means which can be used equally well for good and bad. The human will enters at every point in the development of technology. The stream of evolution is actually made up of those who are told to swim in the same direction. What would happen should we decide to swim in the opposite direction?

A structuralist-determinist view of social change cannot explain the emergence of a high-technological society. Human consciousness and will have been decisive elements in the process. Society is not just reproduction and adaptation; it is also creation and self-production, to use the words of Alan Touraine.[14] Society is not what it is, but what it makes itself to be. It must be seen as the outcome of struggles between actors with different visions of desirable futures of which some are dominant during a particular historical epoch. In fact, the present industrial society is a partially realized utopian society, in which a number of projects are pursued which are abstracted from the concrete situations and only adequate to conditions lying far off in the future. This is the only way to explain big investments in risky non-profitable projects like space travel and nuclear power stations. The fact is that mainstream Western society is propelled by a utopia to the same extent as the vast number of counter-movements which have tried to build utopian communes throughout Western history. The only difference is that the 'mainstream utopia' is backed by power.

The utopian dream of the technological society has its roots in the scientific movement at the beginning of the modern age. It could still stir the imagination of people in the early 1960s, as the following quotation from a 1963 speech by the then US President John Kennedy shows:

> As we begin to master the potentialities of modern science we move towards an era in which science can fulfil its creative promise and help bring into existence the happiest society the world has ever known.

The natural or positive sciences have been one of the most important formative forces in the development of modern society, and its vision of a materially advanced society based on 'objective' knowledge has been realized to an unbelievable degree. The very success of science is its main drawback because the negative side-effects of its programme are now visible for many. The science-based society has entered into an acute crisis of legitimacy. This interpretation explains why the Green attack on modern society is targeted at the cultural rather than the economic level. It has turned into a revolution of consciousness. It tries to construct another world view. It is searching for counter-utopias.

As long as we believe in evolution and progress, there is no need for an elaborated normative concept of development. The stream of evolution will automatically carry us to the promised land. As soon as we realize that we are caught up in a stream which runs in the wrong direction, there is a strong need to make a clear distinction between a descriptive (the direction of the stream) and a normative concept (the desired direction) of development. The question arises, on what to ground a normative concept of development?

The specificity of the Green view of the global problematique derives from the effort to see and to examine the world in a radical humanistic perspective. The concept of development must be defined in human terms if it is to have any relevance at all. Thus E.F. Schumacher wrote about development economics as if people really mattered.[15] The goal of development is basically defined as the full realization of the individual in every aspect of its being. This is, of course, only a preliminary formulation which will be elaborated in a moment. It is, however, already strong enough to rule out a number of other goals, such as economic growth, technological development, scientific growth, social revolution, serving a particular class, serving the national interest, the state, or God.

These values could at the most be seen as second-order goals or as means to the ultimate end. Even a value such as the conservation of nature which is so dear to the Green view is not a goal in itself. 'What is involved is not to preserve nature while forgetting men, but rather to manage nature in such a way that the men of our generation and all future generations will be ensured of the possibility of developing.'[16] There is, however, a radical version of the Green view which defends the principle of biospherical egalitarianism. According to this principle the concern for humanity should be extended to all other forms of life.[17] Humanity has no right to exploit and suppress other species for its own pleasure. The moral force of this argument increases, of course, when we move into the animal kingdom and especially as we approach the 'higher' sentient animals. Vegetarianism seems to be a congenial attitude within the Green movement.

The idea of human self-realization is based on a particular theory of personality which has deep historical roots. In recent years it has been developed further by humanistic psychologists like Abraham Maslow, Erich Fromm, and Carl Rogers. These authors see the modern individual as basically alienated or estranged from others and from its true nature. Instead of trying to adapt the individual to society, they suggest that we should do it the other way around – adapt society to the individual. Modern society in its entirety is insane, because it does not allow people to develop their potentialities.[18] But what are our potentialities and how do we develop them?

The concepts of self-realization and alienation assume the concept of basic human needs. They do not make sense if one believes in the almost complete malleability of human nature. Prevailing theories look upon the human individual as a product of socialization. They recognize deviant individuals and sub-cultures, but never a deviant society.

The concept of a deviant society, however, is the key concept for the alienation tradition – a society whose structure is contrary to human nature and does not allow the satisfaction of basic human needs. If they are to be satisfied, society will have to be restructured and quite fundamentally.[19]

What are our basic needs and how do we satisfy them? (The concepts of basic human needs should not be confused with the concept of specific instincts, desires, wishes or market demand.) Nearly everyone can agree that the human being has basic material needs, such as physiological needs for food, shelter, warmth, sex and so forth. The debate is all about the existence of basic non-material needs such as the needs for love and belongingness, self-esteem and recognition, orientation and meaning, self-actualization and self-transcendence. There is by now plenty of evidence for and very little against the thesis that these needs exist, and that they are fundamental to the very survival of the individual.[20]

The ways in which the basic human needs are satisfied vary from society to society, but their existence is a historical constant. They are inborn in every member of the species *homo sapiens*. The species-nature of the human being is not a product of history, but of natural history. According to the biological theory of evolution, which is different to the socio-cultural one discussed above, humanity is genetically adapted to the conditions of life prevailing at the time when we emerged as a species – that is to say, during the millions of years when the hominids descended from the trees and began to live on the ground as hunters and gatherers. Species-nature is therefore adapted to certain basic features of the hunting and gathering society. It should be kept in mind that this society consisted of about fifty individuals living together for their whole life in a natural community with minimal division of labour, centralization and stratification, and in very close relation to each other and to nature. The development of strong social bonds of unselfish solidarity and care were important for the survival of the group. It is not strange that the corresponding need structure has been for ever ingrained in our species-endowments.

There has been no significant change in our genetic endowment since the human species emerged more than 100,000 years ago. Our species-nature has in no way adapted to the fateful changes in the conditions of life which followed the agrarian revolution 10,000 years ago, the urban revolution more than 5,000 years ago, and the industrial revolution 200 years ago. These changes have successively brought about bigger and bigger deviations from the environment from which we evolved, with dire consequences. Some of these effects already revealed themselves in the urban revolution. The breakthrough to civilization was not an unmixed blessing. Intellectual, artistic and other achievements were bought at a high price in terms of human fulfilment. Slavery, patriarchal despotism, authoritarian government, organized violence, imperialism and warfare, human sacrifices and environmental devastation are all signs of the destructive forces within humanity which civilization brought into being.[21] The fact that most of these problems are still with us today and that they were almost unknown to the early hunters and gatherers justify two important conclusions.[22] The first one is that these problems have deep roots in our culture. As they originated thousands of years before the emergence of capitalism, it would not be sufficient to abolish that particular economic system. The Green view therefore goes far beyond the usual Red interpretation and delivers a civilizational criticism rather than a simple criticism of a particular mode of production. Secondly, the optimistic view of human nature, which is an important element in the Green view, can still be maintained. Like a fruit-tree growing up under favourable conditions, the human being will realize its potentials and develop into a positive creature producing beautiful mental and physical fruits. If the environment is disadvantageous, however, neither the tree nor the human being will realize their optimal development. The Green view does not deny the potential destructiveness of humanity which has been so amply demonstrated in the records of history. There seem to be no limits to the follies of man. The thesis is simply that his destructiveness is a second nature which develops if his basic needs are blocked.[23] When there are no outlets for love and creativity, man becomes a stunted creature characterized by a life-inhibiting syndrome of sado-masochism, greed, egocentricity, and callousness.

We suggest that the trauma of civilization has much to do with the pathology of hierarchical authority-structures, with compulsive order-liness at the bottom and delusions of grandeur and paranoia at the top.

> With every increase of effective power, extravagantly sadistic and murderous impulses erupted out of the unconscious, This is the trauma that has distorted the subsequent development of all 'civilized' societies.[24]

This analysis gives some credence to the very Green proposal of the anarchists that we should rely less on gigantic structures of remote control and more on natural, small-scale, horizontal communities based on voluntary cooperation between people in face-to-face contact.

We have reasons to believe that modern industrial society is still more deviant from human species-nature. The destructiveness of modern humanity, which has manifested itself in two world wars, in Auschwitz, in the Amazon valley, and above all in the callous preparation for a nuclear holocaust, points in this direction. The existence of serious diseases of civilization in all industrial societies are other signs of the same phenomena (the most important of the new diseases are mental disorders, cardio-vascular diseases, and malignant tumours).

This makes nonsense of the very idea of progress as an attribute of industrialization and modernization. The so-called developed societies are to a certain extent responsive to our material needs, but when we introduce the concept of non-material needs, the whole picture is turned upside down. The so-called underdeveloped countries are from this perspective seen as more 'developed'. Schizophrenia, for instance, is much less common in the Third World. Is this because these societies still have viable natural communities such as strong families and villages?

In the poor countries people cry for bread. In the rich contries there is a hunger for meaning and identity. The unprecedented material progress during the post-war period has not made people happier. The biblical thought is worth considering: 'What shall it profit a man if he gain the whole world and lose his soul?'. Numerous people in the industrialized north long to get away from the achievement-oriented society, away from soulless jobs on the factory floor, away from the grim climbing up the career ladders. There is a longing for a softer society, a secret desire to drop out, to be free, to begin to live at last.[25]

Industrial society thus suppresses our basic non-material needs, especially those for love and belonging, because it is incompatible with viable natural communities. The family and the local community started to disintegrate with the advent of industrialism in which more and more people are organized in factories and offices functioning according to impersonal bureaucratic rules. Large-scale enterprises may lead to increased productivity but they also take their toll in terms of depersonalization and anonymity. This shows up in mental diseases, but also in the pathology of normality. 'Society highly values its normal man. It educates children to lose themselves and to become absurd, and thus to be normal.'[26]

Defining the goals of development in terms of basic human needs is only a starting point for a full definition of social development. Most authors within the Green tradition tend to include a number of second-order values when they move from the individual level (human development) to the societal level (social development). The following values are usually mentioned in this context:

- Cultural identity (the social unit of development is a culturally defined community and the development of this community is rooted in the specific values and institutions of this culture).
- Self-reliance (each community relies primarily on its own strength and resources).
- Social justice (the development effort should give priority to those most in need).
- Ecological balance (the resources of the biosphere are utilized in full awareness of the potential of local ecosystems as well as the global and local limits imposed on present and future generations).

There are many possibilities of priority conflicts between the sub-goals of development. Nevertheless, they by and large reinforce each other and do indeed form a coherent whole. The idea of endogenous development stemming from the heart of each culture and from the particular problems of each local ecosystem is, of course, completely at odds with dominant universalist thinking. In contrast to the latter, for the Green tradition there are no models to emulate. A 'backward' country should not look for the image of its own future in the 'advanced' country, but in its own ecology and culture. There is no universal path to development. Each society must find its own strategy.

The emphasis on cultural identity is absolutely essential in this context. To ask people to abandon their own native culture if they want to develop is a contradiction in terms. Development by destruction has nothing to do with the idea of human development and of becoming master or mistress of one's own fate. Besides the value of cultural roots as a basic human need, cultural identity is a *sine qua non* for becoming active in the world. Without common culture there is no common action. A culturally fragmented and atomized mass is the worst conceivable source material for the development process as defined here. Development is a cooperative venture requiring communication and deep understanding between people. All participants must have access to a common code of meaning of else the whole project will simply repeat the biblical story of the Tower of the Babel.

In mainstream development thinking, the state is always seen as the social subject of the development process. According to the theory of modernization this is the unit on which the entire process of social evolution is operating. This perspective also lingers on in dependency theory (compare axiom A4 on p. 210). Even though the world-system approach has shifted the focus from the nation-state to the world capitalist system as a whole, it nevertheless treats development strategies as state strategies.

From a Green perspective, human beings or small communities of human beings, are the ultimate actors. Most states are, after all, artificial territorial constructions, usually the result of internal colonialism and international wars. The concept of nation-state implies that the territorial boundaries of the state coincide with the boundaries of a culturally homogeneous nation. This is the exception rather than the rule in a world with about 1500 peoples or nations but only 150 states.

If development is envisaged as the result of voluntary cooperation and autonomous choices by ordinary men and women there is no way of escaping a cultural definition of the social unit of development. If it is difficult for people to cooperate with each other politically when they are divided socially and culturally, why should they stick to the state? The tribes and nations of the world are much more basic units of development, because they allow for the forging of a genuine consensus between their members. Normative convergence can only be obtained where people share a framework of social reasoning. It requires a common universe of discourse. The principle of national self-determination should not be used as a defence for artificial states. It should rather allow different national groups to govern themselves and to develop separately. (Green authors tend to visualize the future as a world of cooperating and federated natural communities without strong centre-periphery gradients between them.)

The principle of cultural identity and diversity is not limited to nations. It has to be applied to all sorts of cultural units, such as local communities, ethnic groups, religions and civilizations. The Green view believes in the unique virtues of each and every specific culture, however 'backward' or 'advanced' they may be in a technological sense. There are, for instance, many examples of habitats in which tribal people have been able to eke out a sustainable livelihood while the modern way of life is ecologically devastating and not sustainable in the long-run. Lévi-Strauss observes:

If the criterion chosen had been the degree of ability to overcome even the most inhospitable geographical conditions, there can be scarcely any doubt that the Eskimos, on the one hand, and the Bedouins, on the other, would carry off the palm.[27]

The principle of cultural identity does not mean that cultures cannot be criticized. If all cultures on earth are to survive, most of them have to change some of their basic elements in order to become compatible with each other. Cultural relativism has a limit as exemplified by cultures condemning such forms of behaviour as genocide, torture, racism, and exploitation. The examples of Hitlerism, apartheid and the extermination of a number of aboriginal populations all over the world demonstrate on which side of the technological gap we have to demand most of the changes.

Self-reliance is a key concept in the Green definition and strategy of development. It has been a popular concept in the international debate about development issues in the 1970s. This was partly due to the breakthrough of the dependency paradigm, self-reliance being the antithesis to dependency. The concept, however, acquires a slightly different meaning in the Green context. Therefore there is need for some clarification.

A well-known formulation can be found in the Cocoyoc Declaration of 1974. A typical passage from this document reads:

We believe that one basic strategy of development will have to be increased national self-reliance. It does not mean autarchy. It implies mutual benefits from trade and cooperation and a fairer redistribution of resources satisfying the basic needs. It does mean self-confidence, reliance primarily on one's own resources, human and natural, and the capacity of autonomous goal-setting and decision-making. It excludes dependence on outside influences and powers that can be converted into political pressure.

This formulation, which clearly emphasizes the potential value of trade and cooperation, seems to be restricted to *national* self-reliance. Furthermore, it emphasizes the economic and political aspects of the strategy. In the Green view, the approach should be widened into a fully-fledged and more radical development strategy, providing guidelines for almost all fields of action on different levels of society.[28]

We may distinguish between local, national and regional levels. It is with reference to the local and regional (often called collective) level that we find the new and particularly the Green theoretical contributions, whereas national self-reliance is an old Red and Blue political goal. National self-reliance, which basically implies a strong *state*, is perfectly consistent with a dependent or even enslaved people.

The state level is, however, in certain respects a precondition for self-reliance at the local level; some economic planning will always be necessary even in a decentralized economy, the national centre must provide the infrastructure for cooperation between the local units, the state may have to intervene in order to correct the imbalances in resource endowments, and the local units must be protected from external penetration, for example by the multinationals. Thus, in order to achieve self-reliance in the Green sense of the world, it is necessary to combine all three levels.

Most spokesmen for the strategy of self-reliance emphasize that SR must not be confused with autarchy, but should be seen as a precondition for meaningful (i.e. symmetric) cooperation, which leads us to the problem of *degree* more specifically. The Dag Hammarskjöld report (a very Green document) underlines the concept of *seletive participation*. Different conditions among Third World countries will require a variety of selections not only by different countries but also by any country at different times. The only guidelines that can be formulated are the following ones:

1   There is a minimum number of links required to sustain the development process.
2   There is a maximum number of links beyond which no effective sovereignty can be maintained.
3   There are affirmative links which reinforce self-reliance.
4   There are regressive links which weaken self-reliance.

We believe it to be one of the most important tasks of a Green development theory in the years to come to provide the necessary theoretical and empirical base for *the strategy of selective participation* with the aim of promoting self-reliance on all levels, particularly regional and local.

The record of development in the Third World since the 1950s has been a dismal one if development is defined more comprehensively than sheer economic growth. Some early 'success stories' later proved to be 'development catastrophes' which suggests some connection between a forced process of growth and increased political and social tensions. The post-war period was a period of rapid economic growth but it was also a period of increasing disparities. This is admitted even by mainstream development economics:

> It is now clear that more than a decade of rapid growth in underdeveloped countries has been of little or no benefit to perhaps a third of their population. Although the average per capita income of the Third World has increased by 50 per cent since 1960, this growth has been very unequally distributed among countries, regions within countries, and socio-economic groups. Paradoxically, while growth policies have succeeded beyond the expectations of the first development decade, the very idea of aggregate growth as a social objective has increasingly been called into question.[29]

The Green view on social justice goes considerably beyond the policy of 'redistribution with growth'. Monetary compensation for marginalization and alienation is not enough. A deeper approach must go into the institutional patterns of access to wealth, knowledge, decision-making and directly gratifying jobs. It has to deal not only with the appropriation of goods and services, but also with the appropriation of creativity, freedom and authority. This fits in with the emphasis on self-reliance and cultural identity.

Ecological thinking is one main source of inspiration behind the Green view. As we all should know, industrial society has for a long time been unaware of its base in nature. The industrial growth-machine has operated on the assumption, firstly that natural resources are unlimited and secondly that the biosphere can be treated like an infinite rubbish dump. Neither of the assumptions is valid.

In the long-run we simply have to confront the need for action: to put an end to the production and use of poisoning chemicals and waste products and to conserve materials and energy, which means recycling and a switch over to renewable resources. Neither is easily done without basic changes in the very structure of industrial society.

To get an idea of the problems involved imagine agriculture without pesticides and insecticides! Farming without chemical controls is not compatible with a highly mechanized production system or a rigid system of monoculture. We have to adapt flexible mixed farming, encourage the use of organic controls and rely on labour-intensive methods. This suggests that the industrialized countries will probably have to reintroduce some agricultural methods used by our ancestors.

When the reckless exploitation of our irreplaceable fossil resources has come to an end either because the deposits have been depleted or because the increasing concentration of carbon dioxide in the earth's atmosphere has caused highly disruptive effects on world agriculture, we will more or less be forced to rely on renewable energy resources, most of them emanating from the sun. This will have important consequences for the structure of future society. Fossil fuels are concentrated in discrete locations which can be owned and controlled by corporations and governments. Their extraction requires big capital and a high level of technical expertise which are not at everyone's disposal. Renewable resources like sunlight, windpower and biomass are, on the other hand, almost evenly distributed throughout the globe. They are therefore capable of increasing the self-reliance of regions and small communities. The development of simple, small-scale methods for the collection of solar energy could, as Aldous Huxley saw clearly more than 35 years ago,

> be made to contribute greatly to the decentralization of production and population and the creation of a new type of agrarian society making use of cheap and inexhaustible power for the benefit of individual small-holders or self-governing cooperative groups.[30]

What we need is an alternative technology which is small-scale, possible to control by autonomous groups, directly gratifying to work with, compatible with the local culture and the local eco-system and geared to the production of use-values and basic life-necessities.[31]

Green thinkers and activists have moved considerably beyond the exclusive concern with pollution and resource depletion into a total reconceptualization of the relation between humanity and nature. The conception of humanity as masters of nature has been replaced by the idea of partnership. We have to foster a deeper reverential attitude to nature. It is not enough to fight against pollution and resource depletion. We should also be concerned about ecological balance, the equilibrium of natural ecosystems as a value in itself. In this view, the present rate of extinction of species is intolerable.

According to one estimate, 'between half a million and 2 million species – 15 to 20 per cent of all species on earth – could be extinguished by 2000, mainly because of loss of wild habitat but also in part because of pollution. Extinction of species on this scale is without precedent in human history.'[32] The deeper concern with the ecological balance touches upon the principles of diversity, self-regulation, symbiosis, decentralization and autonomy. They are also supposed to be applicable to social systems. Ecologically inspired attitudes therefore favour diversity of human ways of life, of cultures, of communities, and of economies.

Development economists have been spoken of the 'take off' into self-sustained growth. An aeroplane, however, cannot stay in the air for ever. It has to go down to the ground before it runs short of gasoline – a non-renewable resource. It is a strange phenomenon that the thinkers who invented the metaphor of a 'take off' never pondered the problem of landing. This gives us one more example of a paradigmatic blindness, this time with regard to ecological factors, which characterizes both the Red and the Blue views of the world. The real problem is not the 'take off' but the 'landing'. Will we be able to steer the industrial mega-machine down to the ground before the engine stops or will there be a crash landing? The Green movement is eagerly searching for a way down to Mother Earth.

Elements of a non-deterministic model

Mainstream development thinking is deterministic: 'The progressive march of civilization follows a natural and unavoidable course, which flows from the law of human organization' (A. Comte). The Green approach is the antithesis of this view. The future is supposed to be fundamentally open and the Green activists point to a new destination inviting everybody to join in the march. Voluntarism, however, is just as problematic a position as determinism. In this section we will lay the foundations for a synthesis.

The Green movement has thus often been accused of utopianism. There are many structural hindrances on the narrow path to the Green valley and the old road to the supertechnological society has already been paved by earlier generations. If we leave it in a headlong manner we may end up in a marsh. After all, the fascist movements in the 30s started out with some unmistakably Green characteristics. As Ashby Turner has commented, the Nazis launched a comprehensive attack on the modern society:

> In their eyes, modern industrial society was wholly and unavoidably incompatible with what they held to be the only true wellspring of social life: the folk culture . . . While most visionary revolutionaries of modern times have looked to the future, to a new world, the Nazis sought their models in the past . . . What they proposed was an escape from the modern world by means of a desperate leap toward a romanticized vision of the harmony, community, simplicity, and order of a world long past. Their thinking seems best characterized as a utopian form of anti-modernism – utopian in the double sense of being a visionary panacea and unrealizable.[33]

Will the Green movement prepare the ground for a revival of fascism? The potential is certainly there and one should take it into account when designing the Green strategy.

Utopian thinking is needed but that is not enough. What we need most is realistic utopianism, that is, solutions that are radical but founded on critical analysis of the strength of the various anti-systemic forces. Thus we do not want to jump from a position of determinism to a position of complete voluntarism. To see only actors without a system is just as wrong as to see systems without actors. We have to work with the idea of actors in a system. The actors are neither completely free to do what they want nor completely overwhelmed by the laws of the system and its structure. For this reason we have to construct a theory about the structural and historical conditions for a Green development. The world-system approach is a good starting point in this endeavour but it has to be elaborated in a more voluntaristic direction. We should look for those social forces that are working toward a Greening of the world. This necessitates an analysis of actors and their strategies in a long historical perspective.

As a preliminary step towards the construction of a model we will say a few words about the first axiom of evolutionism. Is it true that the general change of history is directed and cumulative? Looking back on humanity's long journey from the stone axe to the moon rocket the idea of evolution carries immediate conviction. However, it is important to keep in mind that we tend to estimate the achievements of earlier ages by the provincial standards of our own culture. In the last two centuries a power-centred technology which Lewis Mumford calls megatechnics has taken command in one field after another. The preceding millenium did not show much development along this line. Thus, it is seen as a period of technological stagnation. But technology was not stagnant. The point is that it advanced according to a different set of criteria. Mumford discerns a biotechnical line associated with the domestication of plants and animals and a polytechnical line associated with all sorts of handicrafts.

According to Mumford the alternative technologies reached an unsurpassed height towards the end of the Middle Ages:

> A genuine polytechnic was in the making capable of reconciling the order and efficiency of the megamachine with the creative initiative and individuality of the artist. But within a few centuries the whole system was undermined by the new impersonal market economy and the resurrection in a new form of the totalitarian megamachine.[34]

The development of technology is not cumulative but rather alternating between different lines of development. The advance along one line is often bought at the price of a regression along another line. As an example we would like to mention the enormous loss of practical knowledge and human skills which followed in the wake of the science-based industries. The megatechnics of the engineers destroyed the polytechnics of the artisans and workers.

The idea of cumulative or linear change is not valid for the whole span of human history. It applies only to particular dimensions during limited periods of time. What makes the idea of evolution so persuasive is precisely the fact that we live in an epoch which has been characterized by growth and expansion along a number of selected dimensions for a very long time. Throughout the last four or five centuries the West has witnessed geographical and demographical expansion, growth of trade and monetary incomes, increasing size of productive enterprises, growth in cities, expansion of central bureaucracy and state power, expansion of science and higher education, growth of megatechnics and so forth. At the same time we have experienced the decline and breakdown of an alternative social and technological order based on local communities and extended households, subsistence economy and mutual aid, biotechnics and polytechnics, folk knowledge and religion.

This strongly suggests a dualistic or dialectical model of social change comprising the following elements:

1 The existence of a dominant system/order during a particular epoch.
2 The existence of one or more countersystems/orders to the dominant one. (On this point we are very much influenced by W.F. Wertheim's model of social change in his *Evolution and Revolution*, Amsterdam, 1971, chapter 4.)

3   The assumption that the expansion or contraction of the dominant system/order is a result of a continuous struggle between actors which are anchored in the different systems/orders.
4   The assumption that the social systems/orders themselves are human products, that they emerge from the concepts, ground rules and utopias of innovating actors and movements and that they are elaborated and modified by later generations.

We do not believe that there has ever existed an all-inclusive social order which determines every social activity. There are always cracks in the dominant order which allow for other rationalities to creep in. The normal state of affairs should be analyzed as a more or less fragile balance between orders which stand in dialectical opposition to each other. Thus, in every formal organization there is an informal network which to a certain extent functions as a defence mechanism against the demands of the formal system.

The existence of competing orders provides people with opportunities to choose between alternative actions in their everyday life. Social change, then, is neither a simple process of reproduction of the established system nor a momentary transition from one system to another. It should rather be seen as a shift in the balance between the dominant order and the counter-order, which is much affected by the autonomous choices of ordinary people.

In the final analysis social orders themselves are human products. They should be seen as emerging out of the categories of thought and social projects invented by extraordinarily creative groups and movements. The great system innovations are usually made in rather short periods of time by a few creative elites in response to a big challenge or crisis in the old order.[35] The crisis provides fertile ground for the new rationality to grow. Ultimately, however, people have to make a choice between the old and the new. This in turn, implies a struggle between actors with different stakes in the two orders. Thus, our model appears in rough outline – a model of social change which avoids both the pitfall of evolutionism–determinism, and the stumbling-block of utopianism – voluntarism.[36] We are now going to develop it further in order to arrive at a view of the potential for the Greening of the world.

The world-system theorists believe that the capitalist world-economy has been the dominant social system throughout the modern epoch and according to Wallerstein it will continue to be so for the coming 50 to 200 years. This is the time needed for the internal dynamics of the system to reach the limits of its own expansion. The system can only survive as long as it is expanding in terms of the human and natural resources which are drawn into the process of capitalist accumulation. There are two ways in which the system expands:

1   *Geographical expansion* The outer boundaries of the world economy expand through imperial conquests, colonization, trade wars,

and the building of neo-colonial bridge-heads. This process which has continued for about 500 years, has been nearly completed by now. There are at present very few spots on the globe which are not incorporated in the global division of labour.

2 *Socio-economic penetration* More land, more labour and more goods are commodified, that is, they are treated as commodities which can be exchanged according to the rules of the market. The commodification of labour implies that the producers become wage-earners or proletarians without autonomous access to the means of production. The commodification of land and capital means that these resources are controlled by actors operating according to the logic of capital.

It is easy to see that the process of socio-economic penetration is far from complete. There is a large counter economy in which people do not primarily work for money and in which goods and services are not provided by money or even financed by taxation. (In industrial societies the counter economy is called the informal economy, in Third World countries it is more often called the subsistence economy. The so-called black (illegal) economy is sometimes included in the informal economy. It is unregistered and untaxed but often closely related to the money economy.) This part of the economy consists of the domestic (household) sector but it also includes mutual aid between neighbours and unpaid work for different kinds of associations. The market does not operate in this sector, nor do the universalistic distribution mechanisms which are used by the modern state.

The informal sector performs socially useful work, but it does not figure in the gross national product. In the Third World today, the informal sector is probably crucial for the majority of the population. People survive without spending any money, as they earn practically none. In the rural areas the bulk of the population partly survive on subsistence-farming. Even in the cities a large proportion of the inhabitants support themselves on the production of use-values. Most of the urban poor live in shanty towns where they themselves build their squatter shacks. They keep a small kitchen garden, some chickens etc. They rely on the pooling of the total resources of their extended families.

The informal economy is significant even in the industrially advanced contries. People have plenty of work to do in their households: cooking, washing, cleaning, care of children, maintenance work, gardening and in some lucky cases wild berry picking, hunting, and fishing. If measured in labour hours, the informal economy is about the same size as the money economy.

According to Wallerstein, the world is capitalist. All countries are incorporated into the system, and there is nothing left of pre-existing systems. This is certainly a simplification. Elements of pre-existing systems continue to be reproduced. In recent marxist thinking most countries of the world are seen as articulations of at least two modes of production – a capitalist and a non-capitalist mode – in which the capitalist one is increasingly dominant over the other.[37] The idea of capitalist penetration, of the deepening of capitalism, presupposes the existence of a counter system which is penetrated. Thus, we are back to the concept of dualism, introduced by the decried theory of modernization.

Production for ones's own consumption, mutual aid, the exchange of gifts, the immediate care for the needs of family members, voluntary work for social ends follow a social logic which differs from production for a market. The former principles are very much older than the capitalist system, and they were once the dominant principles of economic organization. They presuppose that both participants in the transaction belong to a moral community. The transaction is actually submerged in this social relationship and subjected to a number of overriding non-economic considerations. The market institutions separate the purely economic motives from the broader social context. It 'liberates' the actors from non-economic demands and responsibilities. It is an impersonal social mechanism.[38]

This distinction is not a sharp one but a matter of emphasis. Production for markets could be included in the informal sector to the extent that the profit motive is restrained by community norms. This is most likely to happen in local markets. The larger the market, the more anonymous the actors, the less they care for each other as persons. However, even the modern welfare state can to a certain extent be seen as a moral community. It is based on solidarity towards the interior and egoism towards the exterior. The quality of the solidarity is severely diluted because of the size and bureaucratic nature of the welfare state. If loneliness and social isolation is the problem, ordinary human concern by friends and relatives cannot be replaced by the almost purely material support offered by civil servants. There is even a risk that the institutionalized charity of the state undermines people's direct responsibility for each other. We quickly pass by the beggar in the street and appease our conscience with the taxes we pay to the social insurance system. For this reason the redistributive mechanisms of the state belong to the formal economy. The main difference is between expansive large-scale and mechanically organized social institutions on the one hand and contractive, small-scale and personalistic social institutions on the other. The Green view favours the latter, while the Red and the Blue favour the former.

Modern society, whether socialist or capitalist, is dominated by corporate actors, such as companies, government departments, universities, trade unions and political parties. They have been deliberately created to achieve specific goals. They are organized as large-scale depersonalized social machines according to the principles of instrumental rationality and efficiency. This means that the individual is programmed for different positions or functions in the bureaucratic apparatus. They are treated like a replaceable cog in a machine.

Though dominant, the depersonalized system of corporate actors does not control every sphere of action. There is still space for a different form of social life with focus on the person. A family, a work-team, a group of friends, a local community, or a network of informal relations is a small-scale unit, which usually emerges through a process of organic growth. Social relations are personal. The individual cannot be substituted. (Think of a family where the husband is exchanged for another man with the same formal qualifications.)

The Green thinkers believe that the imbalance between the modern large-scale rationalized sector and the non-modern small-scale personalistic sector is one main cause of our troubles. The blame should not be put on capitalism alone but just as much on the nation-state, bureaucratic forms of organization, positivist science, the patriachate and the urban way of life. Reports from the socialist countries in Eastern Europe indicate they they have more or less the same predicaments: war preparations, environmental despoliation, marginalization, powerlessness, and social disintegration. The capitalist societies of the West and the state socialist societies of the East are two varieties of a common corporate industrial culture based on the values of competitive individualism, rationality, growth, efficiency, specialization, centralization and big scale. The dominating position of these values and their associated institutions is only partly explained by economic factors. Their roots have to be sought, ultimately, in the cultural projects of Western civilization.

This is why the concept of a modern project appears so persuasive. Once we abandon the assumption that modernization is the final goal of humanity, we are free to use this concept in the description and explanation of what has happened in the world during the last 500 years. *The modern project* is an integrated project which emerged out of the totality of Western culture at the end of the Middle Ages (compare the fourth element in the above model of social change). It was related to the universalist humanism of the Renaissance, the Protestant work ethic, the scientific movement, the emergence of absolutist states, the bourgeois revolutions and so on. It was promoted by the new elite of capitalist, central bureaucrats and scientists, and it was met with resistance from numerous traditional groups and elites. The interrelated institutions of capitalism, state bureaucracy and university were the main vehicles of the transformation. Together they form the dominant order as defined above. It is interesting to notice that all three institutions originated in Europe at about the same time. Feudalism was replaced by capitalism. The states became the dominant political units. The religious world-view was challenged by a new materialistic philosophy based on natural science. It was also at this time that the Europeans started to conquer the rest of the world. A singularly expansive power complex came into existence.

The three dominant institutions in the dominant order reinforce each other. The state fulfils essential functions for the capitalist economy – it must maintain or create the conditions in which profitable capital accumulation is possible. The capitalist economy, on the other hand, fulfils equally important functions for the state by producing a free-floating surplus which can be taxed by the state. The capitalist economy and the state reinforce each other, and it is impossible to give causal priority to one of them.

A closer look shows the scientific-educational system to be part of the system. Both the state and the capitalist economy are crucially dependent on the services provided by the technical experts who have considerable *de facto* power – not in terms of legal ownership or position of administrative authority, but in terms of technical knowledge and competence.

It is easy to see that all three institutions operate according to a similar social logic. The modern project has only one overriding value, the value of domination – expansion – growth – efficiency. In this respect the logic of capital accumulation, the logic of state expansion and the logic of scientific growth all coincide. The modern mind is almost exclusively bent to the service of instrumental rationality. The ultimate ends or purposes of the growth of instruments and technologies are not subjected to intensive discussion and scrutiny. Modern society has therefore acquired all the inhuman characteristics of a social machine. We are locked in an 'iron cage' of our own making, says Weber. Behind it all lies a particular world-view – the mechanical world-view – which was first propagated by the pioneers of science at the beginning of the modern age.[39]

The essence of the modern mind is its scientific and technological attitude. Science is thought of as objective knowledge, independent of culture, ideology, personality or prejudice. This myth is of fundamental importance to the depersonalization of the modern world. The myth of objective knowledge is the myth that there is a way to obtain knowledge which is cleansed of all subjective distortion, of all personal involvement. Thus the scientists cultivate a state of consciousness which is ideally suited to the merchants' quantitative calculations with standardized monetary units as well as to the functionaries' conception of themselves as impersonal agents of corporate actors. The objectivity of science corresponds in fact to the depersonalization of the bureacracy and the market.

The modern project was first embarked upon by elites in Western Europe and then imposed on the internal and external periphery through state-building, colonization, trade, missionary activity, etc. Modernization should be seen as a transnational process of penetration reverberating throughout the world with the expansion of the capitalist world-system and its associated institutions. The 'national' centres of

Third World countries were more or less linked to the global super-centre of the modern world-system. They have become nation-state builders and modernizing agents transmitting the modern institutions further down to their own peripheries.

With the continuous expansion of the modern institutions of capitalism, state and science, each reinforcing the other, the earlier institutions had to retreat. Modernization always implies the decline and disintegration of natural communities. This is a very significant feature of the modernization project. No other civilization ever tried to eliminate their local communities. Traditional imperialistic societies like those in Imperial China, Tsarist Russia and precolonial India had strong centres supported by tributes from their peripheries, but they did not penetrate and transform their peripheries to any large extent. A thin layer of merchants, priests, bureaucrats and landlords gathering around the king or emperor stood on and over a large peasant mass living in more or less self-sufficient village communities. Extensive parochialism and transformation of these local communities began with the advent of modernization.

The project of modernization, if pushed to its theoretical limit, will eradicate all pre-capitalist social formations, all extended households and all local communities. The world-system theorists seem to believe that this is bound to happen:

> What we shall probably see in the next fifty years is the last expansion of the world-economy. The ground will be prepared by world-wide agricultural reorganization during the downward cycle and then, in about 1990 or whenever the world-economy expands again, the shift to wage employment, the proletarianization of the work force, may become virtually universal.[40]

When all land, labour and capital have been drawn into the orbit of capital accumulation, the system is supposed to enter into a worldwide crisis. Without further possibilities of expansion, the system will simply break down, and with all direct producers incorporated in a huge proletariat servicing a more or less 'fully planned single productive organizational network in the world economy', the final transition to a socialist world-government will be but a minor step.[41]

We have a number of objections to this prognosis. The capitalist system will reach its limits of expansion long before all non-capitalist modes of production have vanished from the earth, that is before all producers have become proletarians. Domestic and communal modes of production cannot be abolished without abolishing humanity itself. The social costs of alienation, clientization, crime and mental disorders would simply be unsustainable. It is already obvious that modern welfare states can no longer afford to tackle these problems by the usual method of bureaucratization.

The capitalist economy is in fact a parasite on the non-capitalist economy because it does not pay the full cost of the reproduction of labour-power, nor does it pay for the reproduction of natural resources. Capitalism therefore has been compared with shifting cultivation: as soon as the social and natural soil is exhausted in a particular area, capital moves to a new area which has been, 'left fallow for regeneration through the vegetative powers of non-capitalist . . . modes of production'.[42] In a parasitical system of this kind there is an upper limit to expansion. Like parasites who stop themselves from spreading by killing off too many of their hosts, the capitalist world-economy will stop expanding long before the non-capitalist modes of production have been completely exterminated. The modern project will never be carried to its extreme.

There is a second objection to the effect that the capitalist economy does not have to end in a general breakdown followed by a socialist order. The system has expanded slowly during a period of five hundred years. Is it not possible to envisage a correspondingly slow decline in the coming five hundred years without any particularly dramatic events at the turning point? The fact that this possibility is not considered is a direct product of the evolutionist and expansionist assumption in mainstream development thinking. However, expansion is not an inherent tendency of the world-economy. The expansion of the system during the modern epoch should not be seen as an automatic process but as a result of a struggle between modernizing forces and a continuous resistance.[43] So far, the modernizers, both Red and Blue, have been victorious but it is now evident that resistance is increasing very rapidly, preparing the ground for a Green strategy.

At the point of maximum development of the capitalist world-economy, the world will still contain a sizeable sector of non- or semi-proletarian producers. Thus, we are not reassured that the socialist project of the proletariat will be carried out. So far the peasantry has been the mobilizing group *par preference* in the revolutions of the twentieth century, and it has tended to embark on a different – much more Green – project. Most peasants in the Third World depend on the domestic and communal modes of production for their livelihood. Their original reaction has always been to defend their traditional way of life against the encroachment of the modern system, capitalist or socialist (compare the third assumption in our model of social change presented above).

Thus, there are two very different roads to a post-capitalist world:

1 *The Red road of continued modernization* The idea is to carry the modern project to its logical end – a socialist world order under the jurisdiction of a single world government. This order will be implemented by the proletariat when the capitalist world-economy has expanded to its ceiling, that is, when every corner of the world has been modernized.

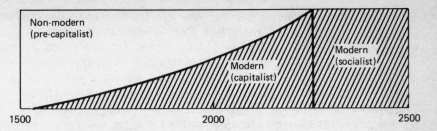

2 *The Green road of demodernization* The idea is to withdraw gradually from the modern capitalist world-economy and launch a new,
non-modern, non-capitalist development project based on the 'progressive' elements of pre-capitalist social orders and later
innovations.[44]

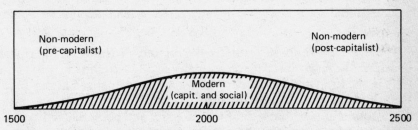

Which are the social and historical conditions for a Green development? What sorts of actors and movements will implement a Green
strategy? Where in the capitalist world-system will they be placed? The
main sources can be derived from our model which now contains the
following essential elements:

1 A socio-economic dualism between modern and non-modern institutions.
2 A modern project (Red and Blue) aiming at control-expansion-
   growth-effiency, legitimized by evolutionist thinking.
3 A Green project aiming at human development (the realization of
   the species-nature of humanity).
4 The incompatibility between modernization and human development.

Our main hypothesis is that the global Green movement derives its
strength from three rather different sources:

1 *The traditionalists*, who resist modernization because they have
   access to a non-modern way of life which they want to defend.
   Modern *penetration* in the form of commercialization, industrialization, state-building and professionalization is the main cause of
   their mobilization. The resistance will derive its strength from some
   sort of *counterpoint*: non-Western civilizations and religions, old
   nations and tribes, local communities, kinship groups, peasants and
   independent producers, informal economies, feminist culture, etc.

2 *Marginalized people*, who cannot find a place within the modern
   sector. The basic process could be called *marginalization*. People
   are either pushed out of the system or not let in. Thus, they have to
   fall back on the non-modern sector in one way or another. To this
   group belongs the unemployed, temporary workers, women, youth,
   the uneducated, the mentally ill, the handicapped, workers with
   soulless jobs (who are marginalized in a psychological sense).
3 *The post-materialists*, who question the modern project as they are
   searching for their own true nature and they also have the resources
   and opportunities to pursue their own projects. The process of self-
   emancipation lies partly outside the field of sociological analysis,
   but it has much to do with opportunities provided by an affluent
   modern society. Thus we find many sons and daughters of the
   modern elite in this group. They are young and well-educated and
   committed to non-material values. They tend to choose person-
   oriented rather than thing-oriented occupations.

These three groups are differently placed in the centre-periphery
structure of the world. The traditionalists will be found disproportionately in the local and global peripheries, the marginalized at the middle
level, and the post-materialist near the centres. This is a very crude
description but it reminds us of the diversity and potential width of the
Green world-movement. These three groups have to forge an alliance
against the modern technocratic elite and its main structures of support. In what follows we will take a closer look at the anti-modern
forces beginning with the non-Western world and the global periphery.

The east wind prevails over the west wind

Having in a somewhat abstract way identified the social actors and
forces which can be seen as working against the 'modern project' we
shall proceed with a more contextual analysis, starting with the non-
Western cultural areas. As the title of this section, borrowed from Mao
Zedong, indicates, to put a stop to the 'modern project' means to stop
Western penetration. We therefore start with an assessment of the
possibilities for a more balanced relationship on the level of civilizations, that is, socio-cultural units that often include a number of nation-
states. We find the real strongholds of the 'modern project' on the level
of the state since the processes of westernization and commercialization
are supported by state structures dominated by 'modern elites'. The
question we put here is thus whether the power of the state and modern
elite is diminishing and, implied in this, whether the local community – our third level of analysis – is reasserting itself. Our thesis is that
the 'Green project' necessitates stronger institutions on the global and
local levels whereas the level of the nation-state is one of the greatest

obstacles to the 'Greening of the world'. As the main power base for modern elites in the Third World, its maintenance is not only extremely resource-consuming but also the arena for a power struggle among fractions of the modern elite and an excuse for repression against the non-elites, that is, the people. Apart from this, there is competition, suspicion and fear among the different elites ruling over neighbouring territories and this provides the destructive dynamics of rearmament and international conflicts.

Restoring the civilizational balance

From the Renaissance, when European expansion began, to the zenith of Western hegemony four centuries later, the Western world-view has been presented as *the* world-view, claiming universal validity. All colonized or penetrated countries were stigmatized as inferior in culture, religion or race. Western man did not bother to listen to the African shaman, the Indian guru or the Chinese scholar.

However, two World Wars, a continuous process of resistance in the colonies and gradual internalization of Western science and technology in the new independent nations have undermined Western hegemony. After 1945 the colonial powers had to withdraw from Asia and Africa. Non-Western countries like Japan and China entered the world arena strengthened by their own indigenous solutions and achievements. Today, we witness the restoration of a number of non-Western cultures which have survived the many centuries of Western suppression. Thus for the first time since Europe embarked on its programme of expansion, cultural cleavages have come to the fore in world politics.

The countries in the Third World that have a real option to choose indigenous rather than Western solutions to their problems are those with access to a strong cultural heritage. After all, the westernized communities do not amount to more than a quarter of the population of the planet. Three-quarters of humanity still live in rural areas which are closer in their economy and way of life to a neolithic village than to a modern city. In most Third World countries the modern elite, though westernized, is rather small, and its control over the rest of the country somewhat uncertain, particularly in periods of deep structural change. Thus, there is always a possibility that indigenous traditions and institutions will reassert themselves.

When have ancient nations and civilizations been able to survive the Western onslaught? A first indication is given by those few countries which managed to avoid colonization by Western powers for a prolonged period in modern times. To this group belong Japan, China, Iran, Turkey, Afghanistan, Ethiopia and Thailand. In the last three cases inaccessibility and isolation probably played a more important role than traditional civilization strength. In the other cases internal strength was decisive. A closer look at the history of these cases reveals that China, Japan and Iran established the territorial and cultural base of their states many centuries before they were confronted with the Western challenge. A second indicator of indigenous potential is therefore obtained by adding those 'new nations' which, even if colonized, have been able to preserve the territorial integrity of an ancient nation, for example, countries like Egypt, Morocco, Vietnam and Sri Lanka. With the exception of Muslim separatism, this is also true for India.

It is a striking fact that most 'new nations' which were founded on ancient nations or civilizations have engaged in a deep national and social revolution or transformation through which they have been able to maintain parts of their cultural heritage. China, Iran, Egypt, Vietnam, principally, but among others Mexico, Turkey, Japan and India also more or less belong to this category. They can therefore be seen as the main sources, actual or potential, of alternatives to the Western model of development.

The Third World can be decomposed into different macro-cultures, groups of societies sharing a common social cosmology. Below an attempt is made to distinguish between Western and non-Western cultural areas. In this context, 'Western' is a cultural concept comprising both the Western core areas and those areas where a Western social cosmology predominates. That this framework is a tentative one should be obvious.[45]

The Western Worlds
1. Western Europe;
2. Eastern Europe (including the Russian part of the USSR);
3. Euro-America (Canada, United States, and 'Latin' Latin America);
4. Euro-Oceania (Australia, New Zealand).

The Non-Western Worlds
1. The Arabic-Islamic world;
2. Sub-Saharan Africa;
3. The Afro-American world (the Caribbean and part of Brazil);
4. The Indo-American world (particularly Central America and Peru);
5. The Islamic Orient (Persia, Pakistan, Indonesia);
6. The Indian subcontinent;
7. The Far East (China, Japan, Vietnam).

Some elements of Western social cosmology were discussed in the first section of this chapter. A detailed discussion of the cosmological context of various civilizations is not, of course, possible in this context, but it should be emphasized that the methodology of exploring social cosmologies (still somewhat tentative) will influence the way we identify them and how we conceive of their interactions.[46] For example, the Islamic world could be seen as part of the West since Islam and

Christianity have the same roots. However, religions spread and interact in different ways, and in the process they take on characteristics
which cannot be solely explained in religious terms. Thus, there are
obvious differences between Arabic and Oriental forms of Islam, and
Christianity may in fact be described as an Afro-Western religion.[47]

South America is marked by three different cultural orientations –
Indian, Latin and African – which only roughly can be described in
terms of geographical areas. For example, the concepts of *Ladinos* and
Indios refer primarily to language and life-style and the same person
may in fact choose one or the other, depending on the context.

Thus cultures and civilizations do interact in very complex ways and,
as was mentioned in the first chapter, one single culture may contain
different orientations that interact in a dialectic way, as the mainstream
counterpoint distinction in Western development thinking.

Taking a longer historical perspective, Johan Galtung has made a
similar distinction between an *expansion mode* and a *contraction mode*
where the former roughly corresponds to the Mainstream and the latter
to the Counterpoint. Galtung makes the prognosis that the contraction
mode will mark the next few hundred years. This raises the question as
to which cultural forces will fill the global vacuum created by Western
contraction.

There are four centres of cultural creativity on the Euroasian
landmass: Europe, Middle East, India and China. They have all developed advanced civilizations, empires and religions. For more than a
millenium they have been the main areas of the great world religions:
Christianity in the West, Islam in the Middle East, Hinduism in the
South and Buddhism in the East. During the long period from 500 A.D.
to about 1800 their interaction pattern looked like this.[48]

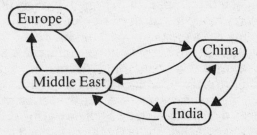

When Europe gained the upper hand in the 19th century the world
looked like this.

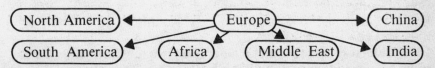

Though all non-Western cultures had to learn from the West, especially in the fields of science and technology, and to go through

veritable revolutions in thought and action, it is a fact that most of them have been able to adjust and recover through a process of rethinking and selective borrowing from Western culture. Some Asian cultures have even been able to launch a counter-attack on Western culture.

It is now common to find denunciations of the modern ways of life by authors and thinkers in the Third World. A statement like the following is fairly typical among culture-conscious intellectuals in these countries:

> Despite the great affluence in American and Europe, crime and anomie are not decreasing there; on the contrary, they are increasing. The pragmatic attitude and logic of the progressive culture is not able to give meaning to the life of the individual. More and more leisure time has become available to the average man because much of his work has been taken over by machines and innumerable gadgets, but he is not much happier and has the tendency to use his free time for unhealthy adventures, experiments and superficial entertainment. He has become more and more insensitive and is continuously asking for more excitement and more thrills.[49]

However, Western culture cannot be wished away. There will be many cultural challenges from non-Western cultures in the years to come but their impact will depend on several factors, economic and demographic in particular. These factors point in a certain direction.

At present the initiative thus lies with the Far East rather than with any other non-Western culture. Here we find the great civilization of China and her offshoots in Japan, Korea, Vietnam and other parts of South East Asia. Europe and China are the two opposite poles of the cultural magnet of the world. There are many reasons to regard the Far East as the main alternative to the West. China contains almost one quarter of humankind. In spite of repeated foreign invasions and internal upheavals, China has remained a politically united and culturally integrated entity for more than two thousand years. She has probably preserved the identity of her traditional culture to a higher degree than any other comparable civilization. China, of course, had to respond to the challenge of modernity and she has done so in an original and creative way. She has come up with her own strategy of development: self-reliance, or 'regeneration through own efforts'. The strategy of self-reliance stood at its height during the sixties and especially during the Cultural Revolution of 1966–1969. After Mao there has been a renewed interest in large-scale and advanced technology and 'foreign ways of doing things', but the basic self-reliant structure has already been built and will probably remain the ground-floor on which the rest of the edifice is to be constructed.[50]

It should also be noted that China belongs to a wider cultural area, which also includes Japan and South East Asia. These countries have already become major competitors to the West in the economic field and may, in fact, emerge as the future capitalist core, which underlines the fact that the Greening of the world presupposes challenges to the Western project but also that not all such challenges can be described as Green politics. In fact, governments may often be very hesitant in carrying out non-Western civilizational projects. This leads us to the problem of the modern elite.

Weakening of the state and the growth of counterpoint movements

The impulse to resist penetration of world capitalism is generally much weaker on the state level than at the level of civilization or the local community – which we discuss below. This reflects the ambiguous position of the modern elite which has seen involvement in the world-economy as one way of expanding its resource base, at the same time as the creation of a national community and a nationalistic consciousness has been necessary for reasons of political legitimacy. Thus, a state which may be seen as a political, administrative and military structure at the disposal of the modern elite has an external and an internal power base. Generally, external dependence will raise internal opposition and similarly, attempts at expanding the internal power base through political mobilization and inward-oriented development strategies will provoke external opposition and destabilization programmes. This is clearly exemplified by those countries trying to increase their autonomy during the 1970s. These attempts at self-reliance have admittedly not been very successful and therefore world-system theorists have, as noted above, tended to rule out this development option. But are the problems encountered by the Chiles, the Jamaicas and the Tanzanias in the 1970s sufficient evidence for this conclusion?

The concept of 'modern' elites is admittedly ambiguous and problematic. The social group that we have in mind is connected with a very specific situation: the emergence of colonial political systems and the need for indigenous officials in the lower echelons of colonial administration. Colonial systems have commonly been divided into those which are *directly* ruled and those which are *indirectly* ruled. In the latter type the colonial power centre made use of traditional ruling groups and interfered as little as possible with indigenous political structures and value systems. In the former, the traditional elites were done away with and a new elite – *the modern elite* – was educated to run their countries as 'brown sahibs' in accordance with the intentions of the colonial power. The recruitment of the modern elite is, of course, immensely important for understanding the dynamics of the anti-colonial power-struggle. We may divide this struggle into four typical phases: the war of resistance, the resistance of the traditional elites, the opposition from the modern elite and mass-mobilization. The length of the first phase to a very large degree depended on the political organization of pre-colonial society. In the second phase, there were sporadic rebellions expressing the incompatibility between the logic of colonial society and persisting traditional values. The later opposition from the modern elite in the third phase did not primarily reflect the contradiction between Western and non-Western values, but rather the feelings among the modern elite that they did not hold a position in colonial society concordant with their Western-style education. The fourth phase of mass-mobilization, usually leading up to independence, was characterized by an alliance between the modern elites and the masses, an alliance that for the modern leaders presupposed a quasi-populist platform. This compromise between the imported values of the modern elite and the more traditional values of the peasant masses was an uneasy one, which explains some of the tensions in the post-colonial era. We may regard this as the fifth phase of liberation – the liberation of the non-elites.

This phase implies a weakening of the state since the non-elites generally identify with sub-national systems, such as regions and local communities, while conceiving the state, the modern economy, the political parties and the other macro-organisations as dominated by the westernized elites. We shall call the non-elite counter mobilization *non-party politics* for lack of a more distinct concept. What we basically mean by this is spontaneous organisation and networks emerging from the economic and political crisis that in some cases is manifested in increased exploitation of humanity and nature, in other cases shows itself in the disappearance of government. At the same time, the counterpoint movements also represent a revitalization of suppressed value systems and traditions.

Modernization generally has the effect of undermining the traditional forms of life in the periphery. The self-supporting household, the village council, the kinship structure and the traditional culture, all tend to disintegrate when penetrated by the modern system. The first impulse of peripheral groups is to fall back on their old institutions. This is the key to the explanation of peasant activism. The peasants have always risen in defence of their traditional forms of life. Peasant mobilization is ultimately a conservative reaction against modernization, which in a later stage – and this is a paradox – often assumes a revolutionary character and brings further modernization. Eric Wolf formulates this paradox in a beautiful way: 'It is the attempt of the middle and free peasants to remain traditional which makes them revolutionary'. Thus, many of the autonomy resources are undermined but not completely exhausted. A weakening of the modern infrastructure and the modern elite will imply a relative strengthening of local autonomy.

Peasantry has been described as a 'way of life' and it is therefore obvious that it is not only economic autonomy that is threatened by what has been called 'modernization'. In terms of political autonomy, the peasants, as mentioned above, usually possessed some form of village councils, but super-imposed on these we find the typical patron-client structures that set the limits for political autonomy and have made the peasants subject to the interests of the local or regional elite. This implies that peasants often are *used* in politics (objects) rather than being political actors (subjects) in themselves. This is particularly the case in those Third World countries that still possess a democratic-parliamentarian political system. Even in revolutionary movements, these structures of patronage have, however, probably been more operative than is usually recognized.

In terms of social autonomy, peasants possess community resources like kinship and other forms of primordial loyalties. These are based upon immediate kin connection but they also extend beyond kinship to religious community, a particular language or a larger group following particular social practices.[54] The political implications of primordial loyalties are not easy to generalize, but a *vertical* primordial orientation usually implies social control, a *horizontal* (in which case the primordial sentiments can be very difficult to distinguish from class sentiments) implies a mobilization potential. A cognitive process replacing primordial loyalties (particularly vertical) with class solidarity is often taken as a necessary ingredient of mobilization. In any case, community resources can generally be held as a very important element in the mobilization potential of peasants and especially so since the processes of modernization (for example, the Green revolution) under-mine vertical rather than horizontal primordial loyalties.

As far as cultural autonomy is concerned, peasants represent what Robert Redfield has termed 'the little tradition' in conflict with, but at the same time, adapting to 'the great tradition', spreading from the urban centres. Wertheim has interpreted the 'little tradition' as an ideological counterpoint to the centre, and it should be noted that our use of the concept of counterpoint mentioned above has been inspired by Wertheim. In his most recent formulation, Wertheim describes counterpoints as follows:

> In all social units there are value dissensions, although they are not always manifest. One distinct value-system may dominate, adhered to by the holders of political power, 'the establishment'. But usually one can discover disguised counter-values, which function as a kind of counterpoint to the dominant values. Such counterpoints express themselves, for example, in religious values opposing the existing hierarchy of power, status and wealth. They can also assume the apparently more innocuous forms of folk tales in which the prevalent social order is more or less reversed (as when the poor swineherd marries the beautiful princess), or of myths in which the weaker groups may recognize themselves as masters of yesterday and victors of tomorrow (as, for example, in the widespread animal fables).[55]

Now, this implies that counterpoints can be seen as an ideological resource at the disposal of the periphery, particularly if the periphery coincides with the peasant culture, which most often is the case. These counterpoints have (since they may take religious or artistic forms) a high capacity for survival even under the most repressive systems and when the objective conditions 'are ripe for revolution', the necessary subjective ingredients will be provided by the ideological counterpoints. The peasant setting (the 'resistance to change' among peasants) is always conducive for the wintering of ideological counterpoints and as long as they stay in that setting, the peasant will always be guaranteed a certain degree of ideological autonomy.

The national space is monopolized by the modern elite who enforces its position by the development of a functional system, which in turn undermines territorial life (to use John Friedman's terminology)[56]. The non-elites can easily be manipulated from the 'commanding heights' of the functional system. Non-party politics is the only force that can counter the power of the modern elite.

To speak of non-party elites may seem to be a contradiction in terms since politics is usually defined as struggle for political power, and counterpoint movements often are characterized by avoidance of power in the conventional sense of the term (positions in the economic and political hierarchy). However, power can also be 'power over oneself', i.e. autonomy against economic, political and cultural penetration. Reactions to penetration, undermining the autonomy of local communities, classes and ethnic minorities have occasionally led to dramatic rebellions by for instance peasant and tribal populations, but, on the whole, non-party politics, expressing the citizen's concern with the exploitation and corruption that typically form part of the functional system, on a more permament basis, has, until recently, been quite rare in the Third Word. This is explained by lack of democratic traditions on the national arena (as distinct from the local) which in turn of course is explained by the fact that such an arena has not existed for very long. In the Third World the 'national space' has been occupied by the macro-organisations to the point of complete domination. This situation is bound to change.

The issue and manifestations of non-party politics differ from party politics in that they are extremely heterogeneous, and therefore defy all efforts at systematization. Besides, this is an almost totally unresearched field, not only because it is so recent but also because it does not fit well with the boxes Western social science is made of.

First a few general observations. The emergence of non-party politics is the result of *both* the increased inherent strength of various associations, networks and other group formations, *and* a weakening of government power, and ultimately the state. State power in the Third World is typically challenged from two directions (if we confine ourselves to internal challenges). The first type of conflict is *horizontal*, i.e. the struggle between elites operating in the national space, on the one hand, and regional or local elites, on the other. The efforts of the latter to achieve autonomy represent a tendency towards decomposition of the national system. The second type of conflict is *vertical*, i.e. the struggle of the political elite to retain state-power. To the extent that these groups represent interests that are different from those of the political elite this type of mobilization expresses a tendency towards transformation of the political system and the power structure. Non-party politics may be seen as a third type of challenge, since only power over oneself is sought, but this ambition is usually interpreted by the ruling elite as one or the other of the more conventional forms of political struggle. Of course the borderlines are difficult to draw even for an outside observer.

The power of the state may be bolstered by military force, police force and – most commonly – the mixture of the two called paramilitary forces, and as this happens the power of the state may for a casual observer not seem to be on the decline. However, an increase in coercive power, relative to remunerative and normative power, may be taken to imply a long-run decline in overall power.

Another general observation that can be made is that the growth of non-party politics in the national space evacuated by state power usually implies new conflicts previously kept down by a strong state heading for national unification. These conflicts are sometimes quite ugly and may make many prefer the repressive state power to, for instance, ethnic wars and extremist religious clashes. We are taking a sympathetic view of non-party politics but a note of warning against idealization and a priori acceptance must be made.

A third observation is that non-party politics is related more to the territorial than to the functional principle, although the political issues may be trans-local. For example the environmental issue is often dramatized in the local space but the sources of pollution and exploitation as well as the solutions must be looked for in larger, even transnational, systems. Functional organizations representing the poor have largely been failures from the point of view of the poor, while being instruments for elites challenging and trying to get access to state power. For this reason, and for the reason that the problems of the less privileged groups cannot be compartmentalized according to the functional principle, non-party politics tend to have a territorial base.

Let's now see what concrete non-party political formations we may find in the case of India, where the 'role of the State in social transformation has got undermined'[57] and where there is clear evidence of 'the incapacity of the macro-organizations of the poor – the political parties concerned, the kisan sabhas, the trade unions – to act effectively.'[58] In this situation India has in the last decade seen a spectacular growth of non-party political formations. The vitality of this new kind of grass-roots movement must however also be seen against the background of Gandhian politics which made an impressive comeback in the mid-70s. The failure of the Gandhian movement then was due to its mixing up with party politics which immediately killed the fire. This mistake will probably not be repeated. Furthermore the struggle is not limited to economic and political demands. It also covers ecological and cultural issues, since the basic issue propelling all these different groups into action is survival. Just to mention one example (India's underworld of grass-roots politics defies all attempts at systematization), *Jharkhand Mukti Morcha* is struggling for the protection of forests in Chota Nagpur and the economic and cultural survival of the tribal population of the area. This is a very clear case of a group trying to achieve autonomy *vis-à-vis* the functional systems: state administration, forestry department, political parties, paper industry, forest contractors, smugglers etc. It is very difficult to foresee what impact such groups may have on the macro-system, but it is quite obvious that their potential impact is underestimated simply because of the heterogenity of the phenomenon. On the other hand one should also not underestimate the problems they are facing.

There is already quite an impressive tradition of non-party political agitation in India, going back to Gandhi's rise to power. This happened with the Indian National Congress but, as is well-known, Gandhi was against the idea of transforming the Congress movement into a political party. During the last decade one could mention the Gujarat and Bihar agitations in 1973–74, the struggle against the Emergency in 1975–77, the famous agitations in Tamil Nadu, Karnataka and Maharashtra during 1980, and the textile strike in Bombay.

Counterpoint movements are not only movements of protest. Even more important are the constructive projects carried out by spontaneous network and voluntary organizations in the Gandhian tradition of 'constructive work'. The experiences of these activities provide new models for development. However, as long as these projects lack political analysis and vision and appeal to the benevolence of the power holders their impact will be limited. According to Harsh Sethi there is a trend towards politicization, though:

> Charity and welfare groups are displaying a development consciousness, while development groups are moving towards a struggle orientation. The more political groups are seeking new allies. These recent changes in the various developmental, non-political, transformative, and semi-political groups, and the growing interaction amongst them indicates that they have a potential for moving towards a new politics of the future.[59]

To the issue-oriented localized movements should be added the demand for regional autonomy which is growing dramatically in India and creates extremely difficult problems of control for the central government (Assam, Kashmir, West Bengal, Punjab, and the whole South). The dynamics of the 'regional phenomenon' is also very diverse and it is not possible within the framework of this overview to go into details. Besides, not enough research has gone into all these manifold challenges to the state. The regional agitation is largely a manifestation of party politics, but undoubtedly the outcome of the struggle will have implications for the future of the non-party political process.

The Indian case is now fairly well-documented because of a long tradition of counterpoint movements and a relatively sophisticated social science tradition where there is room for original and unconventional research.[60] To get an equally concrete picture of what goes on in other parts of the Third World is more difficult. Just to exemplify consider some cases from the late Roy Preiswerk who was a keen observer of achievements in local self-reliance (for him the most important level).[61]

- In Cameroon (where government action in water supplies is limited to towns with more than 10,000 inhabitants) thousands of villages have built their own water installations. Village Water Councils collected money and organized a collective work programme.
- In Senegal a farmer organized a vast movement of 20,000 villages who through their own cooperatives buy their supplies and market their products.
- In Columbia the campesinos have created autonomous zones (some of them called 'independent republics') where land has been redistributed and where the aim is basic needs satisfaction.
- Self-help organizations in Venezuela have emerged in situations of conflict with government, for example when bulldozers bring down the barrios, when unemployment rises, or when minimal public services fall below a tolerance point.
- In Trinidad Servol (Service Volunteered for All), started after the Black Power uprising of 1970, has become a large organisation with so called Life Centres all over the country with self-trained masons, plumbers, welders and carpenters.

There are thousands of examples of this kind. Some may be idealized, some may not exist any more, some may depend on external funds. As Preiswerk's examples also show, their relations with state power vary from cooperation to opposition but since they all reflect a struggle for self-reliance some contradictions will turn up sooner or later. This is in fact an enormous field of comparative research. The first problem is to get an overview over initiatives undertaken outside the formal economic and political systems, since they rarely are dramatic enough to be covered by the news media and they escape the attention of social scientists, who are biased towards putting too much emphasis on the macro-organizations. Another problem is that the viability of the new organizations cannot be asserted without a very deep understanding of the dynamics of the local organization. Thirdly, it is not easy to know whether apparent manifestations of the non-party political process is a true expression of people's power or if this process is manipulated from above.

The self-transformation of the West

The crisis of the West is something much deeper than an economic misfortune. Even if the growth machine regains its earlier momentum, a number of serious problems will remain: the environmental crisis, exploitation of poor nations, militarization and war, marginalization or the loss of a meaningful function in society, powerlessness, social disintegration, psychological and spiritual crisis, structural vulnerability and so on. These problems cannot be solved by applying the old liberal (Blue) and socialist (Red) recipes from the nineteenth century. This is the reason why we now have a whole set of new social movements trying to articulate a third (Green) vision of the world. We are referring to the ecological, solidarity, peace, feminist, communal, regional, youth, personal growth and new age movements and a host of other alternative movements.

What do the new movements have in common? Will they grow into a big wave of popular participation in the years to come? How do they differ from old social movements – that is, the labour movement? How did they emerge? Which groups are drawn into the movements? How do they organize themselves? What is their relation to established society? Will they succeed in solving our problems? We will not be able to answer all the questions here. Our intention is only to arrive at a preliminary understanding of their Green potential.

It is our thesis that the new social movements in the West are part of a worldwide current defending natural communities and searching for alternatives to modernization. Thus, there is a distinct similarity in the underlying pattern between these movements and the peasant movements of the Third World. Both types of movements should be analysed with two main ideas in mind, the concept of socio-economic dualism between modern and non-modern institutions and the idea of periphery mobilization as a reaction to penetration from a modernizing centre.

Table 7.1 *Social movements in western history*

Period	I. Pre-industrial	II. Industrial	III. Post-industrial
	Early modern period from the end of the Middle Ages	Intermediate period from the second half of the 19th century	Late period from the 1960s
	Penetration – modernization		
	State-building and commercialization	Industrialization	Professionalization, automation
Typical movement	Peasant movement	Labour movement	Alternative movement
Type of mobilization	Local and defensive mobilization against the modern-formal sector	Local and national offensive mobilization to conquer desirable positions in the modern-formal sector	Primarily local defensive and offensive mobilization to recreate the informal sector
Main actions	Tax rebellions, movements against conscription, food riots, land occupations	Demonstrations Strikes Electoral campaign	Alternative ways of life
Lower social base	Peasants, craft workers	Workers	Marginalized people
Organization	Local networks	Trade unions, political parties and other voluntary associations national in scope	Local networks and voluntary associations
Ideology	Populism	Liberalism-Socialism	Neopopulism

Note: The tinted area represents the extension of the modern-formal-rational sector. The white arrow stands for penetrations and the black for mobilization.

If we look more closely at the dialectics between modernization and resistance in Western history, we are able to discern at least three stages (see Table 7.1). For hundreds of years people reacted against modernization (phase I) but some time after 1850 they decided to take advantage of it instead (Phase II). Since the 1960s a new wave of resistance has emerged (Phase III) but this time the modernization process has gone so far that the movement has more or less to invent a new counter-structure to the formal-rational structure of modern society.

The first phase shows some similarities to what is now going on in many parts of the Third World, even if the conflicts had another content at the concrete level. During the Middle Ages people lived in small communities with traditional non-capitalist institutions. Life revolved around the family, the manor, the village, the small town, the church or the monastery. Towards the end of the Middle Ages the traditional way of life came under increasing pressure from merchant capitalism and emerging state structures. Wars were a major factor in this development. They increased the pressure for taxation and promoted the emergence of a rationalized state bureaucracy. It was the peasants and the craftsmen who most vigorously protested against the encroachment of the state. Tax rebellions, food riots, movements against military conscription and other forms of local civil disobedience were common all over Europe from the sixteenth to the nineteenth century. We see how people everywhere stood up for their traditional forms of life and their time-honoured rights against the demands of the modern central power for taxes, soldiers, food deliveries, and law and order. In the end, however, they were defeated.[62]

The labour movement in decline

With the industrial revolution, the modern rationalized system penetrated still deeper down in society, and the old organic forms of life in the rural villages moved towards disintegration and break-down. People were pulled out, roots and all, from a 'Gemeinschaft' society based on self-sufficiency and mutual aid and pushed into a 'Gesellschaft' society, founded on wage-labour in a rationalized factory environment. This change was far from voluntary. In support of our model of penetration from above, we would like to quote Barrington Moore Jr:

> There is no evidence that the mass of the population anywhere has wanted an industrialized society and plenty of evidence that they did not. At bottom all forms of industrialization so far have been revolutions from above, the work of a ruthless minority.[63]

With the decline of family, community and other primary groups came a huge increase in the aggregate of social needs. The industrial worker was thrown out in an alien world governed by impersonal market mechanisms and distant power centres. Lacking any recourse to independent means of support, and unprotected by a natural system of mutual aid and social security, workers had to develop a new strategy of survival: they decided to put their cards on the modern industrial state.

The great change in the forms of collective action occurred somewhere in the second half of the nineteenth century when the industrial system had become deeply rooted in most European countries.[64] Local and defensive action based on communal groups was replaced by national and offensive actions based on complex organizations. People began to lay claims to rights and positions within the modern system. The leading movement of its time – the labour movement – demanded the right to vote, equality and social security from the government, higher wages and better working conditions from the industrialists. By and large they also got it. Wages increased, working hours became shorter, the state was democratized and later transformed into a welfare state.

The system went through an unprecedented period of economic growth and people became assimilated and incorporated into the system, partly due to its ability to deliver direct material rewards.

Organization was the secret behind the success of the labour movement. As we will see in a moment, it is also the secret behind its decline. Lacking the ties of traditional social organizations, the workers had to develop new ones. The voluntary association became their major instrument. Uprooted people from the working class and the lower-middle classes joined the free churches, temperance societies, political parties and trades unions in great numbers. With workers' parties represented in parliament and trades unions participating in negotiations with the employers' associations, the working class has been firmly incorporated in the industrial capitalist system.

The workers' project is an integral part of the modern project, not only with respect to the goals – a welfare society – but also with respect to the means – the mass organization and the state. It is worth remembering that even though a voluntary association is a self-governing body, independent of the state, it is not based on personal relations – only a few members know each other personally. It is a national organization which covers the same territory as the state. It has a decision-making machinery which makes it a corporate actor. Its executive structure is organized according to the same bureaucratic principles of instrumental rationality and efficiency as all other modern organizations. It has a hierarchical structure of authority.

Organizations of this type do not allow for direct participation. They do not encourage people to become personally involved and active. They even tend to develop goals of their own – goals that are different from the personal goals of the individual members. The distance between the organizations and their members tends to increase. The more powerful the organizations become, the more powerless their individual members. Therefore the slogan: 'Unite and get strong!' has come into disrepute. People, both to the left and to the right, are now afraid of increasing the sphere of collective decision-making. They realize that they are going to lose power as individuals and not the reverse as they have always been told.[65] The idea of representation as a channel of personal influence is now seen as an illusion and this has affected all the old movements in the West. Though the old mass organizations may play an increasingly important role in national politics, they tend to decline if measured by the activeness and loyalty of their members. They are no longer living movements but ossified shells. This has affected the old mass organizations in most Western countries. Union membership rates and church attendance have been falling. Traditional political party loyalties are also weakening. The so-called crisis of legitimacy strikes not only at party bosses and company managers. Virtually all leaders of modern organizations are hit by this phenomenon.[66]

Many explanations can be invoked. One is in terms of size. Direct participation is not compatible with a mass organization which is national in scope. Let each member talk for five minutes in a meeting! After three hours in a plenary session, not more than 36 persons will have been able to take the platform. A still more basic explanation emphasizes that all modern organizations are based on a ground rule or fiction, which defines their specific nature. This ground rule, which is comparable in its ramifying implications to the commodity fiction of capitalism, says that organizations shall be treated as collective personalities. Like natural persons they have a right of ownership, rights to engage in transactions, a right to make and break contracts and so on. All these rights are legal rights ascribed to so called juristic persons and guaranteed by the state.[67]

The consequences of this seemingly innocent fiction are staggering. Anyone who invests money in a corporation in fact gives up effective control over the use of the invested capital to the corporation itself. In a similar way, the worker who joins a union gives up the rights of negotiating their wages and conditions of work. They have no voice in the day-to-day operations of the union, which is now managed by the union officials. The power moves from the natural person to the collective personality. It does not move from one person to another, but to a fictitious person, the corporate actor. The leaders of the organization have very little personal power: their power derives from position. They have to do what the organization demands. This fact becomes visible when an officer loses his position.

Power has become depersonalized. It is built into the power apparatus as such. The bureaucrat is never responsible – merely a replaceable cog in a social machine. The governing class, therefore, does not consist of governing individuals. They themselves are governed by the functions they perform for the corporate actor. This is the reason why workers' organizations cannot transform society into a socialist order by capturing the state apparatus. When the representatives of the workers capture the state, they themselves will be captured by the state. When they have entered the state apparatus, they will govern more or less in the same way as the earlier rulers. The only alternative is to dissolve the power apparatus itself. The great refusal, the great withdrawal of support, is a much more realistic road to a fundamental transformation of society.[68]

The main strategy of the labour movement has been to control the capitalist entrepreneurs through mass organizations and the state. The state is expected to step in and clean up wherever and whenever the private companies have made a mess. When people lose their jobs they get allowances from the state; when drug addiction increases, the state builds more clinics; when the environment is threatened by pollution, it sets up a national environment protection board. We do not deny that this strategy until now has had substantial effects in a particular historical situation. There are, however, inbuilt limitations to bureaucratic solutions and they will become more visible the longer we proceed in the same direction.

The solutions we apply in our industrial society tend to treat the symptoms, not the causes. The treatment of crime is a case in point. We know that the increasing crime rate is partly due to social disintegration. The point is that the modern society cannot provide the means for restoring the integrity of communities and primary groups. On the contrary, modernization itself undermines all natural communities. What the modern industrial society can provide is more policemen and more prisons, but these external means of control are poor substitutes for the myriad of informal self-regulatory processes which operate between people in small closely-built groups.[69]

The expansion of the state is in itself a threat to informal economies and local communities. This is so because state intervention requires financial means and the informal economy cannot be taxed. Thus, it is in the interests of the state to let the capitalist economy penetrate into the local communities. This will destroy the local informal economy and make people dependent on further state intervention and so on, in a vicious circle. The workers' demand for state intervention is, therefore, just one more factor adding fuel to capitalist penetration and modernization. If capital, state and science have been continuously reinforcing each other for five hundred years, why should we think of the state as a counterweight to capitalism? The whole political debate between the left favouring the public sector and the right who favours the private sector is, in fact, a minor quarrel between husband and wife.

Marx believed that a revolutionary consciousness would develop out of the maturity of capitalism, but so far workers have only been committed to a radically different social order during the early phase of industrialization, when they reacted against the rationalized factory system because of their earlier personal experience of peasant life. During this period the anarchist movement developed a vision of economic life as organized on the basis of federated communal units rather than on the basis of big factories.

Present-day workers are wedded to the large-scale industrial system and to their own organizations who tend to reproduce the same rational and formal features as the modern system itself. It follows that their parties and trade unions are no threat to the established system. Their incorporation has rather stabilized the institutional structure of the capitalist order. It can even be stated that reformist 'social democracy is the normal form taken by the systematic political inclusion of the working class within capitalist society'.[70]

However, one should never say never. If it is true that nothing will mobilize a group more than the defence of resources and rights which they are on the verge of losing, we should expect the industrial workers to become really militant when they are threatened by mass unemployment caused by two important trends in the capitalist world-system which should be noted in this context.

The first trend is the technological revolution of robotization and computerization. It will eliminate more and more jobs in production, distribution and administration. Millions of people will either be forced to leave their factories and offices in the coming years or else drastically reduce working hours and income levels. According to one estimation about 60 per cent of all occupational groups fall in the risk zone. With ever-increasing productivity, fewer and fewer workers are needed to keep the economy going.

The second trend is the emergence of new competitors in the world market for industrial products. The industrial revolution in some parts of the Third World, especially in South East Asia, is a formidable challenge to the old industrial metropoles in the West. A deindustrialization process has already started in the traditional industrial branches (footwear, textiles, steel, ships, watches, cars, etc.) in some of the metropoles. This will affect workers in different ways. The work-force in the technologically most advanced branches have less to fear from the newly industrialized countries and also from automation as they belong to an expanding sector of the world-economy. Their organizations will probably stick to the old model of economic growth through export and free trade. Workers in the most severely affected branches will demand protectionist measures, that is, protection from the world-market. A third group, the 'so-called unorganized workers, principally women, youth, temporary immigrant workers, so-called "marginal groups" of all kinds, will seek to develop as much autonomy as possible from capital and create ways of living and working which run counter to the process of total commodification'.[71]

The twin processes of automation and deindustrialization will shake the working class to its very foundations. A growing part of it will in all probability be open for the demodernization project of the Green movement, though the organized 'core' will stick to the old project.

The alternative movements in the West

The expansion of the modern complex has occurred in three steps. The first one was dominated by state-building and commercialization of agriculture. Industrialization was the second step. The third step, which is a post-war phenomenon, has been given different names: post-industrialization, technocratic society, programmed society, service society.[72] Each of the three steps has been associated with a particular type of popular movement; the first with traditional peasant movements, the second with the labour movement, and the third with a new type of social movement. It is our contention that this new type can be characterized as a Green project. The new movements have abandoned the modern project for a radical humanist approach. This can easily be seen from a brief outline of their emergence.

The first tendencies appeared during the 1950s in the form of protests against nuclear weapons. This represented a militant pacifism which, however, lacked a clear vision of an alternative society. The break with the establishment had more to do with new and unconventional methods of struggle, such as sit-ins, teach-ins, demonstrations, boycotts, and street theatre. An entire spectrum of non-violent direct action in which ordinary citizens could engage was developed. It is to be noted that already at this stage Gandhi, a key figure in the Green tradition, gained widespread attention.

Towards the end of the 1960s these movements turned into a second stage characterized by a more deep-going protest against the centralized and technocratic society and its ideals of mass consumption, especially among students and intellectuals. The foremost expression of this was the so-called New Left which was critical of modern industrial society, both in its capitalist and state-socialist form. It wanted to substitute the one-sided economic-technical rationality of industrial society with radical humanist values. The new Left actually contained many ideological currents. One of them was marxism, but it is probably correct to characterize the main current as a crude form of Green socialism. This was especially the case in the USA, where there are strong populist traditions, as compared to continental Europe where marxism has been the dominant ideology of opposition for a long time. However, even in Europe the New Left felt a strong attraction towards the pre-marxist period in the socialist movement. Utopian socialism, anarchism, syndicalism and guild-socialism were revived because of their critical attitudes to universal industrialism, and their ideas about how to integrate advanced tools and machines into a local community structure.

The new ideas derived not only from the Western cultural sphere. It was strongly influenced by the liberation movements in the Third World where the peasant socialism of Mao was a particularly influential example of a development model 'in which people really mattered'. A feature was the marked orientation towards Eastern philosophy in such forms as Zen Buddhism, tantric yoga, and transcendental meditation within the so-called counter-culture. Thus, we can distinguish between two branches of the new movement. The New Left was a challenge to the establishment on a political and intellectual level (the macro revolution) whereas the counter-culture challenged the socio-cultural and emotional poverty of Western society. It tried to bring about a revolution of consciousness in everyday life and to work out alternatives in living (the micro revolution). The two were fused in the protests against the American war in Vietnam.

The new currents in the industrialized countries entered a third stage in the 1970s. The ideas of the 1968 student rebellion are spreading in ever broader circles, especially in the middle strata. As examples, we could mention the remarkable growth of environmental movements, the women's liberation movements, local action groups, new life-style movements and new religious movements. The new trend is also evident in parliamentary politics through the growth of Green parties as well as eco-political tendencies within the established parties.

In the 1970s the Green movement began to develop and practice its own alternatives: solar collectors and windmills, macrobiotics and organic gardening, parent-cooperative daycare centres and voluntary simplicity in life-styles, bicycle holidays and spiritual travels in the vast regions of our inner life. Much of this was stimulated by the struggle against nuclear power.

To all this we should add the reform movements within the established institutions. The 1970s has been a period of small-scale experiments with radical alternatives in health care, education, research, administration, town-planning, industrial democracy and so on. In almost every institution a few dedicated persons have been able to break new grounds for alternatives based on humanistic and holistic approaches. Suffice it to mention the wave of radical therapy, pedagogical experiments with student-centred teaching, the quality of working life movement, and the anti-positivistic and interdisciplinary movements in the sciences.[73]

Intra-institutional innovations are particularly important in the sphere of technological development. Here new ideas materialize into devices with an obvious impact on the daily life of ordinary people. There is no doubt that the main innovations still fit into the prevalent megatechnics, but an increasing number of inventors and entrepreneurs (in the broad sense of the term) have set their minds on a different path. They have, for example, discovered that micro-computers hold out a strong potential for a home and locality-based economy.[74]

The reform movements within the institutions can be interpreted as a response by the establishment to the turbulent protest movement of the 1960s. The spokesmen are often former protesters now working within the institutions. There is, of course, a risk that the activists will be coopted by the establishment and in the end give up their ideas. So far this does not seem to be case. The experience of a new consciousness and a new way of being cannot easily be taken away from a person. The process is more or less irreversible.

At the level of ideas the breakthrough is even more impressive. Few people are against ecology, decentralization and the quality of life. Even within the establishment, surprisingly Green ideas turn up now and then. This must be seen against the background of a deep crisis in our dominant culture and institutions. The average person is experiencing growing disbelief in the viability of big companies, the state bureaucracy, the representative system, one-dimensional science and technology, the overgrown medical complex and so on. The general distrust has been reinforced by the present world economic crisis. The system is now not even able to deliver the material goods or non-material qualities that people are longing for. Such a situation may easily lead to a desire for a strong hand to take over. There are, in fact, many signs that we are drifting towards authoritarian control. The anti-authoritarian movements we have dealt with so far are not alone on the scene. A true picture of the present situation should include the neo-conservative current, the revival of fundamentalist religion, violent youth cultures and racist movements.

Though the new social movements contain many different ideological currents, it is evident that the Green one is the main innovatory force. All the new movements have in one way or another articulated the non-modern vision of a functionally integrated communal society founded on direct personal participation. The environmental movement, for instance, is itself a heterogeneous phenomenon containing liberal, socialist, conservative and even fascist currents. The most deep-going current, however, is the protest against the industrial-growth society on the basis of a new holistic and reverential attitude towards nature, towards other beings and towards oneself. This branch of the movement maintains an ecosophically inspired world-view based on the principles of organic wholeness, diversity, autonomy, decentralization and symbiosis.

A similar analysis could be made, for instance, of the women's liberation movement. There are liberal and socialist currents within the movement but the dominant current today is a feminist branch rejecting the goal of equal distribution of sexes in modern male-dominated organizations as totally inadequate. The feminist current attacks modern society on the bases of a particular counterpoint, the more or less suppressed and invisible female culture. This culture, which stems from women's participation in unpaid production, emphasizes specific values such as motherly care, the life-giving spirit of Mother Earth, human warmth and closeness, and being rather than having or doing. The feminist current is parallel to the ecopolitical current of the environmental movement. Both belong to the Green Utopia of complete human beings living close to nature and to each other in small-scale communities with a high degree of self-determination and self-reliance.

Table 7.2 *The Green movements in the West*

	Crisis	Movements	Alternatives
1.	Environmental crisis	Environmental movement	Renewable resources, local recycling and partnership with nature
2.	Exploitation of poor nations	Solidarity movements	Self-reliance
3.	Militarization and war	Peace movement	Civilian-based defence
4.	Repression	Human rights movement	Person to person support
5.	Consumerism	Consumer movement	Voluntary simplicity
6.	Marginalization	Youth Feminist Pensioner Regional Labour Client ⎬ movements	Meaningful production, informal economy, radical technology
7.	Powerlessness	Decentralization movement (local action groups)	Participatory democracy, self-management, cooperatives
8.	Community crisis	Community movement	Communes, primary groups
9.	Spiritual crisis	New Age movement	New paradigm, self-produced knowledge
10.	Psychic and physical illness	Human growth movement Health movement	Self-realization, non-material needs, alternative ways of life

Table 7.2 shows, in abstract terms, the typical alternatives put forward by the new movements. It was found that they all converge towards the small-scale logic of functionally integrated communal societies based on direct participation and self-management. In this type of future society, the scope of capitalist growth, central bureaucracy and techno-science would be considerably reduced. It was also found that this type of society would solve a number of problems in an integrated way.

There seems to be nothing wrong with the vision itself, but how do we go from here to there? Is it not completely unrealistic? This is not seen as a serious objection by Green people. (The strategy debate between the Red and Green poles is summarized below.) They do not suggest that we will enter the 'garden city' after a short, once-and-for-all smashing operation at the right historical moment. This would be unrealistic indeed. What they offer is a new project and a new destination for humankind. The modern world was not built in one day by a well-organized social movement. The Green project will also require a long period of uncoordinated actions before it will reach its near completion. It will never be fully completed, however, because new projects will certainly emerge some time in future history. The important thing is that the Green project catches people's imagination and inspires their daily actions. There is no right historical moment to begin the struggle for a decent life. It has to start right now.

Modern society has allowed the means to dominate the ends. The technological means are everything, the ends nothing. The Green movement tries to avoid this mistake. It seems to believe in means-ends consistency. If the means determine the ends, the ends must be the means. 'There is no road to community. Community is the road' is a favourite expression within this tradition of strategy. The building of communities should be promoted wherever and whenever we see the opportunity. The determinist has got an excuse for his or her inactivity. The laws of capitalism exclude the possibility of socialist islands in a capitalist sea. The Green movement, however, believes in a margin of freedom. Within this margin, some local experiments are possible. Together they will form a 'liberated zone' to use an apt expression from the vocabulary of guerilla strategy. This zone will be extended successively and in the end comprise almost the whole world.

How should the Green movement be organized? The modern road of building formal, mass-organizations in order to capture the big companies and the state apparatus does not lead to a fundamental transformation of society in the direction of human and social development. The old labour movement has chosen the modern road and it has become incorporated in the formal-rational complex, and is now losing its momentum as a creative force.

The Green strategy is rather to achieve autonomy by mass withdrawal from the formal system. Thus, the movements tend to organize in decentralized networks of small primary groups. They avoid the concept of the organization as a reified collective personality in which the individual is a mere function. The stress is rather on personal development and direct participation. The organization is seen as the means and the ends at the same time.[75] This new mode of participation is now spreading very rapidly among Western publics. More and more people are drawn into small issue-oriented ad hoc groups based on personal involvement. Their aim is not the simple one to support their leaders, but to cooperate towards concrete goals and at the same time to associate with friends and to grow as persons.[76]

The road to demodernization does not go via the modern complex. The labour movement went this road in the belief that formal labour is the foundation of everything in society. It organized the working class at the big industrial production sites. The Green project turns to the places where people live; the homes, families, the neighbourhoods, the local communities. It wants to bring back the basic life-sustaining

functions from the scientifically planned labour process in the factories
to the autonomous sphere of production in the households and residen-
tial areas. The new project is not to take charge of the programmed
labour process but to abolish it.[77] This cannot be done by workhorses
who have made eight-hours-a-day-work their central interest in life.
However, most working people have an instrumental attitude to work.
Their central life interest lies outside the workplace. They may, therefore, be willing to participate in the Green project.[78]

Granted that we live in an alienating society, how do we make it more
responsive to basic human needs? The society will have to be fundamentally restructured, but how to bring it about? Here we agree with A.
Etzionis' dictum that 'there is no way for a societal structure to discover
the members' needs and adapt to them without the participation of the
members in shaping and reshaping the structure'.[79] The Green position
then is ultra-democratic in seeing direct participation as a major instrument of social development.

However, the problem is not that simple. We have to ask what comes
first, the social transformation or the personal transformation? In an
alienating society we cannot take for granted that people know their
own basic needs. 'In the new Freudian perspective the essence of society
is the repression of the individual and the essence of the individual is the
repression of himself', says Norman Brown in his book *Life and Death*.
Too many in our society voluntarily put on the strait jacket provided by
the industrial-corporate system. They keep up a pretence to themselves
and others that they are the type of person they are expected to be. Their
sense of identity is rooted in external matters like possessions and social
roles. When asked 'Who are you?' they answer with a simply reference
to their occupation, community, family or possessions. Their own true
nature is suppressed under a heavy layer of internalized identities.
Because of a strong self-censorship their basic deprivation remains
hidden even to themselves. They participate in social life without self-
reflection, without really knowing themselves. Their attitudes are generally conventional or authoritarian.

We cannot expect these people to agree to a fundamental transformation of society, which will destroy the external support structures for
their self-image for which they have given up so much of their own true
nature. A deep social revolution would throw them into a state of
complete disorientation and unreality. They would be the first to join
behind the banner of the counter-revolution in order to rescue as much
as possible of their wrecked ego-structure. Their revenge on the revolu-
tionaries would not be particularly mild. Suffice it to remind the reader
that middle-class mothers of the first hippies, who dropped out of
American society and engaged in an alternative mode of existence, cried
for the police to stop the movement by any means, shooting included.

It seems to be clear that the social transformation must go hand in
hand with a personal transformation. You cannot move the social

structure closer to true human nature if you do not recognize that nature within yourself and others. Social emancipation therefore presupposes a kind of self-emancipation – an effort to liberate oneself from a derived sense of identity. Each individual is faced with an existential choice between these two ways to define their own identity.[80] Self-emancipated people have a low level of self-censorship. They are in touch with their internal state and feelings, even those which are painful. Their identity is anchored at this level of their consciousness. They are often intensely aware that they wear a mask, play a role, that they are not the persons they act like. They see through the social conventions and the little games people play. The life of normal people in our society gives them a sense of absurdity and unreality. They know something about themselves and are prepared for real change.

The distance between the actors and their roles is the ultimate mark of their autonomy *vis-à-vis* the social structure. They have a margin of liberty. They do not have to reproduce the existing society in all their actions, because they have access to an independent base from which to transcend that society.

It follows that the emergence of self-emancipated and authentic persons cannot be predicted solely on the basis of an analysis of social structures.[81] The whole phenomenon is partly situated outside the social field. It has its roots in an existential struggle going on in every human being. This does not mean that it cannot be facilitated by social means. On the contrary, the Green movement and especially the so-called counter-culture is deeply involved in group experiments, which allow for authenticity, freedom and openness in human relations.[82] It tries to break down the barriers of communication between people. It is suspicious of all formal roles and rules which impede honesty and authenticity. The ideal is a society where we have thrown away our artificial masks so that our naked selves confront each other directly. The counter-culture has developed a number of techniques of deprogramming to get out of 'straight' society (drugs, meditation, therapy, rituals, artistic activities etc). Some of them aim at the personal level, others at the group level. They all initiate a process of unilateral or multilateral disarmament of ego-defences so that people can move out of their ego-prisons set for them by the system and search for their own true nature.

Table 7.3 *The Red and the Green strategy*

	The Red strategy	*The Green strategy*
Oppressive system	The capitalist economy	The technological culture
Enemy	The capitalists	The technocracy
Social vision	The socialist society	The communal society
Method	The organizations of the working class conquer state power and introduce socialism from above (the macro-revolution)	Many small groups withdraw from the system and introduce or defend autonomous ways of life (the micro-revolution)
Locality	No socialist islands in a capitalist sea	Local experiments, liberated zones
Time	The right historical moment	The whole life, permanent revolution
At stake	Material interests, collective identity, ownership	Existential needs, personal identity, autonomy
The new person	Social transformation before personal transformation	Simultaneous social and personal transformation
Leadership	Intelligentsia	Postmaterialistic elite
Social base	Working class	Marginalized people (youth, women, deviants, unemployed, self-employed, people in peripheral districts etc) .
Institutional base	Big industrial working sites	Small local communities, (neighbourhoods, circles of friends etc)
Organization	Centralized, formal organization	Decentralized, informal network
Ideology	Abstract, rational dogmatic	Concrete, intuitive, open
Basic problem	The organizations of the working class will reproduce the oppressive system	Fragmentation, cooptation and reintegration into the system

   To summarize the forces behind the emergence of a Green movement in the West we hold that the main source so far has been the *post-materialist* elite close to the centres of the modern society. Because of the opportunities provided by an affluent society many young and well-educated people have been able to transcend the programmed society and create a counter-culture aiming at *self-emancipation* and authenticity in social relations. The student rebellion in the late 60s was a real break-through for this new culture and this can largely be explained by the fact that the university was the first modern institution in which the post-materialists became a majority. The university also provided enough freedom for small groups to liberate themselves from the subtle controls of the rationalized system.

The post-materialist elite has been the main innovating force within the Green movement. The fact that women have played such an important role in this process calls for a specific explanation. We have referred to the female culture as a *counterpoint* to the male-dominated modern sociey. The specificity of female culture stems from women's participation in unpaid labour for their families and relatives. This culture has come under heavy pressure from the dominant culture in the last two decades. It is a significant fact that the modernization complex has invaded new fields of activity in the post-industrial period. It has penetrated into the sphere of reproduction. The welfare state has taken over more and more functions in the fields of upbringing, education, care of old people and social security in general. Many of these tasks were earlier performed by women according to a different social logic. Even more intimate and private areas of life have become the object of legal regulations. They are now under the control of professionals with a formal scientific education. The autonomy and stability of the family institution and of local subcultures have been severely curtailed by this last expansion of the modern complex and a great part of the Green endeavour can be seen as a defence and rescue operation for this type of group and institution. The new social movements can, therefore, be explained as reactions against the new encroachment of the programmed society on the everyday life of its members. 'Defence of the identity, continuity and predictability of personal existence is beginning to constitute the substance of the new conflicts.'[83] Thus, the process of *penetration* is still a main causal factor behind the emergence of Green movements not only in peripheral countries but also in the metropoles of the world.

Most observers agree that the third pillar of modernization, science, has increased in relative importance under late-modernism. This is seen in the increasing predominance of professionals, scientists and technicians. Scientific research has become a principal force of production. The scientific institutions are now a major system of legitimation and stratification. This is the reason why so much of the Green attack on modern society has been directed towards science, technocracy and the myth of objective knowledge. A part of the Green endeavour has been to develop a new metaphysical basis for the future society and to encourage autonomous learning processes outside the formal system of education.[84]

Though of minor importance for the Green movement today, the process of *marginalization* may well prove to be decisive in the long run development of the Green project. It hits the broad masses of the mega-technological societies. Marginalization is not only unemployment. It is the process in which people gradually lose a meaningful function in the mega-machine. Because of increasing productivity, rationalization, automation and computerization the system will use less and less of the time, energy and creativity of ordinary people. The worker is physically present at the assembly line but his mind has left the factory long ago and with increasing robotization he will soon leave even in the physical sense, at least for a part of the working day. This, we think, will be a decisive factor in the years to come.

Summary

The purpose of this study is to clarify the intellectual content and the political relevance of what has come to be called the 'Green' alternative in world development. It is our contention that the 'Blue' (market, liberal, capitalist) and 'Red' (state, socialism, planning) options can be seen as varieties of a dominant Western development paradigm, whereas the Green development thinking represents a fundamental opposition against this paradigm. Mainstream perspectives such as modernization theory, dependency theory and world-system theory share an underlying view of development as a predetermined evolutionary process which is immanent in the nation state or the world-system. Thus, they have no need for an elaborated normative definition of development.

The Green view on the contrary assumes that the future is ultimately a product of our own choices. It introduces a normative concept of development which defines development in human terms and it works out a voluntaristic strategy of development, which is ultimately carried out by individual human beings. We admit that the Green approach easily sidetracks into a utopianism divorced from reality. The utopia is necessary both in theory and strategy. However, what we need is a realistic utopia which is anchored in actual global forces, however weak they may look in a short term perspective. Thus our purpose is to develop a non-deterministic model of the world, making use of the world-system approach but focusing on the antisystemic forces with a Green potential. This necessitates an analysis of actors and their strategies in a long historical perspective.

The expansion of the world-system during the modern epoch (modernization) is not seen as an automatic process but as the result of a struggle between modernizing forces and a continuous resistance. Modernization was first embarked upon by elites in Western Europe and then imposed on the internal and external periphery through state-building, colonialism, trade, and missionary activity. Modernization should be seen as a transnational process of penetration reverberated throughout the world with the spread of North Atlantic capitalism and associated institutions such as the central bureaucracy, the military, the university and educational system, and industrial forms of production. This process has been in progress for a period of five hundred years by now and it has always met with some kind of resistance in different parts of the world. So far, the modernizers, both Red and Blue, have been victorious but it is now evident that resistance is increasing very rapidly thus preparing the ground for a Green alternative.

We point to a Green potential among a number of actors and structures, such as non-Western civilizations, old nations and tribes, local communities and informal economies, peasants and self-employed people, marginalized people in general, the post-materialist elite in the West and so on. We also put emphasis on the fact that the modern world-system is ultimately defined by a cultural system of reference which cuts through civilizations, nations, communities, classes and individuals. From this point of view the imputed dominance of the world-system is somewhat of an illusion. After all, most people in the world live most of their lives outside this system. All Westernized communities do not amount to more than a quarter of the population of the planet. Three-quarters of humanity still live in rural areas which are closer in their economy and way of life to a neolithic village than to a modern city. In most Third World countries the modern elite, though westernized, is rather small and its control over the rest of the country somewhat uncertain, particularly in a situation of world economic crisis. Thus, there is always a possibility that indigenous traditions and institutions will reassert themselves.

We see two possible outcomes of the present world crisis. One is suggested by the world-system approach; out of the crisis a new revitalized world capitalism will emerge. On the other hand, and this is the option we investigate here, a new Green project will catch on as a result of the conscious choices of numerous actors.

Notes

1 Björn Hettne, *Development Theory and the Third World*, SAREC Report R2, 1982.
2 A. Walicki, *The Controversy over Capitalism*, Oxford University Press, London, 1969.
3 Robert A. Nisbet, *Social Change and History*, Oxford University Press, London, 1969.
4 J.B. Bury, *The Idea of Progress. An Inquiry into its Origin and Growth*, Dover Publications, New York, 1955 (1932).
5 A.D. Smith, *The Concept of Social Change. A Critique of the Functionalist Theory of Social Change*, Routledge & Kegan Paul, London, 1973. I. Roxborough, *Theories of Underdevelopment*, Macmillan, London, 1978.

6 M. Blomström, B. Hettne, *Development Theory in Transition, The Dependency Debate and Beyond: Third World Responses*, Zed Books, London, 1984.

7 Interview in *Monthly Review* (1981).

8 Andre Gunder Frank, 'Dependence is Dead, Long Live Dependence and the Class Struggle', *World Development*, Vol. 5, No. 4 (April 1977), p. 357.

9 Immanuel Wallerstein, *The Modern World-System I. Capitalist Agriculture and the Origins of the European World-Economy in the Sixteenth Century*, Academic Press, New York and London, 1974.

10 Immanuel Wallerstein, *The Capitalist World-Economy*, Cambridge University Press, Cambridge, 1979.

11 Immanuel Wallerstein, 'The Future of the World-Economy', in Terence Hopkins and Immanuel Wallerstein (eds.), *Processes of the World-System*, Sage Publications, Beverly Hills, 1980, p. 176.

12 To give just one piece of evidence, according to the National Science Foundation, one half of the expenditure on research and development in the United States is for military or semi-military purposes, four-tenths are industrial R & D, and about one-tenth is carried out in universities. Even of the last two items, a large share is directed towards military purposes.

13 A searching analysis of the social functions of modern technology and its legitimations is given by David Dickson, *Alternative Technology and the Politics of Technical Change*, Fontana, London, 1974.

14 Alan Touraine, *The Self-Production of Society*, Chicago, 1977.

15 E.F. Schumacher, *Small is Beautiful. A Study of Economics as if People Mattered*, London, 1973.

16 Ignacy Sachs, 'Civilization Project and the Ecological Prudence', *Alternatives*, III, No. 1, August 1977.

17 A. Naess, 'The Shallow and the Deep, Long-range Ecology Movement. A Summary', *Inquiry*, Vol. 16, No. 1, 1973.

18 Erich Fromm, *The Sane Society*, 1955.

19 A. Etzioni, *The Active Society*, New York, 1968, p. 623.

20 Experiments with sensory deprivation show that people who are cut off from continuous sensory inputs from the environment rapidly develop grave mental disorders. Social isolation and loneliness cause severe psychic suffering. Comparative research about nurseries for abandoned babies shows that love is a condition for human development and survival. Where the babies received little stimulation and love from the nurses their physical and emotional development was retarded. Even though they received perfect nutritive, hygienic and medical care, they had a higher mortality rate (E. Chinoy, Society, 1964).

21 No other author has opened our eyes to the trauma of civilization as effectively as Lewis Mumford in his many books on the history of technology. See especially, *The Myth of the Machine, Volume I: Technics and Human Development*, New York 1966, and *Volume II: The Pentagon of Power*, New York, 1964.

22 Records of armed strife are, for instance, almost totally absent before the agricultural revolution (R. Leaky and R. Lewin, *People of the Lake*, 1978).

23 Erich Fromm, *The Anatomy of Human Destructiveness*, 1973.

24 Lewis Mumford, *Technics and Human Development*, New York, 1966, p. 204.

25 R. Inglehart, *The Silent Revolution*, Princeton University Press, 1977, documents the important shift of values from an overwhelming emphasis on material values to greater concern with the quality of life which has occurred among all Western publics during the post-war period.

26 R.D. Laing, *The Politics of Experience*, Penguin Books, Harmondsworth, 1967.

27 Claude Lévi-Strauss, 'Race and History', in *Race, Science and Society*, Allen and Unwin, London, 1975, p. 113.

28 J. Galtung, P. O'Brien and R. Preiswerk (eds.), *Self-Reliance, a Strategy for Development*, Bogle-L'Ouverture, London, 1980.

29 H. Chenery *et al.*, *Redistribution with Growth*, Oxford University Press, 1974, p. XIII.

30 Alduous Huxley, *Science, Liberty and Peace*, London, 1947.

31 David Dickson, *Alternative Technology*, 1974; Godfrey Boyle and Peter Harper (eds.), *Radical Technology*, 1976; Amory Lovins, *Soft Energy Paths*, 1977.

32 *The Global 2000 Report to the President*, Penguin Books, 1982, p. 37.

33 H.A. Turner Jr., 'Fascism and Modernization', *World Politics*, 24, 1972.

34 Lewis Mumford, op. cit. Vol. I. *Technics and Human Development*, New York, 1966, p. 255.

35 Arnold Toynbee, *A Study of History*, in one volume, Oxford University Press, London, 1972, Parts II and III.

36 Our model is partly inspired by the theoretical work of Alain Touraine. See his *Production de la Société*, Edition du Senit, 1973.

37 See, for example, John G. Taylor, *From Modernization to Modes of Production*, London, 1979.

38 K. Polanyi, *The Great Transformation*, Beacon Press, Boston, 1944.

39 J.H. Randall Jr. *The Making of the Modern Mind*, Columbia University Press, 1976 (1926). This book is still, after more than 50 years, a goldmine for unravelling the historical roots of the modern mind.

40 Immanuel Wallerstein, *The Capitalist World-Economy*, p. 129.

41 Immanuel Wallerstein, *Patterns and Prospectives of the Capitalist World-Economy*, United Nations University, 1981.

42 Folker Fröbel, *The Current Development of the World Economy*, United Nations University, 1980, p. 42, reprinted in *Review*, Spring, 1982.

43 Eric R. Wolf, *Peasant Wars of the Twentieth Century*, Harper & Row, New York, 1969.

44 It is necessary to stress 'progressive elements' in this formulation. We are aware that there are small-scale pre-capitalist orders of an extremely vertical, exploitative and dehumanizing nature. On the other hand, we believe that horizontal and human-centred social orders have to be small scale. Thus, the set of pre-capitalist orders includes the two extremes, the best as well as the worst.

45 We acknowledge several important sources of inspiration: Arnold Toynbee, *A Study of History*, London, 1972; Joseph Needham, *Science and Civilization in China*, Volumes 1-4, Cambridge University Press, 1954-1971; Anouar Abdel-Malek, *Civilizations and Social Theory* (Volume 1 of *Social Dialectics) and Nation and Revolution* (Volume 2 of *Social*

Dialectics), Macmillan Press, London, 1981; Johan Galtung, 'Social Cosmology and the Concept of Peace', *Journal of Peace Research*, Vol. XVIII, No. 2, 1981.

46 According to Johan Galtung (1981, op. cit.) the exploration of a social cosmology should be based on information on the following six entities: space, time, knowledge, person-nature, person-person, person-transpersonal.

47 A.A. Mazrui, 'Eclecticism as an Ideological Alternative – An African Perspective', *Alternatives*, Volume I, No. 4, December 1975.

48 See William McNeil, *The Rise of the West. A History of the Human Community*, University of Chicago Press, 1963.

49 Takdir Alisjahbana, 'Socio-Cultural Creativity in the Converging and Restructuring Process of the New Emerging World', EIC, United Nations University, 1980.

50 There is no denying that Mao was a marxist. However, as has been convincingly argued by Maurice Meisner ('Leninism and Maoism. Some Populist Perspectives on Marxism-Leninism in China', *The China Quarterly*, January-March, 1971), the relationship between marxism and maoism is a rather ambiguous one. The influence of marxism never completely overwhelmed the populist strain in China and furthermore, a powerful populist impulse was to become an integral component of the maoist of marxism. One of the fundamental characteristics of maoism is the still unresolved tension between leninist-type elitism and the populist belief in the spontaneous socialist consciousness of the peasantry. Thus, according to taste, maoism could be described as a sinification of marxism, or as marxism perverted by populist impulses.

51 Björn Hettne, 'Self-reliance versus modernization: the dialectics of Indian and Chinese development strategies', in E. Bark and Jon Sigurdson (ed.), *India-China. Comparative Research*, Curzon Press, London, 1981.

52 Björn Hettne, 'Soldiers and politics: the case of Ghana', *Journal of Peace Research*, No. 2, Vol. XVII, 1980.

53 Basil Davidson, *Africa in Modern History*, Allen Lane, London, 1978, p. 289. See Kwame Nkrumah, *Africa Must Unite*, Panaf. Books, London.

54 Geertz (ed.), *Old Societies and New States*, New York, 1963.

55 W.F. Wertheim, 'The Rising Waves of Modernization', in Emanuel de Kadt and Gavin Williams (eds.), *Sociology of Development*, London, 1974, p. 319.

56 J. Friedman and C. Weaver, *Territory and Function. The Evolution of Regional Planning*, Edward Arnold Ltd., London, 1979.

57 R. Kothari, 'The Non-Party Political Process', *Economic and Political Weekly*, 4 February, 1984.

58 H. Sethi, 'Groups in a New Politics of Transition', *Economic and Political Weekly*, 18 February, 1984.

59 H. Sethi and S. Kothari (eds.), *The Non-Party Political Process: Uncertain Alternatives*, UNRISD/LOKAYAN 1983.

60 See for example publications from the Lokayan project such as Sethi and Kothari, op. cit.

61 R. Preiswerk, 'Self-Reliance in Unexpected Places', *IFDA Dossier*, 30, July/August, 1982.

62 See Roland Mousnier, *Peasant Uprising in Seventeenth Century France, Russia and China*, London, 1971.

63 Barrington Moore Jr., *Social Origins of Dictatorship and Democracy*, Beacon Press, Boston, 1967, p. 506.

64 This has been demonstrated by the Tillys in their pathbreaking work *The Rebellious Century 1830–1930*, Harvard University Press, 1975.

65 The relationship between members' influence in their organizations and the organizations' influence in society is probably curvilinear. Initially, members' influence increases to the same extent as the influence of the organization does, but after a certain point the relationship becomes negative.

66 See R. Ingelhart, op. cit., chap. 11.

67 J. Coleman, *Power and the Structure of Society*, New York, 1974.

68 A more detailed argument concerning this point can be found in André Gorz, *Farewell to the Working Class*, Pluto Press, London, 1982.

69 This line of thinking has been developed by Mats Friberg *et al.* in *Hur Sabart är Sverige* (How vulnerable is Sweden? – available in an English abridged version), *The Swedish Secretariat for Future Studies*.

70 Anthony Giddens, *The Class Structure of the Advanced Societies*, London, 1973, p. 285.

71 Folker Fröbel, op. cit. p. 44.

72 For an overview of theories about post-industrial society, see K. Kumar, *Prophecy and Progress. The Sociology of Industrial and Post-Industrial Society*, Penguin Books, 1978.

73 Quite a number of alternatives for prevalent practices are described and analysed by Carl Rogers, *On Personal Power*, Delacorte Press, New York, 1977; Mark Satin, *New Age Politics*, Delta Books, New York, 1978; Marilyn Ferguson, *The Aquarian Conspiracy*, 1980.

74 For a vivid description of this trend see Alvin Toffler, *The Third Wave*, William Morrow and Co., 1980. Toffler shows that much skilled service work can be done in the home if they are provided with computer terminals. He also points out that computerized production does not have to be mass production of standardized units. Each unit can be designed for the particular needs of the consumer. Thus, it is no longer necessary to concentrate large numbers of people in big factories and towns. Technologically advanced production can be integrated in the local communities and town districts in the form of small workshops.

75 There is ample evidence that person-centred approaches to organization are more effective than the traditional production-oriented approaches in a number of fields from politics to education and administration. See Carl Rogers, *On Personal Power*, Delacorte Press, New York, 1977.

76 R. Ingelhart, op. cit.

77 André Gorz, op. cit.

78 Mats Friberg, 'Dominant and Alternative Ways of Life', Department of Peace and Conflict Research, Goteborg, 1981.

79 A. Etzioni, op. cit., p. 626.

80 This choice is beautifully spelt out by the Swedish humanistic psychologist Claes Jonssen, *Personlig dialektik*, Stockholm, 1975. His theory integrates concepts from Jung, Fromm, Adorno, Maslow, Laing, Berne and others.

81 Class analysis has contributed very little to the explanation of this phenomenon. Self-emancipated persons turn up in the most unexpected social positions.

82 See Frank Musgrove, *Ecstasy and Holiness*, Methuen & Co. Ltd., 1974.
83 Alberto Melucci, 'The New Social Movements. A Theoretical Aproach', *Social Science Information*, 19, 2 (1980), p. 218.
84 See Theodor Roszak, *The Making of a Counter-Culture, Reflections on the Technocratic Society and its Youthful Opposition*, Faber & Faber, London, 1970.

8

A Propos the 'Green' Movements*

Samir Amin

1.

The 1960s saw the development of movements of 'contestation' – to use their own term – amongst Western youth, expressing revolt against the forms of life imposed by capitalism, then still engaged in full-blown expansion: alienating work, the patriarchal family, militarization. Although very diverse, these movements shared a common rejection of the traditional forms of action and organization of the left and labour movements which they regarded as 'recuperated' and 'integrated into the system' – a judgement responded to with scorn, and sometimes hostility. 1968 provided the momentum for these movements: they acquired a theory based, amongst others, on the works of the Frankfurt School and Herbert Marcuse, starting from the proposition that the Western working class had lost its revolutionary role, which had passed on to the peoples of the Third World – Fanon's wretched of the earth – and marginalized sections of the population in the West (immigrants, youth, women). The integration of the Western working class required a revision of the theory of exploitation, and of the strategy for liberation. The rediscovery of Reich directed attention to the mechanisms by which the domination/submission couplet was reproduced – a relation seen as antecedent to that of exploiter/exploited. With the disappearance of any illusions about the nature of the Soviet system, sympathetic glances began to be directed at Mao's China, which two years before 1968 had seemed to prefigure the events of that year in the Cultural Revolution.

The crisis of the 1970s brought with it the end of the vista of unlimited 'consumerism'. A new theme – not unconnected with this crisis

*Translated by Pete Burgess and Christine Blower

– emerged: that of 'ecology' and the planet's limited resources. The end of the war in Indo-China and the restoration of order in China also put an end to the West's enthusiastic Third Worldism: the struggles of the peoples of the Third World, which had entered a less dramatic phase, were not merely forgotten, but in a turn-around not untypical of opinion in the West became targets of the hostility grounded in lost illusions. The intensification of the arms race between the superpowers and the proclaimed aggression of the New Right in power in the USA were to give another dimension to the European scene – anti-nuclear pacifism. Possibly the only movement to have attained any degree of constancy over the two decades as a whole is the women's liberation movement. Moreover, we consider that the impact of this movement is more fundamental than that of the other currents, which are surrounded by an ineradicable air of being a succession of 'fashions'.

Given these conditions, it is difficult to treat the sum total of these movements as representing a homogeneous political current. In fact, they offer only a negative definition of themselves: they are neither 'Blue', by which they mean the forces of the classical right who regard capitalism as basically a satisfactory system and who continue to use those criteria of the system's performance which enable such approval to be shown, nor are they 'Red', by which they mean the traditional forces of the workers' movement in its diverse forms – social-democratic and soviet communist. According to the ideologists of the Green movement, Blues and Reds share the same fundamental vision of social organization: in contrast the Greens locate themselves beyond what they believe to be the limited debate between traditional right and traditional left. They are 'Greens', although their choice of this colour does not reduce the meaning of their movement solely to that of ecology.

The defenders of the 'Green cause' would therefore condemn the following observations in advance as not pertinent to the issues. Nevertheless, we shall try and consider as broad a spectrum of Green opinion as possible, and as the basis for this we therefore take a number of coherent ideological texts from the Green movement – notably by Johan Galtung, Mats Friberg and Björn Hettne, and Rudolf Bahro.[1]

2.

The objective of the Greens is a society liberated from class exploitation and state power, whose members – equal, free of prejudice and a number of diverse forms of oppression (patriarchy, the family etc.) – can develop their full humanity without the constraints of scarcity, the impoverishing division of labour etc. The Green's counter-system will involve the abolition of exchange-value and the state, and the organization of society on the basis of the direct production of use-values. This, at least, is what Mats Friberg expressly tells us, although in reading his contribution it is difficult to refrain from adding in the margin – ' = the communism of Marx'.

In other words, if our critique is guilty of any prejudgement, it is one which is favourable to the Greens. Such a commonality of objectives clearly places us both in the same camp, and is certainly more important than any mutual criticisms we can make. And although we greatly regret the fact that the Greens – mistakenly – do not acknowledge that their counter-society is in fact nothing more than the communism espoused by Marx, our present age is undeniably in need of a reminder of this objective. It is all too true that the forces of the traditional left, such as they are, have either postponed this objective into the indefinite future, if not simply renounced it by categorizing it as 'utopian', or have deformed it, as in the practice of Soviet communism. Finally, the Greens have raised a number of new problems only embryonically touched on in marxism. However, raising them does not necessarily imply opposition to marxism – but rather its enrichment.

The objective of the Greens is not, therefore, a new one. Nor can marxism itself be credited with the invention of such objectives: the revolt of the oppressed and exploited has always produced the ideology of a just, equal and mutual counter-system.

Peasant communism is not specific to any particular society, and one can discover the essential elements of it in the history of all peoples. Utopian socialism had transferred the objective of this society to the developing industrial world before Marx. And neither Utopian socialism, nor Bakunin's anarchism, distinguish themselves from Marx in terms of this objective but rather in the means of attaining it. Again, it is all too true that social-democracy and Soviet communism have deformed the historical significance of the contribution of these strands, overhastily dismissing them as 'peasant egalitarianism' (as if socialism was an apologia for inequality!), as 'petty bourgeois', and even indeed as 'reactionary' Utopias – a process in which Marx and Engels's own assessments have been ripped out of context and misused.

The debate does not therefore concern the nature of the objective, but the theoretical character of its content and substance: former peasant communisms claimed to be the correct interpreters of the Divine message; they opposed the Christianity of the Church of the propertied, the Islam of the Khalifal state and the Confucianism of the Empire with Christ, the prophet Mohammed and the Taoist mystics, invoked to re-establish justice on earth. After the eighteenth century this theoretical justification gave way to an areligious humanism. From Abbé Mably to J.J. Rousseau, the affirmation that the Human Being is by nature good, and that it is society which corrupts it, allowed a view of liberation to be advanced based on the reform of the individual. The Utopians pursued this strategy in Fourier's *Phalanstères* and other model societies.

Marx proposed another type of explanation both for the nature of the social order under criticism, and for the 'counter-system' (a term which Marx avoided). Marx's theses were based on an analysis of the commodity and value, and the opposition between the mode of functioning of pre-capitalist societies (feudal, among others), and that of the capitalist social order. The fundamental concepts of historical materialism (modes of production, class, state, base and superstructure etc.) were elaborated in the course of this analysis. This is not an appropriate point to recapitulate the essentials of Marx's theses, of which there are numerous and often divergent interpretations.[2] Commodity alienation occupies a central position, since it takes into account both the nature of the dominant ideology in the bourgeois system, and specificities of the base-superstructure relationships which characterize this system, in contrast to preceding modes of production. As an explanation of capitalist as much as of pre-capitalist class societies, we have to confess that we are not aware of a richer or a more scientific foundation.

Such an acknowledgement does not necessarily imply either that the question of alienation can be reduced to that of commodity alienation (for the capitalist epoch) or that it is necessary to reject the existence of a form of human alienation which transcends society.

Some of Marx's writings can give rise to this impression. In advancing far beyond his starting-point in Feuerbach's critique of religion, and replacing the latter by a critique of commodity fetishism, Marx kept to the progressive view of his age that there were no such transcendents. Nineteenth century scientistic positivism firmly believed that Nature had been dominated by Man. But this domination can only be relative: the Human Being remains a living creature, part of nature and, as such, finite and mortal. Questions which transcend its existence as a social being are therefore perfectly valid. Historical materialism does not respond to these questions; it does not ask them; it cannot answer them. The action of social transformation does not imply or require them. Such a position holds open the door of reintegration into the social-transformation camp to those who continue to be preoccupied by transcendental questions, but who do not reduce the future of humanity to a passive reflection on these questions.[3] This is not a matter of political tactics but of fundamental conviction. After all, marxism is not the radical prolongation of the Philosophy of the Enlightenment, which proposed to deal with social reality in the same way as Nature; it is a decisive break from this philosophy. The vestiges of scientific positivism which marxism was able to use, and which were reinforced over time within the clasp of the II and III Internationals are not to be defended but in fact expunged – in the name of Marx.

What, then, do the Greens propose as the fundamental method for analysing social and human reality? What they suggest represents a return to the dogma of the goodness of Human Nature of the eighteenth century and the Utopian socialists, and an attempt to theorize history in cultural terms as a substitute for an analysis in terms of the social forms of the organization of production, together with an occasional appeal to transcendental reflection. Does what at first sight appears to be a return to pre-Marx really represent an enriching step forwards under the conditions of today?

3.

The assertion that there is a Human Nature independent of society, even pre-existent to it, constituting the logical condition for social existence, that this Nature is good, and that Society is anti-natural and obstructive to the development of this Nature – an explicit claim made by many Greens – invites neither confirmation nor refutation. The unfortunate thing about theories of human nature is that they are unprovable since they transcend what can be known – society. Deciding in advance that this nature is good does not take us very far: it is enough to know that Society is bad. In a paradoxical article, the Yugoslavian writer Svetozar Stojanic[4] arrives at the same conclusion – that Society is bad – by setting out from the 'pessimistic' hypothesis that human nature is bad. In our view, to pose these questions in terms of human nature is ask a needless question which adds nothing to our knowledge of the world or our capacity to transform it.

Moreover, the Greens themselves are not very satisfied with this answer. They still have to specify which society – or societies – they mean when they call for revolt. Marxism describes them as 'capitalist'; the Greens describe them as 'European'. This is the embryo of a cultural theory of history.

The Greens stress the 'Utopia of the total mastery of Nature' which constitutes the motor of 'our' civilisation and characterizes current socialist reality (that is, the Soviet Union) as much as it does capitalism. This Utopia is explicitly attributed to European culture and its religious beliefs (Christianity). As the key to understanding the world, the Greens propose to replace analysis in terms of precapitalist modes of production (feudal, tributary, communal etc.), the expansion of capitalism on a world scale (with its central poles and peripheries), and its 'revisionist' (to use a Maoist term) and 'socialist' supersessions, by an analysis couched in terms of the cultural manifestations of religious bases: Christian, Islamic, Hindu, Buddhist.

Unfortunately the germ of explanation which this approach provides does not constitute a satisfactory *theory*. Not because religious and cultural facts are not social, and important, facts, but because these facts are not in themselves historic, given once and for all. Instead of such a cultural explanation of history, historical materialism is able to offer a historical theory of cultures.[5] Although the impoverishing dogmatism which has led marxism into denying certain social realities has meant that this is has not yet been accomplished, nothing in marxism's method prevents it.

In Mats Friberg, the Greens offer the following typology: Christianity (together with Judaism and Islam) which makes Man, as the reflection of God, into the Master of Nature; and the other religions (Hinduism and Buddhism) which regard Man as an integral part of Nature. This is very meagre inasmuch as several major ideologies are left out of the schema: Confucianism (which is not a religion but a political morality) is considerably more important in Oriental Asia than is Buddhism. And the schema also ignores the animisms of Africa and animist interpretations of nature (Taoism, the animist dimensions of Hinduism and practical animists in peasant cultures, including those in Christian and Islamic countries). It is also meagre inasmuch as official dogma concerning the Divinity – Humanity – Nature relationship is not invariant in the actual reality of the cultures under consideration. Although the Judaeo-Christian-Islamic conception of these relationships seems to proclaim the domination of nature by humanity, might not this interpretation be an *a posteriori* reconstruction? Beginning from their origins in a number of Egyptian ideas, these religions progressively crystallized into the form in which they now appear to us. The dogmatic element is only one element among several: it developed and acquired dominance along with capitalism, the development of the productive forces which this facilitated, and the conquest of other peoples. There are no grounds for thinking that this version of Christianity was the version lived out by the European peasant, monk and feudal warrior of the tenth century. Religious belief is flexible; it embraces various dimensions, and, depending on the circumstances, one or other of these takes precedence. Were this not the case, it is impossible to understand why Islam, which shares this dogma with Christianity, did not open the way to an earlier form of capitalism. We are back at the old debate about Weber's thesis: capitalism, fruit of protestantism, or protestantism, revision of Christianity in a form more compatible with nascent capitalism? To go even further, would not Confucianism have been an ideology for the domination of nature *par excellence*, also opening the way for capitalism? And can Hinduism be reduced to its conception of humanity as an integral part of Nature? What is the relationship between Hinduism and the totality of Indian reality, the caste-system for example?

The way in which the Greens pose these questions on cultures and religions is reminiscent of the Islamic fundamentalists, whom we have criticized elsewhere.[6] For them too, the expansion of capitalism – and of its brother, 'actually existing socialism' – is not the product of the innate laws of the capitalist mode of production, but simply the expression of European expansionism. And viewed superficially, this is, of course, true: since capitalism was born in Europe, capitalism's expansion in Asia and Africa is also that of Europe. This is not without importance in terms of its political effects, not only in the East, but in Europe itself, including the forces of the Left and the workers movement. But is this sufficient reason to refrain from wanting to go further, to go beyond this surface appearance – however real it may be?

Historical materialism's conceptual resources, and above all, its breadth as a method, and hence its capacity to integrate all aspects of social reality, are an invitation for us to enrich, not abandon them. In our view, the replacements proposed by the Greens represent not progress, but a step backward. One notes, for example, the repeated use of such vague terms as 'modernization', 'individual', 'small groups', which do not have an invariant content throughout history. We also consider that the false history of Europe which the Green thesis leads us to construct is even unjust towards Europe. To say, as some Greens claim, that bourgeois development has reduced the role of the individual is to forget the positive, if limited character of the bourgeois liberation of the individual, and to deny the reality of feudal oppression.

Some of the 'Green' strands have drawn forceful attention to the ecological aspects of the contemporary problem (and hence the choice of colour). Many of their observations and analyses are perfectly correct. Capitalist development is generally based on an irreversible destruction of nature, singularly restricting the potential available for future generations. The basic reason for this is that it is in the nature of capitalist economic calculation to be rational, but for this rationality to have an extremely short-term time horizon, as we have observed elsewhere.[7] And what may be termed 'soviet marxism' has also simply denied that any such problem exists by the peremptory assertion that 'the earth's riches are unlimited', drawing on a tradition of the II International which had its origins in the scientific optimism of the nineteenth century. Marx himself, as always, had a keener eye for reality. If, in some aspects, we can observe him flowing with the current of optimism of his time, in others he raises the question of the relation to nature with characteristic profundity. Nothing stands in the way of developing this analysis further, in full cognizance of the dialectic of the relationship between Society and Nature: on the contrary, we are exhorted to do so.

4.

What appeared as weaknesses in the theory of society re-manifest themselves as weaknesses in the strategy proposed for the transformation of society.

In particular, we have to ask whether the Greens are not perhaps making their task too easy by acknowledging only two strategies – the Blue and Red – which are, in fact, not much more than one, and by excluding any socialist alternative different to the one whose existence they recognize.

By definition, the 'Blues' are evidently satisfied with the system. But sometimes the same ideology is expressed in the language of marxism. Bill Warren, of whom we have made a critique elsewhere,[8] represents one currently fashionable and important trend in Western 'marxism', according to which capitalist expansion into the underdeveloped countries is a reasonable way to tackle the problems of under-development, since the development of the productive forces which capitalism brings about necessarily works to the benefit of the mass of the population. But this reduction of a social problem to the develop-ment of the productive forces is not, all the same, generalized throughout the 'Red' camp. Although there is no doubt at all that some social-democratic currents have succumbed, the globally negative judgement made by the Greens is once more an unjust one: redistribu-tional measures, social security and decentralization cannot be reduced to their 'bureaucratic' aspect. And although the Soviet conception of marxism undoubtedly comes close to a vision of 'capitalism without capitalists', it is unfair to reduce marxism to Soviet practice. In our opinion, Marx himself had another vision of communism, and of the transition to socialism, as evidenced in his observations on the Gotha and Erfurt Programmes.

Maoism constitutes the alternative option which the Greens pass over too lightly. Many of the themes which sustain the 'Green' movement have their origins in maoism, a fact acknowledged by the Greens: self-reliance, decentralization, critique of technology as non-neutral, delinking and so on. According to Mao himself, quite correctly, it is not a matter of new inventions but of a return to a Marx disfigured by revisionism. However, maoism employs these principles under condi-tions which cannot simply be erased from the analysis since they relate to real problems: where the development of the productive forces is not an absurd luxury, where 'transition' has to be accomplished in a world-system in which the dominant forces remain hostile. Moreover, these contradictions are ineliminable because they are in real life: 'relying on your own forces' requires a strong state, be this popular or decentral-ized. In wanting the 'good side' of Maoism without the 'bad side', are the Greens not bringing back the spirit of Proudhon, who was criticized by Marx – and entirely properly in our view – for lacking any sense of the dialectic in advancing such schemas?

The Greens' strategy starts from their theoretical premises: the evil – European culture; the means to fight it – the immediate estab-lishment of partial systems which allow us to liberate ourselves from it. But at this point the balance sheet of what has been achieved, their scope and perspectives leaves us still in doubt. For example, are not eulogies to 'small groups' somewhat ill-considered and in contradiction to the reality of the family as 'the source of many evils'? Does praise of decentralization take account of historical experience: after all, all the great progressive changes in history have been effected by centralized social forces, while decentralization has often reinforced conservative power controlled by local notables and, consider Switzerland and the USA, contributed to depoliticization? Why should communes and other contemporary variants of the Phalanstères have any more chance of succeeding now than previously? As Andre Gunder Frank neatly expressed it during a discussion of these strategies, the essence of the Green position seems to be: 'Stop the system, I want to get off'.

No doubt this – on the whole negative – judgement will seem unjust since the Greens do not constitute an organized and homogeneous movement, and it is undoubtedly unwarranted to group together movements of different natures and scope under the same heading. Our excessively global discussion of strategies would have to be replaced by a case-by-case examination which would lead, more often than one would think, to a convergence of political views. For example, the European pacifist anti-nuclear movement must be judged in terms of the current political and military conjuncture. The Greens also frequently support struggles of resistance against capitalist expansion, in particular peasant struggles. These are progressive because the criterion of the forces of progress is opposition to capitalist expansion (aren't wage rises also in conflict with the immediate exigencies of accumulation?), rather than acceptance of the forces of production in the name of progress through forgetting, like Bill Warren, the capitalist character of these forces. It does not matter that populist motivation does not convince everyone (Mats Friberg makes explicit mention here of the case of the Narodniks). For us, for example, peasant resistance to capitalist expansion – in the Third World a crucial social fact – remains double-edged: both anti-capitalist – because it is capitalism as it functions which is concretely in conflict with the interests of the peasants – but also the expression of another capitalist path, based on peasant revolution. Under current historical circumstances, this resistance should be supported because it could become a decisive element in the anti-capitalist popular alliance, opening the way to a transition to socialism. One could cite many examples of the convergence of partial strategies, despite theoretical differences as to their signification and place in the global perspective. The most crucial area of this deeprooted convergence is beyond doubt the women's movement, which cannot be annexed to the logic of the 'Greens' any more than to any other, since there are feminist movements which are perfectly compatible with capitalist logic, while others subscribe to the logic of socialism, taken in its broadest sense ranging from social-democratic reformism to Maoism.

The debate here is about the theoretical character of these movements' propositions, and the general lines of strategy necessary for keeping strategy consistent with objectives. It is not about tactics and the immediate means of political action. It would be truly pretentious to furnish 'recipes': to build a mass party, or to opt for single-issue or diverse 'movements', for example. We can simply note that the task – nothing less than the radical transformation of society – is sufficiently enormous to require of us that we do not underestimate its proportions. On this score, the Green movements leave us a little worried. Some large mass movements on specific issues gather together people of all political hues (like the current peace movement), and risk not surviving the emergence of ideological positions; but there are very few attempts to construct an integrated force with a proper political strategy adapted to concrete social reality. Is this realistic?

No strategy arrives complete with a guarantee as to the outcome – especially one as ambitious as the radical transformation of society. Mats Friberg reminds us of the reality of the threatening apocalypse with the image of a river carrying us towards the waterfall. But is it reasonable to hope that we can swim against the current through a purely voluntarist declaration, to the effect, as is sometimes claimed, that the will of the actors can fashion the world in conformity with their wishes, independently of the system. The choice is not between swimming with the current or against the current: the question is *how* to go against the current – marxism does not pretend to exclude the possibility of apocalypse, since in the absence of socialism, it holds that barbarism will set about resolving problems in its own way.

The appearance of political currents bearing the name Green is no surprise. It is the manifestation of the failure of the strategies operated by the European left over several decades. As such it demands a serious self-criticism, and represents a positive phenomenon. We can observe much the same process in the Third World, where the failure of revisionist strategies of supporting the national bourgeoisie in the name of liberation, instead of popular-maoist strategies of national liberation under the banner of socialism and the autonomous control of the exploited classes explains the appearance of renewed fundamentalisms, such as those of Islam. This is a fact which requires self-criticism.

Moreover, the reactions in both instances present striking similarities. Like fundamentalist Islam, the Greens locate themselves within the renewal of the religious spirit. It is not by chance that their successes are almost exclusively in Northern Europe, marked by the Protestant tradition. Galtung and Bahro's explicit comparison of the response of primitive Christianity to the crisis of the Roman Empire and movements of transformation inside western imperialism reinforce this ideological aspect, a point already discussed elsewhere.[9] We do not rule out that this transition, whose outcome is uncertain, might take place in the form which we have characterized as the process of decadence, as distant from that termed revolutionary, whose outcome is less uncertain.

In this sense, the appearance of the Green currents, and other forms of religious fundamentalism, do not appear to us as solutions to the crisis, but rather as symptoms of it.

Notes

1 Mats Friberg and Björn Hettne, 'The Greening of the World – Towards a Non-Deterministic Model of Global Processes', Chapter 6, above. Rudolf Bahro, 'Who can Stop the Apocalypse?' WFSF, *mimeo*, Stockholm 1982; and various works by Johan Galtung.
2 See Samir Amin, *Class and Nation*, Monthly Review Press, New York, 1980, Chapter 1.
3 See, for example, the works of Francois Houtart, of the University of Louvain.
4 Svetozar Stajanovic, 'Reflections on the Crisis of the Marxist View of Power', WFSF, *mimeo*, Stockholm, 1985.
5 An expression used by George Aseniero in the course of a discussion of this subject.
6 Samir Amin, 'Is there a Political Economy of Islamic Fundamentalism?', *Journal of African Marxists*, No. 3, London, 1983.
   See too the work by Hassan El Dika (in Arabic) 'Samir Amin and the marxist writing of history', Beyrouth, Dar el Fikr el Arabi, 1981.
7 Samir Amin, 'Le statut de la rationalité économique, la critique de la micro-économie', in Amin, Franco and Sow, 'La Planification du Sous-Développement, Anthropos, Paris, 1975.
8 Samir Amin, 'Expansion or Crisis of Capitalism,' *Third World Quarterly*, Vol. 5, No. 2, London, April 1983.
9 *Class and Nation*, op. cit., 'Conclusion: Revolution or Decadence? Thoughts on the transition from one mode of production to another', p. 249 ff.